MARKETING BEHAVIOR AND EXECUTIVE ACTION

MARKETING
BEHAVIOR AND
EXECUTIVE ACTION

WROE ALDERSON

ARNO PRESS
A New York Times Company
New York • 1978

Editorial Supervision: JOSEPH CELLINI

————◆————

Reprint Edition 1978 by Arno Press Inc.

Copyright © 1957 by Richard D. Irwin, Inc.

Reprinted by permission of Richard D. Irwin, Inc.

Reprinted from a copy in the Pennsylvania
   State Library

A CENTURY OF MARKETING
ISBN for complete set: 0-405-11156-8
See last pages of this volume for titles.

Manufactured in the United States of America

————◆————

Library of Congress Cataloging in Publication Data

Alderson, Wroe.
   Marketing behavior and executive action.

   (A Century of marketing)
   Reprint of the ed. published by R. D. Irwin,
Homewood, Ill.
   Bibliography: p.
   Includes index.
   1. Marketing. I. Title. II. Series.
[HF5415.A39 1978]   658.8   78-222
ISBN 0-405-11162-2

MARKETING BEHAVIOR AND EXECUTIVE ACTION

A Functionalist Approach to Marketing Theory

MARKETING
BEHAVIOR AND
EXECUTIVE ACTION

A Functionalist Approach to
Marketing Theory

By WROE ALDERSON

Alderson and Sessions

1957

RICHARD D. IRWIN, INC.

HOMEWOOD, ILLINOIS

First Printing, February, 1957

Library of Congress Catalogue Card No. 57–6769

PREFACE

As the student begins to use this book he is invited to observe the way it is organized. Awareness of its structure will help him in mastering its content.

There are fifteen chapters organized in three parts, each playing a distinct and essential role in the communication of a functional theory of marketing. The parts are presented in what is presumed to be the natural order for the graduate student who is trying to organize what he has learned about marketing from other books and relate it to a background of knowledge in the other social sciences. The marketing executive with substantial experience behind him might prefer to start with Part III and cover the book in reverse order.

Part III is devoted to principles of action which have general validity in the management of marketing operations. This part is the culmination of the whole book for either the student or the executive, since functionalism holds that the final purpose of theory in marketing is to achieve a better understanding of action and to make it more effective. Each of the four chapters deals with an aspect of the executive function and with the tools and techniques available for discharging the responsibilities of management in marketing.

Part II may be regarded as the core of the book since it deals with the nature of marketing processes, with the way in which market structures evolve to serve marketing functions, and with the way in which both buyers and sellers enter the market place in an effort to solve their problems. In other words, this core of the functional theory presents a generalized picture of the marketing environment in which the executive will develop his plans and make his decisions. The principles of action presented in the final chapters are priniciples for dealing effectively with this environment. The eight chapters in Part II present a dynamic view of market opportunity and marketing effort and the major factors in their continuous adjustment.

If Part III is the culmination and Part II the core of the presentation of functionalism, then Part I lays down its foundation. The author holds that market behavior is typically group behavior and that individuals generally seek to achieve their purposes through the functioning of organized behavior systems. He draws upon such varied fields as sociology, psychology, anthropology, and political science for the elements of a theory of group behavior. Building on Part I, the functioning of groups in the market place is presented in Part II, and principles of executive action for making group operations more effective in Part III. The three chapters of Part I attempt to build up a comprehensive view of group behavior by starting with what seems most primitive and fundamental and moving toward the complex activities of the fully developed organized behavior system.

This preface is intended to give the reader an understanding of how the major parts of the book fit together. Similarly a prefatory note or abstract is provided at the beginning of each chapter. These notes are not intended to summarize the detailed content of the book nor can the reader expect to learn what is in it merely by reading these fifteen introductory statements. Their function is to indicate what the author is driving at in each chapter, how the chapter is expected to contribute to the exposition as a whole, and what the reader should be looking for, chapter by chapter.

The author's indebtedness is too diverse for detailed acknowledgment except as references occur in the text. Aside from published materials, the author has profited greatly from discussions with many of the writers mentioned in the text, with the men and women who have participated in the annual Marketing Theory Seminars, with his colleagues at the Massachusetts Institute of Technology during a brief period as professor at the School of Industrial Management, and with the partners and staff members in his own consulting organization.

WROE ALDERSON

Philadelphia
January, 1957

TABLE OF CONTENTS

PART III.   EXECUTIVE ACTION IN MARKETING

INDEX

Part I

MARKETING AND THE BEHAVIORAL SCIENCES

The conception of an organized behavior system is the starting point for the present approach to marketing theory. Given only the elements of power and communication which characterize every group, the system may discharge certain primitive functions and exhibit survival value. All marketing activity is an aspect of the interaction among organized behavior systems related to each other in what may be described as an ecological network. Operating systems are a subclass of behavior systems distinguished by inputs and outputs and the structuring of processes to achieve efficiency.

The functionalist approach is concerned with the functioning of systems, and the study of structure is incidental to the analysis and interpretations of functions. Every phase of marketing can be understood as human behavior within the framework of some operating system. Several types of systems are of special importance in marketing. Survival and growth are implicit goals of every behavior system, including most particularly those which operate in the market place.

Chapter 1

THEORY IN SCIENCE AND PRACTICE

The book begins with the discussion of several meanings of the term "theory" appropriate to various scientific fields. Some place greater stress on internal consistency and others on relevance to facts. It is argued that since marketing is oriented to action, marketing theory should provide a perspective for practice. Theory as perspective for action is not inconsistent with the conception of theory as a means of organizing and interpreting an advancing body of knowledge.

An effort is made in this chapter to convey the essence of the comprehensive but somewhat illusory concept of functionalism which is the approach to marketing theory followed throughout the book. There is a discussion of functionalism as it has developed in the various social sciences and more recently as the basis for the movement toward integration and the establishment of a general science of human behavior. This treatment of the various aspects of functionalism should enable the reader to assess its potentialities as an approach to the solution of marketing problems.

The chapter closes with an analysis of the nature of systems and a summary of the theoretical position to be presented in the following chapters. The concept of the organized behavior system is the foundation of this position. The summary suggests only briefly the pertinence of this concept to the various aspects of market behavior and executive action which are to be discussed later.

BEGINNINGS OF MARKETING THEORY

The last ten years have seen a rapid increase of interest in theory in the field of marketing. An important turning point seems to have been a special meeting of the American Marketing Association, held in Pittsburgh in 1946 and devoted to the subject of theory in marketing. Subsequent developments included the publication of a book under the title *Theory in Marketing,* sponsored by the American Marketing Association. The authors of these essays and many others have continued to advance their theoretical interests in a variety of ways. Today there are courses in marketing theory given in a number of universities, and an increasing number of articles of a theoretical nature are appearing in the *Journal of Marketing.* Beginning in 1951, a group interested in marketing theory has held a week-long seminar year after year. Some of the theoretical concepts discussed in this book were first presented at these seminars. Readers of the monthly *Cost and Profit Outlook* and of other writings by the author will recognize some familiar ideas now appearing in expanded and integrated form.

Until quite recently both marketing teachers and practitioners were inclined to avoid the use of the term "theory" and were apparently fearful of being identified as theorists. On the academic side such caution was related to departmental organization in the universities. Any theoretical approach to markets or marketing was assumed to be the exclusive province of the economics department. The function of the marketing department tended to be that of offering a detailed descriptive treatment of marketing institutions and processes in a manner not covered by economics.

Marketing analysts in business avoided the label of "theory" for fear that they would be regarded as impractical. Marketing research is still quite new in many business firms. Sales and advertising executives who have acquired their knowledge of marketing solely through experience often view these new techniques with skepticism, and look askance at the professionally trained marketing man as an alien and academic character rather than as one of their own number. To gain acceptance, some marketing research directors adopted the mannerisms of two-fisted line executives and even tried to suppress the fact that they had earned advanced academic degrees.

It is an ironic paradox that the ever-increasing demands from business executives have forced marketing men to become more theoretical. The kinds of questions executives are asking call for rigorous techniques in problem solving, which in turn need to be rationalized in terms of some general theoretical perspective. The marketing teacher finds that he cannot equip his students for effective work in marketing simply by imparting a sound body of knowledge concerning marketing institutions and processes. The most important fact of all is change. Here again theoretical perspective is essential if the marketing man entering business is to grasp what is going on in a world of change. Two professionally trained groups in the field—namely, teachers and marketing analysts—found that some theoretical perspective was required for understanding one another, and growing acceptance of theory is making them a more effective team in furthering the marketing viewpoint throughout the business community.

THEORY IN SCIENCE

The term "theory" is used in a variety of ways, including its use as an epithet for a viewpoint which the speaker does not like. Among those who are favorably disposed, the meaning varies from something that is quite definite and precise to a vague and general expression of a personal philosophy. Even among scientists usage varies according to the degree of precision which is customary or feasible in each field. Nevertheless, it is possible to state a definition for "theory" which is valid for science in general. Theory is a set of propositions which are consistent among themselves and which are relevant to some aspect of the factual world. Some theorists are more concerned about consistency and others about relevance, but both are essential to theory in an empirical science.

At one extreme is the conception of theory appropriate to symbolic logic. This type of theory begins by assuming certain postulates to be true. Various statements or theorems are derived from these postulates. The test of truth for any of these theorems is the proof that they are consistent with the postulates and with each other. Precise logical formulation of theory has advanced quite far in the physical sciences. Many physical laws are stated as mathematical equations expressing the way in which one quantity varies with another. One of the most famous and well known is Einstein's statement of the relationship between energy and mass, $E=MC^2$. One of the consequences resulting from this statement of a physical law has been the development of the atom bomb. With the ushering in of the Atomic Age, it is impossible for even the most hard-bitten executive to assume that theory is divorced from practice, at least so far as physics is concerned.

Many working in other scientific fields regard the logical and mathematical precision of physics as the model they should attempt to follow. It is granted that this can only be achieved in the distant future because of the great complexity of data which must be handled in such fields as the social sciences.

Biology has achieved secure status as a science and has borne many practical fruits in application. Yet there are few principles of biology which can be stated in the mathematical form of Einstein's law of energy and mass. Central to general biology is the theory of evolution, which is a set of propositions concerning genes, mutations, the struggle for survival, and other factors which are believed to effect the development of species. Only a few aspects of the general theory can be expressed in mathematical form. However, statistical methods are increasingly useful in the kind of experimentation which is bringing about extensions and revisions of the theory of evolution.

Still further away from the quantifiable statements of theoretical physics are the current theories about human behavior and its motivation. Pre-eminent among psychological theorists is Sigmund Freud, who seems to many to loom as large as did Charles Darwin in biology. Psychoanalytic theory as developed by Freud consists of a series of daring and sweeping statements about the sources of human desire and the difficulties encountered on the way to emotional maturity. His famous model of personality structure utilizing the concepts of id, ego, and superego were not fully worked out until Freud was in his seventies. The ramifications of libido and the death instinct, of repression and defense mechanisms, of symbols and the interpretation of dreams were suggested by Freud's experience in the treatment of mental illness. Many of these concepts have yet to be subjected to the test of statistically valid research. Most of the entities Freud described are not subject to direct observation but can be investigated only through inferences based on the observation of human behavior. In this respect the situation is parallel to that in physics. In both cases the scientist draws inferences about entities such as atoms, electrons, and protons which are not visible to the naked eye. The real difference lies in the unique character of human personality and the many limitations which are placed on experimental techniques. As one physicist has remarked, it is possible to blow up an atom to see how it is put together and still leave an infinite supply of atoms of identical structure. Parallel techniques are not available to students of human personality or behavior systems.

Economics, among all the social sciences, has gone farthest toward approaching the model of theoretical physics. In fact, pure economic theory resembles logic or mathematics in giving priority to consistency. Empirical research concerning markets has generally pertained to the problems of individual firms or industries, and has had little connection with the elaboration of economic theory. Millions of dollars are being spent annually in such investigations, with relatively little contribution to an underlying science of marketing. It is true that marketing has been increasingly scientific in its methodology, though largely lacking in explicit theory. It has participated in the movement toward quantification of social data and perhaps even deserves some credit for leadership. Rapid progress has been made in such fields as sampling and questionnaire design. There is also an earnest effort to go beyond the asking of questions toward truly experimental procedures, particularly in the investigation of consumer motivation. Marketing is not wholly barren of laws or generalizations derived from these empirical studies. It is well recognized in marketing that its laws are not positive but are only statements as to the probability of an occurrence.

Some philosophers of science say that the most fundamental scientific goal is the progressive reduction of error in the statements of laws or principles. That view is entirely appropriate to marketing along with its adoption of statistical methods for determining central tendencies and the reliability of these results. The progressive reduction of error in marketing is beset by special difficulties. While the marketing facts vary, they do not vary at random. The difference between one marketing situation and another may arise precisely because a significant determining factor is present in one and absent from the other.

Adequate theoretical perspective should aid the student and the market analyst in understanding these differences and in making corresponding decisions about the course of action to be followed in each case. Marketing theory under this conception is definitely relevant to marketing practice. In some instances it can be an immediate guide to action. In many more cases it can give direction to the research effort needed to develop the facts on which to base a course of action. In the longer view, theory should facilitate the accumulation and integration of a body of knowledge, so that what is learned through coping with one set of problems can be brought to bear on others.

Theory in the Advancement of Science. A science is the orderly investigation of some class of natural phenomena. The body of a science consists of statements of laws or generalizations and of the descriptive facts and results of crucial experiments which sustain these laws. There can be no science in any field without both the formulation of laws and the accumulation of facts. The term "science" is sometimes extended to cover fields, such as symbolic logic, which have no immediate reference to facts or to areas of factual investigation such as marketing. The study of marketing until very recently has had little explicit theory or even broad generalizations of fact. Theory without factual content offers little promise of practical application. Accumulation of fact without theoretical structure is an uncertain foundation for an advancing knowledge and mastery of a field. Once scientific study begins in a particular area, the task of science is never ended. New facts suggest new generalizations or revisions in the body of theory. New developments in theory lead to new areas of investigation or types of experiments.

The term "theory" pertains to the whole conceptual framework of science. More limited statements about the relationships among variable phenomena might be designated as theorems in accordance with the practice in mathematics. A theorem may be regarded as a hypothesis which can be tested by reference to fact. The usual stages in scientific investigation are those of setting up a hypothesis, designing a research program or a set of experiments which will confirm or disprove the hypothesis, and finally considering whether the research results may require revision of the general theory. The more formal types of theory tend to emphasize consistency as compared to relevance. Economic theory discusses a formal system built on a series of assumptions, including the principle of scarcity. One would have to go to an institutionalist such as Veblen to find general statements about economic behavior parallel to the biological theory of Darwin or the psychological theory of Freud. Yet the writings of Veblen are scarcely accorded the status of theory at all in the sense in which the term is currently used in economics.

The use of the term "theory" in marketing pertains to something which is less formal and more comprehensive than economic theory in its search for relevance to actual behavior. An adequate theory of marketing at the present stage is likely to resemble the statements of Darwin, Freud, and Veblen more than those of Ricardo. Yet marketing men are also concerned about systems of action and are eager to apply the tools of economic analysis which many of them became familiar with in their basic training. The problems of the market analyst are essentially economic problems, since he also is concerned with the utilization of resources to produce the maximum of consumer satisfactions through goods and services. The reader, however, should not expect to find here a set of propositions as precise or as fully integrated as those of economics. The marketing analyst or executive is interested in matters which are of relatively little concern to the general economist. In his daily practice he is looking for solutions which can lead to marketing decisions in many specific and concrete situations. He must seek these solutions without limiting himself to those procedures which one might expect to find in marketing when considered as a division of economics. He must be equally open to draw insights from applied psychology, sociology, and anthropology, since these sciences of human behavior are demonstrating their ability to contribute to the solution of marketing problems. Marketing theory must provide an adequate perspective for marketing practice or for the education of those who plan to engage in marketing. The version of marketing theory which is presented here may be regarded as an aspect of the general theory of human behavior. It is related to economics, since it is concerned with the efficient correlation of means and ends. It is more allied to the broader social sciences in its conception of the social setting within which the individual or the operating group seek to achieve their ends.

Churchman has given a comprehensive picture of the advancement of science and of the interplay between theory and factual investigation which constitutes this advance. The advances of science consist in giving better and better answers to important questions. The significance of these questions lies in their bearing on man's knowledge of his world and the efficient use of his resources in pursuing his objectives. The goals of science are often discussed under the three headings of explanation, prediction, and control. The scientist first tries to understand what is going on in the area he is studying and to explain why things work out as they do. From this study of current or past events, he hopes to discover regularities in nature or functional relationships which will serve to predict what will happen in the future or under certain stated assumptions. Finally, science provides the basis for controlling or redirecting the course of events so as to produce results of human value.

Marketing as a science adheres to these same goals. It emerged as a separate discipline in the twentieth century and was oriented to immediate results in the business world. Perhaps its greatest weakness, until recently, has been that it had concentrated on the attempt to establish control without giving adequate attention to the companion steps of explanation and prediction. This has tended to make marketing research an opportunistic approach to concrete problems.

In beginning to develop a general body of theory, marketing is only now reaching the stage at which it can become a steadily evolving science. Advocates of theory in marketing feel that marketing can scarcely be regarded as a science until it possesses an organized conceptual framework for ordering and interpreting its factual content.

Theory in the Application of Science. The laws or principles of action which are the fruit of marketing science find application in the solution of concrete marketing problems. This happens in a variety of ways and can be related to the functions of explanation, prediction, and control already described as the goals of science. A comprehensive explanation or interpretation of marketing finds its application partly in the training of market analysts and marketing executives. Such background is of help in recognizing aspects of market structure or marketing processes. It may supply the analyst with a stock of analytical models from which he can select one to fit the particular case. Experienced executives make many of their marketing judgments through the use of such models, even though they may not be consciously aware of the process. In fact, acquiring such a set of analytical tools is perhaps the essence of meaningful experience.

The scientific function of prediction is related to the business function of planning. However, market planning begins with some forecast of what is likely to happen or what can be made to happen by taking appropriate steps. For example, the forecast might pertain to the growth of demand for a given class of products when a given plan has been devised for the application of effort to this market potential. The next step in prediction is to evaluate the probable outcome of the plan.

The scientific function of control is related to the element of organization. The possibility of control in a marketing situation cannot be realized without the effective mobilization of effort. The marketing executive attempts to exercise control over the attitudes and reactions of people such as wholesalers, retailers, and consumers, who are outside his own organization. Marketing science attempts to define the limits and conditions of control which must be implemented through appropriate forms of organization.

The Solution of Specific Problems.   In addition to these various avenues of scientific application, a field such as marketing illustrates another quite different relationship between science and action. The intensive studies which are frequently made to solve individual problems are scientific in spirit and methodology, but show a sharp contrast with science in the way these tools are used. The objective in a marketing study undertaken for an individual firm is to bring about a wiser decision on the immediate problem. The market analyst in this type of study looks at all aspects of the concrete situation, since all may have to be taken into account in plotting a future course of action. A marketing study undertaken from the viewpoint of pure science, on the other hand, might look at a single aspect of many concrete situations. The purpose might be to develop principles of action for such recurrent problems as the determination of an advertising budget. The general principles developed in this manner may then be made available as a guide to the decisions of marketing executives in many firms.

The writer at one time suggested that it was useful to distinguish between science on the one hand and the orderly study of concrete situations on the other. In an article for the *Philosophy of Science Journal,* he suggested that the term "systematics" be applied to the latter type of investigation. This term applies to systematic procedures for gathering and analyzing facts, even though they are not directed toward the development of general laws or principles. A large part of marketing research undertaken on behalf of business firms is of this character. Marketing theory should be broad enough to provide perspective for this type of investigation as well as for the purely scientific approach.

The market analyst has need of a general theory of problem solving to guide him in analysis of data directed toward the solution of a specific problem. The mere accumulation of information, however sound the statistical treatment, may not lead to a wise solution in the absence of such a conceptual framework. To be truly meaningful, statistical data should be organized in such a way as to test some hypothesis in the concrete situation. The market analyst is not usually engaged in testing a scientific hypothesis derived from a general explanatory theory. There is in the concrete operating situation, however, a source on which the analyst can draw for hypotheses. This source lies in the operating assumptions which necessarily guide the day-to-day decisions of the marketing executive. These assumptions may have to do with the size of the potential market for his product, the rate at which the market is growing, the part that his product plays in the operations of wholesalers and retailers, and the kinds of motivations and appeals which induce consumers to buy his product.

Operating assumptions may be either positive or negative, in the sense that they indicate the direction in which the executive feels free to move or the limitations which restrict his freedom of action. As long as everything is going well, he operates as if all of these assumptions were correct. If sales fall off, if his profits decline, or if competitors make unexpected inroads on his market position, the executive begins to feel uncertain about some of these assumptions. It is these uncertainties concerning a future course of action which constitute marketing problems. It is the function of the market analyst to identify the crucial assumptions the executive has been making and to design research procedures that will test these assumptions. From that point forward the testing of an operating assumption in all the research techniques employed is similar to the testing of a hypothesis derived from a general theory. In fact, it might be said that the marketing executive has been operating in terms of a theory about his business that covers its opportunity for growth and its capacity for effective effort in exploiting opportunity. This theory or set of assumptions in the mind of the executive might be regarded as a special case of what economists call "the theory of the firm." A central purpose of this book is to present a richer and more suggestive version of the theory of the firm which will provide perspective on marketing problems for the market analyst and the marketing executive.

By adopting this conception of a special operating theory tailored to the particular firm, the relationship between theory and practice becomes parallel to that which exists in pure science. Marketing theory thus has a twofold impact on marketing practice. On the one hand there is the possible application of principles of action derived from an expanding body of marketing science. On the other hand there is the use of scientific techniques in the orderly investigation and solution of marketing problems in concrete situations.

The Behavioral Sciences. The various disciplines which together are known as the "social sciences" are often contrasted with the physical sciences in method and content. The French philosopher of science, Comte, attempted to arrange all of the sciences in order like a series of building blocks placed one upon the other. There seems to be some merit in this classification scheme until the level of the social sciences is reached. Physics as the science of energy thus may be in a certain sense prior to chemistry, which treats the various forms of matter and their transformations. Chemistry, in turn, might be regarded as prior to biology, the study of life forms making use of chemical processes. Possibly psychology may be regarded as a fourth layer, but thereafter this vertical method of relating scientific fields seems scarcely adequate or appropriate. Once the level of human action is the subject of discussion, the fields of scientific interest divide more along horizontal than vertical lines. The anthropologist and the political scientist may look at the same human society and each report on the aspects of group behavior which are of special interest to him.

For the author, sociology is the most fundamental of the social sciences, although others would argue just as strongly for psychology. Giving priority to sociology has some advantages from the standpoint of classification. If general sociology is regarded as the study of all aspects of the life of man in society, then each of the other disciplines may be regarded as a more highly specialized development out of that field.

THEORY IN PRACTICE

The conception of sociology employed here is that of a broad study of social processes and social structure. From this viewpoint, many courses in sociology are really concerned with what might be called "applied sociology," or the study of a series of chronic social problems such as divorce, juvenile delinquency, and social conflict in neighborhood groups. The kind of sociology which is basic to social science in general is concerned first of all with the normal functioning of groups, with the basic elements making for group coherence, and with the satisfactions which groups produce for their members and which account for their perpetuation. The functioning of a group is determined by the constitutional character of its individual members. Psychology, which treats of individual adjustments, is a necessary adjunct to the study of group relations and the adjustment of its members to each other. For a market analyst with a sociological orientation, it appears hazardous to start with individual psychology as the most fundamental approach to human behavior. The most important entities in the environment of any individual are other human beings like himself. It is slightly unrealistic to deal with individual reactions except as they occur in a group environment. The interdependence of these two fields has been recognized in the emergence of social psychology as an intermediate area of study. The insistence on group behavior as a fundamental starting point is inherent in the basic premise of this book—marketing is a phenomenon of group behavior.

The choice of a starting point for a general science of human behavior is not an easy one to make. There is something to be said for starting with cultural anthropology in laying the foundation for a theory of marketing. Anthropology deals with human culture and emphasizes the attitudes and the ways of doing things which are passed on from person to person or from generation to generation within human society. Sometimes a culture is said to comprise all of the physical goods employed by a social group—its tools, weapons, garments, household furnishings, and ornaments. Somewhat more carefully defined, culture does not embrace the artifacts themselves but the ideas behind the artifacts which enable a people to design and produce the goods it needs and desires. Human culture undergoes constant change, and the rate of change with respect to the physical goods employed has been vastly accelerated in modern times. Certainly one major aspect of deliberate marketing effort lies in the field of applied anthropology, since the marketer attempts to modify the ideas of the consumer as to what is needed or wanted, and to gain acceptance for new classes of goods. Such a starting point in marketing theory would be useful but not sufficiently comprehensive. Marketing undertakes to study not only the changing material culture of modern society but also the process by which marketing objectives are achieved. An understanding of group behavior is needed to interpret an evolving material culture, rather than the reverse. The goods which are used by a family or a society manifestly fit together and complement each other. The coherence of such assortments of goods is wholly derivative, resting as it does on the goals and preferences of the people who use the goods.

The three behavioral sciences of widest scope—sociology, psychology, and anthropology—have shown the greatest tendency to join together in the development of a general science of human behavior. Several teams of scientists drawn from these three fields have engaged in seminars or protracted research programs with this end in view. Some of the more specialized studies classified as social science have participated to a lesser degree in this movement toward integration. Political science is relatively remote from this stream of contact between the disciplines, but primarily because it continues to be regarded as a study of governmental activity. Viewed more fundamentally, political science is the study of the power structure in any human organization, large or small. Political science seen in this light is pertinent to the development of theory in marketing. In fact, it is an essential aspect of the theory of organization which may be regarded as the core of general sociology.

Of all the social sciences, economics is perhaps the one with the greatest tendency to keep to itself. Many economists are scarcely ready to accept a classification of their field as an aspect of a general science of human behavior. Several generations of economists made psychological assumptions which were abandoned when the advancement of science showed them to be poor psychology. Some leading economists have derived insights from the other behavioral sciences, as for example Veblen from anthropology or J. M. Clark from political science. Other economists, however, might assert that they are not concerned with people but with goods and money in relation to the problems of scarcity and exchange.

One economist, still living, went so far as to say that economics, unlike the other sciences, has no references to factual data. Since its central concern is the problem of value, it had no access to such matters through observation and hence necessarily proceeded on a purely deductive basis, like logic or mathematics. This apology for a purely abstract approach to economics could only be matched by a statement from a physicist that he would confine himself to the deductive approach because of the invisibility of atoms.

The marketing executive is thoroughly aware that he is dealing with people. The market analyst finds it essential to formulate most of his problems in terms of group behavior. While his final objective is the movement of goods, he soon learns that group action is the key to his problem. At every level, marketing is concerned with various types of groups, whose behavior will be discussed in this volume. Consumption, which is the end and aim of marketing activity, is a highly socialized process. Most consumer goods are bought to serve the needs of the household, and all industrial goods are· bought to serve the needs of some operating organization. The average individual eats most of his meals in company with other people, and he is influenced by the reactions of other members of his group even in the purchase of such personal articles as clothing and accessories.

Of equal importance with consuming groups in the market place are the producing or distributing groups which supply the consumer. Marketing, of course, is the exchange taking place between consuming groups on the one hand and supplying groups on the other. In addition to these groups which persist over a period of time, there are temporary groups which engage in the negotiation of major transactions. It is important to recognize groups engaged in carrying out marketing transactions as organized behavior systems, even though they are usually dissolved when the transaction is completed. Some of the same principles of social interaction apply to transactional groups and to groups of more permanent character. All three of these types of groups have a formal structure. That is true at least to the extent that each individual involved is aware of his status as a member of the group and grants the same status to others with whom he is associated.

Aside from these groups which are marked by a consciousness of membership, there are other interactive groups in which individuals are bound together functionally in the performance of an operation, even though they have no consciousness of group membership. A major example of such a group is what is known as a "trade channel." A trade channel may exist as a distinct entity only in the mind of the manufacturer who is using it to reach the consumer. His distributors may be more inclined to class themselves with other wholesalers and his dealers with other retailers. Nevertheless the successive stages in the channel are interrelated functionally in such a way that principles of interaction valid for formal groups would also apply for trade channels.

Another interactive group of significance in marketing consists of all the firms making up a local trading center. Such a group is a functional entity serving the consumers in the area and reacting with them. Some of the retailers in such a trading center may be especially conscious of this aspect of group membership, while others are more disposed to think of themselves primarily as members of their respective retail trades whatever the location of the retailers involved.

Finally, there is a type of functioning entity, very loosely bound together indeed, which constitutes the national market for a given class of products. Both economics and marketing assume the possibility of exchange functioning on this national scale. Whether a national market actually exists is a more crucial issue for marketing than for general economics because of the various alternatives for market organization. In the marketing of flour, for example, the distribution of the output of each mill was at one time largely restricted to the immediate locality. Later on the market came to be dominated by large mills shipping their products throughout the United States. Under this latter form of organization the way is opened for producing a greater variety of specialized flours to meet particular needs. Generally, in the marketing of any class of product, production may be localized and product differentiation restricted, or production concentrated geographically but with product differentiation offering a greater variety of choice to the consumer.

The national market as a behavior group and principles of group interaction at the broader level are of special significance for marketing. The general economist has been interested in competition over a wide geographical area mainly as it affects the price-making mechanism. While recognizing the importance of price equilibrium, the marketing man is interested in the issue of local versus national markets for other reasons—including its consequences for product differentiation.

Functionalism and Integration. Functionalism is that approach to science which begins by identifying some system of action, and then tries to determine how and why it works as it does. Functionalism stresses the whole system and undertakes to interpret the parts in terms of how they serve the system. Some writers who are actually advocates of functionalism prefer to speak of the holistic approach because of emphasis on the system as a whole. Functionalism generally recognizes that the operation of a system is likely to change over time and that the essence of science is its dynamic aspect. To signify this attitude, some who accept the viewpoint of functionalism in general describe their perspective as the holistic-dynamic approach. Functionalism is continually striving to maintain an adequately comprehensive view of its field of study. Sometimes it may appear to attain breadth of view at the expense of sharpness of focus. Critics of functionalism assert that it does not have an integrated and internally consistent body of theory.

Instead it is charged with being completely eclectic and taking what it needs wherever it finds it, even from types of theory which were never intended to go together. The functionalist can cheerfully admit this charge, since he is not interested in theory for its own sake but as a conceptual tool which will help him to deal with factual data and with problems of action.

It is true that functionalism, like any other scientific approach, has its own particular hazards which its advocates must guard against. Sometimes excessive zeal is shown in trying to prove that some part of a system is functional when it really should be regarded as the fossil remains of some previous operating system. Again the particular institution or artifact may be an innovation which has not yet been fully established in the operating system. The stress upon function may lead the investigator to ignore malfunction. The latter danger has been pointed out by students of abnormal psychology. While accepting these admonitions, the functionalist is entitled to retort that it would not even be possible to conceive of malfunction except in terms of some functioning system.

The functionalist may also need to be cautioned to give adequate attention to structure. Actually, a sound functionalism in the social sciences necessarily concerns itself with the structure of operating systems. Both function and structure are embraced in the subject matter of scientific study; but the functionalist believes that function basically determines structure in group behavior, rather than the reverse. However, he recognizes the existence of the opposite situation (which may become pathological from the viewpoint of a theory of adjustment), in which a group is acting in a way that is not truly functional, because of its internal structure. Even here he does not feel that he understands the situation if he goes no further than to describe the existing structure. He is impelled to find out what functions it is performing and, even more fundamentally, how the group will have to function in order to survive. This brings us to the final difficulty of functionalism, which is also its greatest challenge. It is scarcely possible to give a correct interpretation of the functioning of a group unless the student begins with a recognition and understanding of its actual or potential functions.

If this sounds like something verging on a normative science rather than a purely descriptive one, the functionalist can only accept the charge and learn to live with the problem. He can still hold up his head as a scientist if the norms he applies are inherent in the systems he is studying and not imposed from without. Thus the majority of systems seem to operate as if they were trying to survive, to grow, and to produce some kind of surplus or output. When the scientist observes pathological behavior in some system, he is judging it to be abnormal in terms of his conception of how a healthy system operates.

Perhaps some may regard functionalism as only one of many strands of scientific thought in man's effort to understand his universe. What makes it so important for marketing, as well as for a general science of human behavior, is that it is the one common factor to be found in all the social and biological sciences. The connection is not so simple as was imagined by Herbert Spencer and his followers, who tried to extend the principles of Darwin to an evolutionary sociology. What is common to all social scientists is the desire to understand and explain the totality of human behavior, each contributing from the standpoint of his special interest. Each human group has a culture and hence might be studied by the anthropologist. Because of the group's internal organization and adjustment to its environment, it is an appropriate subject of investigation for the sociologist. Finally, any attitude held within a group or any decisions reached are, in the last analysis, the attitudes and decisions of individuals—thus the group is brought within the scope of psychology.

Functionalism has had a checkered career in all of the social sciences. American psychology has been essentially functionalist from the days of James and Dewey, even though many psychologists have repudiated the label. Today a neofunctionalism is emerging which has absorbed many of the insights of Gestalt, psychoanalysis, and stimulus-response psychology. The sociologists, perhaps more than any other students of human behavior, have concentrated their attention on the functioning of groups, large or small. It is true that there have been distinctive points of emphasis in their attempts to explain group activity such as geographical determinism and cultural determinism. Through it all the central emphasis has been upon the way that groups are formed, why groups persist, how they adjust to an environment, and what types of surplus they produce for their members, as compared with unorganized activity. In anthropology the functional viewpoint was relatively late in making a formal appearance. Several generations of anthropologists fought the battle of evolution versus diffusion as alternative explanations of cultural change. The functionalist viewpoint tended gradually to resolve this issue as it developed in the hands of Malinowski and others. The overriding concept came to be that of a cultural complex with a strong internal coherence but never entirely closed. With respect to diffusion of culture, the complex served as a selective mechanism through which a society accepted some cultural traits offered through contact and rejected others. With respect to evolution as the source of new cultural features, the complex served to stimulate the invention of what was needed and to promote the adoption of the innovation.

The functionalist viewpoint has inevitably appeared in the foreground of major efforts toward integration of the social sciences. Two books which are the fruits of such efforts will be utilized frequently in this discussion. One of them is called *Toward a General Theory of Action* and represents the collaboration of nine scholars from the fields of sociology, anthropology, and psychology under the leadership of Talcott Parsons. The other book is the product of seven scholars from the same fields, edited by John Gillin. The latter book is called *For a Science of Social Man* and has the significant subtitle "Convergences in Anthropology, Psychology, and Sociology."

Functionalism in Economics. Economics and marketing share a basic concern as to what goes on in the market place. The stimulus behind organized study was quite different in the two cases, economics being originally concerned with affairs of state, as indicated by Adam Smith in the title of his book, *The Wealth of Nations.* Marketing was not recognized as a separate field of study until the twentieth century and arose because of the distance which frequently separated the producer and the ultimate consumer. The study of agricultural marketing grew up because the produce of specialized farming areas had to be shipped many miles to market. Organized study of the marketing of manufactured products arose in the effort to guide the attempts of the producer to reach the consumer through advertising. Geographical distance might or might not intervene between the manufacturer and consumer, but there is a kind of distance consisting of the intervening channels of trade which do not always share the manufacturer's desire to maximize the sale of his products. While economics began with the study of a national economy, it was later extended to problems of the individual firm. Marketing, by contrast, began with the problems of individual firms or producing groups and went much further than economics in its study of the detailed processes by which goods were moved from producer to consumer.

Economics as the older science has developed an impressive body of theory and a more conscious awareness of its underlying assumptions as to the nature of science. A central issue long debated is whether economics is to be regarded as a purely descriptive science or as a normative science. It is sometimes asked whether the theoretical model presented by economics represents the best available picture of the way the economy actually works, or whether it is to be regarded as an ideal of the way it ought to work. Stigler has been so bold as to say that it is both, at one and the same time. This seems to be a paradox —equivalent to saying that the present system is the best of all possible worlds, but it may be possible to resolve the conflict. As indicated above, the scientist is justified in applying standards to the operation of a system if they appear to him to be inherent in the nature of the system itself. On these terms Stigler is making two assertions concerning his model, the first being that it portrays the way in which the system would operate if allowed to function without interference. The second statement implied is that since the system is doing the best it can to function in the manner indicated, no other model could provide a better picture of what is actually going on.

Another fundamental issue in economics has been that between the classical school and institutionalism. The former, from the days of Ricardo down to the present, has worked on a largely deductive basis, engaging in a continuing elaboration of a set of models intended to portray the functioning of the economic system and of subordinate entities such as the individual firm. The institutionalists have taken the opposite approach of looking at actual economic arrangements and attempting to build up a series of generalizations based on these factual data. The weakness of the classical approach has been that little effort was made to test its theories through empirical research and even in the bold assertion in some cases that factual investigation was irrelevant in economics. The weakness of the institutional school has been in replacing the carefully constructed classical models with sweeping generalizations to explain the entire evolution of economic activity. The emphasis on institutions was associated with an interest in the way that institutions were constantly being modified in the course of economic and social adjustment. The notion of conflict came to be as central for the institutionalist as was the concept of equilibrium for the classicist. Karl Marx, as the forerunner of the institutionalists, built his economic theory on the concept of class struggle and the gradual movement toward a classless society. Later institutionalists such as Veblen drew the line between good and evil even more sharply. This struggle of the powers of light and the powers of darkness is as dramatic as that in the theology of ancient Persia.

Veblen balances the businessman against the engineer, the profit motive against the instinct of workmanship. The struggle between good and evil for Ayres is the fight between technology and the embodiment of culture lag in what he calls "ceremonialism." Wesley Mitchell draws a contrast between making goods and making money. Mitchell's real importance in the development of institutionalism, however, is the scale on which he put into practice its preference for factual investigation as compared to purely deductive reasoning in economics.

John R. Commons accepted the institutionalist label, and even gave his last great work the title of *Institutional Economics*. He was not an institutionalist at all in the Veblenian sense of rejecting the classical analytical apparatus, nor in the sense of adopting a devil theory of economic conflict and change. Commons illustrates better than any other economist what the present writer calls the "functionalist approach." It is true that he dealt with economic institutions, but he was interested in them as the framework for social action. He talked constantly in terms of "collective action," which is roughly equivalent to the term "group behavior" as used in this book. He is pre-eminent among economists in his understanding of the business firm as a functioning whole, an insight which was given luminous expression in his phrase, "the going concern." He was a prodigious investigator of actual economic conditions and utilized the classical concepts insofar as they served his analytical purposes. The fact that bargaining is not readily amenable to the classical treatment did not blind him to its importance in the concrete problem situations he confronted. He brought a fresh understanding to the marketing process and had some interesting things to say about its dual nature. He discussed the technology of the physical movement of goods, comparing it with the use of productive effort in agriculture or manufacturing. By contrast he saw the change of title from one owner to another as the essence of exchange involving scarcity and coercion, controlled only by the bargaining limits inherent in the situation.

Some contemporary economists are contributing to an understanding of how business actually functions in one way or another. To mention a few, J. M. Clark brought a new understanding of the realities of business policy in his study of overhead costs. Chamberlin opened up new vistas in his discussion of monopolistic competition, calling attention to the fact that the specifications of the product and the means for promoting it are just as essential in marketing policy as is price determination. Knauth has provided a new conception of the managerial role in describing the way in which the executive constructs and operates a system of action reaching far beyond the limits of his own organization. Boulding in his recent writings has recognized the importance of survival as a business goal. It is to be hoped that he will go further in the development of insights he has drawn from the field of animal ecology in which competition is no longer atomistic, but represents the struggle between populations of firms to survive and to prevail. An Austrian economist, von Mises, gives his definitive works the title *Human Action*. He defines action as purposeful behavior. He believes that the primary role of economics is to develop principles of action which can make purposeful behavior more successful. He suggests the term "praxeology" for the study of such principles of action. The later chapters in this book will deal with principles of efficient action applicable to marketing. The earlier chapters are intended to develop understanding of collective action or group behavior in marketing as a foundation for the later treatment of principles of action.

Functionalism in Marketing. Functionalism has been a central tendency in the efforts to develop marketing theory in recent years. Marketing teachers and theorists are more consistent in their use of the functionalist approach than they are in their terminology. Sometimes the term has been used in marketing in a narrower sense than in psychology and the other social sciences. Marketing teachers have discussed three alternative approaches to describing or explaining the marketing scene: the commodity approach, the institutional approach, and the functional approach. Those who adopt the commodity approach are impressed with the great differences in the detailed marketing processes as they have developed in various commodity fields. They feel that the only way to present a realistic description of the marketing of steel and steel products is to confine the exposition to that class of commodities. They contend that there is little resemblance between the marketing of steel on the one hand and the marketing of cosmetics or machine tools on the other. Any attempt at generalization across commodity lines becomes so abstract as to be meaningless. The institutionalists in marketing prefer to start their descriptions of marketing behavior with the various types of firms and government agencies which participate in marketing. They devote chapters or sections of their books to the description of retailers, wholesale merchants, brokers, and commodity exchanges. Writers of this type in marketing are not necessarily committed to a particular explanation of institutional change as are Veblen and others in economics. Perhaps this is because so much of marketing discussion is still at the level of description, while the effort to develop a theoretical framework is relatively recent.

Functionalism is the most promising approach for theoretical development in marketing because it begins with concepts which can be applied to all types of commodities and all types of firms which participate in marketing. The first step is to identify the marketing functions and then to show how they apply in one situation after another. One difficulty to date is that lists of functions offered by different writers vary as much as the lists of instincts which once were so prevalent in psychology. Another hazard is that a writer may assume that he has developed a marketing theory when he has merely engaged in classifying functions. This is only the beginning and not the consummation of theoretical development. Functional analysis can be used either as interpretation or in the solution of marketing problems. The classification of functions must be shown to have relevance to the various kinds of groups or organized behavior systems which carry on marketing operations. A true functionalist must not overlook the other aspects of business in emphasizing marketing and hence fail to grasp the whole through magnifying a single component. Marketing should be regarded as a vantage point from which to understand business policy as a whole rather than as a single and narrowly specialized interest.

Most of the writers in marketing today who exhibit a special interest in marketing theory can appropriately be classified as functionalists. Aspinwall has developed the most comprehensive conceptual framework, including an analysis of many of the major types of organized behavior systems in marketing and the way they function. Unfortunately, he has written very little, so that his work is known only to his students and his personal friends. McGarry has provided the most precise and thoughtful treatment of the marketing functions. Converse has devoted himself largely to a single type of behavior system, the local trading center. Grether, by contrast, has been primarily concerned with producing regions and interregional trade as the starting point for theory in marketing. A symposium under the editorship of Clewett has made a beginning in the development of a theory of marketing channels. Cox has pursued similar concerns in his treatment of the flow of products through various stages from producer to consumer. Joel Dean, an economist who has had a wide experience with marketing problems, has made a major contribution in showing how the analytical tools of economics might be applied to concrete marketing situations. A variety of insights which may eventually contribute to a body of theory are being brought into marketing by men with background in other fields such as psychology and sociology. The present effort attempts to draw on all of these sources in developing marketing theory as an aspect of a general theory of human behavior.

Alternatives to Functionalism. The functionalist viewpoint has been emphasized so repeatedly in this chapter that the reader may begin to wonder what alternatives there are. In American psychology one of the early alternatives was known as "structuralism." Titchener and his followers felt that the functionalists were erecting a superstructure before they had established the proper foundations. They felt that the question of how a system works should be preceded by the question of what the system is. In other words, it was premature to try to deal with function until a long period of scientific observation had built up an adequate understanding of structure. More generally, this question as to where science should start raises the fundamental issue of the relation of science to action. On the one side is the pragmatic view that a science should begin as quickly as possible to handle its data in such a way as to produce practical results. On the other side is what might be called the "existential" view, that science is concerned first of all with the nature of reality and that questions of human purpose are secondary. The present view is that marketing would not exist as a separate field of study except to promote practical objectives, and that any theory that will provide a useful perspective for this field is necessarily pragmatic or functionalist.

There are still other differences of opinion, which may affect theory, as to the nature of science and of the relation of science to action. The most radical rejection of purpose or function as a central concern of science is that represented by the positivists. They contend that the whole business of science is to record and measure the phenomena observed in a given field. They are loath to recognize any qualitative distinctions or any relationships between variables which cannot be stated in quantitative terms. In subdivisions of sociology such as sociometry, they have shown ingenuity in finding methods for quantifying relationships which were previously discussed only in descriptive terms. Stuart Dodd has developed an impressive scheme for specifying all the variables in a social situation, but he seldom uses the term "system" or assumes that these variables are functionally related.

At the other extreme are those social theorists, including a few economists, who appear to consider organized factual information as so much excess baggage so far as the development of theory is concerned. In fact, some go so far as to say that such testing is impossible because of the extreme complexity of the facts or because the facts are irrelevant for theory. In the latter group are those who have regarded economic theory as purely deductive and as being constructed on the basis of assumptions concerning the nature of value and the nature of action. These truths they hold to be self-evident and not requiring substantiation through factual investigation.

The main body of contemporary economists are functionalists in the sense of concerning themselves with systems of action and how they operate to achieve the objectives of their participants. Marketing theory differs from received economic theory mainly in visualizing a more flexible functionalism which is concerned with a variety of systems and subsystems involved in the movement of goods and service.

Functionalism stands somewhere between the extremes. Functionalism tries to maintain the rigorous standards of the empiricists as to what to accept as facts and to appreciate the analytical power of the deductive methods developed in economic theory. The present writer characterizes his viewpoint as functionalism but is not unaware that this viewpoint also has its limitations and its hazards. The choice may be due in part to his sociological leanings and hence a tendency to take group behavior as fundamental. There are other compelling reasons which are not related to this personal background. Functionalism is the approach which is most in evidence in the attempts to integrate the social sciences. Meanwhile, it gives marketing a conceptual framework which will facilitate its borrowing from these other fields. The marketing teachers and market analysts who tend to be most interested in marketing theory can fairly be classified as belonging to the functionalist school. Finally, the functionalist emphasis on how things work and what is involved in making them work better makes it suitable as a theoretical approach in a field such as marketing, which is concerned first of all with the solution of practical problems.

Key Concepts of Functionalism. Among the key concepts of the functional approach are "group" and "organized behavior systems." These concepts are closely related but not identical. An organized behavior system is a group taken in conjunction with the environment in which it moves and has its being. The system may be regarded as including the instruments and resources utilized in its operations. Such material adjuncts are not part of the group, which consists only of the human beings present in the system; but these adjuncts belong to the system in the sense of being within its possession and control.

Of course, instruments or artifacts belong to a behavior system only to the degree that they are used by individuals in the processes of their behavior. The term "operating system" will also be used from time to time, but this implies a slightly different shading of meaning with emphasis on the inputs and outputs of the system. The notion of subsystems will be employed to designate sequences of behavior which are closely linked, even though they do not constitute an independently functioning entity in time and space.

The general idea of a system is familiar to any student of science as a whole consisting of related component parts. Sometimes the components are very different from each other, and their relationship consists primarily in their common or complementary participation in some operation. One of the most luminous discussions of systems in general is by Ross Ashby in a book called *Design for a Brain*. Ashby's treatment constitutes an important extension of the idea that a system consists of a set of elements which tend always toward some point of balance or equilibrium.

He is looking for something beyond the simple mechanical model, exemplified by the thermostat which maintains a steady temperature indoors by reacting to outside temperatures and controlling a source of heat accordingly. There are many physiological mechanisms in the human body which function in a similar way, such as that which maintains body temperature at 98.6° F. or that which stabilizes the degree of salinity in the blood. This is the type of internal control which Cannon called "homeostasis."

In developing a model for the action of the brain, Ashby recognized that it was equipped to handle many more variables than any of these relatively simple stabilizers and sometimes to bring about immediate adjustment to radically changed conditions. He employs the term "ultrastability" for the organism which is able to achieve adjustment in the face of sudden environmental changes.

The Ashby model for a functioning system will be relied on at various points in the discussion. It is not, however, completely adequate in mirroring the major features of the behavior system springing from a human group. Members of a group can disagree on either ends or means and reach a compromise by debating the issues or by gathering and analyzing further information. Conflict may result in a group breaking up or dividing into two groups. Discrete groups may choose to work together on some project or merge into a single group. The most fundamental difference between a human group and a mechanical system lies in the ultimate bond which holds the group together. This is the element of common expectations. In fact, a group may be defined as two or more individuals linked together by positive expectations concerning the outcome of their association.

SYSTEM AND STATUS

The type of mechanical system which Ashby has been studying is only one of the major possibilities for a system of behavior. Ashby went so far as to design an electronic machine which he called the "homeostat" and which was purely mechanical in its operation but had the ability to adjust to sudden changes originating outside the system. The essence of a mechanical system is that all of the parts are positively connected with each other, and the behavior of the mechanism is completely determined by the rigid structure relating the components.

The Atomistic System. The model which has been preferred in classical economic theory has been described as atomistic because the components are not held in a rigid structure but react with each other freely and at random. The origin of this model is the analysis in physics of the interaction of moving particles, as in the case of a gas enclosed in a sealed chamber. The physicist defines an equilibrium state for his closed system. He is able to describe by mathematical formulas the processes of interaction by which the particles approach or maintain the equilibrium state. The particles collide from time to time and thus reach an even distribution throughout the enclosed space, but the particles are not paired or connected in any way. That is to say that there is no force inherent in the particles or no feature of their structure which causes them to cling together or to react in a well-defined pattern. They constitute a system solely because they cannot escape from the sealed chamber, and they suffer collision with each other simply because each particle continues to move in its established direction until it meets an obstacle.

Students of social and economic life who admire the precision of physics have attempted to show that human society can also be interpreted in atomistic terms. This type of model has had an especial appeal for economists who have sought to interpret free competition and equilibrium prices. The atomistic model in economics has come to be associated with a doctrine of how an economic system should work as much as with a description of its actual functioning. This type of analysis says, in effect, that if there are so many competitors in an industry that no one firm has a significant part of the business, and if each supplier serves the prospective customers at random rather than enjoying an established trade, then something called an "equilibrium price" will emerge from competition and the processes of exchange. The significance of the atomistic model for this analysis is that it lays the foundation for assuming a smooth and continuous adjustment between demand and supply, so that the system is always kept at equilibrium. This is accomplished by complete flexibility of prices, so that when demand exceeds supply, prices will rise just enough to stimulate supply or to restrict demand until the two sides of the market are again in balance. Similarly, when demand at the going price is less than supply, prices will fall to restore equilibrium.

The Mechanical System.   Market analysts as well as economists accept these laws of supply and demand but find that the atomistic model does not carry them very far toward understanding aspects of exchange other than price, or toward the solution of the many practical problems involved in the movement of goods. There is considerable temptation for the marketing man to go over to the other extreme and adopt a rigid mechanical model in which the component parts are positively related to each other. He may picture the free market economy as a vast machine for moving goods in which there is a flow from one stage to another in the channels of distribution, and where time, place, and possession utilities are produced and added to the utility inherent in the physical nature of the goods. In fact, some expositions of the institutional approach in marketing read as if their chief mission were to describe just such a machine.

The analogy to a machine is even more apt when the marketing man is looking into the internal operations of a single firm. The marketing and management consultant is obliged to go beyond what is called in economics the "theory of the firm," which is chiefly concerned with price policy from the viewpoint of the individual seller. The consultant undertaking to improve a marketing operation looks at all the components of the system and their relationships to each other in much the same spirit that an engineer might look upon a problem of machine design or improvement. A component must be effective in the subfunction it is expected to perform, but it must also be in balance with all of the other components. Thus an expensive advertising campaign, however much it influences the consumer, may not be worth what it costs if the company does not have adequate retail coverage for displaying its products to consumers.

Many disparities and even active conflicts arise in the distribution system for any class of products. The major causes of these difficulties lie in the fact that the system is not actually a machine, since the major components are human beings with some independence of motivation and judgment. It is just this fact which accounts for the strength and flexibility of a marketing system as well as for its characteristic defects.

The Ecological, or Group Behaviorism, System. The third type of system is the one which co-ordinates group behavior in all human and animal societies. This type of system has been thoroughly analyzed in ecology, the division of biology which deals with animal societies and their adjustment to their natural environments. The system of co-ordination which binds such a group together in an established pattern of behavior may be called an "ecological system." The term "human ecology" was adopted some years ago but has chiefly been applied to patterns of group behavior that were determined primarily by geographical proximity. This whole book could be understood as an exercise in human ecology if that term were given the same broad scope as in the discussion of animal societies. Instead the term "group behaviorism" is adopted to characterize the investigation of the formation and persistence of groups, the analysis of group structure and function, and the internal and external adjustment of groups to meet changing conditions. It is in these broad terms that the understanding of group behavior is taken as the foundation for marketing theory.

The relationship between the components and the system is what distinguishes the three types of systems from each other. In the atomistic system the particles are held together only by the boundary which confines the space in which they move, and they interact only by colliding as they move freely in this restricted space. In the mechancial system the parts are held together by a rigid structure, and the machine continues to function as a whole or breaks down completely if a vital part breaks down. In the ecological system the relation of the components to the system as a whole stands somewhere between these two extremes. Components are not associated in a merely random fashion as in the gas chamber, nor are they rigidly connected with each other as in the machine. Instead there is a tendency for each part to occupy a certain position or status in relation to the others. This means that it will react most frequently with other components which lie adjacent to it either physically or in relation to the flow of process within the system. Another term for "position" is "ecological niche," which might be defined as the opportunity to participate in a specified way in the network of life processes in some animal community. In the ecological system it is possible for a position to remain unoccupied for a period without causing the system to cease functioning.

At the same time the existence of a niche creates an opportunity for some individual or subgroup qualified to fill it. An ecological system operates something like a machine with the unique capacity for repairing or remodeling itself.

The common rabbit found such an open niche or opportunity when it was imported into Australia. Having no serious rivals for its chosen type of food and no predators to limit its natural increase, it multiplied so fast that it soon became a pest from the standpoint of the human population of Australia. In a well-balanced animal society it may be assumed that all of the principal niches are occupied or, in other words, that all of the major opportunities for life are being exploited successfully by existing species.

The Factor of Status. A somewhat similar structure can be observed in every human group, including those engaged in marketing. Each individual who is a member of the group occupies a position or status with respect to the other members. On the basis of status in the group each member harbors expectations concerning his participation in group activities, and the other members in turn entertain expectations concerning his behavior. In short, to belong to a group or enjoy status in it is to be a party to this network of expectations. So long as the individual accepts his status and in turn is granted his status by the other members, his interaction with them follows a pattern resembling the interaction of machine elements more than the random collisions of the particles in an atomistic system. On the other hand, an element of freedom and uncertainty is introduced into the system through the exigencies affecting individual status. A vacancy may occur through death; the individual may be forced out of his position by pressure from other members; or he may achieve a higher position in the structure of the group, leaving his previous status as an opening for others. This notion of status is a key concept in the analysis of group behavior and hence a foundation stone for the theory of marketing.

The fundamental importance of the factor of status lies in linking the individual to the system, and each subsystem in turn to the larger system of which it is a part. An individual may have status within the sales department of a firm. The sales department may be engaged in trying to realize its full opportunity within the company, while the firm itself is functioning as a component of a system of production and distribution, supplying consumers with a given class of products. Each may play an essential role at a given time but prove to be replaceable if it disappears from the scene. An ecological system thus has the remarkable character of being closed and open at the same time. It is closed in the sense of providing a co-ordinated operating structure for the discharge of its functions. It is simultaneously open to expansion by the addition of components or to improvement of its efficiency by the dropping or replacing of components. The dual nature of the system accounts for the distinctive features of group behavior which enable the system to function in a changing world. At the same time it is this dual nature which creates many uncertainties and tensions and presents many problems to the market analyst and the marketing executive.

How does the individual achieve membership in the group? Some groups are biological in origin, so that the individual is already a member when he is first confronted with the fact of interaction. A child is born into a family, and the family is still one of the most fundamental groups for social science and, of course, for marketing. The status he is able to achieve within the family, the demands he makes upon others, and what they expect of him in return depend both on the previous structure of the family and on the child's own inherent traits. Other groups come into being through simple geographical propinquity. Thus the residents of a neighborhood, both adults and children, inevitably form an interactive group. Casual contacts may ripen into congenial association or, if unfavorable, may arouse dormant suspicion and hostility. Both animal and human groups can quickly form a defensive front to repel what they regard as an invasion of their territory. The danger may be a direct threat to the lives of group members, or only appear to threaten the social and economic order of the community. The point here is not the reason for solidarity but the fact that the individual under some circumstances is drawn into a group without consciously seeking or accepting membership.

In human society many groups, by contrast with the family or the neighborhood, are constituted originally through the purposeful action of their members or recruit new members by a conscious and deliberate process. The individual may seek membership voluntarily or feel when it is conferred that he has achieved a new and significant status. The outlook changes for him because of the new expectations associated with his status as a group member. He now looks forward to participating in the activities of the group and receiving a share of its output. Since nearly all economic activity is group activity, the individual has no economic basis for his life except as a member of a group. The young adult, when he leaves the protection of the ancestral family, must establish his own base for economic survival. Similarly, he must join in the formation of a new conjugal family to assure socially accepted sexual satisfactions.

Some of the associations which the individual first enters into on a voluntary basis are relatively stable and permanent. In economic organizations in a free society, including those engaged in marketing, the presumption is that the individual can withdraw if he is disappointed in his expectations or if a better opportunity appears. Another presumption of economic democracy is that any member may aspire to rise to a higher status within the system. Expectations as to improvements in status are commonly a major inducement for the individual in considering alternative opportunities for group membership. There is a continuous interaction between the individual and the group surrounding this expectation of status improvement. The group or its official agent emphasizes this prospect in an effort to obtain its choice of recruits. If the group gets the type of man who is interested in progress, it may not be able to hold him if progress is too slow in coming. The prospective recruit, on the other hand, judges a group such as a sales organization by such factors as its rate of growth, which indicates the likelihood of advancement. If he bases his hopes on expansion, he and other members of the group must try to make it happen in order to reap the rewards.

SUMMARY

The functionalist approach to marketing theory begins with the study of organized behavior systems. Marketing functions are discharged by behavior systems or by individuals acting within systems. The type of system of interest here is classed as an ecological system because of the peculiar nature of the bond among the components. They are sufficiently integrated to permit the system to operate as a whole, but the bond is loose enough to allow for the replacement or addition of components. Many marketing systems are also ultrastable in Ashby's sense that they are able to modify their manner of functioning to meet sudden changes in the environment. Neither mechanical systems nor atomistic systems have these characteristics.

Such considerations may appear in the beginning to be far removed from the flow of exchange transactions which is a major aspect of market behavior. The transaction will be given appropriate emphasis in succeeding chapters. The interpretation of transactions will regard them as events taking place within or between behavior systems. It is believed that this view promotes greater understanding of market transactions and suggests practical programs for increasing transactional efficiency. The central role in market behavior assigned to sorting and to the routinization of transactions grows naturally out of the treatment of marketing systems.

Much of the content of marketing theory necessarily covers the same ground as economics. What is presented here will generally be found to be consistent with the main stream of economic thought. Yet there is a difference in perspective related to the difference in the ends to be served. A familiar parallel is the fact that the psychologist and the sociologist may each apply his special techniques and seek his own distinctive objectives in examining the same phenomena of human behavior. The discussion of competition and of consumer buying relies heavily on contemporary economics but with a different emphasis. The writer usually attempts to reflect the attitude of the participants in marketing activity as compared to that of an outside observer. The ulimate objective is to understand how firms and households attempt to solve their problems in the market place and to discern some principles by which they might do it better. Interest in the marketing economy as a whole is primarily in the way it continues to evolve through the activities of its components.

The final chapters on executive action might appear to go beyond the scope of marketing theory proper. Surely they are appropriate in a book on marketing theory which holds that the chief function of theory is to serve as a perspective for practice. Every marketing executive is a theorist, consciously or unconsciously, since he must use some general framework in marshalling facts to reach a decision. Even these final chapters are theoretical in the sense that they picture decision making as a process taking place in organized behavior systems and present some general principles for problem solving and market planning.

SELECTED REFERENCES

ASHBY, W. ROSS. *Design for a Brain.* New York: John Wiley & Sons, Inc., 1952.

COX, REAVIS and ALDERSON, WROE (eds.). *Theory in Marketing.* Chicago: Richard D. Irwin, Inc., 1950.

COMMONS, JOHN R. *Institutional Economics.* New York: Macmillan Co., 1934.

PARSONS, TALCOTT and SHILS, E. A. (eds.). *Toward a General Theory of Action.* Cambridge, Mass.: Harvard University Press, 1951.

GILLIN, JOHN (ed.). *For a Science of Social Man.* New York: Macmillan Co., 1954.

The first seventy-five pages of Ashby's book are probably the best discussion to date of the nature of systems in general. Ashby is more hopeful than the author of this book of eventually explaining all systems in terms of mechanical principles. Yet most that he has to say about systems can be applied to ecological systems as well.

The concept of the organized behavior system, developed in this chapter, was first presented in one of the essays in the symposium edited by Cox and Alderson. The various contributors reflect considerable diversity of opinion as to the nature and scope of marketing theory.

The last two references are among the more notable efforts to achieve a synthesis of the social sciences into a general science of human behavior. There is an increasing tendency for teams from the various fields to work together. A new scientific journal, devoted to human behavior in general, has just been established; but its initial plans do not recognize marketing as a separate aspect of this general science.

Chapter II

FORMATION AND PERSISTENCE
OF GROUPS

The chapter attempts to explain the nature of a group whose interrelated activities constitute an organized behavior system. The members of a group associate themselves together to obtain some surplus of satisfactions or expectations as compared to isolated individual action. Attention is centered on power and communication as fundamental in all organized behavior systems. These factors can be seen most clearly by concentrating at first on primitive operations, namely, those which do not involve inputs and outputs.

The interrelations of power and communication are considered, showing the various ways in which the power structure and the communication structure are interdependent. The power principle is introduced to help explain the tendency of behavior systems to survive and to expand. The treatment of survival leads to the statement of three theorems or basic principles governing survival.

The discussion of growth proceeds in terms of the life history of a business enterprise. The three characteristic stages of establishment, expansion, and consolidation are described. Similar stages of growth and the typical problems of growth apply in a general way to other organized behavior systems as well as to the business firm.

SUBSYSTEMS AND PRIMITIVE OPERATIONS

The organized behavior system pertaining to a group can be broken down into subsystems comprising specific aspects of behavior. These subsystems are not so much parts of the whole system as ways of looking at its total functioning. In four of its major aspects a behavior system may be regarded as a power system, a system of communication, a system of inputs and outputs, and a system of internal and external adjustments. The aspects of power and communication are the most primitive elements constituting a behavior system. These elements are the necessary and sufficient conditions for systematic action. In fact, there are some primitive operations which take place within animal

35

and human societies which do not involve inputs or capacity for adjustment to a changing environment.

A power system evolves directly out of the factor of status, which has already been discussed. It imposes a pattern upon the use of the physical and intellectual energies of the participating members. The pattern may be formulated as a set of rules or standards accepted by the group in the case of human societies. But behind the rules lies the sanction of coercion or persuasion by the group or a leader acting as the agent of the group. Coercion may take the form of bodily injury, expulsion from the group, or loss of standing within it. Membership status gives the individual some security against such measures so long as he does not violate the accepted pattern. Leadership often carries special privileges and immunities but also imposes the responsibility of exercising initiative and command on behalf of the group.

Communication at the most primitive level consists in exhibiting and recognizing marks of membership in the group. Members are recognized by peculiarities of appearance or odor and by signs devised for the purpose. These signs may take the form of gestures or of vocal utterances. Primitive communication also embraces symbols of differentiation within the group such as rank, age, and sex and the acceptance of these symbols in determining appropriate behavior responses. In a formal organization such as a military unit, symbol and response are made explicit and include the shoulder insignia of officers, the hand salute required of subordinates, the password in response to the sentry's challenge, and the distinction in type of uniform for male and female personnel. In less formal groups equally numerous distinctions are recognized and maintained by more subtle means. Rank is symbolized in part by personal bearing and manner of speech, and its acceptance is signalized in part by deferential demeanor on the part of subordinates. The point here is that all of these signs and symbols are communication whether or not they are given linguistic expression.

The remainder of this chapter will be concerned with primitive operations which can occur in a group, given only the foundation of power and communication. The next chapter will move on to the more advanced operations which require inputs and result in outputs. The economic activities of both production and marketing take place in input-output systems. The fact that a system handles inputs and outputs reacts in turn on the aspects of power and communication. The interaction of the cardinal features of subsystems will follow naturally after an examination of the more primitive group operations. An attempt to understand the evolving behavior of groups engaged in marketing is the ultimate goal. To understand group adjustment, it is first necessary to understand both primitive and advanced operations as they develop and are conditioned by the factors of power and communication.

Primitive Operation of Rationing. The first primitive operation is rationing. Even if a group occupies a favorable habitat in which no group activity is required to satisfy its needs, a social order is still essential to the enjoyment of the bounty of nature. Assume only that the principle of scarcity is operative to the extent that the food supply would not permit satiation of all individual appetites, even though it is ample for subsistence Without rationing the strong might be satiated, but the weak die of starvation. In fact, there would be no security for the strong unless they adopted rationing among themselves, since they might kill each other off in the struggle for the choicest morsels. In the most primitive tribes, drawing on a common supply of food or raw materials, the determination of shares is a major function of the leader or the elders of the tribe. Sometimes rationing is facilitated by taboos which in effect break the group down into subgroups for purposes of sharing. Some foods are reserved for women and children by making them taboo for men, and vice versa.

Another field for rationing is in the distribution of sexual satisfactions. Many societies, even at the most primitive level, gravitate toward monogamous relations, perhaps in response to the approximate numerical equality of males and females among humans. Lifetime mating occurs in many animal species as well as in man. Extremes in the organization of sex life are carried further perhaps among some animal societies than in man. Witness the unrestrained promiscuity of the howling monkeys of Panama or polygamy as practiced among the fur-bearing seals or the Olympic elk of the rain forests of Washington. The bull seal or the bull elk collects a herd of cows during the mating season and guards them jealously for his own use. Many males in both species must remain bachelors until they are able to conquer one of the herd masters and take over his herd for themselves. While human societies may not match these extremes, there is a great diversity of patterns regulating sexual deprivation or indulgence. It would be beside the point to explore the functional basis of such divergent patterns as permissive indulgence before marriage, wife lending, and polygamy. The interest here is in the allocation of sexual satisfactions as a primitive group operation.

The rationing process in a primitive group often recognizes various shadings in rank and status. The leaders who administer it usually keep a larger-than-average share for themselves. In accepting smaller shares, the weaker members are assured of getting something, while they might lose out entirely if they acted outside the group. In accepting sexual deprivation, the weaker male gains access to the minimum means of survival and escapes bodily harm from the master of the herd. The power structure remains stable and the group remains intact under two conditions. One is a continuing acceptance of the respective shares, the larger share for the leader presumably being in line with what it is worth to the whole group to have the rationing function performed in an orderly way. The other condition is that the scarcity ration should vary within moderate limits, unaffected by either catastrophic decline in supply or sudden abundance of alternatives for the individual.

Another rationing or allocating function of the leadership lies in controlling the status system of the group as compared to distributing goods in relation to status. This is partly a matter of formal regulation of age and sex groups and a recognition of approaching maturity in such customs as puberty rites. In some societies the individual achieves improved status and even distinction simply by growing old. Becoming an elder is an achievement in itself in the primitive struggle in which most die young. Aside from the biological and conventional basis for advancement in a primitive society a strong leader tends to project an element of hierarchy upon the social structure, originating in his own preferences. Among the elders are some who are distinguished from the others by his special favor. Similarly, both his favor and that of his favorites radiate downward through the group and affect the power structure.

No matter how strong the leader is, he is not entirely free to create his own hierarchy. He cannot wholly disregard such inherent grounds of status as seniority in choosing his advisors and lieutenants. Those passed over will find means of open or passive resistance which they will exhibit, if not to the leader, then toward the others to whom he has delegated authority. As previously stated, the group is held together by the network of mutual expectations. The leader is taking serious chances with the maintenance or efficient exercise of his power when he commits too great an offense against the expectations of the group. Moreno has said that the distinguishing characteristic of the leader is a kind of spontaneous vitality. Other members look to him for the solution of problems, for decision in times of uncertainty. More broadly, it might be said that the leader, through his own drive or dedication to a goal, enhances the expectations of the group. To thwart their expectations needlessly is to betray the role of leadership. Maintaining the pattern of expectation while enhancing it in some directions is part of what Barnard had in mind in saying that the leader projects a morality by which his group can live.

Primitive Operation of Defense. Another primitive operation which may even be prior to rationing in subhuman societies is defense. Animals menaced by predators are in some cases able to co-operate for their mutual defense. Another danger from the outside is the intruder who attempts to break into the territory occupied by the herd and to share its resources. Joint defense efforts are designed to protect either life itself or the basis of life. Animal ecology has established the tendency among many species to defend territorial boundaries and to respect the boundaries set by others except when driven to migration by famine.

The chief interest in group defense, so far as the theory of marketing is concerned, is in the defense of resources. Within a great national economy, such as the American market, the defense of small operating groups is chiefly undertaken by the state. Predators such as criminal gangs are not usually bent on taking life as their principal objective. Their aim is to seize or extort money or other liquid resources, and slaughter is incidental. Insofar as economic groups engage in the defense of resources, this activity might be regarded as an extension or a supplement to rationing. One step is the internal action of determining shares, and the other is the external action of protecting the goods or resources that are to be shared. Both actions might be required at the primitive level for the survival of an isolated group with the minimum resources for maintaining life, as long as they were not subject to depletion by invasion.

To persist, a group must produce some sort of surplus for its members. That means that they must feel that their expectations are higher as members of the group than they would be outside. It has been shown in this section that a surplus can be created in this sense by the primitive operations of rationing and defense. That is not to deny that still greater enhancement of expectations can arise in an input-output system, and these potentialities will be discussed fully later on. The discussion so far may seem remote from marketing, since exchange cannot arise until groups exist which are producing specialized outputs. The point is that the primitive operations are still present in the activities of the most advanced groups and affect profoundly any economic processes undertaken. To start with inputs and outputs would be to minimize major factors promoting group solidarity.

POWER AND COMMUNICATION

The two primary subsystems in any system of group behavior are the power system and the communication system. At the human level they are so closely bound together and so interdependent that it is almost a matter of arbitrary choice to give one priority over the other. Neither one could function without the other, but the power system has been presented first in this discussion as a matter of convenience. There is also a presumption, based on the study of animal societies, that a rather fully developed power system can come into being in a group in which communication is still at a very rudimentary level. It is the power system which is more directly comparable with a mechanical system or with an atomistic system in which particles interact within an enclosed space. Building on the previous section, this section will give more attention to communication but will discuss power and communication as interdependent features of behavior systems which interact with each other, even though each has inherent dynamics of its own.

The existence of a well-developed medium of communication such as human language has a marked effect on the structure of power in any social group. Communication consists of the transmission of a series of signs or signals and their interpretation by the recipient. The nature of various classes of signs has been analyzed by several writers, including C. W. Morris. Most of these classes of signs assume the habitual and continuous association within groups rather than mere casual contact of individuals. The class of membership marks, which have already been mentioned, consists partly of biological features and partly of arbitrary symbols. The existence of spoken and written language greatly expands the scope of membership marks. An important sign of common membership is the ability to speak the same language. Smaller groups can be distinguished and recognized by their manner of speaking or enunciation. A famous illustration is the one in the Bible in which the Israelites recognized an enemy group and slaughtered them because they could not pronounce the word "shibboleth." Even today gradations in human society are detected through equally subtle distinctions in manner of speech. Such distinctions are not without importance in business and in marketing. Every branch of trade tends to develop its own vocabulary, and dealings with any member of the trade are facilitated by knowing this special language. Also, as a matter of historic development, it often happens that the members of a given trade or industry have a common social background which is reflected in manner, dress, and speech. Thus membership as it pertains to social groups may operate as a barrier, or at least present a problem, in trying to combine individuals of diverse backgrounds in the same operating group.

Of more direct significance to production and marketing is the kind of signs which may be designated as operating signals. The purpose of an operating signal is to indicate that some sequence of behavior should begin or should terminate. In some operating situations, answering signals are expected in order to indicate (1) that the operating signal has been understood and (2) that the operation has been completed. Communication of this type is indispensable in the co-ordination of operations, particularly if the individuals involved are so numerous, so scattered, or so differentiated in function that direct imitation of the leader will not serve to keep them working together. Modern marketing as well as production has all these characteristics of size, dispersion, and diversity which make effective communication so essential. Operating signals may pass in various directions through power structures. They may pass at the same level among individuals who are engaged in one of the successive stages of a sequence of activity but who do not exercise authority over each other. They may pass from the top of the structure downward and thus have the force of commands transmitted from superior to subordinate. They may pass upstream from the subordinate and thus give notice that some event is happening on the periphery of the system which calls for decision at the center.

Instruction and Information as Types of Communication. There are two other kinds of communication in a complex operation. These are instruction and information. Instruction takes place before the event and often before the individual becomes a full-fledged member of the operating system. The meaning of instruction with respect to an operating system is to teach individuals how to interpret operating signals which they will later receive and be expected to act upon. In a modern production plant where the operation proceeds in a well-ordered pattern, advance instructions can take care of nearly every contingency which may arise and enable the individual to give appropriate responses to operating signals from whatever source they are received. In marketing, it is practically impossible to foresee all contingencies, so that instructions given in advance must provide the salesman, the distributor, or the dealer with decision rules. In other words, the recipient is not told how to act but is given some principles which will help him decide among courses of action for himself.

The handling of information in a behavior system will be considered from many angles throughout the course of this book. It is introduced here to round out the picture as to the types of communication which are necessary to the co-ordination of a marketing system. Information is essential in any power system of considerable size, even in carrying out the primitive operations of rationing and defense. The leader performing the rationing function must know how large the supply is and the number and type of individuals who are to share it. The leader directing defense must know the location of the enemy and the disposition of the enemy forces and his own during the course of the engagement.

The Power Symbol. The impact of communication in its broadest definition is particularly felt in the elaboration of power symbols. This is especially evident in political affairs, as illustrated by such symbols of royal power as the throne, the crown, the scepter, and special forms of speech in addressing the king. Symbols of power are widely prevalent in business organization. The size of the individual's office and the type of furnishings are common symbols of his place in the power structure. In marketing, millions of dollars are spent in building up the power of symbols such as trade-marks. Many practical advantages flow to a firm from recognition as the first in a field or at least being numbered among the leaders. Sometimes the advertiser who spends so much money in making the brand name of his product familiar to many people has objectives beyond that of influencing consumers to buy. He may have an eye on the stock market and possible investors, on the morale of his own employees, or on other factors concerned with maintaining the power structure. One of the aspects of modern times is the increasing radius over which power can be exercised, whether in marketing or in other operations.

The increasing radius of power springs in large degree from the enhanced facilities for communication. Spoken language was a barrier as well as a bond until some individuals began to learn more than one language. Written communication opened up new possibilities as to precision and certainty in the transmission of symbols and also as to overcoming the barriers of time and space. Records were made which facilitated the communication of the whole body of culture from one generation to another. Today the world is united through instantaneous communication by wire and radio, and all of these new facilities are being used with great versatility in marketing. An event like the battle of New Orleans being fought after the War of 1812 was over is no longer possible. Neither is it possible for oranges to rot on the trees or to be dumped into a market that is already oversupplied because the grower is unaware of active demand in other cities.

Another important aspect of communication in relation to the power structure is the extent to which symbolic behavior can be substituted for force in maintaining the power system. Persuasion takes the place of coercion; and even though the leader has the authority to take more drastic action, he endeavors to bring the individual into line by changing his attitudes and expectations. Communication of this type deals with both negative and positive expectations. In other words, the exercise of power through the medium of communication deals largely with threats and promises. The individual may be threatened with expulsion from the group before he is actually expelled. A more subtle form of the same approach is to discuss an individual's situation with him and to point out that his present behavior constitutes a threat either to his current status or to the position which he might reasonably expect to achieve within the organization. Similarly, executive leadership employs several kinds of promises concerned with the individual's compensation and the resources which will be made available to him for the performance of his function. Another type is more vague and general and deals with the stake that the individual has in the success of the organization, assuming an optimistic picture of its future.

Distortion in Communication. Just as communication has an effect on power, so also does power have an effect on communication. This is not always a favorable effect, since communication and power necessarily flow through the same channels to a large extent. Trying to communicate along a line of authority in an organization is not too different from trying to send telegraph messages over electric power lines. The fact that power is being transmitted over the same channel often distorts the message. If a command must move through several stages from the top down to the subordinate who is expected to take action, it can be altered along the way to suit the interest or convenience of individuals at intermediate positions in the channel. In marketing, such distortion of messages frequently happens in distribution channels. Even if the message is not distorted, the intermediary may have an attitude of indifference resulting in a weak signal at the terminal point. Marketing executives adopt various methods to overcome this difficulty. They engage in sales training to provide some assurance that the signal or sales message will be strong and clear when it enters the trade channel. They devise merchandising plans to serve as amplifiers or booster stations along the way. They set up alternative channels, such as advertising, for reaching the consumer as a means of establishing partial independence of the trade channel as well as some control over the character of the message which the trade channel will transmit.

There are also characteristic difficulties in transmitting information upstream in a power structure. This is particularly true if the structure is authoritarian and the pattern of behavior tends to be reduced to command and obedience. The individual at the terminal point may carry out the order as well as he can but try to suppress any evidence of failure. He may hesitate in particular to transmit bad news of any kind, such as reporting an attack along the periphery. This caution was justified in ancient and medieval times when it was common practice to put to death a messenger bringing bad news. Such drastic measures are not common today, but a subordinate often finds it a sticky and hazardous matter to inform a strong-minded executive of the things he ought to know. One function of outside marketing consultants is to present facts which are not always pleasant and to present them more forcefully than could be undertaken by a member of the organization.

The tendency for a signal to die out and to become too weak to provoke action is as great or greater moving upstream as moving downstream. Here again there are possibilities of distortion arising from the fact that the message is moving along a power channel. Intermediaries may temper any bad news in order to protect a subordinate. A less responsible intermediate executive may present the information in such a way as to make the subordinate the scapegoat for a mischance which is actually his own responsibility. There is also the possibility that the intermediate executive will seize upon good ideas and present them as his own without giving proper credit. Sometimes there is no willful deception, since the intermediary may develop the idea into a more acceptable plan and even forget where the germ of it came from. Modern organization practice employs various devices in trying to overcome these defects of communication upstream. One such development is the use of personnel psychologists and the employment of outside management consultants. Of special importance for the purpose of this book is marketing research, which may be regarded as an alternative channel for communication upstream from the consumer and which avoids complete dependence on communication through trade channels.

Positional Behavior in the Power Structure. The combination of a power structure with facilities for communication lays the basis for important aspects of behavior within the group which will be designated as "positional behavior." This term refers to the kind of behavior on the part of the individual which is addressed primarily toward influencing his position within the group. Wherever there is hierarchy or rank, there is rivalry among the members at one level for promotion to the next level. Generally, this structure is in the shape of a pyramid, so that fewer individuals can belong to the next higher level. The typical organization structure is a direct refutation of the old saying that "there is always room at the top." There is never room at the top for all who would like to be there. The germ of truth in this bit of folk wisdom is that those who have the ability and drive to reach the top will find it no more crowded or competitive there than at the more thickly populated lower levels. The attitude it expresses is useful socially, since the whole power structure might weaken and crumble if there were not a constant upward thrust on the part of the more energetic and talented individuals. Ideally, the force of this thrust should be kept in nice balance with the needs of the system. The consequences of the thrust being either excessive or deficient will be discussed later in considering the pathology of organization. At this point it is sufficient to register the idea that there is a principle of scarcity at work with respect to status as much as with respect to goods. In an organization made up of vigorous people, the opportunity to achieve higher status in a pyramidal structure is never equal to the demand. If, for example, the leader of a group has six principal lieutenants who all expect to succeed him, only one out of six can fulfill his expectations upon the death or retirement of the leader. That precise situation and the resulting power struggle was presented in the novel, *Executive Suite*.

In a primitive society, as among the red deer of Scotland and other gregarious animals, the right of succession is frequently settled by physical combat. After the appearance of language as a flexible medium of communication, competition for status is manifested in less violent forms but is frequently no less deadly. The individual who displays some skill or craft in positional behavior does not risk his life or future continuously by throwing his entire mental and physical force into the effort to displace those above him.

Instead he watches for openings and takes action only when a careful weighing of the opportunity indicates that it is worthy of the risk. This type of behavior on the part of the ambitious individual is usually frowned upon by the community. Community disapproval is implied by the use of the word "opportunistic" in this connection. It is doubtful whether the situation would be improved if positional behavior were crude and clumsy any more than if the upward thrust faded out completely. It is the kind of opportunity which the power structure leaves open to individuals, as much as the form which rivalry takes, that makes the difference in the consequences for the group as a whole.

One form of self-promotion utilizing the channels of communication is that of tearing down possible rivals. This means reporting their mistakes or failures which they might otherwise succeed in suppressing. If one candidate for advancement in any group seems to be well in the lead, his rivals may conspire to undermine him in order to leave the field open to themselves. This does not mean that their rivalry will be any less intense once the leading contender is eliminated. This type of competition has been recognized in the theory of games. Special games have been invented to serve as models for these types of positional behavior in which the leader is always killed off by conspirators, until only two contestants remain.

Collusive forms of positional behavior are not always directed against rivals at the same level. Sometimes a conspiracy is formed for the purpose of displacing a superior. Usually, this occurs only when there are pathological stresses in the power structure which interfere with its normal functioning. The stresses and strains arise when the superior is unduly harsh or oppressive in his treatment of his subordinates and thwarts their expectations by failing to exercise the leadership expected of his position. Short of violent attack on the individual they hope to displace, the conspirators may attempt to communicate with those at still higher levels of authority or in some cases appeal to the whole group. The common basis of appeal is the presumption of disloyalty or incompetence in carrying out objectives which are recognized by the group as a whole. In a totalitarian power structure these collusive efforts may often be the only means of remedying an unhealthy situation.

Positional behavior is not restricted to rivals or conspirators at the lower level. It is often exercised at the top by those who possess superior power and wish to retain it. If the leader suspects that others are trying to displace him, he may dispose of rival claimants by playing one off against the other. He may arouse suspicion in each by telling him what the other has said about him or plans to do against him. The contrasting device is that of building up a new rival by showering him with favors and opportunities from the top if one claimant seems too far out in front. Some measure of positional behavior is an inescapable aspect of supreme authority. In fact, management of the power system for the good of the system as a whole will be discussed later as one of the primary executive functions.

The executive undertakes to keep aspiration for progress active at all levels and yet to keep it within reasonable bounds. His legitimate objectives include those of keeping effective control in his own hands and maintaining a balanced and vigorous organization. This part of the discussion may strike the reader as dealing with the elements of the theory of organization rather than the theory of marketing. The present view is that one is essential to the other, since marketing is an aspect of group behavior. A marketing executive or market analyst is not equipped to solve marketing problems unless he can think in organizational terms. Marketing plans which are conceived only in terms of money, goods, and their physical movement are doomed to fail. A marketing plan must be executed through sales organizations, distribution channels, and other organized behavior systems which can only be understood as power structures. The management of these behavior systems is a major aspect of the marketing practice for which this book undertakes to provide theoretical perspective.

Communication within organizations is a subject worthy of separate and intensive study aside from its connection with the power structure. There is a developing theory of communication with which the names of such engineers and mathematicians as Shannon and Wiener have been associated. This theory so far has dealt largely with the transmission of signals through electrical circuits. The theory is not wholly applicable to the kind of communication which is of primary significance in marketing. Nevertheless, it can be the source of some useful analogies and models and can be helpful in formulating principles which apply to communication in any form of human organization. Ideas of the writers mentioned will be drawn upon at various points in this study. At this point it is sufficient to present the key concepts about communication which are obviously applicable to organization and marketing theory.

Message and Noise in Communication. Communication engineers divide all sounds coming over an electrical circuit into message and noise. They are concerned with such problems as the speed and accuracy of transmission both in noiseless circuits and in those with various noise levels in relation to the message. The message is the portion of the transmitted sound which is intended to convey information and to stimulate action. Noise is the portion of the sound which constitutes accidental or deliberate interference with the transmission of the message. There is an obvious parallel in this classification of transmitted signals to what has been said above about the difficulties of communication within a marketing organization. Certain signals carry the official or authorized message which in a healthy organization serves to facilitate the performance of normal functions. Other types of messages, such as those connected with the opportunistic form of positional behavior, tend to disrupt and confuse the transmission of authorized messages. In managing a power structure and trying to provide good communication within the organization, the executive is confronted by problems similar to those of the communications engineer. He may attempt to eliminate all communications which he regards as noise—a very difficult task indeed in human organization. On the other hand, he may resolve to live with some level of noise represented by unauthorized messages and work toward making the official message effective in spite of the noise. If such compromises merit consideration in dealing with electrical circuits, they are inescapable in the case of communication through the power structure of a human organization.

Redundancy in Communication. There are several factors to be considered in making an official message effective in the presence of noise. One, which was first discussed by Shannon, is the degree of redundancy in the message. This means the extent to which the message contains signals in excess of what would be necessary for transmission in a noiseless channel. A redundant message may still come through with enough of the original pattern intact so that the recipient can guess correctly what was intended. Redundant messages are simple and repetitive rather than complex and discursive. Effective communication in management and marketing often seems to the disinterested observer to be underscoring the obvious. Mass advertising may seem painfully repetitive to the person who is not in the market for the product advertised. The most comprehensive and intensive management and market research sometimes leads to rules of action which sound like simple platitudes. Nevertheless, the choice between one rule of action and another may be of crucial importance. Once the choice is made, little is gained by embroidering the rule with qualifications or with involved reasoning to support it. The management usually wants a direct statement of what should be done, which takes on the force of an imperative when endorsed by the top executive.

Information and Ignorance in Communication. Communication theorists have had some interesting things to say about the relation between information and ignorance. A message does not convey information if the recipient can predict in advance what the message will be. There is the qualification, of course, that the recipient may be expecting a particular message such as an air-raid warning and is ignorant only of the time it will be received. Since timing is essential to action, such a message would still convey important information. While a significant message presumes some degree of ignorance on the part of the recipient, a state of complete ignorance would be inconsistent with effective communication. The recipient must have a stock of information in hand to interpret the message, including a knowledge of the code in which it is transmitted. Rapid communication requires that the recipient know a great deal about the situation to which the message applies. The message simply fills in some point concerning which the recipient would otherwise remain in ignorance. Effective communication rests on a correct evaluation of the degree of ignorance and the amount of information in the minds of the recipients. A message may fail because the recipient is not aware of the background to which it pertains. On the other hand, an important message may be ignored if it is embedded in information already familiar to the recipient, so that he jumps to the conclusion that the message does not contain anything new.

Phatic Communion.   This emphasis on information in authorized messages does not imply that messages must convey information to be significant aspects of group behavior. Some years ago a writer, whose identity has been forgotten by the author, proposed the term "phatic communion" for socially acceptable messages which do not convey information. A common illustration is the discussion of the weather with which many conversations begin. Much of what is called "small talk" consists of messages of this type, which nevertheless appear to perform a useful social function. Phatic communion is in much the same category as the symbols of membership which have already been discussed. It serves the purpose of indicating that individuals accept each other tentatively as members of the same group. Membership in a common group may be limited to the particular social occasion. On the other hand, the trivialities of social exchange serve as an instrument of exploration by which individuals place each other in the social scale and determine their attitudes toward more permanent association. While phatic communion is most in evidence in purely social activities, it has a place of some importance in operating organizations. Investigation years ago by Mayo and others found that it makes for greater group solidarity and effectiveness to permit an indulgence in phatic communion so long as it does not interfere with the transmission or reception of operating messages.

Feedback in Communication.   Another concept in communication theory, largely due to Wiener, is that of the information loop or feedback circuit. Wiener says that effective control depends upon return messages from the point at which action takes place, a principle which is illustrated in electronics by servo-mechanisms.

The first impulse toward action may not be well adjusted to the need, but adjustment takes place through successive approximations. Feedback circuits, according to Wiener, are also fundamental in the operation of the human nervous system. This concept is highly suggestive for management action in marketing. Too many times an executive depends on one-way communication and assumes that action has taken place in accordance with instructions. Marketing management has been increasingly aware of the necessity for continuous feedback, and several major marketing research services have developed to serve this need.

Interpretation and Summary of Information. Another concept is that of the transformation of messages at various decision centers within an organization structure. In a large sales organization the messages originating at the periphery are far too numerous and detailed ever to be received and interpreted by a single executive at the center. In an effective organization these messages are summarized and interpreted at various points along the way. Thus a district sales manager may have conversations with a number of salesmen but transmit a summary message to the effect that a certain class of customers is dissatisfied with the company's policy or is going over to the use of competitive products. The head of a sales organization, with the help of his staff, may in turn summarize and interpret messages from all the district sales managers before presenting a picture of the sales outlook to the chief executive. The function of the central command is to perform a major transformation in the flow of communication, receiving information and issuing specific instructions or policy statements. Policies and instructions are in turn interpreted at each of the minor decision centers in order to effect adjustments to local conditions.

Internal Dynamics of Power and Communication. Communication has an inner dynamics quite aside from its services to primitive or advanced operations. Reference has already been made to a form of communication which tends to become an end itself. At a higher level this tendency is exhibited as a concern for symbols for their own sake. Suzanne Langer has discussed the role of symbols and the process of symbolization over and beyond their instrumental value. She believes that the drive to create symbols and to utilize them in shaping new patterns of behavior has the status of a basic spiritual drive. Man conquers his universe and gains some sense of security in the face of mysterious or uncontrollable forces simply by giving them names. Carl Rogers goes still further than Langer and makes symbolization the essence of conscious experience and the basis for the integration of personality. An indulgence in merely symbolic behavior may interfere with the proper functioning of an operating organization. On the other hand, symbolic behavior opens up avenues for human satisfaction which can in some measure overcome the limitations of scarcity as they apply to physical goods. The important role of symbolic behavior as a basis for a full and happy life will be discussed at greater length in Chapter 6, which deals with the theory of consumer behavior.

THE POWER PRINCIPLE

The power drive finds dynamic expression through what may be called "the power principle." An individual or an organization, in order to prevail in the struggle for survival, must act in such a way as to promote the power to act. The power principle is especially important in relation to the expansion of a growing system. As a system grows, it is increasing its power or capacity to carry on its regular processes on a greater scale. The existence of power is a necessary condition for the continuance of many of these activities. Therefore the maintenance and the enhancement of power is an inherent goal for any organized behavior system. A cohesive behavior system operates as if it were animated by the power principle, even though this is only a reflection of the behavior of its leading members. The power principle has a number of specific applications or corollaries which can be observed in group behavior.

Some of the corollaries of the power principle pertain to the control and use of energy or capacity for action. A system may attempt to extend its control over additional sources of energy or to increase its capacity for the various aspects of its operation. In business terms this may mean either buying or selling a new plant or acquiring new mineral or other natural resources. There are also frequent attempts, in line with the power principle, to increase the efficiency of the organization in the use of energy or capacity already under its control. All of these possibilities with respect to greater control or increasing efficiency apply to marketing just as much as to production.

Other consequences of the power principle pertain to executive decision as a general principle governing the choice among alternatives. Economic theory centers attention on alternatives which represent a greater or smaller return in relation to the value of inputs involved. Marketing is also concerned with alternatives which will determine the course of action over a longer period of time and where results of choice cannot be measured in immediate monetary returns. The application of the power principle requires that choice in the current situation will be such as to broaden freedom of choice in the future. The strategy of marketing is concerned with situations in which the wrong choice of method in entering a market may in effect block the opportunity and narrow the range of choice which can be exercised by management thereafter. In developing a new market, the first goal is to establish a beach-head or a foothold, but it is equally important to select the beach-head in such a way that it is possible to move forward thereafter. The best market strategist is usually the one who is able to project his vision further into the future and to foresee the consequences of the initial steps. He is also able to evaluate opportunity more accurately, seeing it as an opportunity for growth in a given area rather than the prospect for immediate sales. Since he is looking forward to the development of a growing market, he tries to avoid rash steps in the beginning which would foreclose this prospect.

The power principle can also be interpreted in relation to risk and the executive function of weighing alternative risks. The greatest risk of all for anyone exercising power is that of losing it by pushing it too far. The power principle suggests a reasonable restraint in the exercise of power, both as to the goals for which it is to be used and as to the form in which it is exerted. This consequence of the power principle should result in prudence but not excessive caution. No system of action can be directed successfully by making avoidance of risk the principal aim. The difficulty is that there is no escape from risk because the risks associated with inaction are often more severe than the risks of action.

SURVIVAL AND GROWTH OF SYSTEMS

The discussion of systems so far has related to the internal structure of systems and the significance of status as the connecting link between the individuals in a group and the organized behavior system to which they belong. The individual or the animal species struggles for survival and the realization of its adult form and function. Our discussion of systems up to this point really treats the system as part of the organized environment in which the individual seeks survival and growth and the performance of his normal functions. This section starts with the recognition that the system also has an environment and that the balance between the system and its environment may change. Economics treats the competitive struggle between economic systems such as business firms; political science deals in part with the struggle of political systems. It is important to recognize at the beginning that the notion of competition among systems is to some extent a figure of speech. A system as such does not have a set of desires and goals like the individual but is at bottom only a means of expressing and realizing the goals of the individuals who belong to the system. In talking about competition among business firms, economists are really going back to an earlier period in which a firm could be regarded as the shadow of one man, called "the entrepreneur." Nevertheless, systems operate in some respects as if they had goals of their own; and it is the purpose of this section to discuss these systemic goals.

Symbiosis, Parasitism, and Competition in Survival. Before discussing the goal-directed behavior of systems, a short excursion into the field of animal ecology will be useful. Reference has already been made to the network of life occupying any natural habitat and consisting of various animal forms, their relations to each other, and their relations to the physical environment. Each animal or animal species affects the survival and growth of its neighbors in various ways. One type of relation is called "symbiosis," or the relation in which two species appear to work together to make better use of their natural resources than one could make alone. For example, there are species of ants which keep certain aphids in their nests and feed and care for them as a farmer cares for his milk cows. The ants are said to milk the aphids, which means that by stroking these small insects, they cause them to secrete a milky fluid which the ants find highly palatable. Probably the most familiar example of symbiosis is the relation between flowering plants and the bees which gather their nectar and simultaneously distribute their pollen. Neither species could exist without the other. Kropotkin, a Russian writer of the nineteenth century, was so struck by this aspect of nature that he developed a theory of mutual aid as the foundation of all animal and human societies. He presented this idea in opposition to both the economic theory of competition and the relentless class struggle of Karl Marx. One view is as limited as the other in overemphasizing only one of the several types of interaction which take place in the ecological setting.

Competition for survival among individuals is probably the most basic and certainly the most primitive type of interaction. Competition arises because of the scarcity of means and the rapid multiplication of individuals seeking survival. The idea of Malthus that population always tends to outrun the available food supply was brought over from economics to biology to serve as the foundation for the theory of evolution. The great majority of the world's population still lives under the conditions visualized by Malthus, and the doom he foretold may yet overtake the world as a whole unless more adequate programs are adopted for the conservation of resources. The main point at the moment is that individual competition for survival and growth still under-lies human activity, even though the qualitative range of growth and self-realization is greatly expanded at the human level, and even though individuals co-operate in many types of organized behavior systems to gain their ultimate ends.

Survival of the Organized Behavior System. Hereafter we shall feel free to talk about competition or other forms of interaction among systems, having first made it clear that systems are only the reflection of their component individuals. A system may operate over a long period of time as if it had a destiny of its own and as if it were guided by inherent goals of survival and growth. A system does not neces-sarily die because of the death of its leader or other members. Like the human body it has the power of repairing and replenishing itself. The process is different, of course, because the system acquires new mem-bers rather than taking in the raw materials for repairing its com-ponents. Some of the recruits accepted in an operating system might, of course, be regarded as raw materials, since they must be trained before they become effective components. In a simpler economy the life of a business firm often depends directly on the life of the founder and owner. Today the corporate form of business organization pre-vails, and there is a presumption of immortality concerning the cor-poration. It is not likely that any of the firms now in existence will really last forever, but many large corporations have been in existence far longer than the lives of any of their present executives or owners.

The struggle for survival among organized behavior systems of all types has transcended some of the limitations of individual competi-tion for survival. Earlier versions of economic theory were modeled directly on the struggle for survival in nature. In any given field many firms were engaged in competition, and the least efficient ones perished like unsuccessful individuals or animal species. New firms were con-stantly entering wherever opportunity existed, and economic evolution was presumed to parallel the emergence of new species under the law of the jungle.

Actually, a firm does not have to die because it is inefficient in its original function. It can be reorganized so that it can perform more efficiently, or it can take on new functions. It may persist for a number of years without such internal adjustments through sheer inertia or momentum. A firm or any other organized behavior system is an ex-pression of the expectations of individuals. Even though the surplus of goods or psychic satisfactions which the behavior system provides have diminished or disappeared, individuals may still cling to it because they have no better alternative. The momentum which keeps a firm going sometimes resides in large part in the energy and determination of the leader or of a small group of policy makers and investors. Expectations in business involve a weighing of risk against possible gains. Thus a firm with only a small chance of success can be kept intact over a long period by the hope of large gains in case that one chance prevails. These are some of the reasons why the outcome of competition with respect to survival and growth is not always what might be predicted on the basis of the theory of pure competition.

Survival through Status Expectations of Subsystems. In ecology an individual or species is presumed to survive because there is a place for it in the scheme of things. That means that the environment offers an opportunity which cannot be exploited so successfully by any other individual or species. This position in the web of life has been variously called a niche, a foothold, or a footing. The importance of this chance for survival in life and in society was dramatically expressed by the sociologist Robert Park in saying that even a blade of grass must have a place to stand. Similarly, a business firm or any other organized behavior system must have a footing or a place to stand in order to survive and prosper. In an earlier statement the writer expressed this condition of survival in what he called the first survival theorem, which reads as follows: *An organized behavior system will tend to survive as long as the footing it occupies endures because of the collective action arising out of the status expectations of its components.*

The individuals or subsystems that comprise a behavior system have a stake in its survival because it serves them as a ground of status. If it is an operating system, their expectations in relation to the system pertain also to the income or goods derived from it. These expectations are dependent upon status expectations, since shares in output are correlated with status. The portion of collective action oriented toward status expectations can thus be identified as the main factor in the preservation of the system. This view concerning the role of status expectations in group behavior is supported by recent developments in social psychology.

Because the system is the ground for status, individuals work for it, scheme for it, and upon occasion are prepared to die for it. They will accept small returns over a long period if they feel that their status expectations will eventually be gratified. Most remarkable of all, perhaps, is the extent to which they will accept group discipline in the remolding of customary behavior to conform to the requirements of

the system. An expanding system tends to require increasing specialization of its members in order to maintain the effective functioning
of the system as a whole. Thus, group discipline may impose a differentiated pattern of rights and duties upon its members but with the
whole complex oriented toward the preservation of the system.

Survival through Competitive Strategy.   Another shortcoming of
the traditional picture of economic competition is that it deals only
with the tactics of competition and ignores its strategy. In other words,
it portrays a continuous and unrelenting battle in which the weaker
contestants are constantly failing and disappearing and reinforcements
are constantly entering the fray. Actually, when a competitor has
gained a foothold, he begins to think in terms of campaigns by which
he can expand his position. Often it is only the campaign which fails
rather than the firm itself. After an unsuccessful campaign a firm is
able to draw back into its original position and await another opportunity to launch a better-prepared attack. It is in the nature of any
ecological niche or position in the market to have a core and a fringe.
The core is that part of the environment which is most completely
suited to the operations of the individual organism or group. Often the
core is relatively free from attack, since no competitor can invade it
without operating at a disadvantage. The fringe is that part of the
environment in which the individual or group can still operate but at
a lower efficiency. The fringe extends out to the point where the particular entity loses its differential advantage and must compete on
equal terms and, at the outside limit, would suffer a disadvantage in
attempting to expand any further. The writer has previously discussed
this phenomenon in what he called the second theorem of survival:
*An organized behavior system may survive the most aggressive attacks
of competitors because it is able to exist at the core of its position
even though losing ground at the fringes and, meanwhile, mature its
own campaign which may utilize strategies that have been overlooked
by competitors.*

To understand modern marketing, it is necessary to recognize that
selling takes the form of campaigns and strategies that must be effectuated over considerable periods of time. The importance of alternative strategies in economic behavior has been pointed out by von Neu-
man and Morgenstern. The fact that a company may be fifth in a
field of five is likely to be interpreted as a challenge by the marketing
strategist rather than as a portent of doom. Even though the company
is steadily losing in its relative position, the strategist may gamble on

reversing the trend if he feels that the firm can hang on until his program has had time to take effect.

In particular, he will examine the activities of competitors in the hope of finding his own opportunity in some weakness of their position. In order to succeed, they have been obliged to take definite stands in their relationships with customers and others. Thus, their choice of certain strategies may make other strategies unavailable to them. For example, the leaders may have differentiated their products in directions that make them more acceptable to one segment of the market but less acceptable to others. It often happens in modern competitive situations that a new firm rises to challenge the leadership in a field because, in reversing some of the policies of the leaders, it is fulfilling a demand that is not being met by the leaders.

Survival through Plasticity. The third type of situation is that in which an organized behavior system persists despite the fact that its original function has disappeared. An effective organization comes to be an important asset in itself to all the individuals who have participated in its activities. Continued group coherence at the human level may rest in moderate degree on the fact that the individuals who make up the group have come to trust each other and to enjoy working together. An organization can grow out of some temporary need. It may persist by taking on another function. One of our great universities was founded because a group of men who had been working together in selling Liberty Bonds in the First World War were reluctant to disband. Having enjoyed working as a team in raising money, they looked around for another good cause and decided to collect a fund to establish a university in their city. There are some remarkable examples among business firms of passing through a series of transformations. One well-known New England firm began many years ago in the manufacture of pumps. During the Civil War it turned to the manufacture of rifles because it was one of the few firms with an adequate knowledge of metalworking. It never got back to manufacturing pumps. The manufacture of rifles took the firm still further in the direction of precision metalworking. Today it is one of the leading machine-tool builders in the United States and seems likely hereafter to expand on that base rather than going through any further radical transformations. The third survival theorem, intended to characterize this situation, is as follows: *An organized behavior system may survive despite severe functional disturbance resulting from environmental changes if sufficient plasticity remains so that new functions may de-*

velop or new methods may be adopted for performing existing functions.

It is a fact of common observation that organized behavior systems frequently survive after their original functions have disappeared. This is true of business firms and government bureaus, among other types of behavior systems. To survive under such conditions requires that the system be able to remain intact during a difficult transition period. This may happen if there is an overlapping between the gradual disappearance of the old function and the establishment of the new function. In some cases the resources of the system are such as to enable it to persist for a time without functioning at all. In any case such a transition calls for a high degree of plasticity on the part of the components of the system.

"Plasticity" may be defined as the capacity for undergoing a reshaping of behavior patterns. A greatly expanded conception of the range of plasticity in human behavior has emerged from the modern approach in cultural anthropology. The fact that such radical transformations in the functioning of a system can happen at all is striking proof of the vitality of systems and the strength of the drive for survival. The more highly specialized the behavior system, the more serious does functional disturbance become. Specialization necessarily arises with the expansion of the system and the increasing range of its activities. In times of stress or unavoidable contraction of activity, versatility is at a premium as compared with specialization. In complex systems, rational planning emerges as a response to the need for accelerating specialization without aggravating vulnerability.

Survival through Growth. The second systemic goal is that of continuous growth. That is to say that systems often behave as if they were driving toward the goal of becoming larger and larger. Sometimes rapid growth seems to be taking advantage of a vacuum in the ecological setting, as in the case already mentioned of rabbits when first introduced into Australia. In human organizations growth may occur in spite of major obstacles or may even seem to be stimulated by them. Here the rate of growth depends on the force of the drive behind it. The expectations of the individuals involved may be heightened by hopes for great gains or relative ease of growth once initial obstacles are overcome. In general, there are two sources of growth for an operating organization. It may expand the volume of its present activities, or it may engage in new activities. In marketing terms this usually means selling more of the same product or adding more products to the line.

The drive for growth is often reinforced by the conviction that growth is necessary for survival. A truism widely accepted in American business is that it is necessary to go forward in order not to fall backward. A firm that becomes overshadowed by its rivals may lose out altogether unless it is content to compete for a very restricted part of the total market. In the early history of man, it is probable that large organizations wiped out many small ones or in some cases absorbed their remnants. Marx assumed the same thing would necessarily happen in free competition among business firms, with an inevitable trend toward concentration and monopoly. The worst results predicted by Marx have not been borne out by history. In the United States the total number of firms continues to increase as fast as the total population, although there have been some important changes in the size distribution, which will be analyzed later.

American business firms range from giant corporations to one-man operations, but growth is an essential aspect of competition for all. Vitality is required even for survival; but vitality is difficult to maintain without growth, at least in the American business climate. The vitality of a firm depends on the vigor and ambition of its members. The prospect of growth is one of the principal means by which a firm can attract able and vigorous recruits. Thus, management in a typical firm is caught in a cycle in which growth is essential even though management may not have an intense desire for expansion. If the firm does not grow, it cannot compete for the more able candidates among executives and workers. If the character of its membership deteriorates, it is likely to lose out altogether in competition.

The growing firm also attracts favorable attention from customers and from suppliers. Suppliers tend to give favorable treatment to any customer firm which is growing rapidly, hoping to retain it as a customer when it has attained a larger size. New types of marketing institutions which have appeared from time to time, such as chain stores, have profited materially from this attitude on the part of producers supplying them with goods. Similarly, the customer who has ventured to buy from a relatively new firm is confirmed in his judgment by its continued growth and is inclined to recommend it to others. Another aspect of growth in operating organizations is its relation to commitments between the top executive and his subordinates. Often he has had to hold out the lure of company expansion in order to get the men he wants. He and they must work together successfully to achieve these goals if the organization is to hold together.

This emphasis on growth is not peculiar to America or to business but applies to many societies and many types of organized behavior systems in which new possibilities are constantly being opened up through technological advance. In fact, the principle would have to be modified only slightly in a completely static society. In this case the commitment between superior and subordinate would relate to the maintenance of the present level of activity and the security of the individual's status rather than the improvement of his position. Even in our own dynamic society, rates of change vary by industry and among firms, as do the relative values placed by individuals upon security and growth.

STAGES IN BUSINESS GROWTH

The life history of a typical business can be divided into three stages, differing as to rate of growth. The middle stage is the period of most rapid growth, with slower growth rates in the earlier and later stages. These three stages in business history provide a convenient starting point for consideration of the strategy of growth. The stages in growth can be labeled as those of establishment, expansion, and stabilization. These words characterize a central focus for business policy in each stage. In simpler terms the most urgent goal in each successive stage might be described as getting started, getting ahead, and getting set. It is not desirable to overemphasize the difference from stage to stage, since the general pattern of daily operation is identical in many respects for large and small business. From the viewpoint of strategy, however, there is a real difference in the relative importance of policy issues as a business passes from one stage to the next. These issues pertain to promotion, pricing, distribution policy, product development, and investment in plant capacity to meet anticipated demand. To simplify the discussion, the subject will be presented primarily from the standpoint of the company producing and selling a single product. These observations about the growth process are believed to hold for all types of organized behavior systems. The discussion will proceed in terms of the business firm in order to make it more vivid for the marketing student, even at the risk of anticipating matters which will be treated in more detail later on.

Stage 1: Establishment. Many of the most difficult problems of business strategy are those facing a company which is just entering business. That is one reason why so few survive beyond their initial effort to get started. In the past it might be said that management was either very farsighted or very lucky in any enterprise that succeeded in getting a foothold. Today it is much more feasible to estimate in advance the prospects of success. The company with a meritorious product and some experience in normal business operation can obtain answers through scientific methods that were at one time available only at the costly basis of trial and error.

The most urgent requirement with respect to the new business or the new product is knowledge of the market. Ideally, the investigation of the market should take place before the final design of the product has been determined. Even though a product meets a definite need, it may fail to achieve acceptance through some minor flaw which might have been corrected. Intimate and detailed knowledge is needed as to the way in which such products are used and as to educational problems in teaching people to use an improved product.

The first and most basic question to be answered is that of how demand for the product is to be promoted. If the idea is new, people will have to be told about it in order to buy the product. The drive to succeed whatever the cost is also a major factor. An operation that was otherwise promising may fail, just before it turns the corner, through the exhaustion of either its assets or the confidence of its management.

Stage 2: Expansion. During the period of expansion the emphasis in the firm's objectives generally shifts from securing a place in the market to excelling and outdistancing competition. The goal of maximum sales is gradually substituted for that of minimum risk. Competitive efficiency in promoting sales and in other aspects of distribution becomes the touchstone of success.

The natural sales trend is sharply upward during this period. The chief goal of management is to accelerate this rate of growth without permitting a corresponding increase in costs per unit. Advertising through mass media may be relied upon increasingly to reach an everbroader public. If so, there will be an attempt to find an advertising formula which fits the product and its market. Numerous experiments may be necessary to find an application of the power of mass media to the selling methods through which the product gained a foothold.

Increasing sales should lead to lower costs per unit. Savings in distribution costs do not arise in altogether automatic fashion from larger volume. The increased scale of operation offers an opportunity for savings through adoption of appropriate methods. Management may or may not discern these opportunities throughout the period of expansion. This applies to production as well as distribution processes. Faster assembly and packaging lines, more specialized use of labor, new devices for increasing the productivity of salesmen, and a greater reliance on mass-distribution channels are among the changes which may be introduced to keep pace with increasing volume.

This is the period in which there is the maximum opportunity to use price as an instrument of sales strategy. Generally speaking, prices on manufactured products tend to be downward over the period. Prices are reduced in the hope of attracting all the new customers who are now ready to buy. Any slower rate of adjustment will encourage competition to enter the field. To reduce prices any faster is to forego gross income which is essential to the fullest expansion of the business.

Many marketing organizations during the period of greatest expansion follow the financial policy of keeping profits down to a moderate rate and plowing the bulk of earnings back into promotional expenditures or other activities directed toward expansion, such as technical and economic research. The chief limitation of this viewpoint is that it may be necessary to pay out some profits as a means for attracting new investors. It may not be possible for the entire increase in working capital to come out of earnings. In many cases, borrowing or new stock issues provide most of the new funds required. The business may have to show steady though moderate profits in order to obtain loans or new equity capital.

Stage 3: Consolidation.   In the third stage of business growth the objective is the most favorable outlook as to stable and continuing profits. The well-established company does not point toward the greatest possible earnings this year or next. The ideal aim is to make a good showing year after year, meanwhile preserving and expanding the assets of the company.

It is not suggested that the company which has reached this stage in its life history will give up all hope of further rapid expansion. Some change in demand or in the technological possibilities of production may initiate a whole new cycle. Management should be ever alert to such eventualities. The established company occupying such a position of leadership is usually obliged to work for two broad objectives. One is to improve conditions for its industry, and the other is to maintain its relative position within the industry. Its requirements as to volume of sales are so large that it directs its promotion to all possible customers. Its advertising is almost certain to create customers for its smaller competitors as well as for itself. Its product quality and its prices set up standards which others may strive to meet in the one case and cut under in the other. Meanwhile, as more and more competitors enter the field, its percentage share of the total market inevitably declines, even though its dollar volume may continue to increase.

The two great periods of danger in the history of a firm are the initial stage in which it is struggling for a foothold and the period when it has attained its major growth and a slowing-down of expansion appears imminent. Some firms which have had a meteoric rise go into an equally dramatic decline. Executives who looked good when they were being carried along by the momentum of steady growth may prove unable to cope with the problems of business maturity. Junior executives and other valued employees may become disaffected because the chances for personal advancement no longer appear so bright. Trouble starts even before the turn occurs if management fails to recognize the approaching change in the trend or chooses to ignore the warning signals. Millions of dollars can be spent in a vain effort to pierce the ceiling on the assumption that the old rate of growth can be maintained. Large advance commitments for advertising and sales organization can be built up on this assumption, resulting in disastrous cutbacks when the change in trend finally becomes apparent.

The stages of growth for the firm have been described in ordinary business terms, but the dynamics of growth arise from the inherent nature of organized behavior systems. A system survives because of the expectations it creates in its members. A system grows in order to meet their expectations more fully, and growth itself creates still greater expectations. The members or at least the leaders within a system are oriented toward growth by means of the power principle. However, they must act to maximize the outputs of the system. There is an overriding rationality in promoting the power to act. With respect to the firm the power principle has direct application to the three stages of its life history. First, there is the objective of gaining a foothold in order to be able to act at all. Next, there is an enhancement of the power to act through expansion. Finally, there is the attempt to maintain it through consolidation.

SELECTED REFERENCES

CLEMENTS, F. E. and SHELFORD, V. E. *Bio-ecology*. New York: John Wiley & Sons, Inc., 1939.

MORENO, J. L. *Who Shall Survive?* Washington, D.C.: Nervous and Mental Diseases Publishing Co., 1934.

HOMANS, GEORGE C. *The Human Group*. New York: Harcourt, Brace Co., 1950.

SHANNON, CLAUDE E. and WEAVER, WARREN. *Mathematical Theory of Communication.* Urbana: University of Illinois Press. 1949.

WIENER, NORBERT. *Cybernetics.* New York: John Wiley & Sons, Inc., 1948.

LUNDBERG, GEORGE. *Marketing and Social Organization.* First Parlin Memorial Lecture. Philadelphia: American Marketing Association, 1945.

Some of the key concepts of this book are drawn from the interplay between economics and biology. Darwin's great hypothesis about evolution was inspired in part by the writings of Malthus, an economist and population theorist. Today ecology is a recognized branch of biology and might be loosely defined as the economics of plant and animal societies. Ecology in turn is currently contributing to a deeper understanding of organized behavior systems in human society.

Moreno's book was one of the first to analyze the membership bonds which characterize group structure. He is one of the founders of the branch of sociology known as sociometry. The book by Homans reports several more recent studies of the structure and function of small groups.

Shannon and Weaver developed their theory as an aid to designing telephone circuits and similar communication channels. Wiener adapted these ideas to a consideration of the human nervous system. They can also be applied to communication within a social system.

The lecture by Lundberg is one of the first formal applications of sociometry to marketing. It initiated a series of annual lectures honoring Charles Coolidge Parlin, marketing pioneer who made use of some of the same notions in an intuitive but effective fashion.

Chapter III

OPERATION OF INPUT-OUTPUT SYSTEMS

Behavior systems may be described as operating systems when they are characterized by processes involving inputs and outputs. The functions of an operating system should determine its structure if the system is to operate efficiently. Thus the concept of the operating structure takes its place alongside the concept of the power structure. There are a limited number of structured elements which can be combined in many different ways in an operating system.

A primary objective of marketing theory is to explore the various roads toward marketing efficiency. This issue is raised for the first time in this chapter. There is a discussion of the division of labor, of versatility and specialization, and of the special role of the decision center in directing and modifying group behavior. All of these are aspects of the relation of structure to function. This relationship is a major concern of functional analysis in marketing. Like the other aspects to be introduced chapter by chapter, it defines one of the dimensions of management effort directed toward orderly marketing.

MARKETING INPUTS AND OUTPUTS

Most of the systems which are pertinent to a theory of marketing are systems which receive inputs and discharge outputs. The discussion so far has deliberately minimized reference to inputs and outputs in order to present a clear picture of other aspects of organized behavior systems which are regarded as more primitive. Inputs and outputs may be viewed as the terminal points of some process. In a continuous process involving whole sequences of steps, the beginning and ending points of the process can be selected arbitrarily according to the convenience of the analyst, and inputs and outputs defined correspondingly in relation to these terminal points. Thus a production engineer might define inputs and outputs as the form in which materials or goods existed at the beginning and the end of the manufacturing process.

For the market analyst the inputs for a firm might begin with the acquisition of materials, and outputs might be measured at the point where goods and related services passed into the hands of customers. In another type of problem the market analyst might be looking at a complete distribution channel. He could define the inputs as beginning in the manufacturer's warehouse and the final outputs as the goods at the time they passed into the possession of consumers scattered throughout the country.

Inputs and outputs both involve transactions between an organized behavior system and its environment. Both inputs and outputs are highly differentiated and are determined both by environmental factors and by factors internal to the system. The location and operating conditions pertaining to each firm vary just as much as the features of the environment in which individual animals or species attempt to gain a foothold. Every organized behavior system is selective in what it takes from the environment and also in the outputs which it produces. The selective factors operating internally with respect to a business firm include its equipment, the technical skill of its labor force, and the background and point of view of its management and owners. The acceptance of an intake from the environment involves a variety of risks and assumptions about the continuity of the operation. It is assumed, for example, that all of the materials acquired will eventually be processed and will emerge at the other end as outputs. The inputs are without value except on the basis of this assumption.

Inputs and Outputs in a Primitive Economy. In a primitive economy pertaining to an isolated family or a tribal group, the outputs would consist of goods which were to be utilized within the group. Inputs have a direct and measurable value under these circumstances. The Stone Age man puts forth the effort to quarry boulders of flint because he expects to fashion them into stone axes and arrows for himself and other members of his tribe. In a slightly more advanced economy some of the outputs will be exchanged for goods produced by another group. An important selective factor in determining the character of outputs is what each group can do best in relation to others. Technical skill and the availability of raw materials are the determining factors.

At quite an early stage in the history of commerce there are examples of starting with what the market required and then taking whatever steps were needed to produce it. The ancient Phoenicians were famous for their Tyrian purple. Fabrics in this color were literally almost worth their weight in gold in imperial Rome. The producers of these fabrics found first one and then another source for the correct shade of dye and in the great days of Carthage were sending ships as far as the Canary Islands to get raw materials for this purpose. Sometimes a special skill seems to have been exercised far beyond the immediate need of either use or exchange. The vast extent of the ruins of the Maya temples in Yucatan and Guatemala suggest that this artistic people built for the sake of building rather than merely to satisfy the realistic needs of their way of life. There are even clearer cases of output for the sake of accumulation rather than use, such as that presented by the Indians of the Pacific Northwest. The Kwakiutl chiefs accumulated scores of blankets to be given away or even destroyed in the ceremony of the potlatch, a most peculiar form of rivalry in the search for prestige. Whether outputs are designed for use, for exchange, or for accumulation, the state of the technical arts is fundamental in determining what they will be.

Inputs and Outputs in a Modern Economy. The inputs entering into economic activities can be classified in various ways. On one hand are the inputs of materials which may be modified or combined into outputs. In modern industry many firms produce semifabricated parts or components which are then marketed to other firms for use in further manufacture. Inputs also include those which are consumed in the process of transformation. Fuel or other sources of energy illustrate this type of input. Industrial development has been determined in large degree by the location of such sources of energy. The ironworks of eastern Pennsylvania in colonial times used charcoal for smelting and sometimes depleted the forests which could be used economically before ore deposits gave out. Another type of input which gets used up in the manufacturing process comprises the whole range of plant equipment. The rate of use is slower than in the case of fuel, but the utility in the machine is used up just as surely by gradual wearing out.

The reason for reciting these obvious facts about production is that they have an important bearing on marketing in several respects. For one thing the sale of goods to industry is of increasing importance in the whole economy. One firm's output is another firm's input, and the marketing requirements vary greatly among the classes of goods which have just been described. For another thing the same categories of inputs pertain to consumer buying, the difference being largely differences of degree. The home as well as the factory buys equipment and has a similar problem of trying to maintain working balance among types of equipment owned at any one time. Both for industry and for the consumer, purchasing a piece of equipment constitutes a major step in meeting anticipated needs. In comparison, a series of relatively small adjustments is required for the purchase of food and other packaged products. Thus the stock of utilities represented by a piece of equipment is suddenly brought to a new high peak by a purchase and is allowed to run down for a long period of time before it is replenished.

Inputs and Outputs in Marketing. A third reason for the preliminary consideration of inputs and outputs is that something similar goes on in marketing but is sometimes more difficult to observe and to trace because the changes are less tangible than in production. Another complication in marketing is that any transaction involves inputs on the part of both the buyer and the seller. That is to say that costs and risks are involved on both sides of the transaction. Just as in production, there are inputs consumed in the processes of marketing, such as the time and effort of both buyer and seller, as well as inputs which can still be identified in the final product. Some major inputs of the marketing system are of an intangible nature, although they are generally associated with the sale of goods. One output by the seller is whatever he does to make purchasing easy and convenient and thus reduce the cost of marketing for the buyer. Another intangible output of the marketing system is represented by the breadth of selection offered to the consumer, which serves to reduce the risks that the product purchased will not serve the consumer's need effectively. Large retail stores may be regarded as producing an output even when the shopper does not buy, since their displays of goods give the shopper a chance to learn what the market affords and to make a decision whether to buy or not.

The tangible values produced by the marketing system are sometimes described as time, place, and possession utility, as contrasted with the form utility which is said to result from production. To create place utility is to offer the goods close at hand so as to cut down the distance consumers have to travel in searching for them. To create time utility is to make the goods available before the occasion for use arises but not so far in advance that the customer would incur additional cost in owning or storing them. To create possession utility is to get the goods into the hands of the consumer on a basis which permits him to use them or have full access to them as the need for use arises. The consumer's control of a product for his own use may be assured through transferring the ownership title or by various types of rental contracts.

The present view is that it is a highly arbitrary procedure to divide the utility provided to the consumer into two parts and to say that one part is created by production and the other part by marketing. A manufacturer can create place utility by locating branch plants in various markets. The producer of toys is creating time utility by making products in the summer and fall so that they can be in retail stores in time for Christmas. The retailer or wholesaler, on the other hand, may change the form of the product as an incident to the individual sale. The apparel store alters the suit to fit the customer. The appliance dealer provides installation service. The retailer may specify the design of a product and thus influence form utility rather than merely accepting the designs offered by the manufacturer.

The attempt to identify time, place, and possession utility with marketing is perhaps intended to show the justification of marketing as a separate activity. Time utility is related to storage and credit, place utility to transportation and the physical handling of goods, possession utility to the negotiation of transactions resulting in a change of title. All of this has a certain convenience and validity for the main emphasis in marketing. There is a fallacy nevertheless in breaking utility down into its separate aspects, since it is really an all-or-none proposition. That is to say that a bundle of utilities with one of the elements such as time or place left out is not utility at all. What is needed is not an interpretation of the utility created by marketing, but a marketing interpretation of the whole process of creating utility.

Application of "Inputs" and "Outputs" to Marketing. Progressive differentiation of products and services is the key to defining the values created by marketing. This approach is based on the assumption that each individual's need is different from every other individual's need in one or more respects. Thus the basic economic process is the gradual differentiation of goods up to the point at which they pass into the hands of consumers. Refrigerators or packages of corn flakes may all look alike as they come off the production line in the factory. The next step in differentiation is the shipment of goods to the various parts of the country. Usually, they are received by some wholesale warehouse and distributed in turn to the various kinds of retail stores which handle them. Consumers differ as to the store where they find it convenient or congenial to buy. They differ as to the day, the week, or the time of the year when their need for a product arises. On major purchases they differ as to the terms and conditions under which they are able to buy. With respect to electrical appliances there are differences in the type of home or the particular place in the home in which the appliance will be installed, and there are differences in the installation problems which arise. Consumers differ about the relative importance of low prices on the one hand and continuous and effective service on the other.

Under this concept there is no basic difference in the kind of utility created by production and that created by distribution. Every step along the way consists of shaping a set of materials more and more completely to fit the needs of specific consumers. When the producer of steel rolls it into sheets, he has relinquished the alternative of forming it into structural steel. When sheet steel moves on to the refrigerator plant, it is one step nearer a definite use, since it is now certain that it will not be used for the manufacture of automobile bodies. When the refrigerator manufacturer in Cincinnati ships a given lot of refrigerators to California, the chance that they will show up in stores in New England is pretty well foreclosed. When the refrigerator is placed on display in a leading department store rather than in a discount house, the prospects who are likely to buy are narrowed down still further.

This step-by-step differentiation of an economic good is the essence of the economic process as recognized by Chamberlin and others. We are likely to think of the mass production of standardized products as the characteristic feature of our economy because an automobile assembly line or a steel rolling mill presents such an impressive spectacle to the uninitiated. Actually, these great plants are only engaged in the earlier steps of the continuous differentiation of economic goods that finally fits them to the individual need. Fitting a good to a need consists of the two phases of shaping and sorting. The first changes the physical character of the goods but does not create any utility in the absence of the other. The second causes the goods to become part of various assortments in the hands of wholesalers, retailers, and consumers. Each assortment exists at a specific time and place. Transportation and finance are facilitating agencies for getting goods into the right assortments. Goods do not really have utility from the consumer viewpoint until they come into the possession of the ultimate user and form a part of his assortment. This conception of the marketing function will be expounded at greater length in Chapter VII, which discusses exchange and the logic of sorting.

The detailed discussion of the marketing inputs of the buyer will be postponed to the later discussion of marketing transactions. At this point it is necessary only to mention the fact that the buyer may exercise substantial initiative. In buying, there is a continuous searching for the goods which will serve the individual purpose, illustrated in its simplest form by consumer shopping. There is also the much greater initiative taken by commercial and industrial buyers, who start farther back in the process to be sure of getting the goods they want. Food packers, for example, contract in advance for the output of certain farmers and supervise the farmers in producing the quality that is wanted. Large merchandisers not only establish standard specifications for the manufactured products they buy but sometimes go back into the plant and offer the services of industrial engineers to make the plant more efficient. The larger firms exercise initiative both on the buying side and on the selling side, so that all of the activities suggested here could take place in a single organization covering the transactions of the firm both as a buyer and as a seller. These issues will be treated in Chapter IX, which deals with the evolution of transactions in the market place.

THE DIVISION OF LABOR

One of the characteristics of operating systems involving inputs and outputs is the division of labor—in other words, the assignment of operating functions to individuals or to subgroups within the larger group. The division of labor creates an operating structure within the group which is not quite the same thing as the power structure, yet the power structure and the operating structure are intimately related. Much of the art of management in marketing, as in other organized activities, consists in maintaining a constructive balance between these two types of structure. Division of labor or the assignment of separate operating functions can take place along several different lines. The problem of organization analysis in either marketing or production often starts with determining the principles which will govern the division of labor and in reconciling inconsistencies where several different principles must be used in distinguishing operating functions within the structure. The major lines along which structuring can proceed are by steps in the process, by segments of output, and by types of input. All of these forms of operating structure occur in marketing organizations, and frequently all three occur in combination.

Division by Stages of the Process. Division of labor by stages of the process is most characteristic of production but also occurs in marketing. Production workers may be situated at successive points along an assembly line or production flow. A comparable sequence in marketing might be illustrated by a wholesale grocery warehouse. First there is a group of buyers who are engaged in the procurement of goods needed from the various manufacturers. Next there are the warehousemen who take the merchandise out of the railroad cars and place it in storage. Then there are the order-pickers who assemble goods for shipment to customers as orders are received. A parallel sequence starts with the salesmen who are traveling in their territories and picking up orders from the customers. When these orders are received at the warehouse, they are usually processed by the credit department and then sent to the assembly floor to be filled by the order-pickers. Before an order is shipped, an invoice has been prepared in the billing department. One copy goes to the customer to initiate the process of collection; and another copy or its electronic equivalent is used for inventory control, so that the gradual depletion of inventory through shipments to customers will stimulate appropriate action by the buyers.

In marketing, division of labor by stages in the process often involves successive levels in distribution channels rather than steps within the same company. Perhaps the most typical marketing channel is that which starts with the manufacturer and proceeds from the wholesaler to the retailer and finally to the consumer. All four of these agencies participate in the marketing process, and there is a sharp differentiation in the type of effort they contribute. The marketing effort of the manufacturer is concerned with product design, advertising, selection of marketing channels, and the co-ordination of the whole process through his own sales force. The wholesaler is concerned with the distribution of a number of products in a single city or region, receiving them in large lots, selling them in smaller lots, and performing the functions of storage and goods handling which are essential at this stage. The retailer displays assortments of goods at a convenient point, publicizes them through local advertising, and assists consumers in making their selections. The consumer does not play a purely passive role but may spend days or even months considering a new purchase, paying attention to advertising and other sources of information, and finally taking the time and effort to visit one or more stores and to consider the various possibilities which are on display. One difference between production and marketing is that production has probably gone further in the differentiation of operating functions within a single firm, while the differentiation of functions among firms and by stages of the marketing process is of crucial importance for marketing management.

Division by Segments of Output. Division of labor also takes place by segments of output. A leather manufacturer making both suede and kid leather may have workers who specialize in each type of product, even though the processes of manufacture do not differ materially in their earlier stages. Similarly, a large company selling both coffee and breakfast cereal may find that it is more effective to have separate salesmen on each, rather than having all salesmen selling all products. As a matter of fact, sales organization necessarily involves some segmentation in relation to output, whether the segments are divided by product line, by territory, or by class of customer. Choosing among these possibilities presents knotty problems of organization, particularly in industrial selling.

Division of labor by type of output depends in part on how far the differentiation of output is carried. A firm may produce its products in a number of different models or price lines to suit different types of customers. This may lead to division of labor within the sales force or within the channels of trade. Sometimes the same company offers an economy line to one trade channel and a more expensive line to another trade channel. The extreme in the differentiation of products is in turning out custom-made articles to each customer's order. The further a producer moves in this direction, the further he will have to go in distinguishing separate functions within his sales force. Division of labor by segments of output is also involved in the competition of firms selling the same class of product. Together they serve the whole market, but each tends to serve those customers he can serve most conveniently or effectively.

Division by Type of Input. Another principle governing the division of labor concerns the type of input. In marketing this means that there are various specialists engaged in physical handling, selling, and advertising. There are many other specialists whose work may be regarded as "marketing," or closely affiliated to marketing, such as that of stylists, product designers, and credit managers. These are specializations by type of input, even though the inputs represent kinds of effort and skill rather than the more tangible inputs of production such as fuel, raw materials, plant equipment, and labor.

Another differentiation which is related to type of input depends on the source of the initiative in the marketing transaction. Sometimes the buyer takes a large measure of initiative which may be carried so far as to specify the design of the product and the materials from which it is to be produced. Sometimes the initiative of the seller is carried to the point of house-to-house calls to reach consumers in their homes. The majority of marketing transactions lie somewhere between these extremes, but the nature of the inputs required from the seller will always depend in some degree on the extent of the initiative taken by the buyer.

Mechanization in Marketing. Any operation carried out on a large scale opens the way for the application of methods which were not applicable in a small operation. Some of these advanced methods involve the application of power, the careful study of the process to eliminate lost motion, and frequently a greater use of division of labor within the operating structure. The methods of large-scale operation have doubtless advanced further in production than in marketing. Certainly there has been a greater opportunity for the application of power because of the amount of energy entering into the transformations which constitute production. At the same time, methods appropriate to large-scale operations and the scientific analysis of processes are having a large and growing impact on operating structure and the division of labor in marketing.

The very existence of great national markets such as that of the United States depends on the availability of relatively cheap transportation. The railroads, ships, trucks, and airplanes which transport goods constitute one of the major applications of power in our economy. There have also been notable applications of power equipment in the handling of goods, particularly since the advent of packaging. In the modern warehouse, fork trucks, conveyor belts, and draglines do much of the work which was once performed by human labor. In retailing, there has been less application of power, but advances similar to those in wholesaling have been brought about by the scientific analysis of the process to be performed.

Rapid communication, perhaps more than any other factor, is responsible for binding all sections of the United States together in one great national market. The possibilities for external communication between business firms and between business and the consumer have been vigorously exploited, although there is still room for progress. Mass advertising has had somewhat the same effect on marketing as the application of mechanical power has had on production. Information and persuasion emanating from the seller reaches an intensity through these new channels which the economy could not possibly afford if it all had to be done through personal selling.

The newer possibilities for the communication of information within a marketing organization are only beginning to be recognized. The flow of information within a retail or wholesale concern is just as vital as the flow of goods, often occupying an even greater number of people. Possibly the most essential function of a marketing firm is that of handling information and acting as a kind of switchboard connecting the consumer who has a specialized need with the specialized product which can satisfy his need. In fact, there are many firms at the intermediary stages in distribution, such as brokers and wholesalers without stocks, who handle information but do not handle goods at all. Even when an intermediary handles goods, the physical handling is not quite so fundamental as having the right assortment of goods on hand, so as to satisfy the majority of customers and yet not incur excessive costs for storage and investment in inventory. Mechanical tabulating equipment of the conventional type has already made major contributions in improving the efficiency of information handling in marketing firms. Far greater strides are likely to come through the application of electronic equipment. Electronic computers and control devices can not only speed up the handling of the minimum amount of information which must flow through a retail or wholesale operation, but can also open up possibilities for an increased amount of control information by making it economically feasible to obtain.

FUNCTION AND STRUCTURE

Social scientists have held diverse opinions about function and structure as appropriate starting points for the study of operating systems. The present view is that function should determine structure rather than the reverse. Perhaps it is not precise to say that function completely determines the structure of an organization. Even the ardent functionalist is obliged to admit that the influence runs in both directions. The structural possibilities affect the method of operation or determine the limits within which a function must be performed. An operating system is subject to the principles of limited possibilities so far as structure is concerned. There are many possible variations in the design of a system as a whole, but all of this range of variation is built up out of a few very simple structural elements. Each of these building blocks or elements of structure which are available must be considered by the organization analyst or the marketing executive in creating or improving an operating system.

Seriality. The first element of structure, which has been implied in much of the previous discussion, might be called "seriality." This is the state of being arranged in a sequence of steps and stages, with the process under consideration flowing from one stage to another. This kind of structure is universal both in production and in marketing. Great advantages arise from offering opportunities for specialization at each stage. It is a practical necessity in marketing because of the very different kind of job to be performed, for example, at the manufacturing and retail level. The manufacturer typically makes a few products to be sold by many retailers in many different communities. A retail store operates in a single community but sells products made by many manufacturers. It would hardly be possible for the same organization to discharge both the manufacturing and the retailing functions in the food industry unless it embraced a complete monopoly of all food production and of food distribution in every community. This statement has some exceptions, such as small bakery shops which produce and sell on the same premises. It generally holds with respect to large-scale manufacture of food products and their distribution on a national basis.

Seriality presents special problems to the market planner, particularly when the separate steps are under separate and independent control. There is a problem of co-ordination and balance in adjusting each step to the next. There is also a problem of motivation confronting any attempt at co-ordination through persuasion. The terminal point on the consumer's table is pretty remote from the fields or orchards in which the farmer grows his product. Thus, it took a long time and intensive organization effort to persuade apple growers to grade their fruit, leaving a large part of the crop on the ground so that only apples relatively free from blemishes would be offered in retail stores hundreds or thousands of miles away. The problem of co-ordination is also complicated by the divergence of interest at various stages in the channel. The small retailer does not always respond with enthusiasm to the merchandising plans which have been developed by the manufacturer and which require the retailer to lavish time and attention on one or two products which make up only a small percentage of his total volume.

Parallelism. Another basic element of structure widely prevalent in marketing may be called "parallelism." The same general type of product may move to market through several quite separate channels, starting with separate segments of supply, serving different segments of demand, and not showing up in the same intermediary establishment anywhere along the way. This separation by parallel channels is partly due to geographical separation of both production and markets. It is partly due to differences among consumers by income classes, or of retailers by type of store. Thus, in the apparel field, various brands of shirts or shoes regularly preferred by certain consumers are made by separate manufacturers and sold by retailers who have exclusive franchises. This kind of arrangement facilitates co-ordination along the successive steps and, in fact, often leads to complete vertical integration in those fields in which separate and parallel channels are feasible. The most striking illustration of all, perhaps, is in the oil industry, in which a number of large, integrated firms present completely separate and parallel channels all the way from the oil field to the gas station which serves the consumer. Parallelism offers the advantages of competition and the hazards of duplication. Every parallel channel may operate vigorously, stimulated by fear of encroachment from its rivals. On the other hand, unnecessary duplication of facilities may exist at some stage along the way if each separate channel is not completely in balance. Thus, there may be small gasoline stations on every corner in some communities where a few large consolidated stations would be more appropriate, if the only consideration were efficiency at the retail level.

Circularity.   A third basic building block for marketing structure may be called "circularity." This is really nothing more than a special case of the seriality which has already been discussed. In other words, circularity is a sequence of steps arranged one after another, but in such a way that the process finally returns to the point from which it started. Circularity in its full exemplification applies to a complete economic system rather than to an individual firm. Every firm produces goods which pass on to other manufacturers or distributing agencies and which may finally reach the ultimate consumer. Other firms meanwhile are manufacturing and marketing goods for industrial use by the first firm, or for consumer use by its employees. There is, of course, a partial circularity in the economic activities of small units such as individual towns and cities. Many of the people in an urban community are engaged in retail or service activities, and the economy of the community rests on an exchange of services among these various types of workers. There are even some special cases of circularity within a single industry or firm, but these are of only moderate interest to marketing. Thus a machine-tool plant may be capable of producing most of the types of equipment which the same plant uses in production. A small part of the plant's output may actually be used for replacing its own equipment from time to time. Similarly, a coal-mining operation may be a substantial consumer of power and thus use a small part of its own output in generating power that will be used in the production of coal.

The main application of circularity in marketing is to the movement of information rather than of goods. Reference was made in the preceding chapter to the requirement for complete feedback loops bringing information back to the point from which the initial impulse started. There would, of course, be no point in the circulation of information if the same information continued to flow unchanged around the circle. Information, like goods, undergoes transformations at each stage along the way, just as in the human nervous system. Information flows out from the central command to bring about appropriate action at the periphery. In achieving the desired result, information flows back that the action has succeeded, or has been a complete or partial failure. The information flowing back is of vital concern in determining the next decision at the command center.

Centrality. A fourth basic element of structure may be called "centrality." This is the kind of arrangement in which the channels meet at a common point and processes flow in or out with respect to that point. A particular process may be convergent in the sense that it flows in toward the center or divergent in that it flows out away from the center. The flow of goods in toward a central point is designated as assembly in marketing. Such a convergent flow may have the job of accumulating a stock of goods at a point which is convenient for later distribution. It may have the job of bringing together the various kinds of materials and components which are to enter into a manufacturing process resulting in outputs to be marketed in a different form. Major examples of assembly in marketing are the primary markets for grain and the great meat-packing centers with the associated terminal markets for livestock.

The divergent flow of goods out of a common center is characteristic of the marketing problem of every manufacturer. A product may be made in a single plant and distributed through various stages from this one point to every city in the United States. In its earlier stages, marketing as a separate field of study developed in two rather separate compartments. On the one hand was agricultural marketing, which largely confined its attention to the convergent flow of farm products to the primary markets. On the other hand was the kind of marketing research which grew up along with the application of mass advertising, which was mainly concerned with the divergent flow of goods from the factory to the consumer. For market analysts in this latter field the terms "marketing" and "distribution" came to be more or less synonymous. Today these separate compartments of thinking are breaking down. Market analysts serving manufacturers are often concerned with procurement problems going all the way back to raw materials, as well as problems of sale and distribution. Agricultural economists have become increasingly interested in what happens to farm products in wholesale and retail distribution. In fact, the relative importance of the central markets for some major products such as grain and live-stock has been steadily declining. Part of the supply has been moving more directly to the markets in which it will be consumed, resulting in a further complexity of the marketing structure viewed as a whole.

Seriality and Concurrence. It may be of some value to regard all elements of structure which have been mentioned so far as falling under the two broad headings of seriality and concurrence. Seriality has already been discussed separately and includes the special case of cir-cularity. Concurrence, on the other hand, includes both parallelism and centrality, and the latter whether the flow of the process is convergent or divergent. Seriality thus pertains to all types of structure in which the steps follow one another and thus must represent a sequence in time so far as any one lot of goods is concerned. Concurrence applies to types of structure in which similar processes can occur simultane-ously, whether they are connected at some central point or remain distinct and parallel throughout. These basic elements of structure would appear to apply to all electrical circuits or mechanical systems as well as to human organizations engaged in marketing. Recognition of these structural possibilities seems fundamental for organization planning in marketing. In planning the utilization of inputs to maxi-mize outputs, management in many operating systems starts with these simple elements as building blocks. There are a number of operating considerations in determining the final design. These include the feasi-bility of fixing responsibility and setting performance standards in the given structure. There is also the basic consideration of maintaining structural balance, including balance between successive elements in a series and balances between the concurrent flows moving in or out of a given center. There is always the underlying problem of power and communication, of making decisions and maintaining control within the system. These elements must somehow be brought into harmony, either by designing the structure to serve the operating function or by giving priority to the power structure and developing the flow of processes accordingly. The considerations which might determine choice in one direction or the other will be developed later.

STRUCTURE AND EFFICIENCY

Despite such an attempt as the present one to find a new theoretical basis for marketing management, it is fully acknowledged that market-ing has a major debt and a close kinship to economics. Both are concerned with the most efficient way of getting things done. Marketing theory turns to fields outside of economics for further insights and for sources of inspiration in finding ways to solve its particular class of problems. Several leading economists have attempted to reduce the essence of their subject to basic principles of efficient action. The viewpoint of von Mises has already been mentioned. Samuelson talks about maximizing behavior or the process of making the most out of available resources, whatever the specific goal. Stigler attempts to formulate the basic postulate of economics in terms of rational action. He says that the rational being engaged in economic behavior will undertake to allocate his resources in such a way as to secure the optimum result with respect to the individual's ends. It will be seen later that allocation is only one of the several possibilities under the broad heading of sorting, and that there are forms of sorting of equal or even greater interest to marketing. In a later chapter a form of the economic postulate will be presented in terms of the concept of sorting, rather than the narrower concept of allocation.

Strategic and Routine Transactions. At this point a principle will be introduced which the writer previously designated as the structural postulate of marketing. This postulate is an attempt to generalize on one form of action with respect to structure which can promote efficiency. An important distinction due to Commons is made between routine and strategic activities in economic operations. Routine activities are those which can be repeated time after time with no essential change in form. Strategic actions are those which pertain to nonrecurring situations. They are strategic because they may affect a whole sequence of activities thereafter and because they may involve major uncertainties as to the future outlook of the firm. Commons was particularly concerned about the differences between routine and strategic transactions in marketing. A strategic transaction might also be described as a fully negotiated transaction, while in a routine transaction many of the terms have already been established by previous negotiations. Obviously, a great deal more business can be transacted in routine fashion with a given amount of effort than where all of the terms and conditions have to be negotiated because the situation is regarded as unique. Similarly, in the internal operation of a firm a great part of daily activity follows established routines as compared with types of decision and behavior which are required to meet the kind of situations which occur at irregular intervals, or perhaps only once in the history of the firm.

This distinction between routine and nonrecurring situations leads to the structural postulate for marketing. Effective management of any input-output system requires that the maximum amount of activity shall be reduced to established routines. "Maximum amount" should be interpreted here as the largest possible proportion of all activity in the system. It is assumed that the whole operation could never be discharged on a routine basis. As the size of an operation increases, the absolute amount of activity required to cope with nonrecurring situations will almost certainly increase. At the same time the increasing scale of the operation usually offers greater opportunities for reducing additional phases of activity to routine. The structural postulate simply says that management will be alive to every opportunity for routinization, and that more and more of the activities of a growing firm will be performed on this basis.

Advantages of Routine. The advantages of routine are numerous and obvious. Repetitive action is subject to improvement to the point where all the waste motion is eliminated. A repetitive action can be divided into segments to permit greater specialization and the development of skill at each step. Once an action has been reduced to routine, it may be possible to invent a machine which can perform it automatically or greatly facilitate its performance by personnel. A routine activity lends itself to the application of mechanical power to accomplish transformations which absorb large quantities of energy relative to output. The economies of mass production and mass marketing generally develop through these successive stages once the possibility for routinizing a recurring activity has been recognized.

Another great advantage flowing from routinization is the relieving of the various command centers of needless detail, and thus the enhancing of their capacity for dealing with nonrecurring situations. The term "routine" in itself suggests something uncomfortable and confining. In reality, well-chosen routines which are effectively carried out have a liberating effect in any organization. Human physiology incorporates many routines without which life and intelligent action would scarcely be possible. The freedom of the individual to walk where he pleases would not be enhanced if he had to make a decision about each individual step. This simple freedom, like many more important ones, rests on the fact that conditioned reflexes have been developed to take care of the details. There are, of course, higher routines involved in the process of decision making itself which the marketing executive utilizes in meeting new situations. The greater his experience and training, the more he may follow an orderly procedure in deciding which problems are worthy of his attention and in pursuing these problems to a final solution. In developing these higher routines, rationality reaches its peak because it is engaged in economizing itself.

Another advantage of established routines either in production or marketing is in the training of new personnel. The individual usually develops the routines in the beginning through the trial-and-error process of learning. In an established organization it is usually a great waste of time and energy to expect each recruit to invent these routines afresh for himself. The period of learning can be greatly shortened by setting before the recruit an efficient routine which has emerged and been gradually improved over the course of past activities. Many routines in marketing as well as in other operations are too complex or too subtle for the recruit to grasp at once. Given an established pattern, he can be led to understand and perform separate parts of the pattern and later learn to assemble and manage the pattern as a whole. This type of training is no different in kind from starting with the rudiments in teaching the student to play the piano or the violin. Routines which have been found effective in operating organizations are usually maintained and enforced by regulations. The individual left to himself can seldom invent a better way of doing a job, and any divergence from the pattern creates problems in co-ordinating his activities with others.

There are some activities which are only semiroutine and which cannot be fully prescribed and controlled by regulations. This is particularly true in such marketing activities as personal selling. Not all transactions are alike, and some transactions may involve elements which neither the salesman nor his superior has ever encountered before. He is usually expected to cope with these situations on the spot and is provided with decision rules for dealing with factors which enter into some, but not all, of his sales transactions. There is commonly an overriding rule requiring him to refer the situation to his superior if its novel features are so great that he does not feel qualified to act under the decision rules which suffice in most cases.

Behavioral Drift and Specialization. Despite the existence of routines, no matter how well designed or enforced, there exists in most organizations a tendency which might be called "behavioral drift." Up to a certain limit, repetition appears to reinforce routines and to develop increasing skills in carrying them out. Beyond that point there is a reaction against routines, either consciously or unconsciously, and a tendency to drift away from the pattern. Sometimes drift is caused by simple boredom and the assumption that it may be possible to get by without performance up to standard. Sometimes it may be due to replacement of the individuals formerly engaged in the routines and the feeling of the newcomers that a slight variation in the established procedure comes more naturally for them. Sometimes the cause for drift lies in changing circumstances which have not yet been recognized by the central command. Individuals engaged in the actual process may be forced gradually to modify their behavior in an attempt to meet a gradual change in the situation.

This kind of drift often occurs in sales organizations if the central command is not adequately informed on market changes. The more orderly procedure would be to hold the line of current policy and decision rules until the central command has analyzed the changing circumstances and issued new decision rules. Behavioral drift is not always a bad thing for an organization; it can lead to progress. Occasionally, the individual who insists on doing things a little bit differently has actually invented a useful improvement. It may be in the interests of group discipline to insist that he report such deviations promptly for consideration by the central command. If the new method is good, perhaps it should be adopted throughout the organization. If it merely diverges from the pattern without constituting a real improvement, it may create confusion out of proportion to any small value in the better adjustment of the individual. Whatever decisions management makes concerning particular deviations, it should be aware of behavioral drift as a universal organization tendency. Most fundamentally, this simply means that every operation has a tendency to turn into something else simply by performing its normal functions. This inherent fluidity of behavior is from one viewpoint a hindrance to smooth operation, but from another it is a resource to be utilized in continuous adjustment.

Specialization and Versatility.   The foregoing discussion of specialization may sound as if the writer advocates maximum specialization in every case. On the contrary, specialization, like other features of organization, has its advantages and disadvantages and should not be pushed beyond the requirements of the particular situation. In a small organization it is easily possible to create too many specialized functions. Some of the functions separately recognized may not be sufficient in volume to keep even a single worker busy. There may also be some resistance on the part of workers who have been assigned to a specialized task to fill in at some other point in the operation when they have idle time. The reference here is to psychological resistance on the part of the worker rather than to union rules, which may also prevent the flexible use of workers.

Even in the case of machines, it is possible to carry specialization too far. A highly specialized machine is most efficient in performing a single task so long as there is no uncertainty as to the task to be performed. Machines of greater versatility can produce numerous variations of products, although possibly they may not be quite so efficient in producing a single type. This difference is well illustrated in the textile industry, in which two types of yarn mills are found. Some of the largest mills in the country are set up to produce a maximum output within a narrow range of yarn counts for which there is a basic and continuous demand. Other mills are equipped with machinery which can be adjusted to produce almost any yarn count which the market may require. The first type of mill can produce at the lowest unit cost so long as demand does not falter, but the second type of mill enjoys greater security in the face of market changes. Both types of operation doubtless have their place in great industries like cotton spinning, if the specialized mills are able to produce the minimum requirement of the yarn counts in greatest demand, while the more versatile mills are able to take up the slack as demand varies from one yarn count to the other.

There are further situations which affect the issue of specialization as compared to versatility in dealing with people rather than machines. Reference has already been made to the psychological resistance to change on the part of the specialist. By contrast, there is also the possibility that the worker assigned to an overspecialized task will suffer boredom and will become careless in his work. The dangers of overspecialization have been stressed by Drucker, who describes some cases in which plant production has been increased by putting specialized jobs back together in order to provide a more meaningful task for the individual worker. One device described is that of giving a worker responsibility for three or four successive steps in a process. He is directed to work on each one for a period before turning to the next one, so that each is performed as an established routine without the lost motion of constantly shifting from one to the other. High specialization presents several problems to management in using it effectively. One is that of setting up appropriate measures of standard performance for each step in the process. Another is maintaining balance between the successive steps to avoid the situation in which one worker in an operating unit is overworked while the next is relatively idle.

The third and probably the most serious of all these problems is that of designing effective channels for communication among the specialized units. The greater the specialization, the greater the amount of communication required simply by reason of the multiplication of the number of units. This is a major problem for the whole economic and marketing system in the United States as well as for large individual plants. Some students of marketing suspect that our economy has passed beyond the optimum point of specialization, so that marketing costs, representing external communication among firms, more than offset any savings achieved by excessive specialization within the operating units. The cost of co-ordination can be separately identified within such market organizations as supermarkets and wholesale warehouses. Other costs per unit of sale such as space and labor costs can be seen to decline as volume increases. The cost of co-ordination, on the other hand, begins to rise perceptively after the optimum size is passed and usually more than offsets any savings in other operating costs which can be achieved thereafter.

It is useful to consider the differences between machines and people in meeting long-run changes in conditions. A machine has certain capabilities and limitations built in by the designer. If the task confronting a company changes too greatly as compared to what it was doing ten years ago, its machines become obsolete and must be replaced. Only to a very limited extent is it possible to have machines rebuilt to meet new performance standards. People have the capacity to learn and to adopt new methods when the old routines are no longer effective. Workers may have to resign because of age, but over the period of their employment they may go through substantial changes in the character of the tasks performed. The ability to adjust to new requirements has been called plasticity. Its plastic quality is one of the greatest resources of human nature, and yet it is exercised within limits determined by experience and native endowment. In biology it appears that the species with the greatest plasticity are usually less specialized than their competitors. In the course of evolution many species died out because they became overspecialized, while man finally came to dominate the scene because he remained plastic and relatively unspecialized. In planning input-output systems, the assignment of personnel should take full account of the factors of plasticity. Some individuals can work best at specialized tasks and, once settled in them, will be unwilling to change. The growth and vitality of a firm in meeting the conditions of the changing market may depend in large degree on the opportunities for diversified experience which are given to the more plastic members of the group.

Versatility and the Relationship of Structures. A key function of management is in relating the operating structure of an organization to the power structure. How well an individual performs in an operating position is influenced by his sense of group belonging or feeling of security in his power status. Management studies by Mayo and his associates long ago revealed the importance of group solidarity in promoting individual performance. Since these early studies it has become more common to reward a group as a whole for meeting or surpassing the established standard in lieu of giving individual bonuses. There has even been a tendency to encourage groups to become self-governing and self-policing rather than administering standards for the individual from outside the group. There are doubtless many individuals who prefer to work under the piece-rate system, where each worker is paid for his individual output. Measurement of individual output is more feasible when the task involves the transformation of materials rather than dealing with people, as in the case of sales or supervisory functions. It is nearly always harder to establish an equitable bonus plan for salesmen than for workers in a plant. Anyone whose job is to work with people and to control or transform their attitudes and reactions is inevitably involved in a power structure and in two-way communication.

The salesman in a territory remote from the home office represents the power and prestige of his company. He is charged with overcoming the resistance offered by customers and the counteraction of his competitors. He has the technical function of presenting the advantages of his products effectively and assisting his customers in their application. At the same time, his success depends upon creating bonds with his customers which bring them within the power structure of his company. Thus, like the executive at the top, he is constantly engaged in extending or maintaining a power structure as well as operating within it. For marketing as a whole, it is a continuous flow of goods which is the most tangible result; but this flow takes place through a set of channels which are not always clearly marked. Creating an appropriate structure and then keeping these channels open and effective is one of the fundamental tasks of the marketing organization.

Since a basic function of marketing is to distribute goods over a wide area, the design of marketing organizations must take account of the problem of geographical dispersion. Geographical structures of various kinds are fundamental in marketing. Some of these organized behavior systems are concentrated in a single city or even in a single building, while others extend across the United States or even into foreign countries. The discussion of the relation between function and structure is not complete without an analysis of these various types of geographical structure. This aspect of organized behavior systems will be discussed at various points in this book, including the chapter on competition.

DECISION CENTERS, COMMITMENTS, AND CONTROL

Most operating systems have at least one decision center for co-ordinating the activities of the system as a whole. In many small firms the power of decisions rests in the owner and manager, who is in direct daily contact with his small group of employees. Large oper-ating systems require multiple decision centers, since too many things must be decided for all of them to be referred to a single center. In the case of multiple decision centers, there is necessarily some type of structural arrangement connecting them. Commonly, there is a hierarchy of decision centers, one of which is central and superior to all others. Radiating out from the supreme center, there are subor-dinate centers which report to it, each of which may have its own subor-dinates in turn. When the need for decision arises, it is referred upward in this structure until it reaches a level where there is adequate authority or informational resources to make the decision. The issue goes all the way to the supreme decision center if the capacity for resolving the is-sue does not exist at any lower level. Once an issue has reached the top, the flow of decision making will move downward by reverse stages. When an issue is in the hands of the supreme decision-making center, its action must take priority in time over all the others. Once a decision on a broad policy issue is made, it may need to be translated or inter-preted into more specific terms at each of the lower centers to meet local conditions.

Decision Centers as a Link between Structures. The type of de-cision assumed in this discussion of decision centers is restricted to those which are incidental to minor adjustments while a course of action is in progress. There are other issues requiring decisions which originate at the top, at least in the sense that the issue is for the first time clearly stated and explicitly considered in the supreme decision center. Decision issues originating at the top may be classified broadly into two groups. On the one hand are the decisions as to a broad course of action to be followed, and on the other hand are the decisions concerning the means for carrying out a course of action. Decisions originating at the top often call for a sharp change in the behavior patterns which have prevailed before. They constitute what Ashby has called "step function adjustment" as compared with the more continuous adjustment through day-to-day decisions. The step may be small or large, representing either a minor or a major break with what has transpired in the past.

A new course of action may be adopted if the present course has been unsuccessful or is expected to fail in the immediate future. Even though the present course of action may have succeeded, management may be aware that new conditions have arisen, making it inappropriate. Sometimes the conditions which threaten future failure grow directly out of current success. In warfare or in economic competition the other side may have devised means of defense, so that new tactics are needed for further progress. By contrast, there is sometimes good justification for continuing the present course of action, even though it has had indifferent success, on the grounds that it is just beginning to work effectively and will succeed hereafter. Determination of a course of action at the supreme decision center is equivalent to defining the behavior field in which all operations at the lower level must take place. Day-to-day decisions are something like those made from play to play by the referees in a football game. The strategic decisions emanating from the supreme decision center are more like the annual changes in the rules which are to govern the games for the following year. Perhaps a more apt parallel for a major change in a course of action would be the decision of the sports director of a college to drop football and have his men compete in soccer the following year. Such a decision would of course mean a complete reshuffling of the members of the team, with each having to acquire new skills and to learn how to fill an unfamiliar position. Something like that occurs in a marketing organization when there is a major change in the course of action. There may be a complete reorganization of methods and to some extent of personnel. Key executives in the old structure may no longer fit into the new pattern. The continuance of some of the others may be conditional upon their ability to adopt new methods and to grasp the aims and spirit of the new course of action.

Under this conception the most significant role of the supreme decision center is to serve as an organ of growth and change. The center is itself a vital part of the operating structure. At the same time it is the source of initiative for changing the structure if the organizaion is not functioning effectively. This power of decision at the center is thus a major link between function and structure. It is desirable usually for the supreme decision center to be relieved of all specialized operating activities, since it must retain the highest plasticity in order to bring about necessary changes in the organization and even in itself.

The means for following a course of action embrace all of the resources available to the operating system. There is always a scarcity of means relative to the ends to be achieved. Even though a marketing organization may have large cash reserves, the means which can be expended in any operating period are limited by the principle of profit maximization. Since the whole aim and purpose of the operating system is to produce a surplus, the means expended must be kept below the level of the gross output. There are exceptional circumstances in which the expenditure of means is deliberately placed at a higher level than the expected output, such as the initial campaign in launching a new product or steps which may be required to meet an unexpected competitive attack. The principle of scarcity is still in force, since optimum use of resources is required to meet the emergency. Resources, including manpower and other necessary facilities, must be allocated to the various phases of the whole course of action.

The allocation of resources is something like the rationing function except that it applies to productive resources rather than consumer goods. In either case the leader making the allocation must take account of the claims of the various persons or operating units which share in the total supply and are often pushing for increases in their shares. The basis of allocation in either case sometimes relies heavily on arbitrary principles, such as past history. There is an increasing practice within operating organizations to make comprehensive studies of the tasks to be performed and to allocate funds or other resources to each operating unit accordingly. It is not always possible to escape arbitrary methods entirely, so that when the requirement for all of the tasks to be performed exceeds the allowable total, the same percentage cut may be applied across the board. Sometimes a decision can be reached by weighing the relative urgency of various projects and deferring until a later date some which are worth-while but not immediately urgent.

Commitment and Structure.   Another aspect of allocation which is sometimes missed in theoretical treatments is the factor of mutual commitment. An allocation is made on the assumption of effective performance on the part of the person receiving the allocation. The supreme commander in a battle inevitably weighs the ability of his lieutenants as well as the urgency of their needs in considering their requests for reinforcements. The executive allocating resources is thereby making a commitment to the individual that he will have the resources in time to meet the occasion for use. The making of budgets as an orderly method of allocation is no mere accounting device but reflects a process of negotiation between a leader and his subordinates. The result is an implicit bargain, with one side promising resources and the other side promising performance. The network of commitments running between the executive command at the central decision point and other parts of the organization is obviously related to the power structure. It represents the manifestation and exercise of power during an operating period and binds the various units in the organization together in a way that parallels the status system. There may not be an exact correspondence between the network of commitments and the power structure in the short run, because of the emergency use of resources which may be required temporarily to support some phase of the operation. In general, however, the power of an executive is correlated with the amount of resources for which he controls or influences allocation. There is some difficulty in comparing the relative status of line and staff executives, since the line executive may have direct authority in allocating a certain volume of resources, while a staff executive may indirectly influence the allocation of a substantially greater volume of resources.

Control and Communication. The effectiveness of control depends not only on the structure of an organization but also on the extent to which it is subject to unexpected contingencies originating outside the organization. A sales executive may regard the wholesalers or retailers who sell his goods as being in one sense part of the system he is attempting to control. Obviously, control is subject to greater contingencies in dealing with these trade channels than in managing employees who are on the payroll of the parent organization. Psychologists have discussed the differences between closed and open groups. Closure for a group depends on the extent to which operations can be completed within the group without involving any outside factors. It has already been pointed out that human behavior systems are both closed and open in the sense that there are some operations which have full closure in the group and others which do not. There is, however, an important range of difference as to the degree of closure. In any organization there is likely to be a closely knit group in the center which has a higher degree of closure and is more persistent as a behavior system than the organization as a whole.

An organized behavior system can be represented by a series of concentric circles with the greatest density toward the center. In a marketing organization the inner circle would represent the executive group at headquarters. The next ring might include other members of the organization, such as traveling salesmen. The outer circle would go beyond the organization proper to include all of the firms making up the distribution channels for the company's products. Control is most concentrated at the center and encounters increasing uncertainties at each step away from the center toward the periphery.

The problem of control is dependent upon the communication facilities within the system. This is one reason for the increasing difficulties away from the center as the communication lines become more attenuated. Despite all of the progress in communication facilities, communication and control are still more favorable under conditions of physical propinquity. Even when all of the members of an organization are located in the same building, communication flows more easily on each floor than from floor to floor. An organization sometimes operates under serious handicaps if it is divided into two parts which are located as much as a block away. No communication facilities which are yet in prospect are quite the equal of face-to-face contact. When an organization is scattered over a large geographical area, time is consumed either by the members having to travel in order to communicate face to face, or in the mechanics of using such communication facilities as mail, telephone, and telegraph.

PATHOLOGY OF ORGANIZATION

This section deals with abnormal behavior as compared to the concentration on normal behavior so far in this chapter. The reader is reminded once again that the word "normal," used here, does not imply any ethical judgments imposed from the outside but refers to that kind of behavior which appears to promote the survival and adjustment of the system itself.

The first type of pathological development to be mentioned is the tendency to substitute ideology for information. This may be regarded as a disturbance in the channels of communication within the system which come to be encumbered with symbols and statements which do not have adequate reference to external reality. The symbols may have other values to the group, such as imparting a greater sense of group power and solidarity. Statements of ideal aims, if recognized as such, are not pathological but may be essential to the survival and growth of the system. It is only when the statement of the ideal or of the desired condition is substituted for statements about actual conditions that it becomes dangerous to the system.

The influence of ideology on group behavior has been analyzed at length by Karl Mannheim. Ideology is that set of statements which a group wants to believe about itself and its destiny. Ideology tends to contrast its members favorably with the nonmembers, whom it may be prepared to exploit or dispossess. Mannheim employs the interesting phrase "sociology of information" to describe the way in which the literal facts are constantly revised and reinterpreted when they come into the field of a power structure.

One consequence of embracing an ideology is to cut the members of the group off from a sense of reality. Government bureaus which have been deprived of their original functions have been observed to maintain internal activities just as if they were operating as usual. In such cases there seems to be a sort of tacit agreement on the part of the members to disregard the unpleasant facts of their situation as though they would disappear by being ignored. The same type of ideological curtain is sometimes drawn between the members of a business organization and the environment in which they are attempting to operate. The organization may be so large that it cannot be sustained by the available opportunity, as in cases where new inventions may have largely displaced the company's product in the market. The organization may be ill-equipped to take advantage of an improved opportunity because its plant equipment and other resources have been allowed to deteriorate for a long period of time. Ideology may obstruct the prompt readjustment that is needed in either of these cases.

Sometimes these persistent beliefs contribute to survival, since the organization may find a solution during the period that it is being kept together by these means. A more rational procedure would be to set a definite interval of time before dissolution was to take place after weighing the remaining assets such as going-concern solidarity against the difficulties facing the firm and accepting that a solution might not be found.

Another condition which can reach a pathological stage is that of excessive expectations within the organization. It is difficult to say at just what point the level of expectations becomes excessive or pathological in individual cases, but in general it is at the point where the level of expectations threatens the survival of the system. Active and even increasing expectations may be favorable or necessary to survival. Excessive expectations can disrupt either internal or external adjustment. Internally, they become a source of conflict between ambitious individuals, each coming to regard the other as an obstacle in achieving his ends. Externally, excessive expectations may lead to ruthless exploitation of the environment so that its resources are dissipated at an ever-increasing rate. While this external maladjustment is more characteristic of the transformation of physical resources, it can also apply to a marketing situation, as indicated by the phrase "spoiling the market." A market can be spoiled by promoting a product aggressively before it has really been perfected for successful use by consumers or before consumers are sufficiently aware of the method of use to feel that they are getting a real value from it.

An aspect of pathology which shows up in all types of organizations, including the business firm, is that which centers around the self-dramatizing leader. This is a situation similar to the ideological fallacy except that it infects a single individual rather than the whole group. The individual is enamored of an ideal image of himself and insists on shaping his behavior according to this image rather than his real character or the demands of his position. He sees himself as the center of attention and adulation of all who surround him. His actions begin to be pathological in the sense that they are designed to perpetuate this image rather than to insure the survival of the organization. A strong and ruthless personality suffering from this malady evokes an unhealthy response in those who surround him. They try to obtain security for themselves by agreeing with what the leader says and otherwise helping him to maintain his image of himself. This condition in an organization may be described as a mirror effect, in which the self-deluded person at the top sees what he wants to see as he looks into the faces of all those around him. The behavior of the individual subordinate is understandable in terms of his own security or maintenance of status, but this type of behavior on the part of a whole group of subordinates is pathological in the sense of perpetuating a condition which endangers the system as a whole.

Power as an end in itself is a pathological syndrome which involves all of the factors of ideology, excessive expectations, and self-dramatization. The self-dramatizing leader is himself caught in a vicious circle in the extreme cases in which he becomes the symbol of ideology for the group as a whole and continually strives to strengthen his own position by methods which lead to excessive expectations on the part of the other members of the group. By pursuing such measures, he unleashes forces which are difficult to control and must in turn attempt to increase his relative power still further to prevent the whole system of action from collapsing. Having stimulated the expectations of his lieutenants to an abnormal degree, he may presently become obsessed with a pathological fear of rivals. He may attempt to dispose of them by setting them against each other or by expelling them from the system. While business organizations do not suffer the blood baths which occurred under the regimes of Hitler and Stalin, they do experience a purging of rivals through dismissal. Such situations are abnormal and relatively rare in business; but here, as in other forms of organization, they can be carried to the point of wrecking the whole system. Survival and adjustment for the system as a whole require a steady progression of new leaders toward the top. Some managements try to insure this progression by making it the full responsibility of each executive to train his replacement.

One of the most universal forms of organizational pathology is the existence of internal conflict, in which an organization is faced with a great central issue for which there appears to be no permanent solution. There is an inevitable tendency for the members of the group to range themselves on either side of this issue. Those who dissent from the official view are not necessarily engaging in conflict for the sake of conflict or in a calculated attempt to promote their own interests. The very arguments urged by the majority tend to stimulate doubt and the fear that the other side of the case is being overlooked. If such individuals were asked to decide the issue themselves, they would have great difficulty in choosing. If the organization appears to be deciding it in one direction, they become genuinely fearful that the other alternative is being foreclosed.

There are many other cases in which the dissenters are less ingenuous and identify themselves with an opposing view as a means for self-promotion, with the hope that if their plan is adopted they will be given an important part in putting it into effect. Sometimes the change they are advocating is beneficial in the long run, but it may be wasteful and hazardous to carry out such reforms through the processes of conflict rather than those of rational discussion and decision. Sometimes dissent becomes a habitual attitude on the part of some members of the group. Psychologically, it appears to be a way of compelling the group to pay attention to the individual and to court his good will as a condition for going ahead with a plan that is assumed to have general group approval. Conflicts can also arise because of a basic incompatibility of individuals who do not like each other and who will not make any effort to get along. The special division of sociology known as sociometry has made an intensive study of the problem of individual compatibility within the group. It has been found that the efficiency of operating teams could be greatly improved by giving attention to this factor. In all types of business firms, including marketing organizations, one important consideration in making job assignments is that of having people in the same operating units who really work well together.

Another aspect of conflict is the fact that the individual is often placed under great psychological strain because he is the center of conflicting loyalties. In a complex civilization every individual belongs to a number of systems, such as his working organization, his family, his church, and his community. The claims made upon him by these various systems are not always consistent. The strains of conflicting loyalties may even be at work within a single organization, such as a business firm. The individual may be a sales executive and thus feel that he has certain interests in common with all the other sales executives throughout a large organization. At the same time the individual may be sales manager for a particular product division and responsible to the head of that division. On the other hand, if the newcomer is brought in to perform a definite but temporary function, it gives him a chance to become accepted by the group, so that there is relatively little resistance if he is given permanent status later on.

Another troublesome condition is that in which an operating group as a whole acquires a psychological fixation in which it either underestimates or exaggerates the capacity of the system. A business organization, like an athletic team, can come to have a low state of morale because of a series of defeats. This cellar-team psychology is self-perpetuating because the group is less able to win a competitive battle simply because it has come to expect defeat. Sometimes this is carried so far that a team in marketing, no less than in baseball or football, has to be broken up in order to change the trend. The group's attitude comes to be a justification for shortcomings and slack performance on the part of each member. A marketing organization in this state of mind may exhibit greater ingenuity in explaining why a sale was missed than in finding means of capitalizing on the opportunities which remain.

At the opposite extreme is the fault of overconfidence, which may be a serious hazard but can scarcely be regarded as self-perpetuating. The overconfident group soon runs into trouble and gains a better perspective on what it will take to assure success in the future. Overconfidence can make the organization vulnerable to unexpected attack while the attitude lasts. It may persist for a considerable time in a large company which is being carried forward by the momentum of past success rather than by the interests of its current executives.

This is in effect an application of the mirror principle to an entire organization. The organization may be so dominant in its field that all of its competitors tend to imitate it, or defer to its leadership. Thus, it sees its own image wherever it looks and may be distracted from basic problems which neither the organization itself nor its competitors are meeting effectively. The solution for the firm or the individual occupying a dominant position is to find a yardstick for performance which is more exacting than that presented by associates or competitors. That means adopting a standard based on an ideal goal or on a level of aspiration which is appropriate to the resources and capacity of the organization.

The final type of pathological condition to be mentioned is that of a top-heavy structure which in business would be described as excessive overhead. Ambitious people in any organization may scramble to get into positions of control and administration, since these appear to be higher up the scale. This tendency is exceedingly difficult to control in a large organization, so that some phases of business no less than government come to be ridden by bureaucracy. This tendency can threaten survival because the members of the group who are a part of overhead constitute an increasingly heavy burden in relation to a shrinking base of truly productive activities. Action may be impeded because some of the bureaucrats feel that their major function is to say "no" or simply because of the time consumed by clearance at successive administrative levels. This type of malady is observed in armies which require an excessive number of men behind the line for each one on the firing line and in business organizations which have too many people engaged in developing and discussing plans for those who are occupied with executing them. This situation may be complicated further by loyalty to the person who first brought the individual into the business or attraction to others in the organization who seem to be offering him a better chance for advancement than his present superior.

An individual may feel that he occupies a place on the border line with respect to the operating system to which he belongs. He may feel that his tenure with the organization is doubtful and may be uneasy from day to day as to when his employment will be terminated. Sometimes he may have given up hope of improving his status and merely tries to hang on until he can become a member of another group. Situations arise in which he is willing to promote his chance of joining a new group by actions which appear treacherous or disloyal from the standpoint of the group to which he currently belongs.

In military and political affairs, treachery sometimes endangers the survival of the group as a whole. In business the consequences are generally not so serious, even though there is still a great concern with commercial security in some business organizations. Trade secrets are of no substantial importance in marketing except for the secrecy surrounding the launching of a new campaign. As to day-to-day operation in marketing, it suffers from a higher degree of visibility and is generally open to full observation by competitors.

SELECTED REFERENCES

WEBER, MAX. *Theory of Social and Economic Organization.* English trans. by A. M. Henderson and Talcott Parsons. New York: Oxford University Press, 1947.

MERTON, ROBERT K. *Social Theory and Social Structure.* Free Press of Glencoe, Ill., 1949.

MAYO, ELTON. *Social Problems of an Industrial Civilization.* Cambridge, Mass.: Harvard University Press, 1945.

GRUCHY, ALLAN G. *Modern Economic Thought.* Prentice-Hall, Inc., 1948.

LEONTIEFF, WASSILY W. *Structure of the American Economy.* 2d ed. New York: Oxford University Press, 1953.

Max Weber was a German economist and sociologist who studied such organized behavior systems as the business firm and the government bureaucracy. He demonstrated that the operations of any economic unit are necessarily influenced by its social structure.

Merton is essentially a functionalist but holds that structure can determine what he calls the "latent functions" of a system. Mayo directed a series of studies showing how the cultural and social relations of an operating group could influence its output.

Gruchy summarizes the views of contemporary economists who share what he calls the "holistic approach." A fundamental concept for most of these economists is group behavior or collective action, as it is called by Commons. Leontieff is prominently identified with input-output analysis, which is a way of regarding the economy as an interlocking set of operating systems.

Part II

THE THEORY OF MARKET BEHAVIOR

Eight chapters are required to present the core of marketing theory. The functionalist approach to competition emphasizes rivalry within and among behavior systems in the search for differential advantage. Negotiation is a major topic in the present view, accounting for what may be called the vertical relationships of behavior systems as compared to the horizontal relationships constituting competition. The treatment of consumer motivation takes the household as the fundamental unit and considers aspects of its structure and functions which determine the course of consumer buying. The discussion of exchange describes the four aspects of sorting which produce economies in matching supply and demand. Price is discussed in terms of the uses and limitations of marginal analysis. Some basic problems of price policy are also discussed, including the overriding problem of maintaining an integrating price structure. The possibilities of creative marketing in stimulating demand are considered with respect to such processes as product innovation and advertising. The market transaction is analyzed to show how it has been modified to increase marketing efficiency. Finally, the dynamic character of modern markets is shown to rest on competitive efforts at market organization.

Two general comments may be useful to the student in relating marketing theory as presented here to economic theory. Economics starts with certain assumptions as to market organization, while marketing in a sense starts further back with attempts to organize the market or to establish the processes of orderly marketing which economics for some purposes takes for granted. Marketing as well as economics is concerned about efficiency. It is directed more specifically, however, toward the drive toward efficiency in marketing as compared to other processes. Marketing theory contemplates a variety of means for advancing efficiency, taking into account the detailed techniques of various marketing functions.

Chapter IV

COMPETITION FOR DIFFERENTIAL ADVANTAGE

The application of ecology to marketing organizations provides a new starting point for the study of competition. It begins with the assumption of heterogeneity in the market as the normal or prevailing condition, rather than building on an assumption of homogeneity as the ideal condition. The emergence of relatively homogeneous conditions at certain stages of the competitive process is treated as a tendency which can be functionally useful for some aspects of marketing operations rather than as an essential aspect of effective competition.

Starting as it does with an analysis of organized behavior systems, the functionalist approach tries to understand how competition of the prevailing type can contribute to the effective operation of behavior systems. This is in sharp contrast to the approach that starts with a competitive ideal and finds itself obliged to reduce behavior systems such as firms to bloodless and abstract entities because the going concern of real life does not fit the pattern. There is no desire, however, to detract from the great achievement of economists in developing their deductive analytical apparatus to the point where it approximates the view of competition which is obtained more directly by making a fresh start from ecology. The substance of the functionalist approach is very similar to what Chamberlin implied by "monopolistic competition" and what J. M. Clark has recently designated as "the economics of differential advantage."

THE ECONOMICS OF DIFFERENTIAL ADVANTAGE

The functionalist or ecological approach to competition begins with the assumption that every firm must seek and find a function in order to maintain itself in the market place. Every business firm occupies a position which is in some respects unique. Its location, the products it sells, its operating methods, or the customers it serves tend to set it off in some degree from every other firm. Each firm competes by making the most of its individuality and its special character. It is constantly seeking to establish some competitive advantage. Abso-

101

lute advantage in the sense of an advanced method of operation is not enough if all competitors live up to the same high standards. What is important in competition is differential advantage, which can give a firm an edge over what others in the field are offering.

Differential Advantage and Dynamic Competition.   It is the unending search for differential advantage which keeps competition dynamic. A firm which has been bested by competitors according to certain dimensions of value in products or services always has before it the possibility of turning the tables by developing something new in other directions. The company which has the lead is vulnerable to attack at numerous points. Therein is a strong incentive for technical innovation and other forms of economic progress, both for the leader who is trying to stay out in front and for others who are trying to seize the initiative.

Departures from previous product designs or patterns of practice will not be successful unless they appeal to needs or attitudes of the buyer. Differentiation by the seller is an adaptation to differences in taste and requirements among consumers. Demand is radically heterogeneous or diversified and quite independent of the actions of the seller. Supply also breaks down into heterogeneous segments according to differences in location, raw materials, plant equipment, and the skills of management and labor. The processes of exchange in the market place are directed toward matching up segments of supply and demand to provide the best fit.

This conception of an economics of differential advantage has important consequences for the analysis of monopoly and competition and for the choice of criteria to determine the degree of competitiveness in a given industry. New firms enter a field because of an expectation of enjoying differential advantage. Their chance for survival depends on whether their expectations were realistic in the first place and whether the original advantage is maintained or wrested from them by others. The profit incentive provides the drive for vigorous competition, but this drive is directed toward differential advantage because of the fundamentally heterogeneous character of markets. The enterpriser accepts the risks of innovation in his search for differential advantage. Success may be rewarded by profits until other enterprisers overtake him. Later sections will develop further implications of this view for both market structure and market behavior.

The term "differential advantage" is currently being used by J. M. Clark, who developed the concept of workable competition. It is adopted here as the term which best characterizes the dynamics of competitive advantage. Much of the underlying analysis was developed by E. H. Chamberlin, who inaugurated a new era in the theory of the firm something over twenty years ago.

Differential Advantage and Monopolistic Competition.   In his formulation of the theory of monopolistic competition, Chamberlin was applying to a wider field and developing with a greater elegance methods of analysis which, in their essentials, are already to be found in earlier economists such as Walras and Marshall. The roots of the economics of differential advantage go back still further, to the treatment of the division of labor and regional specialization by Adam Smith and Ricardo. J. M. Clark makes a fresh start by dealing directly with the struggle for differential advantage as the essence of competition. Chamberlin reaches a similar position in his later discussions of monopolistic competition by beginning with the traditional concepts of monopoly and pure competition and showing how they are usually blended in concrete situations.

Not a few economists join with Chamberlin in the advancement of a theory blending monopoly and competition. Arthur R. Burns in 1936 wrote: "The elements of monopoly . . . can no longer be regarded as occasional and relatively unimportant aberrations from competition. They are such an organic part of the industrial system that it is useless to hope they can be removed by law." W. A. Joehr points out that bilateral monopolies and oligopolies form a part of the competitive system. "Thus even if the existing structure of the present market economy could be called a 'world of monopolies,' its system of coordination could nevertheless be termed a competitive mechanism." It is the opinion of another contemporary, Kurt Rothschild, that the more realistic models of competition advanced by Chamberlin and Joan Robinson seemed to destroy the last nimbus which the idea of competition had managed to save through all the years of skepticism and criticism, by showing that so many adverse features were not occasional blemishes but were part and parcel of the way competition works in our world.

Such terms as "pure competition" and "pure monopoly" have little relevance except for tracing the transition from an atomistic model to what is essentially an ecological view of the competition among business firms. If Chamberlin had been the first major student of the subject, he might have moved more directly toward the creation of an appropriate theory. That would have meant starting with a recognition that markets are radically heterogeneous on both the supply side and the demand side. Under this approach, pure competition is nothing more than a limiting case in which there is a tendency to approach homogeneity. It is only an analytical reference point; and the true norm is effective competition, or that state of affairs which will facilitate the flow of goods in heterogeneous markets.

The fact that Chamberlin started from the traditional view led him to apply the slightly invidious term of "monopolistic competition" to what he recognized as the normal situation..

Preoccupied as they were with the problem of resource allocation, economists of the classical school devised an ingenious framework for the solution of the allocative problem. In the classical system, market structures were classified under either of two mutually exclusive categories, pure monopoly or perfect competition. In capsule form, a perfectly competitive market situation is one in which large numbers of atomistic buyers and sellers exchange an identical product. Since by assumption the quantities purchased or offered by any one buyer or seller do not represent a significant portion of the total amount being exchanged, no individual has an appreciable influence on the selling price. And since in any market the product is homogeneous, buyers are indifferent as to the source of their supply. It is assumed, moreover, that all productive resources are completely mobile and will move promptly to industrial sectors where money rewards are highest. Finally, in a perfectly competitive market all buyers and sellers and productive services are fully informed of available alternatives.

The Functionalist Approach. Within these assumptions (and taking the distribution of income as given), the allocation of resources will be "ideal." Consumer want-satisfaction will be maximized. All productive services will be compensated according to their contribution to the national income. Business firms will be compelled to produce at lowest costs per unit of output in the short run and to adopt the most efficient size of plant in the long run. Should an innovation create economic rents (excess profits), additional resources will flow into the industry until the rents are dissipated. In brief, under static conditions, changes in demand or costs will set in motion adjustments which will bring about a new position of equilibrium.

BUSINESS EXPECTATIONS IN HETEROGENEOUS MARKETS

Chamberlin formulated the principle that the market for every competitor is in some degree unique, thus initiating a drastic revision in competitive theory. This "market uniqueness" he believed to be due mainly to the phenomenon known as "product differentiation," a concept involving both monopoly and competition. Grether and his as sociates, pursuing this lead from a marketing viewpoint, have suggested the equally helpful concept of enterprise differentiation which is implicit in the present treatment. Chamberlin writes that ". . . a general class of product is differentiated if any significant basis exists for distinguishing the goods (or services) of one seller from those of another." The basis may be real or fancied, so long as it is of any importance to buyers and leads to a preference for one variety of the product over another. The market for each seller is unique, for ". . . where such differentiation exists, even though it be slight, buyers will be paired with sellers, not by chance and at random as under pure competition, but according to their preferences."

Product Differentiation. Product differentiation takes various forms. It may be based upon certain characteristics of the product itself: patented features; trade-marks; trade names; peculiarities of the package or container; singularity in quality, design, color, or style. Product differentiation may also exist with respect to the conditions surrounding its sale. Examples of this are convenience of the seller's location, reputation and good will of the seller, services provided by the seller, and various other links which attach the customers to the seller. Product differentiation, broadly interpreted, represents a control over supply in the sense that only one seller offers a product of that exact name and identity. The seller offering a product different from others actually does occupy a monopoly position in that limited sense. A seller in a particular location is a monopolist in more ways than merely the obvious sense that two physical bodies cannot occupy the same space, for his geographical location ties certain customers to him. This is often called "spatial monopoly." The customer's approach and attitude are essential, for it is noteworthy that buyers take the product differences into account when purchasing.

Behind the acceptance of differentiation are differences in tastes, desires, incomes, locations of buyers, and the uses for the commodities. It may safely be generalized that such differences among buyers have always existed, and it follows that products have differed. Of course, the merchandising tools of advertising and promotion, plus technological advances, have emphasized and widened the scope of product differentiation. This differentiation, which is a reality in the economy, leads Chamberlin and others to point out the necessity of substituting for the concept of a "competitive ideal" an ideal involving both monopoly and competition. In the economist's role, and in the immediate situation of public policy, it would be advantageous to measure and evaluate activities in the economy against an ideal which represents something more readily approaching reality. Pure monopoly, on the one hand, is impossible because of substitutability. Pure competition is not possible because of the presence of heterogeneous products and markets.

Differentiation and Monopoly. With heterogeneous products each seller has a "complete monopoly" of his own product. This type of monopolist, however, is not free from outside competition, but only partially insulated from it. The monopolist's demand curve is vitally affected by competing substitutes. Control over total supply of all related products is impossible. Recognition and acceptance of Chamberlin's concept that the real world evidences a complex of monopoly and competition, based on product diversity—a natural consequence of the system of demands—leads to several useful analytical concepts. These include market segmentation, local oligopoly, and multilevel competition.

The economics of differential advantage, building on the foundations laid by Chamberlin, holds that no one enters business except in the expectation of some degree of differential advantage in serving his customers, and that competition consists of the constant struggle to develop, maintain, or increase such advantages. In large part, these efforts in any industry or area, of course, offset each other and cancel out; and to the extent that they do, a kind of "equilibrium" results, consisting of the offsetting of various differential advantages. It is possible under certain restricted assumptions to define with precision an equilibrium situation where a general and complete "balance" of such efforts would be achieved. But in real life, conditions are constantly changing, so that at any particular time some firms will be gaining and others falling back. Any concept of competition which does not include its dynamic aspects would have little relevance to reality.

This summary of the economics of differential advantage suggests several aspects of the theory which require further explanation. It is necessary to examine the following areas: (1) bases on which a differential advantage may be obtained; (2) risk and uncertainty involved in the expectation and exploitation of a differential advantage; (3) entry and exit of firms; (4) industry structure, "balance," and equilibrium; and (5) problem solving by firms and by public administration.

Differential Advantage and the "Product." From the broad definition of "product" it is possible to determine these general bases for differential advantage. Differential advantage today rests on technological as well as on legal or geographical grounds. The legal and geographical grounds account for differential advantages due to trade-marks, patents, and to location (spatial monopoly). The technological basis for obtaining a differential advantage receives increased emphasis in the American economy, in which there has been a shift in relative importance away from geographical advantage to technological advantage. The various aspects of technological advantage are in general related to use requirements, production processes, and marketing methods. An advantage may be obtained by styling a product to meet a particular consumer taste or desire, such as the production of golf clubs for left-handed players. Advantages based on production processes may be exploited by use of unique assembly-line methods, new equipment, or application of results from a time and motion study. Marketing methods offer an ever-widening basis for exploiting an advantage. A differential advantage may be obtained by a new and different distribution system, or by a revised warehousing or inventory control system.

In this kind of competitive process the innovator may enjoy monopolistic profits for a time. When he introduces his new product or his new method of production or marketing, he is a monopolist at least in the formal sense that he is the only seller of the product or process.

Business expectation as to differential advantage is subject to uncertainty. In attempting to exploit any anticipated advantage, the firm risks resources and effort on the possibility that its expectations may be justified. Even if successful, the duration of an advantage is highly uncertain with the present pace of technological change. The chances are good that some other firm will soon find a way of competing away any excess profits by introducing another innovation along the same or some other dimension of differential advantage. It is not necessary for dozens of firms just like the innovating firm to enter the field in order to deprive it of excess profits. There are several dimensions of differential advantage, actual or potential, in any field. All are vulnerable to immediate attack with the exception of those backed up by the power of the state—as, for example, patents. Geographic advantage may, it is true, place an effective barrier around a trade territory for some commodities. But over a period of time it is constantly shifting and being transformed through improved transportation and communication, through technological developments, and through changes in the distribution of natural resources and of markets. In brief, the existence of opportunity creates an almost irresistible attraction to profit-seeking resources.

Differential Advantage and Competition. Competition among problem solvers is inherently dynamic. If a seller is at a competitive disadvantage under present conditions, he is likely to direct much of his organization's skill and resources to redressing the balance. He is in no way compelled to play the competitive game as it stands but is constantly exploring new dimensions of advantage. Sellers' competition is not merely a matter of tactics as in the case of two military forces in fixed positions gradually wearing each other down. Competition is a war of movement in which each of the participants is searching for strategies which will improve his relative position.

Further insights into the concept of differential advantage have been provided in a recent essay by Professor J. M. Clark. Clark points out that active competition consists of a combination of (1) initiatory actions by a business unit and (2) a complex of responses by those with whom it deals and by its rivals. The more aggressive firm will give the buyers more inducement (lower prices, better quality, a differentiated product to suit the buyers' tastes, greater selling efforts). The resulting advantage to the initiator consists of increased sales, wholly or partly at the expense of rivals. A rival's response seeks to neutralize or offset the initiator's advantage by offering the buyers something more effective, establishing a positive sales-increasing advantage for himself. In poker-playing terms, he may "see" the initial move or "raise" it.

Differentiation and the Neutralizing Process. Inasmuch as the initiator's and rival's inducements are confined to price, the neutralizing process—the meeting of price reductions—is conceived as being complete and instantaneous. But with respect to quality (or other variables of "product"), formal theory had previously emphasized the initiating action (establishing of a quality differential) and minimizes the neutralizing process, treating the initiating process as establishing a limited monopoly. The outcome of initiating and responding actions hinges on the relative speeds, or expected speeds, of the initiator's gain and of the neutralizing process whereby rivals destroy or offset his differential advantage, the initiator's actions becoming standard practice.

The initiation and neutralization generally take a substantial time in the case of new productive methods or products (technological advantage along the dimension of consumer uses, production processes). Incentive to innovate or differentiate would vanish if the initiator expected neutralization to be complete before he had recovered the costs of innovation. Thus the elements of risk and uncertainty enter. Fortunately, the pessimistic viewpoint of immediate neutralization is not common. Most innovators expect some enduring residue of advantage. If neutralization were permanently blocked with no further exploitation of a differential advantage possible or permitted, the initiator would have a limited monopoly, in the sense of a permanent differential advantage. To the extent that patent rights, secret processes, or strictly locational advantages exist, such a condition may be approximated.

Instantaneous neutralization occurs only in the case of price reductions on homogeneous or very closely competitive products, with few sellers. But even here, the initiator can shade list prices, vary his discount policies, make forward contracts, or benefit from other market "imperfections," so that competitive action seldom stalls completely unless marketing processes are strongly standardized. As the opportunity to differentiate marketing practices is widely available and attractive, even this qualification nearly disappears.

Clark maintains that the desirable case "lies somewhere between too prompt and too slow neutralization." He does not call this an "optimum" for the reason that the term suggests a precision that no actual system could obtain. "Neutralization needs to take time enough to leave the innovator incentive that is adequate, but not more, and then diffuse the gains as promptly as is consistent with there being ample gains to diffuse." Such neutralization in our terms is the offsetting or destroying of rivals' differential advantages. It may take away the sales gains the innovator has made, or it may merely stop further gains. It may stop further gains quickly and encroach more gradually on gains already made, so that a residue of these gains may last a fairly long time. "If such a residue is expected, it is the innovator's chief incentive, since small but long-lasting gains outweigh large temporary ones."

CONDITIONS OF ENTRY AND SURVIVAL

Entry can best be understood as an aspect of the allocation of resources or the appropriate matching of segments of supply and demand through the processes of the market. The ability and desire to assume entrepreneurial responsibility is a scarce resource no less than labor, raw materials, or capital. Entry is an important aspect of the allocation process for all of these resources. This very complex allocation process starts out with the enterpriser who wants to go into business, who discerns an opportunity and then undertakes to collect and organize the facilities required for the purpose of exploiting this opportunity.

Barriers to Entry. Ease of entry means freedom from artificial barriers which might obstruct this allocation process in the market. Ease of entry does not arise as a problem except as there is a need for new entrants on the one hand and prospective entrants ready to fulfill the need on the other. Lack of entry in a given field does not constitute proof of barriers to entry. Among the barriers to entry most frequently cited are patents, secret skills and processes, monopoly of raw materials, cartel restrictions, and capital requirements.

The desire to become an independent businessman may be considered in two separate phases. One is the general desire to head a separate enterprise. The other is the intention to go into a particular industry in a given location and under other specified conditions. It is useful to consider the sequence of steps which a prospective entrant might follow. Initially, he looks around for an appropriate opportunity, typically an industry in which there is an unusual outlook for growth and profits. According to the economics of differential advantage, he would then consider what he had to offer that was unique or that would give him an edge over established competitors. Then, having defined the opportunity, he would determine whether the costs of acquiring the necessary resources, including a suitable location, raw materials, and labor with the necessary skills, are commensurate with the capital rewards from entry. When he had satisfied himself on all of these points, he would finally approach the problem of the necessary capital. If the capital were his own, he would have to make a decision as to whether the returns in this particular opportunity would be greater than in alternative uses. If the money is to come wholly or in part from other investors, he would have to persuade them to have confidence in his expectations as to differential advantage.

Persuading investors to put money into a prospective enterprise is a marketing operation similar to persuading customers to buy a product. There is no way of compelling the investor or the consumer to part with his money if he does not have confidence in what is offered. In appealing to investors, the promoter must provide the kind of evidence which is acceptable to them regarding the reality of the differential advantage on which he expects to found his business. If the advantage is real, the amount of the funds required is not an insurmountable barrier. It is expensive to put up a steel mill, but if the enterpriser can show a real need—such as a market region which can be served more economically or an innovation in production methods which would assure an edge over existing producers—that kind of money would be available.

In brief, as far as capital requirements are concerned, the only valid barrier to prospective entrants is that the enterpriser or his potential backers do not have sufficient confidence in the expectation of differential advantage. This is the means by which the market allocates both entrepreneurial skill and other resources to the fields where there is the greatest expectation of differential advantage.

A related aspect of the problem of entry is that the optimum size of plant may be very large in the field under consideration, so that the prospective entrant would suffer an initial cost disadvantage if he could not start off working at capacity. The effect of optimum size on entry is complex, and the prevailing type of entry depends in part on this factor. If the optimum is large, there is likely to be a stimulation of entry for complementary firms rather than directly competitive firms. A company turning out a basic raw material, for example, needs an adequate number of fabricators to realize its full market potential and, in fact, often promotes the establishment of such complementary firms. If some of the fabricators get large enough, they may then integrate backward into the production of the basic raw material, provided that they are not obstructed by patents or other barriers to entry.

The Strategy of Entry.   If small units can operate effectively, the way is open for competitive firms to enter by direct simulation of the established firms. That means trying to be as much as possible like the successful firms in the hope of sharing in their success. Simulation is especially common in the retail and wholesale trade, where the successful pattern of operation cannot be kept secret and cannot be protected by patent or trade-mark. When economists talk about economies of scale as a barrier to entry, their comments should be taken as applying generally to a single type of entry—namely, entry by direct simulation.

Entry by differentiation is usually possible, despite economies of scale in existing operations. To achieve great economies of scale, the seller must induce customers to accept a highly uniform product which is susceptible to mass-production methods. To the extent that he succeeds, the demand for individual variations is partially unsatisfied, even though some of these prospective customers might be willing to pay more in order to get something that was more precisely what they wanted. Loss of volume by the mass producer through further differentiation is constantly going on in industry. The production of upholstery fabrics is only one example of a type of production in very large plants where there has been a large amount of new entry through differentiation and dissipation of economies of scale previously enjoyed.

A significant form of entry is that of the existing firm going into a new field. Entry through diversification may well serve the ends of public policy, since it tends to assure the intensification of competition in a given industry even where new firms are not available to enter the field. Not all opportunities are susceptible, however, to exploitation by existing firms. That is a major reason why the number of firms continues to increase from year to year. A firm will hesitate to go into a new field if this step may endanger what it already has. The two fields, that is, may be quite inconsistent and incompatible. A firm that competes primarily on the basis of efficiency in distribution tries to avoid the dissipation of this advantage which can arise from accepting orders for too many divergent products. The existing company may be restrained from exploiting a new opportunity because of established sales policy. Thus a company which has made a virtue of selling only through wholesalers faces serious hazards in taking on a line to sell direct to retailers. Those who have confined their sales to the drug trade often feel that they must pass up opportunities in the grocery trade. There are many cases of firms which operate under restrictions intended to preserve good trade relations and who therefore must leave the opportunity to differentiate to others.

The same considerations hold to some degree with respect to consumer good will. A manufacturer of a product which enjoys great prestige with the consumer may feel barred from bringing out a cheaper item under the same name. Examples could readily be cited, ranging all the way from face cream to automobiles. This consideration also restricts manufacturers in their choice of retail outlets and hence in the extent to which they can develop the market. The prestige of a product is related to the standing of the stores in which it is offered. All of these considerations help to keep opportunity open to the new entrant who differentiates either in product or in marketing methods.

From the viewpoint of antitrust law, the existence of barriers to entry is, then, a question of fact which can and should be determined by investigation rather than inference. For, as previously pointed out, it is highly improper to conclude that such barriers exist simply because of a low rate of entry. That may mean simply that there is no need for new entrants because, for example, product demand may be constant or falling. Again, lack of entrants may merely mean that there is no desire to enter this field on the part of prospective entrants into business.

Expectations of Differential Advantage. Entry into business is made on the basis of an advance estimate of the opportunity or the differential advantage which the entrant will enjoy. After entry has been effected, the expectations of the entrant may turn out to have been either unduly optimistic or unduly pessimistic. To have under-estimated the opportunity creates some problems, but the entrant may be able to adjust to the unexpected opportunities. We are concerned more at this point with those cases in which realized opportunity barely equals or falls short of expectations. What are the factors governing survival and final exit if the firm does not survive?

Effectuating entry into business involves a number of steps and may require a considerable period of time. Exit may be even more protracted, even if it is clear from the first that the conditions for survival cannot be met. In extreme cases the entrant recognizes on the day he opens for business that he has made a mistake. Backing out may be more difficult than plunging in, whatever the problem he faced in entry. One aspect of business entry is that relatively liquid assets are transformed into relatively specialized and frozen assets. This process is not an easy one to reverse. The beginning stage in any new business is one of testing whether the conditions of survival can be met and if they cannot, planning to withdraw with minimum loss.

Conditions of Survival. Successful entry implies as a minimum result that the firm can survive for the indefinite future. That means that the realized opportunity is at least sufficient to yield an income that will defray the current operating costs of the business. To achieve this result, the business must attract customers whose purchases will provide the required revenue. Any business selling goods or services may be regarded as a link between certain suppliers on the one hand and customers on the other. To survive, a firm must offer a preferred route for a part of this flow of goods or services and for the transformation of goods which may occur in the process. The going concern may be said to close the circuit in this flow of economic values. Ability to survive rests ultimately on the fact of closure and whether the volume of goods involved and the margin on these goods are sufficient to meet the minimum operating requirements.

Ability to survive must be combined with the will to continue. Even a profitable business may suspend operations if its owners do not wish to go on. An unprofitable business may continue for an indefinite period if its owners are willing and able to meet its deficits. There are intermediate cases in which a business fails to show a profit in the accounting sense, but can survive for a considerable period without any additions to capital. The owner may be willing to forego all or part of the wages of management and may be using up his original capital by failing to accumulate any reserves for depreciation.

Most fundamentally, what is happening when business firms survive despite their failure to live up to expectations is that their backers have accepted a write-down of their expectations. A new entrant who puts $50,000 into his business and expects to earn a return on that amount may begin to behave shortly thereafter as if he expected a return on only $10,000. The write-down of expectations influences competitive behavior both of those already in the business and of those who might consider entering later. In a stagnant or declining industry their only alternative to accepting a write-down is withdrawal. In the example cited, the owner of the business might withdraw if he could recover $15,000 of his original investment but might accept the write-down to $10,000 if the amount he could hope to pull out was less than that. Such decisions would also be affected by judgments of the future trend in the value of assets. Thus the owner might accept a write-down to $10,000 rather than attempt recovery of a larger amount through liquidation because of a conviction that asset value will eventually equal or exceed the amount of the original investment.

Avenues of Exit.   There are several well-marked avenues of exit from an overcrowded or otherwise unattractive field. Among these are outright liquidation of a firm, movement from one field into another, and sale as a going concern. Outright liquidation is the form of exit which has been implied so far. It may occur even in the case of a prosperous business which has remained the vehicle for the activities of a single individual or partnership. There may be no means of securing continuity for the business upon the death or retirement of the principals.

An organization may enter new fields and then gradually drop out of the older fields altogether. Jones and Lamson, which makes machine tools today, was once engaged solely in the manufacture of firearms and is the direct successor to a company which manufactured pumps. The U.S. Leather Company is really in the oil business. The Huron Milling Company does no milling; it is concerned with the chemistry of wheat flour.

Census statistics may show a largely fictitious exit from one field which should be balanced against apparent entry into another field. The extermination of hundreds of firms by reclassification on their census returns can greatly exaggerate the adverse trends in some industries. For example, let us look at two branches of the grain products industries such as flour and formula feeds. A firm reporting 50 per cent of its volume in flour at one census would drop out of that classification in the next census if its flour business were down to 49 per cent of its total, since the census classifies a firm according to where 50 per cent or more of its business falls. Thus, in related fields the change between successive census years might show a big drop in one and a gain in the other, while the true figures on both exit and entry would be much smaller.

The third way out is sale as a going concern. The prospective purchasers may not be very numerous, particularly in a declining industry. Outside capital is likely to look more favorably on expanding industries. Aside from exceptional cases, outside management would not expect to be able to do better with a company than the experienced people who were trying to get rid of it. The consequence is that the chances to sell as a going concern are most likely to apply to prospective purchasers in the same or related lines. A statute which was interpreted as a ban on all mergers of related companies would thus close off one of the principal opportunities for orderly exit, especially where stagnant or declining industries were concerned. It would be equivalent to blocking the normal process of reducing the number of firms in fields where the firms were too numerous.

THE PROLIFERATION OF OPPORTUNITY

Entry for a firm, like new employment for an individual, depends on the successful exploitation of opportunity. As economic activity expands, opportunity proliferates. That means that potential openings increase in number and variety and in direct relation to what has gone before. An open system is one in which openings are steadily being created, and open competition is a state of affairs in which all qualified aspirants can compete to fill the vacancies. It does not mean that every aspirant will attain the position of his first choice.

The proliferation of opportunity has been discussed in other papers as an inherent aspect of a free-enterprise economy. It has been contrasted with the Marxist principle of capitalist accumulation. Marx assumed that capitalism by its very nature was cannibalistic, that strong firms would necessarily get stronger and thus gobble up their weaker competitors until a single firm dominated each major segment of industry. More conservative economists than Marx have difficulty in avoiding this conclusion for industries with increasing returns to scale. At least one attempt has been made to show that the American economy is experiencing a long-run "decline of competition."

To say that opportunity proliferates is to say that there is an opportunity for the entry and survival of new firms precisely because of the success of existing firms. The firms already in the field help to determine the character of opportunity for the newcomer as well as to make opportunity available.

Proliferation through Simulation. The success of the established firm creates opportunities for new firms in several ways. The new-comer may enter the identical field after the first firm has pioneered production methods and product acceptance by the market, thus re-ducing uncertainty for those who follow. The original firm makes entry still easier if it abuses the privilege of being first in the field through high prices or otherwise takes its customers for granted. It may not be willing to increase its investment fast enough to take care of increasing demand. The new firms may make the same product but exploit a different segment of the market such as another region or community. Even if the pioneer follows an aggressive marketing pro-gram directed at the maximum rate of growth, common experience indicates that his advertising tends to create demand for all products of the given type and not merely the one bearing his brand name.

Proliferation through Deviation. The second aspect of prolifera-tion is the opportunities created for the firm which deviates in strategic ways from the pattern set by the first firm. The pioneer generally as-sumes some definite position as to product characteristics and sales policies. This brings corresponding expectations from consumers and the trade, so that he is not free to deviate from the pattern. The denti-frice manufacturer who puts peppermint in his tooth paste is at a dis-advantage with respect to those consumers who prefer wintergreen. If he has built his business on distributing his products through drug-stores, he is vulnerable to attack by the newcomer who discovers that the same product can be marketed efficiently through grocery channels. Thus the original firm, by taking one specific stand as to products and policies, opens the way for others who are free to deviate from these policies. There is little the first firm can do to prevent others from gaining a foothold in this way.

Proliferation through Complementation. In the third type of opening, the established firm relinquishes a part of its activity to an-other firm which can serve it better than it can serve itself. In the field of marketing intermediaries, in particular, entry is achieved by successful competition with the new firm's prospective customers. A food broker exists because he can sell the goods of some manufacturers more efficiently than they can perform this function for themselves. The wholesaler has to cope with potential competition both from the manufacturer and from the retailer. Each would usually prefer to deal directly with the other unless the wholesaler can show substantial economies in bringing them together. In this third type of opening, the new firm is relating itself to existing firms by performing complementary functions. While this phase of proliferation is prevalent in the creation of marketing channels, it appears in many other fields as well. One example would be the numerous independent parts manufacturers producing components for automobile manufacturers.

The three aspects of proliferation may be summarized by saying that the success of an established firm may create opportunity for its simulant, its deviant, and its complement. These are characteristic types of openings created by the requirements of an expanding system. Attention may now be turned to the way in which the system expresses these requirements or, in effect, lines up new firms to fill these openings.

OPERATING CLOSURE AND OPEN COMPETITION

The concept of closure as developed in communication theory can give somewhat greater precision to the treatment of self-sufficient systems. A system which is closed with respect to a given operation comprises all the parts and processes which are necessary to complete the operation. An operating system such as a telephone circuit may be interrupted by the incident of a broken wire and become a closed system again when the wire is repaired. The concept of closure with respect to an operating system is more or less analogous to concepts in topology and psychology. In set theory a closed set is one which contains all of its limit points. In Gestalt psychology the attempt to accomplish closure, to provide the missing link, is said to be characteristic both of perception and of problem solving. With respect to operating systems, the property of closure is fundamental, since the system cannot function at all without it. To the extent that we regard the national economy as an operating system and not merely a set of random variables arbitrarily selected for study, it is a system only to the degree that it achieves closure. That fact is recognized by economists in such phrases as "the circular flow of economic activity."

Closure for Efficient Routine. The operating significance of closure goes beyond the completeness of the system for the flow of economic processes. Within a closed system it is possible to work out and adopt efficient routines for handling these processes. If the system is made up of independent units, the established routines emerge more gradually from trade negotiation and the general adoption of the procedures which seem to work best. Among the characteristics of a routine that is working well is the economy of attention needed to maintain it. Repetitive operations proceed in accordance with expectations and with a minimum of effort being required to keep them under control. The value of a good working routine in human affairs is so great that it usually is better to let it alone unless a proposed change can effect a very material improvement. Certainly it cannot be kept in a fluid state with endless small modifications, or it ceases to be a working routine. The importance of closure for the system as a whole is partly that it permits closure in the more detailed aspects of the operating structure. Performance of each individual in an operating system rests in large measure on his confidence that others will act in accordance with his expectations. Reliance on expected behavior characterizes relations among business firms as well as parts of the same company.

Openness for Free Competition. If closure is the fundamental characteristic of an operating system, competition must be regarded as a supplementary factor contributing to the efficiency of the system. It is more than a coincidental paradox that free and open competition is generally regarded as a desirable state of economic systems. At first glance it may be moderately disturbing to think that a system must be open in order to be competitive and closed in order to operate at all. Systems may be closed in one sense and open in another. It is more than a play on words to say that an economic system must be open for change even though it is a closed circuit for the flow of economic processes. The system may be closed in the sense that it has all the necessary parts to operate at the present level and open in the sense that its parts may be replaced or supplemented in such a way as to improve the operation of the system. Certainly no one requires that it be open to the extent of permitting random replacements or free entry of additional firms without reference to the requirements of the system.

The desirable state with respect to closure and openness can be suggested by the sign which is frequently displayed by a retail store that is being remodeled. The message reads: "No interruptions to business while alterations are in progress."

The paradox of operating closure versus openness to change pertains to all machines and not merely to systems characterized by competition. A machine must retain a fixed structure for some period of time in order to complete an operating cycle. If the machine is to be rebuilt or adjusted, it usually has to be taken out of operation. There are modern machines capable of moderate adjustment or even self-adjustment with no interruption of operating processes. That is the kind of machine that the economic system is assumed to be. Yet the system is subjected to strains from time to time which appear to transcend its built-in power of adjustment. Some economists would prescribe an extreme degree of competitive flexibility to facilitate adjustment, even at the sacrifice of the operating closure required to maximize production. In fact, the model of perfect competition which is usually adopted as the ideal would largely disrupt operating closure in many places where it seems to be essential for the conduct of business. In a theoretically perfect market, buyer and seller would be paired on a random basis, transaction by transaction, rather than by customary and continuous association.

Resolution of the Paradox.   The resolution of the paradox which has been under discussion lies in the fact that the same system may achieve closure at different operating levels. A plant which has been turning out 10,000 units of a given product may be capable of turning out 20,000 units if additional capacity is provided at a critical point in the production process which heretofore has acted as a bottleneck. The management continues to operate the plant at the lower level until conditions are auspicious for moving to the higher level. There is a minimum of disruption to operating closure in making the change, since the move is from one definite level to another. In the economic system as a whole, changeovers do not occur by the deliberate choice of an executive exercising control over the system, but through the interaction of independent elements which are members or potential members of the system. One function of competition is to effectuate changeovers from one operating level to another in the economic system as a whole, or in its various subsystems.

An obvious model for a system which has the potentiality for closure at various operating levels is the structure of the atom as pictured in quantum physics. An electron revolves around the nucleus in one orbit but appears to shift instantaneously to a different orbit when the energy level changes. There seems to be a finite number of orbits available with a discontinuous step or jump from one orbit to the next. The energy level over time is not a smooth variable but a step function.

Step-Function Corrections and Closure.   The fact that the atom behaves in this way is still a mystery, but there is no mystery as to the fact that most adjustments in small segments of the economy take the form of step-function corrections. In building a bridge across a river, we are not willing to paraphrase the old proverb and say: "Half a bridge is better than none." Since the function of the bridge is closure, exactly one whole bridge is the right amount. Meeting the requirement of increased demand for a product usually takes place in discrete steps, whether the action is taken by established firms or by new firms entering the field. The established firm must build a new plant, broaden its channels of distribution, or adopt new operating methods which are appropriate to a larger volume of business. The new firm must create corresponding facilities and procedures subject to additional uncertainties as to both market acceptance and the operating efficiency of a new organization. More and more it is the accepted practice to spend months in staff planning, trying to make the changeover in one jump when everything is ready. Good planning decisions often make a far greater difference in selling prices than willingness to forego profit. The difference between the best and the worst technologies might make it possible to drop a price by 25 to 50 per cent as compared with the few percentage points usually represented by profit.

THE NETWORK OF COMPETITION

The economics of differential advantage helps to explain why the vigor of competition is a function of the number of levels at which rivals operate. If there were to be only one level of competition, the most intensive rivalry would result if all firms operated on a national level. If there are a number of local companies as well, they are bound together competitively by the fact that they are all in competition with the national firms.

Local and National Competition. The national distributor of any given product may be regarded as a local competitor in each market. His product goes on the shelf beside the products made by local manufacturers. Consumers are free to choose one or the other. If the national brand is chosen, it is because the consumer has weighed its price and quality against the other brands and ended up giving it an edge. The national manufacturer is trying to realize certain sales goals nationally, but he is perfectly aware that he must achieve them market by market in the face of local competition. It is common practice for the national company to analyze its sales territory by territory and to put pressure on its sales force for better performance in territories that seem to be lagging.

The total effect of what is happening to a national firm, market by market, is what determines its national sales policies. Thus, vigorous competition by local firms in half of its sales territories forces the national firm to adopt policies which, when adopted, bring heavier competitive pressure to bear on the less vigorous competitors in its other territories. The national firm is a very effective channel for transmitting competitive pressures from one market to another. With respect to the competition between national firms and local firms, there are some ways in which the local firm has the best of it. The national firm is obliged, both legally and economically, to adopt a policy which is in some respects uniform for every territory. The local firm can adapt itself to its immediate market, deviating from the policies of the national firm in directions which take advantage of the most vulnerable points of the national competitor, but which the latter is not free to meet. This is unquestionably one of the reasons why only two or three firms in an industry may have discovered a pattern which enables them to compete nationally against local competition.

Geographical and Technological Competition. Often there may be more than two distinct levels of competition corresponding to different dimensions of differential advantage. Some firms compete largely on a combination of geographic advantage with the minimum technical facilities for turning out an acceptable product. Some succeed in competing over a greater geographical area by specializing in some dimension of technological advantage. The general trend in the United States has been toward diminishing importance for geographical advantage and the proliferation of various aspects of technical advantage. This is not a one-way trend, however, since some technical developments such as the transmission of electrical power and industrial air conditioning have opened up new possibilities for geographical specialization.

The flour industry in the Southeast is an excellent example of a three-level structure of competition. In addition to local and national millers, the area has the unique development of flour-blenders not found anywhere else in the country. The flour-blender buys flour instead of wheat and blends to specification. His product competes both in the bakery trade and on the grocery shelves with those manufactured directly from wheat by other millers. The average plant capacity of the blender is much larger in terms of end product than that of the local miller, but less capital is needed for entry into the blending business than to establish a modern flour-milling plant.

Multilevel Competition. Multilevel competition in the Southeast is a good illustration of what Chamberlin has called "the network of competition." In a differentiated industry each type of firm is competing for the consumer's dollar by using distinctive methods. Any one competitor has to meet the onslaught of several different types rather than competing only with others like himself. In the simpler and more homogeneous type of competition, a leading firm might be able to rest on its oars if it felt that it was the best in the field. In multilevel competition it might excel along one dimension but be definitely outclassed along other dimensions.

There is the further hazard that the relative importance of the dimensions of competition is steadily changing with changes in consumer preferences and in the technical possibilities. Using flour milling in the Southeast to show how a network of competition operates, four separate groups might be identified, since local millers in the region and millers of less than national scope shipping into the region have a different place in the network. For ease of reference, consider local millers in Alabama and Kansas, blenders in Alabama, and national millers in Minneapolis. The national miller competes with the Kansas miller in selling flour to the blender in Alabama, and also in selling packaged products to Alabama consumers. The national miller also competes with the Alabama miller both in sales to blenders and in sales to the consumer. He competes with the blender as well as with other national millers in sales to the consumer. Here are six competitive fronts facing the national miller, even though only three types of competitors are involved. To complete the network, all the competitive relations involving the other types, but not involving the national miller, would have to be listed. The Kansas miller competes with the blender as well as supplying him, and also competes with the Alabama mill. The Alabama mill also competes with the blender as well as supplying him. Altogether there are nine competitive relations which serve to integrate supply and demand throughout the market. Thus the competitive network is far more complicated and far more effective in transmitting competitive pressures than is immediately apparent from the conception of multilevel competition.

PRICE COMPETITION AND COST REDUCTION

Competition among sellers is the unending process of trying to attract customers by giving the consumer the same satisfaction for less money or by providing greater satisfaction without a corresponding increase in price. This section deals with the first aspect of competition, in which firms compete by lowering price, either absolutely or in relation to costs. The next section deals with the second aspect, in which the competitive emphasis is upon giving the buyer a better or more acceptable product. This second phase of competition has been discussed under the rather unfortunate label of "nonprice competition." It would be more accurate to call it product competition. Actually, product and price rivalry are opposite sides of the same coin, since both price and product enter into every transaction. Both are ways of giving the consumer a better value, one by taking something out of the price side of the balance and the other by putting more in on the product side.

Minimization of Costs. Competition based on price rests fundamentally on the minimization of costs. Cost reduction depends heavily, in turn, on the realization of economies of scale—that is, the progressive reduction of costs per unit of output. The most dramatic of these economies are achieved in production-line assembly and in the mass production of materials or component parts. But, in addition, there may be economies in distribution and marketing; a large organization can enjoy rewards from specialization. Moreover, the larger the average size of customers' orders, the lower is the ratio of sales to the fixed costs of billing and customer contact. Equally, the greater the sales volume, the lower will be the unit costs of staff functions such as technical and economic research. It must be remembered, however, that economies do not arise automatically with a greater volume of business. Large-scale operations provide the opportunity for the adoption of efficient methods, but resourcefulness and good judgment must still be employed in selecting the appropriate techniques. A highly specialized piece of equipment may, for example, represent efficient production if volume has been estimated correctly, but a very high cost of production if it must stand idle much of the time.

The impact of price competition may differ in detail on the various products made by the same company. That is true even when all the products of the firm are joint products of the same process and are derived from the same or related raw materials. The flour-milling industry is a good example, since it is basically engaged in the processing of wheat, although other ingredients are included in some of its products.

Grain product prices are highly responsive to short- as well as long-run changes in the cost of wheat. That is not so true of prepared cake mixes as for flour for the very good reason that wheat flour is only one—and the least expensive—of the ingredients in a cake mix. It is clear that the prices of grain products are interrelated. They compete with each other, so that the price obtained for the major product is a controlling factor in the price that can be obtained for the minor products. The major product today is bakery flour, which accounts for 75 per cent of the tonnage of all flour. The lower the price to the baker, the lower the prices at which he can sell bakery products. Family flour has to compete for consumer favor against the alternative of buying the finished product (bread or cake). Family flour has been losing out steadily over the years in its competition with commercial bakery products. That creates a downward pressure on the price of family flour which bears heavily on those millers who have a higher-than-average stake in family flour. Cake mixes must compete with commercial cakes on the one hand and with the separate ingredients on the other. The consumer of mixes would presumably expect to pay something less than the corresponding price for cake and something more than the price of the raw materials. If the price of the mix should get close to the upper end of this range, customers would be lost in two directions. Some would buy cake because the saving in buying the mix was too small. Others would go back to the separate ingredients because the saving to be obtained in that way was so large. Formula feeds compete with mill feeds and whole grain which would be readily substitutable in many feeding programs, if formula feeds did not enjoy an economic advantage. Thus, while the four product groups are in partially isolated fields of use, all of these fields are alternative users of wheat and hence part of a broader competitive network.

PRODUCT COMPETITION AND CONSUMER CHOICE

An active competitor is always striving to give the consumer a value as good or better than any other seller who strives to satisfy the same need. Measuring competition would be relatively simple if this effort were all expended on identical and unchanging products and took the sole form of initiating changes on the price side of the bargain. The dynamic character of modern competition arises in large part from the fact that sellers also initiate changes on the product side, attempting to outguess each other as to the improvements which induce a favorable consumer response.

Product Differentiation. Product competition tends to create a gradient in market response to each seller's product. To the extent that a product differs from what existed before, it is bound to suit some people better than others. This market gradient is expressed as the demand curve for the individual product. At the left and higher end of the curve are those consumers who, other things equal, get enough extra value out of the product to be willing to pay more for it. Further to the right are consumers who consider it directly interchangeable with other products for the same use, so long as there is no difference in price. Finally, at the extreme right are people who customarily place a very low value on the product but who may purchase it in an emergency if they cannot find their regular product.

The established producer or the prospective entrant with any knowledge of marketing does not embark on product differentiation casually. While he may be anxious to give his product some distinguishing characteristic, he is foolish to do it if the feature selected has no possible interest to the consumer. Only a minor fraction of the differentiations introduced are crowned with lasting success. Both market and technical research are directed toward improving that ratio. One result of research is to eliminate some of the possible differentiations by analysis rather than by trial and error in the market. By whatever means new product features are developed, it is clear that product competition is by no means the easy escape from price competition that it has seemed to some critics of modern merchandising.

Product Competition.   Product competition supplements rather than supplants price competition. Suppose a competitor does not see any way to produce his present product for less in order to sell at a lower price. If, instead of improving his production processes, he is able to improve his product, he is still competing but along a different dimension. Such a competitive move does not lessen price competition but may increase its intensity directly. If the producer making the innovation succeeds in giving the consumer more for her money, his competitors may have to reduce prices on the older product to meet this competition. Later on they will probably find a way to meet him on the product side too by introducing the same or a similar feature. The weighing of price against product still goes on, even though the process is more complicated than that implied by simpler models of competition.

In this context, advertising takes on a meaning quite different from that implied under perfectly competitive conditions. For where product differentiation is regarded as the essence of competition, advertising serves two functions, each of which is consistent with an optimum allocation of resources. On the one hand the advertisement is a means for enhancing the general dissemination of knowledge as to available products and their relative prices. On the other hand, as an alternative method of selling, it may reduce costs to the extent that fewer salesmen, wholesalers, and retailers may be required. In the latter case there may be secondary effects as well, since the use of advertising may compel rivals to reduce their own marketing costs or improve their products, or both.

Expanding Range of Consumer Choice. Product competition tends to assure an adequate or expanding range of consumer choice. Price competition alone cannot accomplish this. Certain products may have been acceptable under past conditions, but consumer requirements are constantly changing. To get new products promptly before the prospective user once they have been introduced is to speed the consumer verdict and to facilitate the continuous adaptation of products and production facilities to the market. The enrichment of consumer choice is illustrated by the case of the consumer who wishes to serve cake to her family. She is presented with a variety of commercially baked cakes by her grocer. He also has available mixes she can use to produce many different types of cake with the minimum of effort on her own part. Finally, she can reject any of these alternatives and purchase a uniform and dependable family flour with which to turn out a cake according to her own special recipe.

The producer accepts basic business risks in taking the initiative in product competition. The projected improvement in the product may not make enough difference to get a response from the consumer market. The added costs of the new feature may be greater than the added value to the average consumer. The new product may be superior to what is on the market, but inferior to what competitors are about to bring out. The market test of a new product may cause the project to be abandoned, but it may be that the real difficulty was with some phase of the marketing program rather than with the product itself. To bring about one new differentiation may be to encourage the demand for variety and hence to undermine the basis for mass production. In the early days of the Ford Motor Company, its reluctance to depart from mass-production specifications was caricatured in the statement that you could "buy a Ford in any color, so long as it was black."

Risks Involved. Having decided to differentiate, there is an inherent risk of judgment in deciding how far to go. High specialization means an adjustment to a narrow segment of the market. The more specialized the product, the more perfectly it may meet the needs of a special group, but also the smaller that special group may become. Thus, if differentiation does not go far enough, there is nothing to distinguish the product from other products and to attract a solid core of enthusiastic customers. If it goes too far, the active market may not be large enough to support an efficient production unit.

The firm which wants to participate in product competition must carefully weigh its position in the industry and its appropriate place in the whole stream of innovations. The large firm often has a reputation for leadership to maintain and cannot afford to let others "scoop" it in the field in which it is supposed to excel. Yet it cannot afford the risks of exploring every plausible idea on a purely trial-and-error basis. It attempts to minimize its risks in several ways. One is to foresee the possibilities some distance ahead by an extensive and continuous exploration of market changes and technical developments. The other is to cover as broad a product range as possible within the limits of the field the firm is equipped to serve. It is thereby able to spread the cost and risk of research and development. If it gets a real winner out of ten potential products, that product can absorb the research costs of the other nine which did not yield a direct return.

Successful Competition. The smaller concern also seeks to minimize the risks of innovation. In the extreme case this is done by following the leader completely and making a new product only after it is fully established. In between are the firms which are willing to take some chances but which must offset with ingenuity and good merchandising strategy the actions of competitors with greater financial and technical resources. Without trying to be absolutely first in a new development, these firms may watch the introduction of a new product very closely and climb on the band wagon at the right moment. They may be content to be known as the first in their own area or the first to make the product available at a moderate price. They enjoy the great advantage of being able to analyze the leader's product and marketing program very exhaustively and to capitalize on any mistakes he may have made. If the new product is protected by patents, the shrewd competitor may attempt to break the patents either by legal challenge or by alternative technical developments. If the initial strength of the innovation is on the marketing side, there is nothing to protect it from either direct simulation or skillful differentiation. The smaller but aggressive firm has the advantage of greater mobility and freedom of action as compared to the large firm which may be the leader in the industry. The smaller organization has less to lose in deviating from accepted marketing methods or in changing its tactics if it gets off on the wrong foot. Sometimes it can seize the initiative by so simple a means as outguessing its larger opponent as to the basic appeals which are going to influence the consumer to buy and incorporating these appeals in its advertising campaign. It can call on skills in technical and marketing research which are comparable to those on the staff of the larger concern. It can minimize the cost of these services, not by spreading the cost of a permanent staff over more projects, but by calling in consultants as needed on particular projects.

In summary, there is really only one kind of competition. That consists of changing the balance between price and product in a direction favorable to the consumer. That is accomplished by either a reduction on the price side or an increment on the product side. The fact that competition is open in both directions greatly enhances its vigor. The variety of competitive measures which can be taken on the product side largely accounts for the dynamic character of competition and the rapid adjustment of the market to changing demand and advancing technology. A balance between price competition and product competition is the desirable condition which Abbott calls complete competition.

Co-operation and Oligopoly. Economists who have been concerned about the threat of monopoly arising from large-scale enterprise have feared that competitors would co-operate or collude with each other to fix prices and market shares. An ingenious extension of this theory of collusive market control was developed by William Fellner. He contends that large companies will usually behave as if each recognized the competitive position of the other and refrained from any invasion of it. Even though no discussion or negotiation has taken place, all parties act as if they have agreed to maximize the profits of the group as a whole. This theory of tacit agreements provides the economist with a determinate solution for the outcome of oligopoly or competition among a few large marketing organizations. It has the weakness of ignoring the forces generated through the vertical co-ordination of marketing channels. There can be no question that the primary interest of the seller lies in co-operating with others in the same marketing channel to maximize the sales and profits which can be divided among all participants. These are open and legal agreements to work together for a common end. To co-operate in the vertical direction and collude horizontally at the same time would create impossible conflicts for marketing policy. Imagine the tire manufacturer who spent millions of dollars to build an effective dealer organization in order to compete effectively and to get his tires to consumers at the lowest possible price. This manufacturer and his dealers are endeavoring to maximize their joint profits even though they gain at the expense of other dealers and manufacturers. To assume that the manufacturer is concurrently engaged in a tacit collusion with other tire manufacturers to maximize joint profits is utterly unrealistic. I involves the old fallacy of trying to maximize two quantities at the same time. The major efforts at maximizing joint profits are clearly conformed to joint opportunity, which means that they usually run in the vertical direction embracing the successive stages in a trade channel.

SELECTED REFERENCES

CHAMBERLIN, EDWARD. *Theory of Monopolistic Competition.* 6th ed. Cambridge, Mass.: Harvard University Press, 1950.

CLARK, JOHN MAURICE. *Studies in the Economics of Overhead Costs.* Chicago: University of Chicago Press, 1923.

INTERNATIONAL ECONOMIC ASSOCIATION. *Monopoly and Competition and Their Regulation.* Ed. by Edward Chamberlin. New York: St. Martin's Press, 1954.

BOULDING, KENNETH E. *A Reconstruction of Economics.* New York: John Wiley & Sons, Inc., 1950.

FELLNER, WILLIAM JOHN. *Competition among the Few.* New York: Alfred A. Knopf, 1949.

ABBOTT, LAWRENCE. *Quality and Competition.* New York: Columbia University Press, 1955.

Chamberlin has been the leading figure in the contemporary movement toward a more realistic theory of competition. His book, in its successive editions, has been very influential in marketing circles.

Clark's contributions are more diffuse but equally significant for marketing. The writer has utilized his work on overhead costs, his concept of workable competition, and his treatment of the economics of differential advantage which is one of the essays in the volume of essays on monopoly and competition edited by Chamberlin.

Boulding, in the reference cited, has a chapter on the ecological approach to competition. Abbott analyzes the competition on the product or quality side which is supplementary to price competition in what he calls "complete competition." Fellner is cited in the discussion of oligopoly at the end of the chapter.

Chapter V

NEGOTIATION IN MARKETING SYSTEMS

Transactions between two operating systems always involve the two factors of economic values and the balance of power. The ideal of a system in which market values alone control is impossible of realization because goods always move through a power structure and not through the neutral type of facility which may be suggested by the term "marketing channel."

Negotiation is the means of relating two systems to each other and not merely a method for carrying out transactions. Routine transactions are those which are completed without raising questions concerning power relations. Fully negotiated transactions are always concerned with the coordination between power systems, even though the sale of goods is the immediate topic of discussion. Negotiation can be either implicit or explicit. Issues may be resolved and the equilibrium of power achieved with or without a formal agenda or rules of procedure.

Negotiation in marketing channels is an essential aid to the orderly flow of products from one step to another. It seems to establish the basis for effective co-operation in the exploitation of joint opportunity. Negotiated transactions can help in reducing more numerous transactions or aspects of transaction to routine. Negotiation itself can be systematized in some degree for greater efficiency.

TRANSACTIONS BETWEEN CENTERS OF POWER

The word "negotiation" has an interesting history in relation to business. The term for business in the Latin language is *negocio*. This word is related in its original significance to the word "negation." In classical times anyone who was in government or the army, in philosophy or the arts, had a recognized occupation. Businessmen were not engaged in any of these recognized occupations, so they were regarded as occupied with negotiating—in other words, doing nothing. The term later emerged as the designation for the activity of carrying out transactions which was recognized to lie at the heart of the business function. Negotiation is a respectable term today despite its negative

130

origin and applies not only to transactions among business firms but to dealings among other types of organized behavior systems, including governments. Another area of negotiation of major importance today affects the relations of management and labor.

There has been a more intensive study of the processes of negotiation in connection with diplomacy and collective bargaining applied to labor contracts than has ever been made in the field of business. It is not surprising that among economists interest in negotiation has been keenest among those who have had some contact with international trade or trade agreements and those who have specialized in labor economics. Commons is outstanding among those who have made an analytical study of negotiation or bargaining. One of his books largely devoted to this subject bears the title of *The Legal Foundations of Capitalism.*

Negotiation in Relation to the Power Structure. One way to look upon negotiation is as a continuous adjustment among power centers. These centers of power may be business firms, national governments, or labor unions on one side facing business management on the other. In order that continuous adjustment be required or take place, it must be true that there is an inherent instability in the relations among centers of power. The process of adjustment is illustrated by the continual grouping and regrouping of nations in military alliances. Suppose that one group of allies obtains complete victory over another, as the United States and its allies defeated Germany and its allies in the Second World War. The war was scarcely over before this alliance began to fall apart, and the powers which still had great military strength began to divide into two camps consisting of the Western allies opposed to Russia and its satellites. The elimination of Germany and Japan as military factors created a power vacuum and precipitated a new alignment to offset its consequences. Similarly, negotiation which takes place in the power structure of an economic system is in part an attempt to maintain a working balance within this structure.

In business, as in diplomacy, the need for redressing the balance is precipitated by the growth or decline of power and the increasing relative power of individual firms or industries. A company grows because of consumer demand for its product and because of the efforts it puts forth in cultivating this potential demand. No company can grow faster than the national economy or the other members of its industry without imposing stresses and strains on the power structure. Some older enterprises may feel that they are being dislodged by the expansion of the newcomer, and they may combine their efforts in various ways to stem the tide. Some of these defensive moves take the form of illegal collusion or appeals for protective legislation or other forms of government aid. Our primary concern here is negotiations within the law which exhibit the form of a defensive alliance. An example would be the development in which wholesale and retail grocers negotiated a form of working arrangement, which came to be known as the "voluntary chain," as the means by which these independent firms attempted to defend themselves against the rising power of corporate chain organizations.

Sometimes the rapidly growing organization takes the initiative in effecting working arrangements with established organizations. Its special facility in negotiation may contribute greatly to its growing power. Possibly the greatest number of negotiations or attempted negotiations related to the maintenance of the power structure represents the attempt of others to negotiate favorable arrangements with a growing organization. When a business firm or an individual is obviously on the way up, there are many who would like to make a connection as a means of facilitating their own progress. Most of these proffered deals have little to offer the dynamic organization. The offers are made because the organization is showing inherent strength. In many instances, it will be able to make better bargains with the same people later on as its own position continues to improve. A promising operation might find that much of its future opportunity has been foreclosed if it made ill-considered agreements in the early stages which paid too high a price for the co-operation of others. It might find that it was working largely to enrich another organization, as in the case of the manufacturer of a new product who makes a long-term contract with a mass distributor out of excessive eagerness to get into mass production. Present agreements may limit freedom of action in meeting future risks or opportunities.

There are types of agreement which might be made between two centers of power in the market. The agreement might reflect the resolution to work together under a stated plan, each performing without stint, in full confidence that the other would do the same. A second and more typical case might be the embodiment of an agreement in a legal contract in which there were provisions by which each side could enforce performance by the other side. A still more limited degree of concord would be the agreement of one party to support another in a specified move or program, but without any long-range commitment or abnegation of alternative courses of action. Finally, there might be the agreement not to oppose a move, or to tolerate it while awaiting further study. Even this very limited type of agreement can be of importance in marketing at critical stages—as, for example, when a supplier wishes to add new channels to distribution without giving up an established channel. Beyond the realm of agreement there can be what amounts to a declaration of war when negotiation breaks down completely and each side feels injured by the refusal of the other to comply with its desires. There have been occasions when major companies, such as a grocery chain and a food manufacturer, have broken off diplomatic relations with each other, so that for months consumers were not able to get the products of the manufacturer in the stores of the chain. Meanwhile the manufacturer was intensifying his efforts with competitive retailers, and the chain was intensifying its efforts on competitive products, each attempting to bring the other to terms. There are elements of business strategy even in the process of breaking off relationships. One particular point out of many sources of friction may be selected as the basis for taking a stand. In business negotiation, as in military action, it can be very advantageous to choose one's own battleground.

Negotiation in Relation to the Operating Structure. Another way to look at negotiation among business firms is as a process of building a system of action. Oswald Knauth has stressed this view of management in his book, *Managerial Enterprise.* He sees the chief executive as constantly engaged in creating, maintaining, or extending a system of action reaching far beyond the limits of his own organization. Management is thereby preserving or perfecting a framework within which his subordinates can operate. Negotiation is thus concerned with the operating structure of business as well as with the power structure. It is the crowning process of business effort, particularly on the marketing side, which makes it possible to maintain an orderly flow of the other processes. At any given time the executive engaged in negotiation may have in mind some design of an action system which represents an immediate objective, although probably not an ultimate ideal. When he measures the facts of his situation against this design, he observes gaps or bottlenecks in the operating structure which reduce the effectiveness of operations. Negotiation may be regarded as an effort to close these gaps or to remove these bottlenecks. If the executive does not have facilities or resources under his control to accomplish closure, then he must enlist the co-operation of some independent organization and if possible conclude an agreement which will give him some assurance on this front for a reasonable time ahead.

Fortunately, it is usually not necessary to negotiate on all fronts at once. Many of the essential elements are already in place, with only one or a few missing links needed to effect operating closure in the system. If any firm, no matter how large and powerful, suddenly found that all of its co-operative arrangements with other firms had lapsed and that it had to negotiate from scratch, it would probably be out of business as of that day. It would be beyond the capacity of the most able executive group to reconstruct a complete action system quickly enough to save the firm. Commons talked about the strategic transactions which were the subject of business negotiation. He identified as strategic factors those constituting the crucial limitations on the activities of the firm at any given time. The strategic factors for any business undergo change from time to time. At one time it may be most concerned about its relations with labor. At other times its strategic limitations pertain to supplies of raw materials or the markets for its products. Negotiation may be regarded as a strategic aspect of business, since it is an attempt to deal with these limiting factors as they arise and to restore balance in the action system as a whole.

Negotiation in Relation to Solving Conflicts.   There is a third view of negotiation which is worthy of separate mention, even though it is closely related to adjustment in the power structure and the operating structure. Negotiation is a manifestation of competitive articulation or of the effort of various participants in a process such as marketing to organize the process to their own advantage. The sharpest conflicts often develop among those who feel obliged to co-operate with each other. While accepting this common necessity, each may insist that the co-operation be carried on in terms which suits his own convenience. Negotiation enters as a means of solving these conflicts. Sometimes there are irrational factors arising from the temperament of persons handling the contact which are constant sources of friction over and beyond any concern for power or for operating closure. Every organization has a stake in the integrity and the effectiveness of any representative handling its negotiations. There should be a sufficient measure of harmony so that relations are not disrupted because of the personal feelings of individuals. On the other hand, one organization may feel that it is paying too high a price for harmony if its representative is completely dominated by the representative of the other side. Among good salesmen, as well as among diplomats, a premium is placed on good manners and agreeable personality. While extending all possible courtesies to his opposite number, it may be the function of a representative to be pushing the other side constantly a little further in the direction of the arrangements which his side is trying to effect. In some types of selling, such as for advertising media or for equipment manufacturers, a salesman may obtain an account for his company only after four or five years of unremitting effort, in which each succeeding interview was an attempt to negotiate one of the many aspects of a complex understanding.

In promoting the articulation of marketing structure, each firm naturally sees itself as the center or vortex of the system of action which it is attempting to create. A buyer looking at the marketing channels through which he is supplied sees them as convergent lines running toward his company from numerous original sources. For the seller, marketing channels for his product are a set of divergent lines running outward from his firm toward ultimate consumers dispersed in all directions. Since the buyer and the seller are engaged in trying to construct quite differently oriented structures, each regards the other party to a negotiation as only one of the building blocks with which he must work. There are, of course, cases in which each is an especially important building block to the other. Extra effort is expended on either side to negotiate an effective and durable relationship. If they can arrive at a wholly satisfactory arrangement, each is in a better position to manage transactions with others. In rare cases each might tower so far above any of his individual competitors that the agreement between the two could amount to a kind of pooling of monopoly power. An agreement between a large manufacturer and a large distributing organization, for example, might pertain to a large enough segment of the whole supply as to affect the actions of all other manufacturers and distributors. Contrary to theories about bilateral monopoly, this kind of arrangement derives its power from the offer of a low price to the consumer, rather than presenting an opportunity to exploit the consumer with a monopoly price. The advantages which the two parties hope to offer each other are low price on the one hand and massive volume on the other. The author has yet to see any real cases in marketing which would support the theoretical possibility of a large supplier and a large distributor each collecting a monopoly return so as to make the price higher than for a fully integrated monopolist.

Negotiation in Relation to Its Outcome. One useful test of the outcome of a negotiation might be the degree of satisfaction which is felt on either or both sides. The result of a negotiation between two equally aggressive and well-informed parties may end with each side feeling that the other drove a hard bargain. In the case of the dissolution of a firm where assets are to be divided, each side probably permits itself to entertain expectations which are unrealistic if the other side is equally ambitious and stubborn at the bargaining table. Probably many negotiations between management and labor end with some feeling of dissatisfaction on both sides. There are other instances in which both sides may be quite happy with the results, each convinced that it got the better of the bargain. That perhaps is the ideal situation which all exchange transactions attempt to approximate. A good bargain is one in which both parties are genuinely better off than they were before. It is entirely feasible for this to happen because each side is giving up something which is more important and useful to the other side.

It is the one-sided bargains, in which both have a feeling that party A gained at the expense of party B, which will probably prove unstable and may be stirring up difficulties for both. The losing side may be resolved to tolerate the situation only so long as it cannot be avoided. The winning side may find itself unable to enforce performance if the agreement is too onerous for the other. In marketing, suppliers sometimes obtain agreements as to the services which their distributors will provide; but the services never actually materialize because of inadequate distribution margins. In a bad bargain the reconciliation of monostasy and systasy has not been achieved. The party on the losing end may feel that a breach has occurred in the system of contact and effective co-ordination.

Negotiation in Relation to Change. Whatever the setting in which negotiation takes place, no bargain can be expected to last forever. There may be an implication of immortality in the modern corporation; but any arrangement between independent, organized behavior systems is just as surely a tentative and temporary arrangement at bottom. A bargain which pertains to more than a single transfer of goods or assets attempts to formalize an appropriate relationship between the two behavior systems. Since the relationships between the systems are bound to change, the results of negotiation between them are essentially perishable. In reaching an agreement, either side enters into commitments based on a necessarily limited view of the future. A time is almost certain to come when one or both parties will be either unwilling or unable to abide by the requirements of these earlier commitments.

Every organized behavior system undergoes changes in both its capacity and its aspirations. It would be sheer coincidence if these changes should occur in unison with respect to two organizations which had a contractual arrangement with each other. Changes in either factor or on either side can upset the balance. A supplier may increase his capacity to produce and need more outlets for his products. The distributor, such as a chain organization, may open more stores and be obliged to turn to new sources for such supplies as fresh produce. A supplier may improve his product to the point where it can command a higher consumer price but through that very fact be less desirable to existing channels which have moved his products to consumers of lower incomes. The distributor may be obliged to sell at a lower price to meet new competition for the consumer's dollar and hence become restive under an existing arrangement even when he has an exclusive franchise in his market for the particular product. New markets and new technologies help to render old agreements obsolete. A manufacturer who has long depended on a single channel of distribution may find that he is missing out on a sudden expansion of demand because his traditional distributors are not able to tap these markets. Finding new channels to reach these markets almost always produces friction. There may not have been any contract or even a verbal agreement in effect. Nevertheless the traditional channel often feels that it has been chiefly responsible for the manufacturer's success and tries to hold him to a sense of moral obligation in continuing to use this channel exclusively.

Agreements, whether explicit or implicit, are quickly swept away by radical innovations in either production or marketing techniques. The firms themselves may not always survive the storm and may have to cut loose from earlier commitments in order to have a fighting chance. Often the shift in technology which undermines the old arrangement happens right within the same company. For example, a manufacturer who has made spring-wound clocks to sell to one channel of trade may move toward the manufacture of electric clocks and find that they can best be distributed through quite another channel of trade. The cycle of business boom and depression results in changing mortality rates among business firms, but a business decline doubtlessly precipitates a much higher rate of mortality as to the external arrangements among firms. Whatever the reputation of a firm for standing by its agreements, considerations concerning its own solvency necessarily come first in times of stress. The only type of external arrangement which is likely to survive in these circumstances is a legally enforceable contract, assuming that the survival of one party to the contract is as dependent upon its maintenance as the survival of the other is dependent upon its cancellation.

Negotiation in Relation to Objectives. Another starting point in analyzing negotiations is to classify negotiated transactions according to their objectives. A negotiation may be concerned with the sale of assets, such as the purchase of a company or its plant and equipment. It may be concerned with the movement of a large lot of goods, and the transaction may be fully negotiated simply because of the quantities involved. A transaction may represent the explicit or implicit negotiation of a supply contract. In either case it would govern the form of routine transaction to occur thereafter. Negotiation may be preliminary to the discussion of any individual transactions and hence be concerned with procedures for moving goods rather than with actual movement. Such a negotiation would result in an agreement as to the basis on which two firms would deal with each other if such dealings did, in fact, take place later. A negotiation may be wholly or largely concerned with the sale of services. Services can move in either direction, since the intermediary buyer can sometimes be regarded as engaged in selling services to suppliers.

The transfer of assets is a highly specialized field of negotiation which is not marketing in the ordinary sense. Yet the effect of such transfers has a major impact on marketing policy and on the structure of marketing organization. Investment bankers would be more likely than sales executives to handle this type of sale, but the market analyst might be brought in to assist in evaluating the assets. One of the results of acquisitions and mergers is a shift in the power structure, which may require a whole program of new negotiations with respect to market organization. A striking example was the merger of two companies selling home appliances under the competing names of Bendix and Crosley. The company had to decide whether to maintain two distinct product lines with their corresponding channels of distribution or whether to merge them in the attempt to obtain production and marketing economies. Having decided on the latter course, the company undertook to develop a consolidated distributor organization, hoping that it could pick the Bendix or Crosley distributor in each market according to which was regarded as the stronger. In practice the company found that many of its most successful distributors for Bendix washing machines did not want to handle Crosley refrigerators and, in fact, were prepared to give up the Bendix washing machine rather than the make of refrigerator they were already selling. Similarly, there were some strong Crosley distributors who for reasons of their own would have nothing to do with the Bendix line. The company was forced to take the weaker distributor in many cases, so that its consolidated distributor organization averaged only moderately better than the two predecessor organizations.

A recent statistical study of mergers indicates that they are on the average somewhat disappointing as compared to advance expectations. One problem that is likely to be given insufficient weight in considering any acquisition is that of integrating two distribution structures which were built up in the first place on the assumption that the lines were competitive. When competitive considerations disappear at the top, it does not mean that they are automatically removed at each succeeding step in the channels of trade.

The negotiation of a long-time supply contract involves opportunities and risks for both sides. There is the advantage of being able to adopt effective routines on either side and, by eliminating uncertainty, provide for a more orderly flow of goods. There are hazards on each side, both with respect to price and with respect to product. A drastic change in the price situation may result in conditions in which one side or the other could do much better in the open market. Similarly, the product which was the basis of the original contract may have been rendered obsolete by new inventions or may be less adaptable than competing products to improved methods of manufacture. It does not require the negotiation of a supply contract to reduce such a transaction to routine or semiroutine. Out of one or a few transactions there may emerge a general understanding which has almost as much force over a period of time as a binding contract. It often happens that an initial order is consciously regarded by either or both sides as a trial run which will set the pattern for subsequent transactions if it is mutually satisfactory.

Sometimes the possible form of future transactions is the main topic of a negotiation. A firm may go to considerable pains to qualify as a source of supply either for a large corporate customer or for government purchasing agencies. Even though no immediate business is in sight, it engages in discussions for establishing its credentials, so that it may be among those to be considered when contracts are to be let. In some such situations in marketing, investigation and negotiation merge rather imperceptibly into each other. A customer looking for a certain type of goods or services holds preliminary discussions with several firms in the course of investigating sources, and any one of these discussions might turn out later to have been the first stage in a successful negotiation. Negotiations or agreements in advance of the sale of goods are especially frequent when marketing services are being sold to the supplier. A prime example is the negotiation of a brokerage contract before the broker undertakes any sales on behalf of his principal. There have been instances in which brokerage contracts were negotiated covering markets throughout the United States before any sales were undertaken by the brokerage organization. Sometimes a salesman undertaking to negotiate the sale of goods is confronted by what amounts to an attitude on the part of the distributor that he is selling marketing services to the supplier. But the salesman must typically refer this kind of offer back to his superior for a decision. If the reaction is in the affirmative, the sale of goods to the customer may proceed. Goods move thereafter within the framework of an understanding as to the type of services which the supplier is in effect purchasing from his customer.

POWER AND VALUATION

The point has been made that negotiation is an exercise in the reconciliation of power centers. If the negotiation pertains to the transfer of goods and assets, it is also concerned with valuation and the attempt to effectuate, through analysis and discussion, the determination of values which are not automatically fixed by the market. The purpose of this section is to trace the connections between power and valuation and to describe some of the factors and practices which emerge in determining values through negotiation. Power in bargaining, as previously suggested, consists of the contrasting phases of the power to take action or the power to refrain from action.

Waiting Power. The power to refrain from action is perhaps the more primitive so far as commerce is concerned. The term "contravalence" has been used as applying to the power which two parties can exercise against each other if they are sufficiently independent to withhold co-operation. With respect to the ordinary course of negotiation in marketing, this may be designated as "waiting power." One or the other party may feel less urgency about the completion of the transaction or may exercise greater discipline in forcing the other to take the first step. There are some obvious advantages in waiting for an offer when the situation will permit. The offer may be more than was expected, in which case it may be accepted with proper care not to seem too eager. It may be lower than expected, giving the party exercising waiting power the option of rejecting it and waiting for a better offer, or taking the initiative at this point in describing an arrangement that would be satisfactory. Waiting power depends on the relative resources of the two parties, and it also depends on how each is affected by the pressure of events. The party taking the initiative may have constructed an entire system of action and need only the co-operation of the other party in this final negotiation in order to consummate a complete plan.

There are some interesting monuments to the use of waiting power, both successful and unsuccessful. In Philadelphia, Gimbel Brothers tried to acquire an entire block in which to build a department store. They were able to get together all the land in the block except for one parcel. On that parcel stood Leary's Book Store, a narrow building running four or five stories high. Since the deal for this parcel fell through, the department store was built on both sides of the book store and above it so that Leary's today is completely surrounded by Gimbel's except for the front entrance.

Initiative. Waiting power is associated with leverage, which is the situation in which the two parties to a bargain retain a measure of independence because of what each has to offer the other. First, each has something that the other really wants. Second, neither is without recourse but has access to other parties with whom it can work. Leverage can be used by the party taking the initiative as well as by the one who is relying on waiting power. Adequate leverage on both sides gives greater assurance that an agreement will be reached and that it will be an agreement with which both parties can live. One of the difficulties encountered in labor negotiation is that neither party has really effective leverage upon the other. Instead, each is completely dependent upon an agreement with the other; and the outlook for each is completely determined by the terms of the agreement so far as the subject matter of the negotiation is concerned. Here, as in domestic difficulties which lead to divorce, an unbearable tension can build up because of the conflicting claims of monostasy and systasy.

The advantages in the exercise of the initiative lie in the opportunity to give shape to the proposal which will be the subject of negotiation and to develop an agenda for the negotiating procedure which may be to the advantage of the initiating party. Quite often one party or the other is obliged to take the initiative because of the urgency of its situation or because of a desire to make a uniform arrangement with a number of people with whom it expects to negotiate. Thus a manufacturer who plans to use food brokers is obliged to develop in advance the structure of the arrangement which he expects to discuss with each broker in turn. Any other procedure would lead to a chaotic situation in which such a variety of deals were in force as to make the distribution organization unmanageable from the viewpoint of the manufacturer.

It is a matter of considerable theoretical interest to determine when the negotiator could take the initiative and when he should rely on waiting power. Sometimes there are structural elements in the situation which point rather obviously toward one policy or the other. A study of the handling of damage claims by transportation companies located in a number of states led to the conclusion that the most effective policy on the part of a company depended a good deal on the legal climate prevailing in its state. In some cases the laws of the state are much more favorable to the plaintiff than in other states. In such states, there has been an unusual flowering of legal practice concerned with handling claims against the transportation companies. It seems wise under these circumstances to take the initiative looking toward an early settlement of all legitimate claims. Reasonable compensation for damages suffered can more probably be negotiated directly with the injured party than with an attorney who specializes in pushing such cases to the limit on a contingent basis. The general rule about taking the initiative in such a situation would necessarily be qualified with respect to major claims where there was any reason to suspect fraud or a connection with the claims racket, which is well developed in some cities. The company might choose to stand and fight in the courts on those cases where it had a reasonable chance of winning or of disclosing that the claims were fraudulent. Where the attitude of both the court and the public is generally favorable to the plaintiff, the company would certainly lose most of its cases if it allowed them all to go into court and would have to pay out more, both in settlement of damages and for litigation. On the other hand, a selection of cases which would result in a reasonably high percentage of victories among those that went to trial would have a chastening effect upon individuals who were faking claims of injury and others who hoped to profit from their claims.

The Strategy of Negotiation.   This aspect of what might be called the "strategy of negotiation" offers an opportunity for the application of the theory of games. As analyzed by von Neumann and Morgenstern, there are in general two basic kinds of game situations from the strategic viewpoint. In one type of game there is a best strategy which is open to the particular player and which he should pursue as a uniform policy. He may not always win, but his chances of winning can be shown to be better by following his better strategy uniformly than by any other policy. The situation with respect to damage claims, discussed above, would probably fall under this category, with some slight reservations. In the other type of game situation a most important consideration is to keep the opponent completely baffled concerning the player's next move. Here it is important to avoid any set pattern of behavior which the opponent might observe and come to rely upon in devising his countermoves. In some cases it may even be desirable to choose one's own strategy by some random method, such as the flip of a coin, to keep the opposition from discerning any orderly sequence of moves.

The attempt to avoid any observable pattern of behavior is particularly clear when there is any element of bluffing in a negotiating stance. This rule about bluffing is just as valid in marketing as in poker. The bluff is no good if it is completely transparent and the opponent can see that the party making the bluff lacks either the resoluteness or the resources for carrying it out. It is better never to be caught in a bluff; but in a game or a commercial pursuit involving substantial uncertainty, excessively conservative play might be equally faulty. The firm which never took a chance on anything that it was not absolutely sure of being able to execute would be greatly hampered in any program of expansion. A businessman may have to conclude a successful agreement with several different parties in order to achieve closure for a proposed operation. In the initial stages he might merely be talking somewhat optimistically to each one of them in turn, even though his agreement with each one was conditional on effecting an agreement with the others.

There is a common use of both threats and promises in negotiations. Some threats can, of course, step over the legal boundaries and become intimidation. Within broad legal limits a negotiator can threaten to withdraw from the entire deal, to start negotiations with other parties unless certain conditions are met, or to withdraw from other arrangements already in force between the two organizations. There is probably a declining tendency to make use of threats, partly because of the adverse reaction on the general trade standing of the company and partly because of the extent to which possible action has been hedged about by trade regulation. Promises, on the other hand, are the essential substance of trade agreements; and the contract is a formal listing of the various actions which each party agrees to perform on behalf of the other. In the early stages of a negotiation, promises may be tentative, conditional, and indefinite. The progress of a negotiation to a successful conclusion can usually be traced in the firming-up of these mutual commitments and arrival at a balance which is satisfactory to both sides. Here again, bargaining can be something like a game of poker, with both sides remaining noncommittal as to the value they place upon various proffered features of the deal, until all of its elements are finally in place.

Valuation Procedures.   There comes a time in marketing negotiations when bargaining tactics have served their purpose and both sides are confronted with the difficult and often technical job of valuation. Valuation procedures are fairly well established for some types of transactions which are recurrent but where too much is involved for them to be considered routine. Valuation procedures might be classified as those established by custom and those which have to be especially negotiated in the particular case. Customary valuation procedures include the development of competitive bids by several possible suppliers who have each been negotiating with the customer. In private business the customer has the option of accepting the lowest bid or favoring another bid, which he considers to be the best price, in view of his estimate of such factors as fidelity in performance. In government buying the purchasing agency is usually obliged by law to accept the lowest bid. Even where there is no competitive bidding, it may be customary in the given field for a prospective supplier to prepare a quotation or to submit a price schedule governing possible variations in price, depending on design of the product or quantities purchased. Sometimes, government or other large buyers prescribe a formal basis of quotation as well as establishing the product specifications. With or without such a formal method of analyzing a price, it is customary to break the quotation down into its various components to permit effective review and discussion on both sides. Another valuation procedure used occasionally in marketing, but more often in other fields, is that of arbitration. This means laying the unresolved issues of a negotiation before a third party for decision. Use is also made of appraisers in establishing a fair value of goods or property of a nonstandard character. This includes real estate, precious stones, and paintings.

Very often the basis of valuation is one of the major topics with which negotiation has to deal. The negotiation concerning the principles and criteria to be used in reaching a decision may be even more protracted than the application of these criteria once they are agreed upon. In negotiations of major importance in which neither side is willing to give way to the other, discussion is likely to move back very quickly from the issues at hand to the criteria to be used in deciding them. When the parties are far apart to begin with, each of these background matters will be fought out just as bitterly as the question which was originally raised. In some extreme cases of this type, it is almost impossible for the negotiators to get past even the initial step of agreeing on the agenda which determines the items to be discussed and the order in which they will be brought up for consideration. This type of difficulty was well illustrated in the bitter and protracted negotiations between representatives of the United Nations and the Communists in Korea. Almost equally difficult situations arise in labor-management negotiations. The problem of agreeing on an agenda for discussions scarcely ever reaches such magnitude in marketing negotiations because of the fact, previously mentioned, that either side can usually get along without the other and will soon turn to other matters if the discussion seems likely to be unprofitable.

Negotiation Procedures. There are two general approaches to negotiation, procedurally speaking, which apply in marketing as well as in other fields. One is the well-ordered negotiating procedure, starting out with an agenda, proceeding to an agreement upon criteria, then to an analysis and valuation of the issues to be resolved between the two parties. This procedure is common practice in diplomacy but is less frequent in marketing. Negotiation in marketing is likely to proceed on more of an *ad hoc* basis. A formal agenda might seem out of character or tend to arouse suspicion. The negotiation is simply regarded in many instances as a continuation of previous discussions between the two parties. Thus, they are in effect starting again where they left off. Even where this is not the case, there is a tendency to make some assumptions about common background with respect to the particular product or trade. Discussion may go immediately to the main issue to be decided, with the criteria for decision emerging out of the discussion. This method may serve well enough so long as criteria are noted and agreed upon as they appear in the discussion. One reason for an *ad hoc* procedure is that neither side feels quite prepared to suggest or impose a negotiating procedure upon the other.

Deadlock is a situation in which negotiators still have unresolved issues between them and neither is willing to give way on the disputed points or able to conceive of a fruitful way of continuing the discussion. When a negotiation has been suspended in a state of deadlock, representatives on either side may engage in a caucus or may report back to their principals for further instructions. These discussions behind the scenes are likely to be concerned with an evaluation of the points still at issue or of what might be gained in resuming the discussion. A way out of deadlock may be found by giving ground on a point of special concern to the other side while asking for some concessions in return. New developments meanwhile may create a greater sense of urgency on the part of one or the other party to the negotiation. The protraction of a negotiation may in itself be the exercise of waiting power by one of the parties, combined with using the opportunity for a close-up appraisal of the opponent's position.

Implicit and Explicit Negotiation. Reference has been made to the fact that negotiation can be either implicit or explicit. This is not quite the same thing as saying that the process of negotiation can be formal or informal. An explicit negotiation is one in which a group meets with the mutually understood objective of making a deal or resolving issues which have been precipitated by one side or the other. The notion of implicit negotiation is meant to characterize those situations in which two groups act as if they were each relying on commitments made by the other, or where there is contact between them which is interpreted by one side or both as directed toward obtaining a working agreement, even though this purpose is never openly mentioned. Implicit negotiation, then, is any sequence of behavior which is directed toward, or may eventually lead to, an understanding, even though the relationships between the two parties are never cast in a formal bargaining framework. A shopper enters a retail store in response to an advertisement and looks over the merchandise offered. She may arrive at a negative conclusion simply through inspecting the merchandise, without any exchange of words with the salesclerk who is standing near at hand to help her. Individuals who are possible candidates for jobs sometimes are looked over by the prospective employer without being aware of it. If the employer decides he has no further interest, the result may be as conclusive as if there had been a formal employment interview. If, on the other hand, he decides to go ahead, his first covert scrutiny of the prospect might well be regarded as a preliminary step leading to the later negotiation. Similarly, retailers are constantly being looked over by consumers in search of merchandise, or by manufacturers or wholesalers in search of outlets. In many of these contacts, both sides are fully aware that a transaction or even an enduring relationship might result from the initial contact.

The importance of recognizing the notion of implicit negotiation is that it offers a way of taking care of certain contactual activities which appear to be separated from the final transaction resulting in the movement of goods. The relation between routine and fully negotiated transactions has already been mentioned. Every routine transaction must have behind it either a fully negotiated transaction or the kind of contacts which have been referred to as implicit negotiation. Salesmen and other representatives of marketing organizations are often granted substantial expense accounts to allow them to live at good hotels and to entertain in the style which will make a favorable impression and may influence business later on. These activities would not be encouraged except for the expectation that they would lead to profitable business in a reasonable percentage of the cases.

There is another aspect of implicit negotiation occurring at a slightly later stage in the contact between two parties. Any discussion which touches on the issues between two parties or the possibility of transactions between them falls in this category, even though one party or the other may have had no intention of getting involved in the negotiation. Any discussion of issues may result in the expression of attitudes subject to interpretation or misinterpretation by the other party. The old adage that "silence gives consent" is often operative in such situations, so that merely to withhold response is not a sufficient safeguard for the individual who wants to avoid the pitfalls of implicit negotiation. Statements are easily interpreted either as implied threats or as implied promises by one side or the other. For purposes of illustration, assume the case of a manufacturer engaged in discussion with his authorized distributor for a given market. He may have been thinking about appointing a second distributor in the same city or nearby but have refrained from mentioning it in the conversation. The distributor may launch an attack on competitors in his area or describe some incident involving another manufacturer and his distributors in that market. This statement might sound like a threat that the distributor would drop the manufacturer's line rather than accept a second distributor in his territory. If the manufacturer does not meet the issue squarely, and if the distributor really intended his statement to be a threat, he may interpret the manufacturer's silence as an implied promise that no such action is to be taken.

It is a matter of personal judgment determining the effectiveness of contact in business or other group activities to decide when issues must be brought out in the open and when it is better to let the occasion pass. The chief executive of a marketing organization has to be skillful in avoiding promises that he cannot fulfill either to his associates or to his distributing organization, and he must be aware that implicit promises can live to plague him just as much as those which were presented as formal propositions. The executive who gains a reputation for being a man of his word is one who does not give it lightly and who refuses to take responsibility for discussing issues unless he is ready and authorized to talk things through to a formal understanding. One of the hard lessons of experience is that words of encouragement offered in a friendly fashion can prove very costly if phrased in such a way as to imply commitments.

Specialized Negotiations. The profession of corporation law which has blossomed so prodigiously in the twentieth century is largely concerned with problems of negotiation and with the frequent need for skilled and specialized negotiators. There are many laws which bear on business negotiation; and, in a complex transaction, legal help is essential in foreseeing all the eventualities and developing the terms of a sound contract. Most fundamental is the law of contracts, which governs the kinds of business relations which can be covered by contract and the rights of enforcement accruing to either party. A transaction, according to Commons, is essentially a transfer of legal rights plus a statement prescribing performance under the agreement. Law and business meet in the elementary unit of business activity—namely, the transaction. Every transaction involves the legal essence of a contract, whether or not there is a written document setting forth the terms of the contract. Any written statement of intent or even a purely verbal commitment may be enforceable under certain conditions. The drawing of leases and contracts is a major activity of the corporation lawyer, together with representing his client in the negotiation of contracts. Aside from a contract which is negotiated to cover a special situation, there is the task of drawing up a standard contract to cover many recurring situations. The burgeoning of trade and labor legislation in the last twenty-five years has placed a premium on professional skill in this field. In marketing the need for standard contracts has been accentuated by the price-maintenance laws and other legislation, such as the Robinson-Patman Act. There are finely drawn issues as to the kind of agreement which can be made without being subject to charges of restraint of trade or of unfair price discrimination. A skillfully drawn standard contract has sometimes stood as a bulwark for a marketing method or channel. The consignment contract, first developed to govern the sale of electric lamps, has been copied or adopted many times and applied to the marketing of other products.

In addition to the negotiations of businessmen with each other, most major business enterprises have many occasions for negotiating with government agencies. One type of negotiation involves contracts to supply a government agency with goods or to undertake a construction project. Such negotiations are similar to those with other large customers, except for the body of regulations and procedures which every procurement agency imposes upon its suppliers. There is hardly any article of commerce which is not bought in substantial quantities by some government agency; but, in general, government procurement has not chosen to follow the established methods of handling transactions in each product field.

Of somewhat greater moment, from the standpoint of its impact on the normal flow of commerce, is the negotiation of settlements with various regulative bodies. A firm charged with actions contrary to some statute regulating business action is not always subject to punitive proceedings. The government's objective in many cases is to cause the marketing organization to cease and desist from the objectionable practice. Negotiation may result in a consent decree by which the firm agrees to abide by a government order with the understanding that there will be no further legal action. An interesting new possibility remains to be tested under Section 7 of the Clayton Act as revised. This section gives the Federal Trade Commission power to act in the case of mergers which are held to lessen competition or contribute to monopoly. The remedy to be exercised by the commission is to require the company making the acquisition to divest itself of all or part of the new assets in order to restore the previous condition of competition. No divestment programs have so far been carried out under this statute. It will be difficult or impossible to unscramble the two companies once they have been merged. The owners who have sold out may have no desire to re-enter business, and it may be extremely difficult to find other competent parties who have any desire to enter the field.

Another area of negotiation with government has to do with the power of the government to confer valuable rights and franchises. Authority to establish a television station or an air line can be an extremely valuable franchise. There are regulative bodies governing communication, aviation, power, and various aspects of natural resources. In any of these fields it is no longer possible for the enterprise simply to discern an opportunity and then to proceed with an operation to develop it. Opportunity in such cases takes the form of obtaining certain legal rights and franchises, and the authorization to proceed is the prize toward which competitive effort is directed. The policy of the particular bureau may lean toward large enterprise or small enterprise, or may specify numerous restrictions as to those who are eligible for consideration. The maintenance of the competitive economy in such fields of activity depends not so much on the ecological struggle as on the administration of policy. The semimonopolistic position of many organizations has depended on patent rights granted by the government. The acceleration of technological advance has reduced the relative importance of such privileges. Of considerably greater importance for the future may be the granting of rights and franchises by regulative bodies in other fields.

NEGOTIATION WITH THE CONSUMER

A genuine negotiation with the consumer resulting in a transfer of goods may be classed among retail transactions whether or not the seller confines his activities to retailing. In fact, it is more likely to be a fully negotiated transaction if the retailer is also the producer. A sale of a suit by a tailor would generally involve a more comprehensive discussion of all of the elements—including material, style features, and workmanship—than would a sale of a ready-made suit. Where the producer and the retailer are separate and distinct, each one is in a sense a party to the final transaction, even though the producer is related to the ultimate consumer only through his retail representative. This division of responsibility and interest on the supply side, instead of making the transaction as a whole more cumbersome, actually provides the opportunity for greater streamlining and efficiency. The contact between the retailer and the consumer tends to be reduced to a routinized transaction. The contact between the producer and the consumer tends toward a standardized approach to prospects through mass media. These two phases of the transaction become more manageable by being separated. Advertising as a form of prenegotiation handled on a mass basis will be discussed later in the section. The main point here is to note how a fully negotiated transaction gets broken down into prenegotiation without the movement of goods on the one hand and the transfer of goods without negotiation on the other.

Prenegotiation.   Prenegotiation and the opportunities for rendering it more efficient will first be discussed as if only the retailer and the consumer were involved. Consumer shopping of the type which represents just looking around can be classed as prenegotiation. This preliminary to a transaction would, of course, include window-shopping as well as shopping within the store. There are some customers who rely heavily on window-shopping with respect to unfamiliar types of goods. This inclination may arise partly from a notion that they are saving time as compared with entering the store and getting involved in discussion with retail salespeople. There may also be a feeling that they are still entirely free of any implied commitment so long as they are only pausing to look at merchandise which the retailer is displaying for the benefit of the passer-by. During such preliminaries, consumers are trying to clarify their own ideas and to be in a better position to deal with the clerk without the uneasy feeling that they are going to be sold something they really do not want. Some consumers experience a slight sense of embarrassment in taking up the time of the clerk or in revealing the state of their own indecision during the stage when the purchase is regarded as possible but not urgent. All the attitudes described are more likely to apply to the young shopper or to the male shopper as compared with the experienced household purchasing agent, who regards buying or shopping as an essential part of her vocation.

For the experienced shopper there are occasions when a prolonged period of searching necessarily precedes the purchase of goods. This is true in buying a dress for a special occasion, in selecting wallpaper or drapery material, or in looking for personal accessories or household furnishings which must fit in harmoniously with a previously established ensemble. Man's earliest attempts to satisfy his needs consisted of hunting or searching for game or for natural objects which were suitable for his purpose. That type of initiative from the ultimate user of a product is still very much in evidence, but today it is exerted mainly through the available channels of trade. Usually, this means searching by the consumer through the displays or stocks of accessible retail stores; or in special cases it may mean a search by the retailer on behalf of a favored customer carried further back toward the sources of supply. The searching activity of the shopper is facilitated by retail advertising. The consumer who is trying to satisfy some very specialized need adopts a more or less efficient searching pattern, guided by experience as to what stores are most likely to carry the goods she wants as well as by the current offers of the stores in their advertising. The searching activity of the household purchasing agent tends to be differentiated to some extent by seasons of the year. The busiest search of all is the search for gifts during the Christmas season. When the Christmas rush is over, the stores begin to offer such features as the January white sales. At other times it is the Easter season, the buying of sportswear and accessories, vacation time, or getting ready for the return of children to school which tend to set the principal goals of the shopping search. The department stores and speciality shops try to facilitate the search by arranging appropriate displays and advertising emphasis as they move through the various stages of the shopping calendar.

Point-of-Sale Negotiation. Once the consumer has entered the store with some serious intention of making a purchase, the ambivalent relationship of consumer and retailer becomes highly significant. The retailer is at one and the same time on the consumer's side and on the opposite side, since he is only the intermediary for the goods he sells. He is eager to make a sale on his own behalf. In completing a transaction, he is representing the original supplier as well as himself. The sharing of returns from the retail sale between the retailer and the original supplier depends on the retailer's purchase price which has usually been settled already and the price that he charges the consumer which may still offer some room for negotiation. On the one hand, the consumer may attempt to get some price concession on the product offered. On the other hand, the retailer may undertake to trade the consumer up to buy a more expensive model with a greater margin of profit for the retailer. Thus, there is always an adverse interest between retailer and consumer so far as the situation leaves some room for bargaining. On the other hand, the retailer may very genuinely serve as an advisor to the consumer; many consumers rely heavily on the judgment of the retailer as to the purchases which will serve them best.

Even though the consumer should depend on a single retail store in the purchase of a given class of products, the pressure of competition still has an impact at the point of sale. Most retailers handle the products of a number of manufacturers, and many of the products in the same retail stock are directly competitive with each other. If price and profit are the same, there is no particular inducement for the retailer to push one item rather than another. He simply presents them during the interval while the consumer is trying to reach a decision, either with complete neutrality or with advice representing his best judgment as to which will serve the buyer more satisfactorily. Price competition as well as product competition is represented at the point of sale. It is quite customary for the same retailer to handle several different price lines of the same product. While he might prefer to trade the consumer up to the higher-priced item, he will usually accede readily to the consumer's preference for the lower-priced product rather than lose the sale. In a sense the retailer is the mediator or co-ordinator of competition among the original suppliers, since all must rely upon him as the final link in reaching the consumer. If he is too obviously acting as an agent of a single supplier, he loses his status as advisor to the consumer; and the consumer preserves freedom of choice among competitive items by shopping in an increasing number of stores.

The Art of Retail Selling. The art of retail selling requires the retailer to give the consumer an adequate but not an excessive range of choice. One of the major topics of negotiation between the retailer and the consumer, usually remaining implicit, is the proffer of advisory service by the retailer and the acceptance or rejection of the proffer by the consumer. If the retailer has only one item in stock which could possibly meet the consumer's requirements, the consumer may react against it, no matter how great its superficial appeal. Reduced to deciding for or against a single item, a buyer lacks a convenient yardstick for comparison. To effect a sale in such an instance, the retailer usually has to be skillful in building up a verbal picture of what the alternatives are or of the background of the store's decision to handle only one brand or model, or to convince the consumer that no genuine alternative is available. This throws a heavy burden on selling and negotiating skills that could be avoided by presenting alternatives. There is the danger at the other extreme of confusing the customer and losing the sale by presenting too many alternatives. At some point in any sales negotiation when alternatives are under consideration, the choice boils down to one preferred item against the field. When this stage is reached, the buyer should be given every opportunity to make the choice final rather than pushing the merits of numerous alternatives in an excessive eagerness to be sure of a sale.

During the process of reaching a final and definite choice, it is well to have in mind that a buyer is looking for characteristics in a product which might be described as absolute and relative values. Absolute value rests on specific requirements which the product must meet in order to be useful at all. For example, a pair of shoes which is otherwise desirable may be out entirely if it is a size too small, while a sofa which attracts the shopper may be eliminated if it is six inches too long for its destined wall space. Relative value, on the other hand, is related to the competitive sense of the shopper in trying to do as well or better than any of her friends or neighbors. The consumer may see an item which meets her absolute requirements and still continue the search for a time before she is satisfied that she is getting a good relative value. In the attempts of a given retailer to negotiate a sale, he needs first to be clear on the customer's absolute requirements and then, if he has two or more items to offer which qualify on this score, assist the consumer in choosing that one which will make her feel that she has obtained the greatest relative value.

Communication in Retail Selling. Transactions between retailer and consumer, whether fully negotiated or not, require communication. Sometimes there are serious difficulties of communication affecting either side. From the consumer side the problem of communication arises partly from the vague and sometimes conflicting nature of consumer desires and inability to put in words exactly what is wanted. Even the available vocabulary is inadequate and inexact with respect to such qualities as taste or odor. While the sensation of being exposed to an odor may make the subject aware at the time of distinctly pleasant or unpleasant reactions, many people would find it difficult to say anything later beyond the fact that something smelled bad or had a pleasant odor. There is evidence that individuals vary greatly in the acuity of their senses of smell and taste and certainly in their attitudes as to what they would regard as pleasant or unpleasant. Even with respect to those qualities such as shape, size, and structure for which descriptive terms or measurements are available, the consumer may not be very articulate in describing what is wanted. Possibly one of the easiest of all products to identify is a book. It is only necessary for the prospective customer to know the name of the book, the author, the publisher, and the date to identify the book beyond any reasonable possibility of confusion. Booksellers can testify that their customers only too rarely order books by these simple and positive specifications. Customer orders without ambiguity are rare in fields where elements of style or design must be described with some accuracy to identify the desired item.

Brand names are the simple answer for product identification in many fields. It is true that the brand name is a device associated with product differentiation and sometimes means a distinction without any real difference. On the whole, brand names are highly functional for buyer as well as seller and flourish for that reason. Consider the ease of purchase of packaged products in a drugstore or grocery store as compared with purchasing in a hardware store. In one case a coined trade name identifies the bundle of utilities constituting the desired package of cigarettes, cereals, or detergents. In the other case the buyer must know what length and diameter he wants in ordering so simple a product as a screw; and in ordering paint, he must specify several features of the product such as color, whether flat or gloss, and whether for inside or outside use.

Another major difficulty of communication lies in the effort of the consumer to picture the setting in which a product will be used. The appeal of products such as carpets, draperies, or bedspreads is largely dependent upon whether they will fit in with other articles in the room where they are to be used. Very few consumers have a sufficiently graphic power of description so as to give the salesclerk a vivid picture of the room they have in mind. In fact, when the individual is not in the room in question and is in the store trying to make a purchase, he sometimes finds to his dismay that he has only the vaguest recollection of the colors in the room, the dimensions of the floor area, or the location of features affecting the placement of furniture such as doors, windows, and radiators. Various devices are used to help bridge this gap in communication. The store may provide swatches of cloth or samples of wallpaper which the consumer can take home and match up with its proposed surroundings. Color charts and suggestive decorative schemes are also used.

Our mass-production economy will continue to turn out standardized products. Marketing problems arise because these products must find their way into use in nonstandardized homes and in the hands of nonstandardized people. Of three aspects of matching supply and demand, we have done pretty well in the shaping and sorting of goods as steps in adapting them to the assortments in which they will eventually function. The final phase of matching—namely, fitting the standardized product to the individual need situation—does not lend itself so readily to mass operations and will continue to constitute a major topic for the negotiations between consumer and retailer. From the side of the seller, there are equally baffling problems of communication in inducing the consumer to believe that the product will serve the specified purpose and in gaining some assurance that the product will be used intelligently. It is not sufficient to assert that a product will perform satisfactorily, since much depends on the way in which it is used. A growing number of products have to be demonstrated to the buyer in order to function. If the use of the product means acquiring new habits or involves any manual dexterity, communication may require the three steps of demonstration, written instructions which can be studied afterward to recall the demonstration, and a practice period on the part of the buyer until he can execute these steps for himself. Negotiations between retailer and consumer can be made more effective by analysis of this two-way communication problem involving the statement of the need on the one side and the demonstration of the product on the other. Where these elements are involved, the transaction is not routine in the sense of the purchase of a package of cigarettes where, commonly, the brand name of the product is the only word that has to be spoken to complete the transaction. Since these communication problems occur over and over, it is possible to devise an efficient and standardized method of handling them which will serve in the majority of cases.

Another factor affecting the efficiency of contact between consumer and retailer is the gradual ripening of a mutual understanding which makes it easier to do business thereafter. This is a contribution to greater facility in negotiation, not through routinization but through the building of confidence. The first contact may be a very casual one indeed, in which the consumer is simply one of many casual shoppers drifting through a store. At the point at which she begins to express some interest or to ask some questions, the retailer begins what may be a lengthy process of evaluating his prospect and trying to understand her needs and preferences. From the initial purchase the shopper may go on to become a regular customer. At that point the customer

is entitled to expect something more in the way of candor and solici-
tude from the seller. A good salesman in an apparel store would not
let his customer buy something which was quite inappropriate for him.
At the very least the salesman should suggest that the style and color
of another suit would be more becoming. A bookseller loses nothing in
the long run by expressing an unfavorable opinion of a book that is
under consideration by a favorite customer. Examples of this kind, in
which the retailer would rather give up a sale than make an improper
one, leave a deep impression on the customer and strengthen the bond
of loyalty to the store. This is a particularly effective device for cross-
ing the line mentioned before and gaining acceptance as an advisor to
the buyer rather than being regarded as an antagonist who is trying to
get the better of him in a bargain.

JOINT OPPORTUNITY AND NEGOTIATION

The concept of joint opportunity was introduced in the chapter on
competition. Expectations concerning the exploitation of joint opportunity are the source of the bond which causes a marketing channel to
behave as an organized behavior system. But in addition to their common interests the several firms which are linked in a marketing channel have diverse interests—in some respects, adverse interests. To the
extent that their interests are diverse, they tend to be indifferent to the
interests of the other. An example would be a large retailer carrying
many lines in his dealings with a supplier whose product could not
make a significant contribution to the retailer's total sales and profits.
To the extent that their interests are adverse, conflicts arise which
interfere with orderly, co-ordinated efforts. An example would be the
relationship between a large supplier and a large retailer in which the
supplier insists on methods of handling for his products which are contrary to the policies of the retailer or may yield what he regards as an
inadequate return on his operation.

Negotiation in trade channels is the means for overcoming indifference or reconciling conflict. The small supplier in the case cited may
be able to show that while the volume of his product is small today,
its growth prospects justify the retailer in stocking it. The large supplier in the situation described may be able to show that the special
services he requires on his product line are offset by favorable marketing characteristics which tend to reduce other aspects of retail handling
costs. Negotiation is thus an essential aid to orderly marketing when
producers must reach the consumer through intermediaries. It serves to
create and maintain a framework for co-ordination between successive

steps in the channel and hence to promote efficient operation of the channel as a whole. By negotiation, crucial features of the transaction become more orderly and efficient. Many transactions can be reduced to routine. Meanwhile, there are possibilities for introducing greater efficiency into the negotiating process itself.

The starting point in negotiation is to recognize that all of the firms making up the channel in supplying a given class of products to the consumer are engaged in the exploitation of joint opportunity. The retailer would receive no income without products to sell. The manufacturer would receive no income without appropriate channels for selling them to consumers. As in the co-operative effort confined to a single firm, there are two basic problems confronting the co-operating firms making up a trade channel. One is that of getting the job done, and the other is that of dividing the returns among the several participants. The members of a co-operating group always have a common interest and an adverse interest. Their common interest centers in joint opportunity. Their adverse interest is resolved through bargaining power. Because of the tension between common and adverse interests, a co-operative arrangement must be maintained through more or less continuous negotiation. This is especially true of the relations among firms making up a trade channel.

The Fully Integrated Channel. The place of co-operation in the marketing of goods may be seen by comparing a fully integrated channel with one made up of independent units. Some oil companies have become fully integrated, starting with the extraction of crude petroleum from the ground and reaching all the way to the final sale of gasoline, lubricating oil, and fuel oil to the final consumer. An integrated channel needs to be well balanced, with enough crude to supply its refineries and enough filling stations to serve as retail outlets for gasoline and oil. Operations at each step must take account of the needs of the other steps. Deliveries to filling stations should be so scheduled that they do not have to turn away customers for lack of supply. Storage capacity at stations should be sufficient to permit delivery in economic lots. If the refinery makes and advertises specialty products, they need to be given adequate display and sales attention in retail outlets. New supplies of crude or new methods of refining will be developed if customers are not satisfied with the product from present sources and methods.

The Nonintegrated Channel. The nonintegrated marketing channel is often in direct competition with the fully integrated channel. In order that the nonintegrated channel may survive, which is a condition for the survival of the independent units which make it up, it must achieve balance and co-ordination in its operation. Lacking a central command, the nonintegrated channel must achieve co-ordination through the processes of negotiation. The case is no different in commodity fields in which there is no integrated channel, but only nonintegrated channels competing with each other. Under the theory of differential advantage, each competitor is always searching for something that will give him an edge over others. One important possibility for attaining differential advantage lies in more effective coordination in one channel than in another. A firm at any point in the channel may take the initiative in seeking improved co-ordination, but attaining the goal involves the co-operation of all firms in the channel.

Trade channels for various products vary in the extent of integration and the means which must be employed to achieve integration. Next to petroleum products, the manufacturing and marketing of shoes is one of the more striking examples of integration. Many shoestores are owned by the same companies which operate the factories. Independent shoestores have the same general incentives for co-operating with the supplier and make similar demands on him to respond co-operatively. They must work together in exploiting joint opportunity, whether or not they are under the same ownership. The problems of diversity in prices, styles, sizes, and in fitting the particular requirements of each neighborhood cannot be solved in an atmosphere of mutual indifference or antagonism between manufacturer and retailer. Quite similar considerations pertain to the marketing of automobile tires, where most dealers concentrate on a single line of tires.

Exploitation of Joint Opportunity by Wholesalers and Retailers. Participation in the exploitation of joint opportunity becomes more diffused in the fields where wholesalers and retailers handle many lines of goods such as drugs, groceries, and general merchandise. Independent retailers and wholesalers were forced to recognize their common interests in many lines because of the coming of the chain organizations, which integrated these two steps. Under the necessity of competing with the chains, the independents found it possible to improve their co-ordination greatly through such means as the voluntary chains and the retailer-owned co-operatives. The initiative sometimes came from the wholesaler and sometimes from the retailer, but in either case they realized that they would stand or fall together in serving a community with a given class of goods.

Co-ordination of the manufacturer's efforts with those of the retailer and wholesaler presents some special problems in a broad field like groceries. The initiative in this instance usually has to come from the manufacturer because he is producing only one or a few of the items sold by the trade. The supermarket could not be expected to develop a plan for the active promotion of each of the thousands of items it sells and then negotiate the acceptance of each plan by the appropriate manufacturer. Neither would it be feasible for the manufacturer to entertain and pass on thousands of plans originating with retailers. A merchandising plan for securing co-operative effort in the sale of a product naturally originates with the firm having the greatest stake in its sale, the manufacturer. This tends to be true whether the trade channels carrying the product to the consumer handle a narrow line or a broad line.

The narrower the line, the more the manufacturer can afford to do in an effort to assure the success of his retailers and wholesalers. Tire manufacturers offer services to independent dealers which scarcely stop short of what they would do for company-owned stores. They help the new dealer to select a site, to design his store layout and fixtures, and to determine the lines of tires and accessories necessary to meet demand. They show him how to set up accounting records and controls, and offer credit and financial support to meet various exigencies. In this and similar retail lines, such as automobile agencies, the representatives of the manufacturer may show up so often and be so insistent on the use of approved methods that the retailer becomes restive and resentful about infringements on his independence.

In trades handling broad lines, the association between the manufacturer and his channels of trade never becomes quite so intimate. The manufacturer still realizes that he has a stake in the success of his retailers and wholesalers, but there are financial limitations as to what he can undertake on their behalf. He is largely limited to promoting his own product and to showing the retailer how he can take advantage of this promotion. On the average, he can expect only a limited amount of time and effort from the broad-line retailer. Some of the smaller manufacturers can scarcely accomplish more than to persuade a number of retailers to stock the product, since it can only make a moderate contribution to each retailer's sales and profits. Larger manufacturers compete for favorable display space and other types of co-operative effort. In a complex marketing system, much of the substance of competition is competing for co-operation.

Strategy in the Use of Marketing Channels. The urgency, from the manufacturer's viewpoint, of getting the trade to accept and co-operate with merchandising plans opens up the general field of strategy

in the use of marketing channels. This subject will be discussed at
length in a later chapter. Here it will suffice to point out the two main
lines in which a marketing organization can take action in competing
for co-operative support in trade channels. One is to work with different
types of units at the same level; the other is to establish bonds with
units at successive levels. A manufacturer often utilizes two types of
retailers, one relatively more specialized than the other. The more
specialized retailer has a greater stake in the sale of the product and
will co-operate more fully and effectively with a well-designed merchandising plan. The less specialized stores provide supplementary distribution in other neighborhoods and areas. Sometimes they can be induced to adopt streamlined versions of the sales methods followed by
the specialists. The use of two types of retailers gives the manufacturer
some protection from exorbitant demands by one group or the other,
but also presents him with an additional problem of co-ordination in
getting the two to work well in double harness.

Advertising and Co-operation. The other general approach to
securing co-operation is to go beyond the immediate customer and attempt to influence his customer or the ultimate consumer. The vast
growth of advertising has been due not only to its direct value in
stimulating consumer demand but also to its indirect value in inducing
trade co-operation. In fact, a bid for a favored display position or other
help from dealers is often premised on current or prospective advertising and on the argument that the dealer has a chance to cash in on the
demand which advertising will create. Similarly, manufacturers whose
customers are wholesalers often utilize most of the time of their salesmen in picking up orders from retailers which are turned over to the
wholesaler. The manufacturer's salesmen also give talks at sales meet-
ings called by the wholesaler and go out with his salesmen on calls
where specialized sales help is needed.

Reference has previously been made to advertising as a form of
prenegotiation. In most cases the advertising sponsored by a manu
facturer has no direct relationship to individual transactions in which
goods are transferred to the consumer. A manufacturers' advertisemen
is not really an offer to sell in the sense of naming a price and telling
the consumer when and how he can obtain the merchandise. Advertising, by its very nature, uses public channels of communication and ma
be heard or seen by many people who have no possible interest in the
product advertised. The best that the advertiser can do is to selec
media which give a better-than-average chance that the advertising
audience will be interested in the product and will be financially able t
buy it. Advertising by the seller is like preliminary shopping on the

part of the buyer. It is an attempt to search out the prospect, paralleling the customer's search for goods. The difference is that the prospective customer must be induced to identify himself. He does that by responding to the advertisement, in some cases sending in a coupon as directed, in other cases visiting the types of store in which he either assumes or is told that he can find the product on display. Media advertising, then, is not negotiation, strictly speaking, since it does not constitute an approach to particular individuals, as in the case of house-to-house selling. Instead of initiating a negotiation, it induces the buyer to take the initiative. The situation is a little different with respect to direct-mail advertising, in which the seller has identified particular individuals as likely prospects and has attempted to initiate a sales negotiation by means of a letter addressed to the individual. Here, also, experts on the subject generally hold that the first letter should not in itself attempt to make a sale but should concentrate on trying to provoke a response which would in effect be the beginning of a sales negotiation.

The concept of prenegotiation is also applicable to relations between a supplier and his trade channel. Advertising directed to retailers and wholesalers through their trade journals can simplify the task of the salesman or other negotiator. Reference has already been made to the impact of consumer advertising on negotiations with the channels by which the supplier reaches the consumer. There are other methods for increasing the effectiveness of trade negotiation and giving it something of the character of a standardized procedure. Salesmen are provided with presentation covering the advantages of a product of the merchandising plan which is being recommended to the retailer. Still other aspects of negotiation as an aid to orderly marketing will appear in the discussion of executive action in Part III.

SELECTED REFERENCES

GAMBS, JOHN SAKI. *Beyond Supply and Demand.* New York: Columbia University Press, 1947.

ZEUTHEN, FREDERICK. *Economic Theory and Method.* Cambridge, Mass.: Harvard University Press, 1955.

GALBRAITH, JOHN KENNETH. *American Capitalism: The Concept of Countervailing Power.* Boston: Houghton-Mifflin Co., 1952.

BAKKE, WIGHT. *Bonds of Organization.* New York: Harper & Bros., 1950.

NICOLSON, HAROLD GEORGE. *The Evolution of Diplomatic Method.* New York: Macmillan Co., 1954.

COPELAND, MELVIN THOMAS. "Dynamic Distribution," *Changing Perspectives in Marketing.* Ed. HUGH G. WALES. Urbana: University of Illinois Press, 1954.

The most basic reference on negotiation in marketing is the writings of John R. Commons which have been cited previously. Negotiation inevitably loomed large in his thinking because of his emphasis on collective action and his interest in law and labor economics.

Other economists who give an important place to negotiation include Gambs, who describes the role of coercion and persuasion in operating systems; Zeuthen, who attempts to bring negotiation within the framework of marginal analysis; and Galbraith, who calls attention to the countervailing power of large firms on either side of the markets.

Bakke is a social scientist with a special interest in labor relations and the bonds of organization in social systems. Nicolson is a British diplomat who describes stages in the development of techniques of international negotiation in the short essay cited here.

The essay by Copeland deals with the problem of the equilibrium number of distributors from the point of view of a manufacturer. The attempt to have enough distributors, but not too many, is a significant aspect of negotiation in marketing channels, for reasons discussed by Copeland.

Chapter VI

THE MOTIVATION OF CONSUMER BUYING

The household is a special type of organized behavior system providing the setting for most of those activities which are classified as consumption. It is the place in which the growing child forms his tastes and preferences and gets his earliest experiences as a buyer. The activities of the household include congenial behavior, which is an end in itself, and instrumental behavior, which is a means to an end. Households fall into several types according to whether their members are compatible in their congenial behavior or well-co-ordinated in their instrumental behavior.

On the side of its economic activities, the household is an operating system with some genuine parallels to the business organization. In performing its functions, it utilizes rational devices such as plans, budgets, and the division of labor. The buying function tends to center in the housewife, and she becomes more specialized and skillful in this activity as forms of production have been increasingly removed from the home to the factory. Consumer buyers no less than marketing executives come into the market to solve problems for the behavior systems they represent.

While rational problem solving is believed to fill a central place in the behavior of the consumer buyer, the presence of irrational or nonrational factors cannot be ignored. Habit and impulse are often more in evidence than rational choice, and efficiency as a buyer is acquired only as the result of considerable experience. The concept of rational ends must be expanded beyond the acquisition and use of economic goods to include such objectives as the maintenance of a favorable self-image.

CONSUMER BUYING AS AN OPERATION

Discussion of consumer behavior has been deliberately deferred until the underlying theory concerning operating systems had been presented. Consuming units such as households are organized behavior systems, but they are systems with a dual aspect. On the one hand, they are operating systems comparable to business firms; and marketing theory must try to understand their operations, particularly those which

163

are directly concerned with buying decisions such as consumer shopping. There are also the activities of the household or individual consumer which lie outside the scope of marketing, but which are presumed to yield satisfactions for the individual and which use up goods which may later be replaced by purchase. Marketing, in effect, needs both a theory of consumer buying and a theory of consumption. Both activities are treated here as aspects of group behavior as exhibited by consuming units. This section emphasizes problem solving in consumer buying as an operation, in contrast with some alternative approaches to the study of consumer motivation.

Rational Problem Solving. One of the basic doctrines to be expounded here is that rational problem solving is a key aspect of consumer behavior. Much of the current work of market analysts on consumer motivation attempts to explain buying behavior by irrational factors such as instinctive and unconscious drives. This tendency is understandable as a reaction against the excessive and exclusive emphasis on rationality by some economic theorists. The present view starts from an analysis of the nature of problem solving and what it means when applied to consumer buying. This view of motivation is able to take full account of nonrational factors such as habituation, ego-involvement, and emotional conflict. These factors can all be treated as aspects of the buyer's problem in the present view of rational behavior.

During the nineteenth century, Bentham and his followers thought they had found the key to human conduct in the pleasure principle. The individual sought to maximize pleasure, to minimize the corresponding pain of effort, and evaluated all goods accordingly. Economic man was assumed to know exactly what he wanted, to have perfect knowledge of what the market offered as to the goods desired, and to carry out with complete precision his calculations as to the net effect of his purchases on happiness.

Still greater refinement of analysis was attributed to the consumer by the exponents of marginal utility. Confronted by a barrel of apples, economic man was able to arrange them instantly and automatically on a scale of descending values from the first apple to the last in anticipation of progressive satiation. The basic decisions made by the buyer were those relating to price and quantity for the same product. The range of wants was fixed by the underlying pattern of needs. This theory of economic behavior really dodges the issue of motivation and merely seeks to explain how the buyer with a given set of preferences will adjust to the supply situation.

Habit and Impulse. Two nonrational factors which have received much attention in efforts to explain consumer behavior are habit and impulse. John B. Watson, one of the founders of behavioristic psychology, entered the advertising business after establishing his place in the academic world and was the great exponent of habituation in buying. In fact, his view of human nature was that we bring little into the world except capacity to absorb our native culture through exposure and conditioning. Our preferences as well as our skills are the result of learning. Constant repetition is a primary means for shaping learned behavior. Identify the people who can buy your product, bombard them with advertising messages, and build up a distribution network which makes it easy for them to buy. Many marketing plans are built on this philosophy and proceed as if habituation were the sole end and aim of selling.

Instinctive Drives. Quite a different approach to motivation, arising in recent years, relies on instinctive drives to explain behavior. Personality and culture are diverse expressions of sexual desire, the will to power, or primary emotions such as rage or fear. For a product to sell, it must be hooked up with the individual's self-esteem or with deep-seated urges he will not consciously acknowledge even to himself. Freudian psychology in its various forms as well as older and cruder instinct theories have been employed in this attempt to search out hidden motivations. Marketing research has responded with a rash of depth interviewing methods, projective techniques, and other adaptations of psychiatric practice. Impulse buying is a major influence in the market, and success awaits those who can plumb the hidden sources of these drives. That is the promise presumably offered by such theories.

Both habit and impulse are undeniably important in a comprehensive view of consumer behavior. Both, however, play their part within a broader pattern of adaptation which cannot be explained by either. Rational decision and rational planning are as vital to the household as to the business firm.

A new conception of consumer rationality will be presented, based on the psychology of problem solving or adjustment, and embracing the nonrational aspects of behavior as problem elements.

PROBLEMS OF CONSUMER PURCHASING AGENT

The new approach draws a clear distinction between the consumer and the consumer purchasing agent. It is the motivation of the purchasing agent which is most directly relevant in marketing. The prospective consumer of a given purchase and the person making the purchase are often two different people. In many cases the purchase is made for a household, and the purchasing agent is only one of those who will share in its use.

Rational Behavior. The distinction still exists in a fundamental sense when only one person is involved. Most purchases are made to provide for consumption at some future time or for use over some future period. Psychologically, the consumer is in a different frame of mind in buying than in consuming. The rational buyer must weigh each purchase against an anticipated pattern of behavior and not merely in terms of satisfactions to be derived from the given article. In our modern American economy, we do not typically sell food to hungry people or clothing to those who literally have nothing to wear. The purchasing agent and those he represents already possess a stock of goods which he is trying to replenish or extend. Only in the case of the dope addict or the alcoholic are the consumer and the purchasing agent merged into one by the drive of an overwhelming desire.

The positions of the consumer purchasing agent and the industrial purchasing agent differ only in degree. Rational behavior is a matter of planning, budgeting, and careful consideration of comparative values. Rationality is exhibited in ability to learn from experience and to adopt new methods. It is exhibited in its choice of issues and in its application to the significant rather than the trivial. Finally, it copes with the problems which arise in trying to provide the goods which will serve as the instruments of future behavior for one or more people, each with several roles to play at home, at work, and in the community.

Habit and Impulse. Returning to the issue of habit and impulse, it becomes apparent that it is immediately clarified by drawing a sharp separation between consumption and buying. Consuming habits are part of the pattern of living, but buying habits are only derived from this pattern. Buying habits, in the sense of repetitive purchase of a given brand or customary trading at a given store, can be broken overnight with no real disruption in the pattern of living. Buying habits, in fact, can more safely be regarded as deliberately chosen routines designed to save time and energy for rational consideration of more important matters.

The distinction between buying and consuming is equally crucial in trying to understand the place of impulse. The term "impulse buying" is widely and hopefully used by students of display merchandising. Close observation of unplanned purchases indicates that display often merely serves as a reminder and that the purchase still falls within an organized pattern. Impulse in the sense of breaking the pattern through the force of desire is a factor, but it happens within definite restrictions. The rational buyer is more concerned with providing for the consuming impulses which may be expected to occur in the future. The impulse to eat between meals cannot handily be indulged unless the refrigerator is stocked with appropriate foods. Ordinarily, the consumer must possess a set of golf clubs if he is to obey that sudden impulse to spend Saturday on the links instead of mowing the lawn. It is true that there are consumer purchasing agents of less rational type who respond with childish abandon to items on display which have little genuine utility for them. This type soon runs up against the imposed rationality of being out of money and having to use some part of the next week's check for necessities before going on another splurge.

Problem Solving. There is no intention here to leave habit and impulse out of a comprehensive view of motivation. In terms of the present view, however, the important thing is habit and impulse in consumption as seen through the eyes of the consumer purchasing agent. The presence of nonrational elements in buying itself is recognized but given a more restricted place. The purchasing agent is essentially engaged in solving problems. While there are differences in ability here as in industrial buying, the performance is fairly good; and the desire and ability to improve are clearly in evidence.

The definition of an operating problem is the same for buyer and seller, for large and small operations. A problem is an issue involving uncertainty as to the course of action to pursue in an operating situation. To solve a problem is to reduce uncertainty to the point where a course of action can be adopted with some confidence. Uncertainty arises either because the operation situation is complex or because the person who must act is confronted with contingencies as to future events which are beyond his control. The consumer purchasing agent, like other problem solvers, faces both complexity and contingency in carrying out her function.

The problem solver is trying to see the essential structure in a complicated situation and trying to make the best gamble in being prepared for future requirements which are subject to chance variations. Complexity in the consumption pattern arises from the many products needed to maintain a high standard of living and from conflicting ideas about the desired standard either among the members of a household or within the mind of a single individual. Uncertainty arises from the requirements imposed on the household from the outside, including the pressures of business and social schedules and the common circumstances of illness or frustration, or of success and maturation. Outguessing the future is hazardous either in the short run or in the long run. Yet that is what the purchasing agent must do as effectively as possible if the household is to have the means of carrying out desired behavior patterns in the light of its opportunities as they develop.

The approach to motivation presented here is believed to have several major analytical advantages. It enables the analyst to deal directly with heterogenous demand or the choice among unlike goods as compared with the choice among different quantities of the same goods. It provides a more effective way of getting at the dynamic aspect of demand and identifying the motives which lead to changes in the pattern of living. An approach which emphasizes current purchase for future use is appropriate to an economy of abundance as compared with theories which were formulated in terms of more stringent assumptions as to scarcity.

BEHAVIOR AS ENDS AND MEANS

Behavior may be classified or categorized in various ways, depending on the interests of the investigator and the class of problems to be solved. For marketing and economics it is consistent to seek a classification of consumer behavior which can be interpreted in terms of ends and means. The aim of the marketer is to sell products which serve as instrumentalities to promote the ends sought by consumers. Many psychologists prefer to talk in terms of the drive or push exerted by a need, rather than the pull exerted by a goal. All, however, recognize that foresight intervenes in human behavior to accumulate the necessary means in advance, rather than waiting for the urgency of immediate need to trigger action. One of the methods by which psychologists get themselves across this bridge is the sign-Gestalt theory of Tolman in which he says that what the individual learns is not mere behavior sequences but signposts along the road to a goal.

Behavior itself can be classified on an ends-means basis. One type of behavior covering a wide range of activities is maintained by the individual for its own sake, since it is a direct source of satisfaction. This type will be called "congenial behavior." By contrast, there are many activities which are carried on primarily because they are regarded as the necessary antecedent of congenial behavior and are expected to lead to it. These activities will be grouped under the designation of "instrumental behavior." Finally, there are some activities and some organic states which have been called "symptomatic" because they neither yield satisfaction in themselves nor serve as an instrumental prelude to congenial behavior. There is good authority in the social sciences for each of these concepts, although they have not previously been combined into an all-embracing classification.

Congenial Behavior. These three types of behavior will first be discussed in terms of their place in the life of the individual person. Consideration will next be given to the interaction of individuals within the family or household as the primary social and consuming unit. Finally, the behavior domain of the family will be related to its cultural setting and the external forces impinging on both the ends pursued and the means employed within the household. Prominent among the means employed are various types of consumer goods, so that purchasing will be treated as a cardinal feature of instrumental behavior. The aim throughout is not merely to provide a comprehensive descriptive model of consumer behavior, but also to point out functional relationships, trends, and tensions which can suggest testable hypotheses to guide basic research.

The term "congenial behavior" is due to the social psychologist, Richard La Piere. He discusses the concept at length in his book on collective behavior. He states flatly that congenial behavior is indulged in for its own sake, enumerates the many kinds of occasions when people get together for no other purpose save to enjoy themselves, and indicates that these activities occupy a large proportion of the total time span of the individuals involved. La Piere begins by using the word "congenial" in the first meaning as applying to relations among two or more persons. Later, when he admits books and magazines as a form of communication among persons, he moves close to the second and broader meaning of the word "congenial" which also admits relations between persons and things which yield satisfaction. The intention here is to use the term "congenial behavior" to cover all activity, whether collective or solitary, which is expected to yield direct satisfaction and hence is pursued as an end in itself.

The individual will attempt to occupy as much of his time as possible with congenial behavior. According to the psychoanalysts, the infant responds immediately to pleasurable excitations furnished by the environment; and his basic drive thereafter is to prolong and perpetuate these satisfactions. The pleasure principle of Freud, unlike that of Bentham, assumes an all-pervading primitive drive rather that a neat calculus of pain and pleasure under rational control. Nevertheless, apart from the sexual emphasis in its earlier versions, it is roughly equivalent to the statement that the individual will attempt to maximize the time occupied by congenial behavior. Freud says that the adult is gradually forced to face the reality of barriers to immediate gratification and the necessity of devoting some part of his time to acquiring the means for resuming pleasurable activities. His most important point for our present purpose is the suggestion that there is a dynamic thrust within the field of congenial behavior whereby patterns of behavior, subject to limitations of individual energy and environmental restrictions, are steadily transformed in the drive for perpetual bliss.

Interestingly enough, mathematical economists have been using the notion of bliss as an analytical concept in some of their calculations. It is generally held that Dante and Milton were more successful in picturing the torments of hell than the pleasures of heaven. Congenial behavior need not reach the level of ultimate and endless joy to serve as the goal toward which instrumental behavior is directed.

It may be required of pleasant experience that it be prolonged, intense, and varied; but these criteria are not altogether consistent. An obvious means of prolonging pleasure is the repetition of experiences which have proved congenial before. But repetition may lead to boredom and a heightened demand for variety, which cause the subject to try new experiences. The attempt to intensify pleasure often carries many hazards and penalties. The thrills of a big night out may be largely offset by an aching head and financial worries the next day. A law of behavior dynamics will now be stated through which these criteria are partially reconciled. For most individuals there is a lifetime trend in congenial behavior from direct experience toward a larger component of symbolic experience.

Suzanne Langer has made out a persuasive case that man attempts to master his universe through symbols. She is not referring merely to the instrumental use of symbols, but contends that symbolization is itself a direct source of satisfaction and even of a sense of security. Certainly, symbols aid man in achieving an economy of time, his scarcest resource, in maximizing congenial behavior. He talks about events, reads about them, and experiences exciting, soothing, or exalted moods created by art, music, and drama. Symbolic behavior takes place at various levels and successive stages. It is more symbolic to attend a prize fight than to engage in fisticuffs on the street; and one stage further removed from direct experience is to watch the fight on television or to read about it on the sports page. It is more symbolic to gossip about the sexual adventures ascribed to others than to seek adventure for oneself. The main point is that increased symbolic content permits a greater depth and breadth of human experience to be compressed into the same number of hours of congenial behavior.

There is another conflict in the field of congenial behavior which is not so readily resolved—namely, between solitary and gregarious enjoyment. Some are drawn one way and some another, while those who enjoy both are forced to make an uneasy compromise. Both forms of congenial behavior occupy time, which can create tension, as one necessarily limits the time available for the other. This conflict will be mentioned later because of its implications for the social structure of the family. It is deeply involved with the individual's sense of freedom in choosing congenial activities. Participation in congenial behavior with others leads to mutual commitments as to schedule, which limits individual freedom.

Instrumental Behavior.   Instrumental behavior includes all activity which is designed to achieve some goal. The target may be the ultimate goal of congenial behavior or some intermediate goal necessarily antecedent to another sequence of instrumental behavior. For instance, a housewife buys food in order to be prepared for cooking a meal. After it is cooked and served, she then joins her family in eating it. Similarly, buying goods generally has the necessary antecedent of obtaining income, usually by one or more earners in the family. Instrumental behavior is always motivated by expectations as to what is to follow, whether or not they are consciously formulated as specific goals. Buying behavior is motivated by expectations either as to other types of instrumental behavior or as to congenial behavior.

One brief but cogent discussion of instrumental behavior is provided by the anthropologist, George Peter Murdock. It appears in a chapter called "The Common Denominator of Cultures" in *Science of Man in the World Crisis.* He says that instrumental acts are seldom innately rewarding in themselves and offers an anthropological example. "Making a spear or pot, for instance, gratifies no basic impulse although at some future time the result may serve to lessen the interval or the expended effort between the onset of the hunger drive and its reduction." He goes on to point out that through social organization other individuals as well as tools or goods can be instruments for the eventual achievement of satisfaction. These comments by Murdock underscore two important aspects of instrumental behavior. One is the tendency to improve upon existing means. The other is the typical involvement of the instrumental behavior of an individual with some organized behavior system in which other people participate.

It is on the instrumental side that consumer behavior is most similar to producer behavior and is subject to some of the same criteria of rationality and efficiency. Given an established goal in either area, it is clearly rational to observe the principle of least effort in attaining it. Much instrumental behavior can be explained in terms of the feedback mechanism whereby any disturbance of a desirable state of affairs leads to action which is just sufficient to bring conditions back to normal. This is the stabilizing process known as "homeostasis," as discussed in earlier chapters. This term is given a broader connotation by Stagner and Karwoski. They distinguish between static and dynamic homeostasis. The first is illustrated by positive inner mechanisms such as that which maintains body temperature at 98.6° F. The latter covers situations in which the energies of the whole organism are mobilized to deal with a problem and to bring about the adjustments which will restore the desired state. The authors then present the rather startling definition of psychology as the science which deals with dynamic homeostasis. The ensuing discussion shows that the drive for equilibrium is so broadly conceived that it includes courting, tool making, and mountain climbing as well as the more obvious instrumental activities such as food gathering.

Valuable as this viewpoint is, it essentially limits psychology to the study of instrumental behavior. Even an advocate of functionalism must grant that this tendency is one of its inherent dangers. That would leave to the student of esthetics or social philosophy the task of describing and analyzing congenial behavior or those pleasurable states of the organism which are said to be the end and aim of all instrumental activity. Aside from congenial behavior, it is not clear that homeostasis can be made to stretch far enough to cover all aspects of instrumental behavior. What it seems to leave out of account is the dynamics which is internal to the field of instrumental behavior. This dynamic tendency is represented by the power principle, which has been discussed in an earlier chapter. Here it is sufficient to point out that the power principle applies to households as well as to other behavior systems.

The power principle, as formulated here, is not the same thing as the will to power, either as discussed by Nietzsche or as imported into psychoanalysis by Alfred Adler. Nietzsche was counseling the superman to assert his natural superiority, while Adler was interpreting aggressive behavior as compensation for an innate sense of inferiority. There is a potential conflict in the application of the power principle, however, which may be resolved in various ways. An increase in power may be judged absolutely in terms of one's own capacity and resources, or relatively by comparison with other people. In one case it might be said that the goal was growth and in the other leadership or degree of control exercised within some membership group.

An adequate view of the relationship between instrumental and congenial behavior is more complex than was visualized in the old hedonistic calculus, in which the pain incurred in achieving a good was neatly balanced against the pleasure to be derived from it. Freed entirely from the demands of instrumental behavior, most individuals would show dynamic changes in the character of their congenial behavior. By contrast, those who restrict their congenial activities to the minimum may show a marked trend toward mastery in their instrumental behavior. It would be a rare occurrence indeed if the same person were to achieve the highest level of refinement in taste and the greatest degree of instrumental capacity. Since both types of behavior occupy time, they not only can displace each other, but great concentration on one also can block or retard the potential dynamic trend in the other field.

Admittedly, congenial and instrumental behavior are not always as completely separated as the previous analysis might appear to indicate. Instrumental behavior may yield satisfaction directly, aside from the achievement of goals or the anticipation of achievement. This is more likely to be true in those occupations with a high symbolic content than in those requiring a sustained and routine application of muscle power. Congenial behavior such as the entertainment of influential friends may have an instrumental objective in the background. An avocation may lead to a profitable vocation, as in the case of Duncan Hines, the eminent authority on where to eat. Eating and resting may be experienced as congenial behavior but be instrumental as a preparation of the organism for resuming other instrumental activities. There are activities aside from earning a living or managing a household which are of mixed character. These would include religious, civic, and fraternal activities, which offer both congenial association and the chance to contribute to some meritorious goal. The types of situations enumerated in this paragraph recall the distinction between manifest and latent functions drawn by the sociologist, Robert K. Merton.

Individuals attempt to reconcile the claims of instrumental and congenial behavior by a life plan more or less clearly visualized. Experience or natural endowment gives some direction and sets some restrictions on both congenial and instrumental behavior. During childhood, instrumental behavior such as going to school, and to some extent the rules governing congenial behavior, are shaped by parents and other adults. The individual coming of age emerges from adolescent dreaming about the pleasures he will enjoy when he is free to choose and the great deeds he will accomplish. Only at this time is he expected to have a more concrete career outlook, a decision which would usually have been made for him long before in older cultures. Association with his age-mates and older people as well as innate tendencies have influenced his pattern of preferred satisfactions. During courtship, he and his prospective spouse explore the things they like to do together and exchange ideas as to what their lives should be like as they go on after marriage. This attempt to negotiate out a mutually acceptable way of life is often all too sketchy, as revealed by the shock and dismay of disagreements later on.

Symptomatic Behavior. The third general type of behavior is neither congenial nor instrumental. That is to say that it neither yields satisfaction directly for the individual nor appears to be an effective means of advancing any of his recognized goals. This third type will be called "symptomatic behavior." The term is due to the world's best known authority on the subject, Sigmund Freud. He defines and develops the concept in *The Psychopathology of Everyday Life,* which is the one of his many works most pertinent to our present purpose. There is a story about Freud's love for mushrooms and his manner of gathering them, reported by his biographer, Ernest Jones. Spying one at some distance, he would sneak up on tiptoe and finally clap his hat over it, as if to keep it from getting away. There is an illustration of symptomatic behavior which was possibly worthy of interpretation by Freud himself or one of his disciples.

The present view is that symptomatic behavior is potentially functional. It may not yield satisfaction directly like congenial behavior. In fact, it may disrupt and displace congenial activity just as the distracting or painful symptoms of physical illness may do. Symptomatic behavior is not instrumental but may defeat or frustrate the individual's efforts to achieve his established goals. Nevertheless, symptomatic behavior may be functional in somewhat the same way that mutations are functional in biological evolution. By disrupting fixed patterns of behavior on both the congenial and the instrumental side, it may throw the individual into what Tolman called a state of "creative instability." That is a condition in which existing habits have been challenged and it is easier to accept new ones. It may happen that a pattern of behavior which appears symptomatic at first is adopted as functional when more fully understood, or that the individual is forced to devise new patterns to meet the challenge.

The second way that symptomatic behavior becomes functional is through the diagnosis others may make based on these symptoms. A perceptive and sympathetic observer may be able to guess the trouble and offer help. Parents and spouses engage in amateur psychiatry fairly successfully, just as they use the first-aid kit for minor cuts and bruises. That is not to say that they should ignore the need for professional help in major behavior disorders any more than they should rely on home medication for cancer or coronary thrombosis. Even such an extreme example as attempted suicide, however, may not express a genuine desire to die but may actually constitute a desperate cry for help. One special diagnostic use of symptomatic behavior is that undertaken by practitioners of motivation research. Projective techniques and many experimental and depth interviewing procedures may be regarded as attempts to provoke symptomatic behavior. The inability or reluctance of the subject to answer direct questions about his deeper motivations is what Freud called "resistance," a concept which he regarded as one of the chief foundation stones of psychoanalysis. Motivation research does not attempt individual cures but is aimed at more general increases in satisfaction through such steps as product improvement.

CO-ORDINATION AND COMPATIBILITY IN HOUSEHOLDS

Most individual consumers or consumer buyers are members of a small social unit, the conjugal family or household. Manifestations of both congenial and instrumental behavior are modified through family membership. As an operating unit, the family involves division of labor, mutual commitments and the discharge of responsibilities, internal communications, and functional relations with the environment. Assuming a typical unit of husband, wife, and one or more dependent children, there can be an almost infinite variety of family behavior patterns based on the aspects of individual behavior which have already been discussed. The possible types of families will be reduced to a manageable number by emphasizing two concepts. They are the compatibility of congenial behavior and the co-ordination of instrumental behavior within the household. Using these concepts, a classification of households will be developed which is believed to be directly pertinent to buying behavior.

Compatibility must start with the husband and wife who established the family and who are responsible for its survival. A truly compatible couple is sexually well adjusted, takes a mutual pride and pleasure in the children who are the fruit of their union, and has a reasonably consistent set of preferences as to other phases of congenial behavior. The last condition does not necessarily mean that they must be inseparable in all activities designed to yield satisfaction directly. It will suffice if they can agree on the appropriate balance between solitary pursuits and those they engage in together or as members of a larger group. Compatibility also implies relative freedom from negative effects of each on the satisfactions of the other. Either may bring to the marriage habits or mannerisms which are extremely distasteful to the spouse. While husband and wife usually come from the same general cultural level, traits drawn from the subcultures of different ethnic and neighborhood groups can reveal distressing contrasts under the strains of daily living.

Sources of Conflict. Only two sources of conflict will be mentioned here because they are especially pertinent to the line of analysis which is being followed. One is difference in attitudes toward time, and the other is differences in the symbolic level at which each is accustomed to operate. If one partner is regularly obliged to spend a substantial amount of time waiting for the other to appear or to get ready for festive occasions, it cuts down on the amount of time which can be spent together in congenial behavior. Most married couples have experienced the dampening effect of tardiness on the spirit of congeniality. Planning for the future can become uncongenial if one tries to project certain events as of a given date and the other prefers to dream about them as nice things which might happen in the indefinite future.

Symbols are the basis of communication and can serve both instrumental and congenial purposes in the family as elsewhere. Communication theorists such as Shannon and Weaver have discussed what they call "the degree of redundancy." This means the excess of the number of visual or auditory symbols above the minimum necessary to convey the intended message. For example, written English of average difficulty is said to be about 50 per cent redundant. In an intimate union such as marriage a large discrepancy in the degree of redundancy can create irritation and misunderstanding. The partner receiving highly redundant communications may find it extremely tedious and fall into the habit of listening with only half an ear. The other partner, unaccustomed to low redundancy, may fail to grasp the message or to recall it when response is anticipated.

Need for Instrumental Efficiency. The human family has always been a significant economic unit. It has been marked by division of labor from its beginning. There has been a steady shift in the roles of husband and wife with changing technology and social organization. These changing patterns in the division of labor are graphically pictured in recent books by the anthropologists, Ralph Linton and Carleton Coon. The process of removing productive activities from the home was also established some centuries ago and has been taking place at an accelerated rate. More and more, the goods needed by the household are acquired by purchase. More and more, the major economic roles in our type of society are those of earning and spending. While both activities may be shared by husband and wife, the tendency today is for the husband to be the principal earner and the wife to be the principal spender.

Instrumental efficiency of the household demands that these two basic activities be well co-ordinated. The means of co-ordination are varied. There may be clear-cut dominance by one partner, with recognition of the special role of the other. There may be a complete family budget or an allowance for recurring household expenditures, with joint consideration of major purchases. The wife may enter into the business or career planning of the husband, while he participates in long-range planning of purchases. Interest at the moment is not in the method of co-ordination but the question of whether it gets done effectively. The favorable case will be referred to hereafter simply as the "co-ordinated" family or household.

Degrees of Co-ordination and Efficiency Achieved by Families. This scheme of analysis obviously leads to a four-way classification by family type. The four classes are as follows: co-ordinated and compatible; co-ordinated and incompatible; unco-ordinated and compatible; and unco-ordinated and incompatible. It seems reasonable to expect quite different types of buying behavior from these four types of families. The classification raises some questions as to the validity of some forms of motivation research which take the individual as the unit, and in which there is no knowledge of the type of family to which the individual belongs. Many depth interview surveys cover only forty to fifty respondents. There could be substantial sampling error in the incidence of these respondents by type of family. Symptomatic behavior provoked by survey techniques might have very different diagnostic significance from one type of family to another.

The unco-ordinated, incompatible family is an unsatisfactory and unpredictable purchasing unit, just as it brings little satisfaction to its members. A typical case would be that in which husband and wife have no sexual or social attraction for each other, and the husband squanders most of his earnings in drinking and gambling. The wife and children live from hand to mouth on whatever income they can pry out of him or derive from other sources. The most ingenious appeals of the seller are largely wasted when lavished on the housewife shopping for this type of family. Such a family is probably headed toward the divorce courts, unless there are religious or personal scruples which prevent this final drastic action. The couple may have appeared compatible in the beginning, but later drifted into projecting hostilities upon each other which arose from other situations they were unable to handle. This case illustrates the position taken by the social psychoanalysts such as Karen Horney. Abandoning Freud's early position that the sex drive shapes all behavior patterns, they point to cases in which anxiety derived from other sources frustrates sexual satisfaction.

The unco-ordinated but compatible family is the typical case of the easygoing but improvident couple who are out for a good time while the money lasts. It might be called the "happy-go-lucky" or "feast-and-famine" household. They share their ups and downs with equal harmony. The wife is genuinely delighted when the husband brings home an expensive bauble for her birthday, even though she knows the money should have gone to pay the dentist's bill. The husband may change jobs frequently, and it may be difficult for the family to settle down in any one community. A clever salesman might be able to sell them almost anything if he approached them at the right time. His problem might be in collecting if it were not a cash sale. This type of family may effect a transition into one of the other types with changing conditions or the maturation of one or both partners. The coming of children may occupy more of the wife's time and make her increasingly uneasy about economic insecurity. The husband may at last find his niche vocationally and, as he becomes more successful, insist that his home be run on a more businesslike basis.

The co-ordinated but incompatible family is one in which the partners have quite different conceptions of congenial behavior but share a goodly measure of common sense with respect to economic matters. Either or both may have strong ties to their ancestral families and have more in common with their parents or siblings than with their mates. The wife, for example, may appear to be tolerating life with her husband from month to month until she accumulates the means and the excuse for the next visit with her kinfolk. One partner may have a stern, puritanical attitude toward the pleasure-seeking activities which others regard as congenial behavior. If both feel this way, they would fall into the category of a restricted form of compatibility. Such a household is likely to be operated on a very businesslike basis, since its main function is to advance the instrumental goals shared by the partners. Joint satisfaction would derive mainly from getting ahead in material terms. As shoppers, members of such families might be especially price-conscious, immune to emotional appeal, and hard bargainers in the effort to get their money's worth.

The co-ordinated and compatible family is the ideal for the household which perhaps 50 per cent attain in some reasonable measure. Similar preliminary guesses as to the relative importance of the other types are: co-ordinated but incompatible, 35 per cent; unco-ordinated but compatible, 10 per cent; unco-ordinated and incompatible, 5 per cent. This distribution may be optimistic, since the last percentage is considerably less than the percentage of marriages ending in divorce. A number of marriages, however, break up after a couple has lived together many years; and it is reasonable to assume that the family fell in one of the other categories during much of the time that the marriage lasted. It will also be observed that this distribution, if true, would reflect greater successs in achieving co-ordination than compatibility. Ours is a civilization which puts enormous emphasis on instrumental efficiency. Most American adults are more adequately conditioned to work than to play. The severe strains on compatibility arising from the complex relations between parents and children will discussed in a later section.

SHOPPING BEHAVIOR AND PROBLEM SOLVING

The shopping behavior which is most worthy of analysis is that of families in the first group, and those in the second who are not wholly incompatible. For this large group, possibly two thirds of all families, it is assumed that the basic function of the household purchasing agent is to maintain or achieve the conditions for congenial behavior on behalf of the entire family. This two thirds of families is especially important to the seller, for it is likely to account for as much as 80 per cent of the family income. Families of higher incomes would tend to be well co-ordinated, although not always compatible. The purchasing agent referred to above is usually the wife, sometimes the husband, sometimes the two together. The discussion hereafter will be in terms of the housewife as purchasing agent, since there is a steady trend toward her specialization and increasing competence in this field. This feminine specialization is in marked contrast with rural America of several generations ago, when the man dominated the outside trading function, selling his own produce, and buying the necessary supplies for the home. Women at that time were largely occupied with the traditional arts of household production.

The Wife's Role. The household purchasing agent has the responsibility for maintaining or expanding an assortment of goods which will provide as fully as possible for all the contingencies of anticipated activities within a household. The principles of inventory control are as pertinent here as in industrial buying. In either case, limitations of money and storage space make it impossible to carry in stock every item which might conceivably be used, or to carry unlimited supplies of items which are regularly used. The buyer attempts to minimize the number of "outs," meanwhile taking advantage of opportunities to buy standard items at a favorable price. The good buyer anticipates occasional needs, and in the household this includes outfitting children for school and preparing for the Christmas holidays or other special occasions. As in industry, the inventory requirements for an item depend on the relative ease of replenishment. Thus, household inventory on most food products is kept low. Nevertheless the logic behind extra storage space, such as a household freezer, is not so much saving on food costs as reducing the number of "outs" on such occasions as entertaining and the arrival of unexpected guests.

The housewife would be performing a miracle of economic analysis if she read the minds of each member of the family, determined just how much value is placed on each type of product by each member, and then weighed these ratings objectively along with her own to arrive at some kind of a priority scale for purchasing. Fortunately, she does not have to do anything quite so complex. On routine purchases of items used over and over, she simply has to follow a schedule which will minimize "outs." Everything else amounts to doing the same thing by a variety of methods. One is to see that the items on hand are kept ready for use. Her husband may get no particular thrill from donning a clean white shirt, but he may feel horribly frustrated if none is available when he is dressing for work. From time to time she may substitute a new product or brand for one she has been using in the hope that it will last longer or give greater satisfaction.

Finally, she may consider items not previously in the household inventory, either alone or in consultation with her husband. The value of these additions is in increasing the potency of the assortment. They can do this in a variety of ways such as saving money or time, improving the level of performance in some instrumental activity, or opening up a new dimension of choice as to congenial behavior. On the basis of greatest enhancement to the potency of the assortment, the next item to be purchased might be an automatic washing machine in a home expecting a new baby. It might be an upstairs telephone in a house with an invalid who is not allowed to come downstairs but is able to answer the telephone while others are away. All of these types of foresight make it possible to utilize the energies of the household more successfully in meeting the probable requirements of future behavior. Not all goods are of the same value, since the contingencies they are designed to meet differ both in degree of urgency and in probability of occurrence. Nevertheless, they are all related to the simple rule of minimizing frustration by reducing the number of "outs." The essential outlines of this part of the theory of consumer buying were anticipated by the Austrian economist, Bohm-Bawerk.

The Husband's Role. The foregoing description of household buying may seem to suggest that the housewife performs her purchasing function in a completely disinterested fashion without regard to her personal preferences. This, of course, is far from the truth. She takes household operation to be her province and does what she thinks is best, subject to some discussion in advance with other members of the family or some attempt to justify her action after the event. In fact, it may be said today that the wife generally determines the style of living and the husband the scale of living. He at least sets a ceiling on the scale by his total earnings. Above the subsistence level he may exercise policy, particularly as to the allocation of income between a savings and investment program and living expenses. When income has been substantially increased, it is sometimes the husband who presses for an expansion in the scale of living. The wife's dominant part in determining the style of living gives her a primary outlet for the expression of her personality. This aspect of our culture may have some offsetting disadvantages. There are homes which might have husbands in them during more of their leisure hours if the furnishings of the home made more concessions to masculine taste.

Product Acceptance. The theory of consumer behavior outlined here has practical implications for several of the basic problems facing a marketing organization. Among these problems are the introduction of new products, the maintenance of brand loyalty, and factors affecting shopper preference for stores. The anthropologist sees the successful introduction of a new product as equivalent to the acceptance of a cultural innovation. Linton and others stress the prestige of the innovator as a factor in its acceptance. The sociologist, George Lundberg, qualified this in the first Parlin Lecture by saying that the person imitated is usually of superior status but not so far above as to appear remote and irrelevant. Another anthropologist, H. G. Barnett, in his study of innovation, takes what at first appears to be a contrary view. He says that the innovators and acceptors of innovation are usually the rebels and nonconformists who are at war with the established social order. On closer reading, he appears to be discussing innovations in modes of behavior at this point, rather than product innovations.

Our own view is that new products are expected to function within the social order, and it is the relatively secure and well-adjusted personalities who are most free to accept them. A special role is performed by the creative shopper, who is able to visualize constructive relationships between new products offered for sale and the goods she already possesses. The possibility of enhancing the potency of her assortment is something she can grasp imaginatively, whether she is looking at a really novel product or seeing an old one for the first time in a new light. Women of this type may be described as the leaders of consumption. Older women who maintain this kind of vision and flexibility play an especially important role in the market place. They have a broad experience in judging goods and in attempting to promote congenial behavior in the household. On the average they have more money to spend and less urgent needs to be satisfied. As a result, their expenditures bulk large in the direction of gift purchases. In their shopping, they are constantly on the watch for something they consider both novel and useful which will fit the pattern for some of the families they know intimately, such as those of their sons and daughters.

Brand loyalty is seldom as great as the sponsor of a product would like to believe. Unless the product has a real advantage for some segment of the market, it is bound to experience an interchange of users with other brands in the same classification. Increasing advertising effectiveness may be the only assurance of at least breaking even in the process of gains and losses. Motivation research may take one of two directions. One is to determine whether a change in the product or a progressive series of changes can give it an invulnerable position in some substantial segment of the market. The other is to determine whether some obscure psychological factor, overlooked by competitors, can become the basis of a more effective promotional appeal. An aspect of product presentation which gives expression to some hidden desire of the consumer can be effective in getting buyers to try it. Such an appeal does not relieve the product from the necessity of measuring up to performance standards set by similar products. Where there is a constant interchange among brands, such a device may help in getting more tryers; but it does not necessarily improve the rate of retention of tryers as regular users. In terms of functional analysis, a product must live up to the consumer's expectations to retain a place in her assortment, no matter how the impulse to try it was generated.

Store Preference. A research program dealing with shopping behavior suggests some tentative conclusions about store preference. The first is that a department store shopper has a tendency to rely on a single store and to shop at other stores only as an occasional check on her basic choice or in response to bargain offers. Her preferred store is one which reflects a view of contemporary life consistent with her own. She wants to buy things which seem to belong together and which fit in with her home or her vision of what she wants her home to be. Both breadth of assortment and depth of assortment facilitate satisfactory choice, but breadth comes first if one must be sacrificed to the other. A conviction that competing department stores have definite personalities has been registered strongly in these intensive studies of shopping behavior.

The shopper approaches the specialty store in quite a different frame of mind. For one thing the proportion of male shoppers is far greater in many types of specialty stores. The customers of these stores are looking for a depth of assortment or a type of assortment in the particular field which department stores could not economically provide department by department. The manager and his assistants are expected to be specialists in their field and to be able to react to the specialized knowledge and interests of the customer. The customer in the specialty store, whether man or woman, is frequently giving free rein to a personal bent or hobby, while the department store shopper is more strictly in the role of household purchasing agent.

Improving Consumer Services. Retailing in the future will need to pay much more attention to motivation and other marketing studies. Stores need to know more precisely what motivates consumers to come downtown or go to a neighborhood shopping center, what makes them feel more at home in one department store or supermarket than another. Manufacturers must broaden their market research programs beyond their own immediate problems to give more help to their specialty outlets which cannot carry on such programs for themselves. Both manufacturers and retailers must focus more sharply on the part of the market they will attempt to claim as their own. The shopping studies already mentioned suggest that the market is sharply divided among groups of consumers whose motivations are different and who will not respond to the same appeals. The theoretical perspective presented here has drawn on a variety of sources in the social sciences in sketching a functionalist approach to motivation research. It is believed to present valid grounds for anticipating basic differences among individuals and among households with respect to consumer behavior.

One final conclusion about shopping behavior is offered: The instrumental side of the American household involves rational foresight and skill in problem solving. The realization that buyers come into the market to solve problems is more reliable than the notion that selling is simply a matter of implanting habits or taking advantage of impulses in passive and muddleheaded consumers. A product, a service, or a retail store must function to survive the test of the market. Marketing men who cynically describe their vocation as the sales or advertising "racket" are deluding themselves when they follow the ancient Latin motto: *Mundus vult decipi.* The world of consumers may be willing to be flattered, cajoled, or entertained, but it does not really wish to be deceived.

CHILDREN AND ADULTS IN THE HOUSEHOLD STRUCTURE

The relation of children and adults within the household is one of the most characteristic aspects of any culture and is involved with its fundamental values as well as with the economic activities of the household. Children were an economic asset as a source of farm labor in an earlier America. Today the varied needs of children weigh heavily on the family budget, while their opportunities to be productive have diminished. Difference in patterns of family relations is strikingly demonstrated by the fact that juvenile delinquency is almost unknown among the Chinese in the United States. Otherwise, delinquency seems to be a universal problem, regardless of the racial or nationality background of the parents. The fact that a major function of the home is that of bringing up children has two major consequences for marketing. One is the direct impact on current consumption patterns. The other is that tomorrow's shoppers are being trained in the homes of today.

The Struggle between Generations. The struggle between the generations has been accepted as a part of Western culture for centuries. It is reflected in Greek and Hebrew literature as well as in the latest modern novel. To the extent that this struggle exists, it is an important feature of family life itself and in addition may become involved with the conflict among the adult members of the household. The problem of achieving compatibility is of quite a different character with and without children. In its mildest form the struggle between children and parents may be nothing more than the resistance of inertia against learning new habits. In its graver manifestations, it may be the source of severe psychic disturbances which will be revealed in the child later on.

Perhaps the most typical situation is that in which the child at successive stages of development rebels against authority and then appears to become adjusted at a new level. Rebellion is directed against parents or those who may exercise authority in another setting, such as teachers. The rejection of authority or the demand that it be moderated could be regarded as a feature of the process of maturation. The child is expected to change by degrees from an initial state of complete helplessness and dependence to an independent young adult who will presently form a new conjugal family. The uneven growth toward independence with occasional violent outbursts can occur in any power structure because of the delay on the part of those in command in recognizing a new level of competence among their subordinates.

The early writings of Freud painted this struggle in a different light, introducing the element of sexuality as the key to its interpretation. He utilized the notion of the Oedipus complex or the sexual craving of the child directed toward the parent of opposite sex. A son, according to the Freudian theory, went through the inevitable stage of secretly dreaming of murdering the father as a rival for the mother's love. Growing up consisted of a transition through a series of dark and sinister mental stages, which the individual would later try to keep hidden even from himself. The Freudian idea of resistance to the disclosure of true motives has strongly influenced some current techniques for investigating consumer behavior.

Freud today is credited with having pioneered the study of motivation, even though some of his interpretations, which were derived wholly from contact with abnormal individuals and from a daring theoretical imagination, are no longer accepted. At the very least, Freud won a new freedom for motivation research by his shocking yet plausible explanations of abnormality resting on such assumptions as infantile sexuality. Some of Freud's followers have asserted that his doctrines are inherently sociological, dealing fundamentally with group behavior and its reaction upon the individual psyche. One might go still further in the present connection and say that Freudian psychology is essentially a theory of interaction within the household, with special emphasis on maturation and the struggle between parents and children.

The Family as a Behavior System. Latter-day psychoanalysis tends to favor a more common-sense view of what is transpiring in the family. Usually, the family with children may be regarded as a behavior system in which more or less mature adults accept as one of their functions the training of others who are certainly less mature than themselves. Psychoanalysis, of whatever version, serves to put us on notice that training is not merely indoctrination in accepted attitudes and useful habits. Instead it must assist the immature in getting through a series of crises which are entailed in the processes of growth. The human individual does not go through such a striking physical metamorphosis as the butterfly, but the intellectual and emotional adjustments at various stages may represent equally radical though less visible changes.

The responsibilities of parenthood in this connection are complicated by various factors. One or both parents may still be insufficiently mature to understand or be of much help when the crises of growth arise. One or both may exhibit aggressive behavior because of their own frustrations. Their failures to achieve adjustment to each other or to their adult environment may be projected upon the children. Harsh or brutal treatment of children is less common today than a generation ago, but it is fair to say that for some children the problem of growing up is partly that of achieving normal development in spite of their parents. The adverse influence of parents may be manifested in overprotective behavior. Sometimes there is an ill-concealed rivalry for the affection of children, which means that no effective discipline can be imposed by either parent.

Because of the mechanisms of bisexual genetics, the child may be vastly different from either parent in its potential characteristics. Parents are sometimes confused and inadequate because they do not know how to deal with the stranger in their midst. They expect the child to react as they do or as they think they remember reacting at the same age. The estrangement of parent and child is often aggravated as the child acquires new associates at school and elsewhere. The child is being inducted into a subculture which is alien to that of its parents. The barrier can reach formidable proportions indeed if the parents are of foreign extraction or if they have been rising in the social and economic scale. The children acquire new ways faster than the parents and become embarrassed over what seems to be quaint or inferior at home. Estrangement can also occur among the so-called "best families" which have tried to give their children every advantage. Here it is usually associated with membership in a juvenile gang which has greater solidarity than the family and may even adopt resistance to adult discipline as an explicit tenet of group action.

Pathological conditions in family life can parallel most of those which develop in other behavior systems. An earlier section dealing with the pathology of organization discussed such features as excessive expectations. Severe tensions can arise in a family because its members in total expect too much. The parents expect their offspring to behave like paragons rather than like average youngsters. The children expect adult privileges and access to goods before they are ready to earn them or use them wisely. The stimulation of demand for high-powered cars and other expensive products through advertising may play a part in adolescent outbursts of violence in the effort to possess them. Marketing has an influence and a growing responsibility for what is happening in family life and for problems of adjustment by the young adult.

The Child within the Family.   Another aspect of the place of children in the family structure is the fact that the rearing of children is in many cases the central enterprise which gives continuity and meaning to the home as an organized unit. Biologically speaking, families would not come into existence at all except for the purposes of reproduction and the rearing of the young. At the human level, the instinctive urge of sex does not lead so directly or automatically to reproduction. Instead, bringing children into the world may be adopted as a deliberate aim, with planning and foresight expended on every stage of their care and development. Parents may be held together by a common stake in this enterprise, even though they are otherwise incompatible and would have separated if there were no children. At the same time, the rearing of children provides new opportunities for disagreement. Homes which are maintained only for the sake of children may, paradoxically, be rent with quarrels over the way children should be treated. In other cases, one parent may tolerate unacceptable methods of handling children in the hope of preserving the family.

The centering of family interest in children is a crucial fact for marketing. For such a family, the effects on the purchasing pattern are striking. Many of the items bought by the parents are determined by the kind of environment they hope to provide for their children. This attitude influences not only such purchases as baby foods, but also major purchasing decisions such as buying a home in what is regarded as a favorable location. To an increasing extent, partly because of the influence of such advertising media as television, many purchases are directly dictated or influenced by children. Even on the basis of minimum provision for the needs of children, the purchasing pattern is quite different than for families without children.

Families might usefully be classified according to dominant interests which give a central orientation to the purchasing pattern. Some families are primarily concerned about their homes or their social position, or may be unusually preoccupied with their automobiles, their pets, or various hobbies. A psychoanalyst might see in some of these activities a substitute for children as objects upon which to lavish affection. Where such interests are shared, they may serve as a means of cementing relations between husband and wife in the absence of children. Lacking such central interests, the family expenditure pattern may be dominated either by the desire for savings or other forms of accumulation or by the pursuit of pleasure from day to day. Given congenial tastes, the pursuit of pleasure can provide the basis of solidarity; but the persistence of such an orientation over a lifetime is more problematical.

In the modern urban home, children—along with old people—tend to exercise no economic function except consumption. Nevertheless, this is a significant contribution to business stability and expansion in a stimulated market economy. Aside from the impact of children on the expenditure pattern, marketing is interested in the training of future consumer buyers as it is proceeding in the homes of today. Basic preferences for food and other products are being established which marketing organizations will either try to capitalize upon or modify later. Some children are provided experience either in buying incidentals covered by a weekly allowance or by participation in selecting their own clothing and other belongings. The consumer today depends on the market far more than in a previous generation. The consumer of tomorrow will need increased buying skills to cope with the proliferation of goods. The home and the school might give more attention to equipping boys and girls to meet their future responsibilities as buyers.

INDIVIDUAL PSYCHOLOGY AND MARKETING

The section will present some concepts which may be useful in explaining both the normal and the abnormal adjustment in the family. The chief reliance so far has been on social psychology rather than individual psychology. The approach to individual psychology adopted here emphasizes the principle of organization as it applies to the individual psyche. This view follows Snygg and Combs in holding that the self wants always to be seen in a favorable light, and that the maintenance and enhancement of the self is the most fundamental of all drives. The kinship of this psychological objective to the power principle will be immediately obvious.

Even in the discussion of behavior which is regarded as an end in itself, there has been an emphasis on the group by relying on the concept of congeniality and compatibility within the household. Before closing this chapter, it is desirable to recognize that individual psychology must provide the answer to some problems of consumer preference, since all groups are composed of individuals. It is not the business of marketing to predict the behavior of the individual or to deal with individual problems of the type involving psychotherapy. Marketing undertakes to predict and control the behavior of masses of people and for most purposes finds it convenient to observe them as members of organized groups or consuming units. Nevertheless, in order to understand both adjustment and maladjustment in group behavior, it is necessary to consider some aspects of individual psychology.

Locke and Leibnitz. There are great difficulties for the market analyst in adopting a psychological position because of the many conflicting schools of psychology. A recent history of American psychology by Roback identified thirty-nine schools which still exert some influence. A drastic simplification of the history of psychology was suggested by Allport in a recent book. He says that there are really only two essentially different viewpoints, identified with the names of two famous philosophers, Locke and Leibnitz. Locke used the phrase *tabula rasa* to suggest that the human mind starts out as a clean slate on which a record is to be written by experience. Under this view the mind reacts in a completely passive fashion to the stimuli in its environment. Action may arise as a response to some of these stimuli, but this is a purely mechanical result of the original stimulus. The schools of psychology which followed in the path of Locke were known as "associationism" and "stimulus-response behaviorism." Some American behaviorists related this theory to the neurological system and attempted to explain the whole process of mental development by the conditioned reflex.

An interesting consequence of this concentration on the reflex arc was the attempt to eliminate consciousness as a proper subject of study in psychology. It was held that psychology could not be scientific unless it confined its attention to observable phenomena such as external behavior. This was a strange outcome for a field of study which had begun with the objective of investigating the nature of conscious mind. This attitude is believed to have been adopted through a false analogy with physics, during a period when physics was generally regarded as the model for all scientific endeavor. While physics deals with matters which are external to human consciousness, it does not confine itself to entities which can be directly studied and measured. Instead it has used its experimental data to make inferences about such matters as atomic structure, which are quite beyond the range of human observation.

The other view of the nature of mind has come down from Leibnitz through Kant to its present manifestation in several leading schools of psychology. This is the view which emphasizes the active and organizing aspect of mind. It holds that the mind does not merely record experiences but accepts or rejects stimuli from the environment and organizes them into patterns determined by its own needs. This general viewpoint, of which Gestalt psychology is representative, emphasizes complete wholes rather than separate elements as the objects of perception. Like psychoanalysis, it emphasizes purpose, goals, and motives rather than mechanical responses to stimuli. Both Gestalt psychology and psychoanalysis, different as they are in their respective points of emphasis, accept conscious mind as a central fact, in contrast with the schools of psychology derived from Locke.

The current trend in American psychology, in terms of the division suggested by Allport, is away from Locke and toward Leibnitz. Most psychologists who once adhered to the stimulus-response approach have come to recognize that something significant must intervene between stimulus and response. Thus, Woodworth came to talk about "S-O-R" with the "O" representing the internal organizing process which intervenes between stimulus and response. Tolman has used the more general term of "intervening variables" to characterize any mental processes which lie between sensory stimulation on the one hand and motor response on the other. Both Tolman and Woodworth are talking about processes which cannot be observed directly but must be inferred from external behavior. Their value is in providing a basis for prediction of future behavior which may vary from the patterns of past behavior.

There is still a reluctance in American psychology to recognize introspection as a means for obtaining scientific knowledge about mental processes. An individual may in some sense observe his own inner processes, but there is some skepticism as to his ability to report them in a way that allows reliable comparisons with similar reports from others. It is an important fact for marketing theory that marketing research still relies very largely on the introspective reports of respondents. In other words, consumers are asked to tell the investigator about their preferences and often to explain the motivations which lie behind the preferences. This fact should be a matter of some concern for those in marketing who like to believe that they are following the more behavioristic and objective point of view in their approach to the psychology of the consumer. The chances are that market research will have to rely on introspection for much of the information it needs for quite a long time to come. Meanwhile, persistent efforts should be made toward the development of experimental methods in market research; but the present view is that these experiments will be most fruitful if they recognize the active and organizing aspect of mental processes.

The Self-Image. The viewpoint concerning individual psychology which is adopted here is largely derived from the Gestalt psychologists and some of the more recent work in psychotherapy. This view emphasizes the phenomenal field as the basic reality for the individual. That is to say that what is real for each individual is the environment as he sees it, and particularly as it involves opportunities or limitations for his own actions. This concept of the phenomenal field in relation to individual action was first fully developed by Kurt Lewin. Later psychologists such as Snygg and Combs have placed an equal emphasis upon the phenomenal self. The individual's concept or image of himself is central to the phenomenal field in which he lives and attempts to satisfy his needs. Further support for this view has come from some of the newer developments in psychotherapy such as are represented by Karen Horney and Carl Rogers. For these psychologists there is one basic drive or purpose transcending all others in the life of the individual. That is the goal of maintaining and enhancing a favorable self-image in the midst of the stream of experience. Snygg and Combs go so far as to say that all of the vital energies are directed toward the survival of the phenomenal self rather the physical self.

The Self and Perception. There are three principal alternatives available to the self in dealing with experience. First, it may accept those parts of experience which are favorable to the self-image and, by organizing them into the existing pattern, achieve the enhancement of the self. Secondly, it may ignore those aspects of experience which do not appear to be related to the self. The ignoring of aspects of experience is essential on grounds of economy, since the available stimuli are infinite in number and beyond the organizing power of the individual to handle. The third method is the rejection or repression of aspects of experience which do not fit in with the self-image. Freud believed that the individual did not actually get rid of unpleasant experiences but simply relegated them to the unconscious mind. Often they remained there as a constant threat to the integrity of the self and might result in pathological behavior. The therapeutic techniques of psychoanalysis attempt to bring these repressed experiences out into the open and finally to dispose of them by dealing with them consciously.

Symbolism. Later psychoanalysts such as Rogers stress the importance of symbolization. The threatening experience is no longer a threat if it can be related to the self-concept through symbolic processes. The completely healthy individual, according to Rogers, is the one who can admit the whole range of his experience into the symbolic structure. To do so, the individual must be able to face up to failure as well as to success, to admit shame as well as pride, and to assign to each an appropriate place in the picture of the self and its continuing effort toward enhancement. Symbolization is regarded by this group as the essence of consciousness. That is to say that to be alive and aware consists of entertaining a series of pictures or symbols derived from experience and reorganized into acceptable patterns by inner processes.

The Phenomenal Self and Learning. It remains to mention the relation of this view to certain topics in psychology which are of special concern for marketing. The first of these is the theory of learning. Marketing is concerned about acquired attitudes such as those which advertising attempts to instill in the consumer, and the habits of both buyer and seller which facilitate orderly routines in the market place. It has been pointed out by Hilgard that the general view which is championed here has been weak in its treatment of learning. Gestalt psychology in its classic form came close to saying that the individual learns nothing, while psychoanalysis states that he forgets nothing but only relegates unpleasant experiences to the subconscious. Most recently, the concept of the phenomenal self has demonstrated that it can contribute to an understanding of learning. This differs from an earlier view which relied largely on repetition as the mechanism of learning, reinforced by rewards and punishments. The new view is more inclined to talk in terms of success and failure as shaping the learning process. It is increasingly recognized that repeated trials d not necessarily result in learning in the absence of adequate motivation. The term "ego-involvement" is used by Cantril and others to characterize those activities which are significant for the phenomenal self and hence may result in changed patterns of behavior.

Introjection. Another topic of basic importance is that of value theory and the way in which the goals of individuals are determined or modified in the course of development. In general, it is believed that the child starts out with values imposed from without. To use a technical term, these values are said to have been "introjected" into the ideal image of the self. Since these values are of external origin, they often become distorted or confused in the process of acceptance. Rogers believes that the life history of the normal individual is marked by a gradual displacement of introjected values and the development of a set of goals and standards which are really consistent with the phenomenal self.

Individual Psychology and Organized Behavior Systems. A major aspect of the self-image is the factor of group membership. The individual's self-esteem rests in considerable degree on a sense of belonging, which may pertain to one or several behavior groups. In order to maintain and enhance the phenomenal self, the individual is obliged to maintain and enhance his status in these organized behavior systems. This is in no way inconsistent with the recognition of individual differences or with the pursuit of a unique personal destiny as a transcendent goal. The reconciliation lies in the fact that organized behavior systems are the necessary vehicles for the realization of individual goals. This is true both of the instrumental behavior which characterizes operating systems and of the congenial behavior which is regarded as the end of all activity. Congeniality, in the last analysis, resides in a mutual sense of belonging and in the capacity of the group to contribute toward the development of self-images favorable to each of its members. The investigation of the congenial states of mind which yield satisfaction directly has largely been neglected by psychologists. The concept of the phenomenal self and its drive toward enhancement is an important foundation stone for the theory of consumption.

SELECTED REFERENCES

MURDOCK, GEORGE PETER, in *Science of Man in the World Crisis.* Ed. by Ralph Linton. New York: Columbia University Press, 1945.

LA PIERE, RICHARD TRACY. *Collective Behavior.* New York: McGraw-Hill Book Co., Inc., 1938.

FREUD, SIGMUND. *The Psychopathology of Everyday Life.* New York: Macmillan Co., 1917.

ROGERS, CARL R. *Client-Centered Therapy.* Boston: Houghton-Mifflin Co., 1951.

ALLPORT, GORDON W. *Becoming.* New Haven: Yale University Press, 1955.

BOEHM-BAWERK, EUGEN V. *Positive Theory of Capital.* New York: G. E. Stockert & Co., 1891.

Three major types of behavior are discussed in this chapter, each of the three terms being due to one of the authors cited. George Peter Murdock defines instrumental behavior as that directed toward achieving an end. This type of behavior is, of course, the central concern of functionalism.

Consumption is related to what La Piere calls congenial behavior, which is expected to yield satisfaction directly. Freud is the leading authority on symptomatic behavior, which he defines as behavior which is not functional except as it is a signal indicating maladjustment.

Carl Rogers represents a new development in psychotherapy which emphasizes the need for the enhancement of the self-image and the use of symbols for that purpose. The psychological viewpoint summarized in the final chapter of the reference cited is very close to that adopted here. The small volume by Allport is a simplified history of trends in psychological theory.

Some of the salient features of the present author's views concerning the behavior of consumer buyers were anticipated by the Austrian economist, Boehm-Bawerk. In particular, he held that the consumer was engaged in accumulating or replenishing an assortment of goods in anticipation of future needs.

Chapter VII

MATCHING AND SORTING: THE LOGIC OF EXCHANGE

Exchange is essentially the act of improving the assortments held by the two parties to the exchange. Without the aid of organized marketing facilities, an individual seeking to acquire a product which could enhance the potency of his assortment was typically faced with a long and difficult search. Exchange was costly in human effort and confined to a very limited range of economic goods, so long as the matching of small segments of supply and demand had to take place through such individual pairings.

Economic progress has consisted largely in finding more efficient ways of matching heterogeneous supply and heterogeneous demand. Matching can be divided into the three phases of shaping, fitting, and sorting, the first two concerned with the form and the specific application of a product. Sorting as a means of accomplishing effective matching is roughly equivalent with the domain of marketing as compared with production. Four aspects of sorting are discussed, each playing an essential part in marketing processes. Among these four aspects of sorting, economics has emphasized allocation or the breaking-down of a homogeneous supply. Marketing theory gives relatively greater emphasis to assorting or the building-up of assortments. An assortment is a heterogeneous collection of products designed to serve the needs of some behavior system.

THE FUNCTION OF EXCHANGE

It is commonly stated that exchange takes place because each party to the transaction has a surplus of one product and a deficit of another. In marketing terms, it is somewhat more precise to say that exchange takes place in order to increase the utility of the assortments held by each party to the transaction. That is to say that the assortment held by A can be improved by adding to it a product in the hands of B. At the same time the assortment held by B gains greater utility from the product received in exchange than it loses from the product which it gives up. Exchange under this conception is a creative function. It creates value in the sense that there is greater value in use for all of the products involved after the exchange than before the exchange. This is directly contrary to the conception held by some that exchange can only represent a transfer of values, and that any gain on one side must reflect a loss on the other. This doctrine of creative exchange is based on the notion that value pertains to assortments in use and not merely to individual products.

The notion of an assortment and its significance for the theory of marketing has already been presented in a preliminary way. The reader will observe that there is an analogy between the term "group" as applied to individuals and the term "assortments" as applied to goods. As with all analogies, it is important to understand its limitations as well as its valid application. A group regarded as an operating system performs many functions which are beyond the scope of the individual. Its entire performance is motivated by what it can contribute toward achieving the goals of the individual participants. A group has a structure and operating functions, but its apparent aims and objectives are entirely derivative.

Assortment of Goods. An assortment of goods has a kind of structure and internal consistency, but it has no purpose except to serve the purposes of the individuals of the group to whom the assortment belongs. A product may have a place in an assortment which is vaguely similar to the status which an individual enjoys in a group. There is, of course, no sense of belonging as in the case of the individual, and no attempt to achieve status as a means of promoting other goals. It is only from the viewpoint of some interested observer that a product fits into an assortment. In the case of the assortment of goods in the possession of a consumer, it is natural to adopt the viewpoint of this consumer in considering whether a given product will contribute to the utility of the assortment.

In some respects it is more precise to speak of the *potency* of the assortment, since the *value* of the assortment as a whole lies in providing against future contingencies facing the consumer. As described in the previous chapter, each consumer unit, such as a household, tries to be prepared for the appropriate type of behavior in view of future contingencies. The contingencies facing the individual vary both as to their likelihood of occurring and as to the degree of urgency in case they should occur. The value or utility of a product is related to both the urgency and the probability of the contingency to which it is related. Between two products, the one of greatest utility to the consumer is the one which will make the greatest contribution to the potency of the assortment. In other words, the product to be next acquired is the one which will most greatly reduce the risks of being unprepared to meet an urgent situation.

Closure of Assortment.   Another parallel between group and assortment is that the concept of closure applies in both cases. A closed group is the one which is complete in the sense that all of the necessary positions are occupied in order to permit the group to function. A closed assortment is one which is complete in the sense that it provides for all of the contingencies for which the owner of the assortment is consciously attempting to be prepared. The closure of assortments is achieved only rarely and temporarily in our type of economy. An assortment which appears complete may quickly reach the stage where one or more of the products essential to closure are exhausted. Thus, consumers are constantly engaged in replenishing an assortment to restore the original state of potency. Assortments are also extended by adding items which they did not contain previously. The extension of an assortment may mean that the consumer for the first time is economically able to provide for some future occasion, or it may mean that for the first time he recognizes the urgency or the probability of some future contingency. A major function of selling and advertising is to bring consumers to recognize contingencies which were previously ignored.

Enhancing Potency of Assortment.   The creative aspect of exchange in enhancing the potency of assortments can be seen most directly in the case of barter. Where one group has more wheat than it needs and the other group has more wool than it needs, the survival of both groups can be promoted by exchange. In a monetary economy the mutual enhancement of assortments is partially obscured. It is clear enough in the case of the buyer who is obtaining some product necessary to sustain his standard of life or to promote some particular objective. In the case of the seller the eventual result is the same, but the process is more roundabout. That is to say that the seller is compensated in a medium of exchange representing a general token of value. He will eventually use these returns to replenish the supplies needed to continue his operations, or will disburse them to the various participants in the process. Thus, they ultimately enable these participants to replenish or extend the assortments in their possession.

The marketing process as the creation of assortments is essentially irreversible. That is to say that at each step along the way a product is approaching the point at which it will become a part of some ultimate assortment. Costs are incurred at each step which cannot be recovered by reversing the process. When goods have finally reached the consumer, they have gained use value but have lost most of the commercial value they had in the channels of trade. That is because of the costs and the other factors which would stand as barriers to any reverse flow of goods from the consumer back into the market.

Irreversibility of Assortments. The stock market and the commodity exchanges are sometimes regarded as the most nearly perfect examples of the way a free market operates. Actually, they serve as great exceptions from the normal flow of marketing transactions, because they are not completely subject to the principle of irreversibility. The same person operating on the stock exchange or the commodity exchange may sell something one day and buy it back the next. The physical commodities or properties represented in these transactions do not change their location or character in any way. They are not involved in the irreversible process of gradually being adapted to the use patterns of the particular individual. The discussions of price making in economic theory have attempted to center on some one point, such as the wholesale market, as crucial for the matching of supply and demand. From a marketing viewpoint the matching of supply and demand takes place through a continuous process, with each item brought closer and closer through a series of stages to its ultimate place in an assortment.

Utility of Assortment Achieved through Sorting. Both marketing men and general economists have discussed the contrast between marketing and production. The general economist has tended to look upon production as the process which creates value. He has been inclined to regard marketing either as a subdivision of production or as a wasteful manifestation of excessive competition. The present view is quite the reverse and holds that marketing is, in fact, the source of all ultimate value in use. Value can be created through exchange even when restricted to products as they occur in nature, without being subject to any manufacturing processes. Manufacturing is a supplementary way of shaping goods to the needs of the consumer. It takes place within the structure of marketing operations rather than the reverse.

Reference has already been made to the distinction sometimes drawn between form utility and other aspects of utility such as time, place, and possession. The notion is here rejected that one of these aspects of utility can be associated with production and the other with marketing. There is only one kind of utility—namely, the value which a product contributes to the potency of an assortment. There are many stages through which products may pass before reaching their ultimate destination, which involve changes other than those brought about by manufacture. All economic activities create a single form of utility, but they employ diverse means toward this end.

This ultimate objective is to match the needs of the individual with a suitable product. The primary methods of matching may be called shaping, sorting, and fitting. Manufacturing and other forms of production bring into being products that are shaped for specific uses. Fitting is the modification of a standardized product so that it will suit the individual or, more precisely, its installation in a particular use situation. Marketing, on the other hand, starts out with the available supply of diversified products and creates ultimate utility through what is essentially a process of sorting. The building-up of assortments through the various stages of sorting is the essence of the economics of marketing. Economics and marketing have distinct points of emphasis in their investigation of these processes. Economics takes its point of departure from the principle of scarcity and the need for coping with the fact that the supply of goods can never be sufficient or serve all possible needs. Marketing, by contrast, emphasizes the unique characteristics of individual need and the objective of achieving the most suitable assortments within the limitations of the goods available.

THE FOUR ASPECTS OF SORTING

Matching aligns a small segment of supply against a small segment of demand. Considering the radical heterogeneity of both demand and supply and the geographical dispersion of the segments which are to be matched with each other, it would not be economically feasible for this pairing to be accomplished one pair at a time. The cost of the search which brought the two segments together, to say nothing of other charges such as transportation, would be prohibitive. Instead of being carried out directly, matching is the end product of sorting in its various aspects. The goal of marketing is the matching of segments of supply and demand. The essential mechanism of marketing by which this end is achieved consists of the four aspects of sorting, which will now be discussed.

An assortment is a collection of two or more types of goods which either complement each other directly or in total possess some degree of potency for meeting future contingencies. The word "supply" in this chapter will be used, by contrast, to designate a collection of identical or similar products. Thus an assortment might be regarded as two or more supplies, even though sometimes a supply would consist of a single unit. Another type of collection will be designated as a "conglomeration." A conglomeration contains two or more types o goods, but it has not been brought together for the purpose of servin the needs of a particular individual or group. This applies to collectior of all types, or of grades of products just as they may occur in nature, anc hence at random so far as the objectives of any individuals or group are concerned.

Conglomerations and Assortments. The whole economic proces may be said to start with conglomerations and end with assortments That is the way that the market must somehow bring together hetero geneous supply on the one hand and heterogeneous demand on the other. The two sides of the market cannot be simply and readil matched with each other because two varieties of heterogeneity ar involved. The kind of mixture which occurs in nature is usually les suitable for human use than if the different elements occurred ir pure form. The facts of heterogeneity of markets were discussed b the British economist, G. F. Shove. He used the example of a jigsaw puzzle to illuminate the process of matching up supply and demand This figure of speech is interesting both as to the way in which i applies and the way in which the parallel breaks down. In solving jigsaw puzzle, an individual starts with a conglomeration of piece and must try to fit them together in a meaningful pattern which re sembles the concept of an assortment. Jigsaw puzzles are usually solvec on a rather naïve trial-and-error basis. The solver may either picl up a piece and look for all the openings where it might fit or observ an opening in the developing pattern and start looking for a piece t fit it. This type of procedure would resemble an unorganized market in which the consumer searches for goods and the suppliers search fo ultimate consumers, without benefit of the intervening marketing chan nels and processes. Suppose that the individual solver were confrontec with a much larger jigsaw puzzle, in the completion of which he coulc make use of several helpers. Perhaps the picture to be put togethe was that of a wheat field beside a forest, with a stretch of sky beyond There might therefore be a large area of the pattern made up re spectively of yellow pieces, green pieces, and blue pieces. The solve and his helpers would probably start out by sorting the pieces int three piles, and then one or more persons would specialize in puttin together pieces which represented the field, the forest, and the sky The economics of marketing is concerned with the possibilities o using such intermediary steps in moving from the conglomeration o the one side to the assortment on the other.

The Four Aspects of Sorting. There are four aspects of sorting, which all enter into these intermediate processes and which result in economies that would be impossible if it were necessary to match every small segment of supply with every small segment of demand. The term "sorting" applies either to the practice of breaking down collections or to the building-up of collections. Sorting also has both its quantitative and qualitative aspects. These two basic distinctions result in four separate types of operations under the general heading of sorting. Starting with a conglomeration, we can perform the operation of *sorting out,* which breaks the collection into various types of goods. Sorting out results in a set of separate supplies which may be regarded as homogeneous in terms of the classification being used by the sorter. Given small homogeneous supplies, it is possible to create larger supplies by adding one to another. This building-up of a larger supply may represent the *accumulation* over a period of time from a single sorting operation, or it may represent the bringing together in a single place products which meet standard specifications but are drawn from different localities. In the latter case it may be that the large demand of a single plant is being matched by the accumulated supply. Once a large homogeneous supply has been accumulated, it may, on the other hand, be broken down by a process of apportionment or *allocation.* Division of the total supply is made in terms of the requirements of various operating units whose claims are to be met. Allocation may take place within a single organization in terms of planning and control, or it may take place through the market and be determined by such a consideration as price. Finally, there is the step of using supplies to build up assortments. This process may be designated as *assorting,* or the putting together of unlike supplies in accordance with some pattern determined by demand.

The four stages of sorting out, accumulation, allocation, and assorting have been introduced in the order in which they most frequently occur in marketing processes. There are, of course, many exceptions and variations; and the sequence is also complicated by manufacture or other changes in form, such as fitting, which may take place at various points along the way. The four types of sorting might also be grouped according to their logical relationships. Sorting out and assorting may be placed together as pertaining to the qualitative aspects of collections. Accumulation and allocation pertain to purely quantitative changes in what is taken to be a homogeneous supply. An alternative method of classification is to group sorting out and allocation together because they both apply to the breaking-down of a collection or a supply. The contrary process of building up a collection or supply is represented by accumulation and assorting.

Assorting in Marketing Theory. Marketing is concerned with all of these aspects of sorting as they appear in the process of matching supply and demand. Marketing theory necessarily places the greatest emphasis on assorting as the final step in meeting the needs of consumers, for which all the other types of sorting are merely preliminary. Economics, with its emphasis upon scarcity rather than the unique character of individual needs, has paid most attention to allocation among the four types of sorting. Allocation has a special fascination for the mathematically inclined, since some problems of allocation are subject to precise solution through calculus and other mathematical techniques. The main hope for analyzing sorting in general, with some precision, seems likely to lie in the direction of symbolic logic. These possibilities will be discussed briefly in a later section of this chapter.

PROBLEMS OF SORTING OPERATIONS

There are some special problems pertaining to each of the four basic sorting operations. Marketing efficiency rests in part on a successful handling of these sorting problems. The four basic processes will be discussed in the order in which they were first introduced, starting with sorting out. The over-all organization of the sorting process will be discussed in the following section.

Sorting Out. Sorting out requires that standard classifications be established in advance. The sorter must have a definite set of criteria by which he is guided in inspecting units and throwing each into one class or another. He must decide how many classes to use and frequently must allow for a miscellaneous class to cover items which do not fit into any of the specified classes. Some characteristics of products or materials are more objective and measurable than others and lend themselves more readily to distinguishing one class from another. Sorting out by grades is one of the foundation stones of agricultural marketing as it has developed in the United States. Apples, for example, are graded by size as well as by color and freedom from blemishes. The culls go into other uses, such as vinegar making or the feeding of animals. Only the best-looking fruit goes to market for household consumption, but it is easier to assure eye appeal than flavor. The effort to maintain useful standards for agricultural produce is fraught with difficulties. Experts in nutrition say that beef with yellow fat should represent first grade because of the vitamin content. Actually, beef with white fat is classified as first grade because it has greater eye appeal for the consumer. Similarly, potatoes are graded by the smoothness of their skins rather than by any measure of their nutritional content. Grades once established are hard to maintain because of the shifting geography of production. It is scarcely feasible politically to administer a grading system which would put the product of one state in first grade and the comparable product of another state in second grade. Anyone familiar with the produce business can testify to the distressing lack of uniformity and quality labeled as first grade that sometimes gets through to the consumer.

Some years ago there was an active agitation for placing all canned or preserved foods under a system of grade labeling to supplement brand names or to take the place of such trade terms as "fancy," "choice," and "standard." Many obstacles developed, aside from the desire of packers to maintain the prestige of their brands. One is the variation in the quality of a crop which may occur from year to year, so that in a poor year no part of the crop might qualify according to rigid specifications. Yet it might be better to place some percentage of the crop in first grade, since some consumers are prepared to pay a premium for the best available. In products like coffee or flour, limitations are imposed by the desire for uniformity in flavor or performance. The standard is maintained by using whatever blend will produce the desired result rather than by sticking to a rigid formula related to the source or grade of the ingredients.

Grading is always having to be adjusted to the realities of supply and to the changing requirements of consumer use or of manufacture. Lumber is typical of the products in which the best available today might not have passed muster as first grade a few years ago. Grades for Douglas fir plywood are enforced by an industry association, but the declining quality of peeler logs makes it very difficult to maintain these standards. At the other extreme, there are cases of companies which built too much quality into their products in terms of durability or other physical characteristics. In the case of industrial raw materials, it quite often becomes possible to use those previously discarded as substandard because of improvements in processing. On the other hand, uniformity of materials often has a major impact on plant operations. The substitution of synthetic materials for such natural materials as leather has been accelerated by the greater uniformity of the synthetic product.

There are certain industrial processes which are scarcely more than an extension of the sorting out which can sometimes be performed by direct inspection of the units constituting the supply. Smelting is a process by which metal is separated out of the ore, leaving such residues as slag. The slag may have some use value also, but usually for very inferior uses and at much lower prices. The entire chemical and petroleum industries in a sense represent a sorting out or a separation of products which cannot be separated by merely physical means. Common salt is indeed composed of sodium and chlorine. The bond between the two elements can be broken down by electrolysis. The commercial incentive at one point might be to serve an active market for caustic soda and at another time to serve the market for chlorine. One constitutes the main product and the other the by-product which must be disposed of in many such cases. In principle, this is no different from the sorting out of first-grade apples, leaving the culls to be disposed of for whatever they will bring. The apples, of course, can be left on the land to rot, while chemical by-products create a more serious disposal problem if there is no market for them. It is rather startling to be reminded in these days of automobiles that gasoline was once a troublesome waste product created in the process of producing the kerosene needed for domestic lighting. The still unsolved problems of disposing of industrial wastes are reflected in the poisoning of streams and the fouling of the atmosphere in many communities.

Accumulation. The accumulation of the smaller homogeneous supplies into a larger supply serves several economic purposes. Possibly the simplest case is that of promoting the ease of transportation. Copra might be accumulated on a Pacific Island until a shipload was ready to be carried away. Coal might be loaded at a mine until a string of cars was ready to move. A similar reason for accumulation is to utilize storage space especially adapted to the purpose. Wheat moves to grain elevators, eggs and other produce to cold storage warehouses, whiskey into bonded warehouses for a certified period of aging.

Many raw materials, after being sorted out or refined, move to manufacturing plants for processing. Accumulation for a large plant must be a continuous flow rather than the periodic gathering of large lots. The working inventory on hand is steadily being used up and must be just as continuously replaced. Supplies may come in from a number of locations, but all must fall within certain limits as to product specifications in order to be suitable for processing. Industrial procurement has the task of enforcing technical standards on a steady flow of materials produced under varying conditions from a number of locations. The economies of procurement often require that mini-mum levels be maintained in the stocks of raw materials. These stocks constitute insurance against interruption in the flow of materials and allow the plant to continue to operate for a period until the flow is resumed. Such accumulations of materials can also minimize market risk as to price fluctuations. Materials may have been bought in large lots to obtain a favorable price. Some raw materials are highly seasonal in production, resulting in the need for accumulating inventory either at the source or at the plant. The decision as to where the accumulation will take place will depend on relative ability to carry the investment, on the degree of perishability of the material, and on the availability of suitable storage space. The final determination will be worked out through the price mechanism. The seller may take a lower price to speed up the movement of materials. The buyer may be willing to pay a higher price in return for a delay in taking possession of the materials.

The greatest urgency is typically on the side of the raw materials producer. The material he produces often has little or no use value to him or others in his immediate community. It may be highly perisha-ble, as in the case of some agricultural products. He may be concerned that others will exhaust the supply first, as in the case of competitively developed oil fields. This urgency of the raw materials producer to sell is responsible for many types of economic regulation in the United States and elsewhere. The problem of farm surpluses has led to vast accumulations of various products either owned directly by the govern-ment or financed by the government. The purpose of such devices is to hold supplies off the market and allow for a more orderly movement later on. The difficulty is that these government arrangements create a new artificial market for the material involved, so that supplies are created to satisfy this market as well as the genuine market.

Raw materials countries provide even more spectacular examples of this abnormal type of accumulation. Coffee has been held off the market by such countries as Brazil until there appeared to be no solu-tion except to dispose of great quantities by burning. Competition among raw materials countries nearly always places a bargaining ad-vantage in the hands of the more industrialized countries buying the raw materials.

Good industrial procurement policies can give more stability to raw materials markets than artificial controls, at least for some favored prod-ucts. The manufacturer who is trying to maximize his market by producing a uniform-quality product is in turn anxious to obtain raw materials of uniform quality. The soup manufacturer contracts in advance for the entire output of farmers producing tomatoes or other crops for his use. Skilled help is provided to the farmers in producing crops of the quality desired. Dairies rely on selected farms to provide milk which meets their standards, and enforce regulations as to sanitation and the care of dairy herds. Large marketing organizations such as chain stores often have standing arrangements with certain farms or farm communities to supply the fresh produce to be sold in their stores. Large printers have long-term contracts with paper mills or even sources of pulpwood. The requirements of mass production thus provide a secure and profitable niche for the raw materials producer in many cases. This runs contrary to the notion that free and open competition makes for superior adjustment. The point is that highly specialized and massive requirements can best be met in some cases by tying up the most favorable sources, with resulting advantages to the producer as well. Here the full force of Shove's jigsaw puzzle is exemplified with the direct matching of a segment of demand and a segment of supply.

This discussion tends to qualify the original statement about the greater urgency on the part of the raw materials producer. The manufacturer has his urgencies also, but they are not served by an open market for raw materials in which much of the supply is not really suited to his needs. Sometimes the manufacturer integrates all the way back to raw materials sources to get the quantity and quality he needs. The intermediate stage of using selected suppliers on a contractual basis represents one of the many variations in the matching and sorting procedures which constitute marketing.

It should be noted that industrial procurement in most firms is concerned with many goods rather than a single material. The industrial purchasing agent may be regarded as building up an assortment to support his firm's operations in somewhat the same way that a household builds up an end-use assortment. The purchasing agent tries to foresee future contingencies, taking account of their urgency and probability. He may stock certain parts or even whole machines because of the urgency of minimizing down-time in the case of breakdown. He may increase his stocks of certain raw materials because of an estimated increase in his company's sales or because of rumors of a strike or price increase affecting the supply. He is not free to judge each source of supply separately, but must sometimes choose one alternative over another in terms of what seems required by balance in the whole assortment.

Allocation. The third type of sorting, allocation, has had extensive theoretical treatment in economics. In fact, some economists define their field of study as that of determining the best allocations of scarce supplies. Allocation in the economic sense takes place both internally as a function of business management and externally through transactions in the market place. Both internal and external allocation mean the breaking down of a homogeneous supply into smaller quantities determined by the requirements of each use situation.

Internal allocation is guided, according to economists, by the principle of marginal productivity. That is to say that where there are two or more possible uses, each unit is assigned to the most productive use until productivity is equal at the margin. In other words, if this principle is followed effectively, the last unit assigned to each of the several uses will be equally effective. In the operation of a marketing organization, internal allocation applies primarily to the deployment of workers or the appropriation of dollars for advertising or other types of promotion. It can apply also to the assignment of such facilities as office equipment, or the time of electronic computing machines. It enters into decisions concerning the use of the end product for such purposes as display, sampling, or actual sale.

The external allocation of the goods produced and marketed by a given firm is guided by the marginal revenue principle. If a company has several sales territories, it will distribute its products among these territories so as to obtain the same revenue from the last unit sold in each territory. Under the marginal revenue principle, the seller will be encouraged to expand his sales in all directions, until the last unit sold produces a revenue which barely covers all the costs of production and selling. This principle might induce him to expand the total area covered, until he reached a point on the perimeter of his sales region where delivery costs were just sufficient to absorb the margin between price and all other costs. He might be induced, on the other hand, to intensify his sales effort closer to home, until the added costs of selling absorbed the available margin. Similarly, the pursuit of profit may induce the seller to make various adjustments to the demands of customers. He may give a price concession in recognition of the economy of a large order. He may vary his price according to the terms of delivery and payment which are convenient to the customer. In the free market the allocation of goods is assumed to be adjusted automatically to all of these varying conditions, and the goods are assumed to come into the possession of just those customers for whom they have the greatest utility.

In an earlier chapter, there was a discussion of rationing as a primitive operation taking place within an organized behavior system. Rationing is a process which is not necessarily guided by marginal principles but may be greatly affected by such considerations as maintaining the power structure. Internal allocation in a business firm is not carried out on a purely mathematical basis but necessarily takes account of the power and capacity of various operating units. In allocating the means of production, the chief executive receives back commitments concerning performance from each of his subordinates. Similarly, rationing is never entirely absent from the external allocation of products. It took the period of wartime scarcity to reveal the fact that the flow of goods is guided by many considerations other than price. There has scarcely been a time since the Second World War when one group or another of major commodities was not in short supply. That means that the people who were willing to buy at the stated price had total demands exceeding the supply. Whenever this happens, something other than price is involved in making the allocations.

The need for rationing under peacetime conditions arises partly from the existence of intermediary sellers. Assume that a manufacturer has only a certain quantity of a new product to sell in a given market, and it is clear in advance that consumers will be eager to buy it. The manufacturer may have been selling his other products to two leading dealers in this city, and either one of them might be able and willing to take the entire initial supply of his new product. It would not be rational for him to settle his problem by selling the entire amount to the highest bidder, since what he wants is an established and continuous business on this product rather than maximum profit from the initial sale. Forced with having to allocate on a basis other than price, the seller will consider such factors as stability and growth for his business. On grounds of stability, he is likely to favor the customer who has given him the most business in the past and thus might be expected to be most loyal in the future. On grounds of growth, he will be inclined to favor the customer who shows the greatest future promise or who has plans for featuring the new product effectively. Sometimes the allocation is made on less rational grounds and represents nothing more than a compromise with the relative amount of pressure exerted by one customer or the other. Each customer may offer reasons why he should be favored, which will presumably relate to the immediate or long-run interest of the seller. Thus, allocation may be brought about neither by the impersonal mechanism or price nor by the deliberate decision of the seller, but become a matter of negotiation.

There are other restrictions on the use of marginal principles for rational allocation. The developing techniques of linear programming are designed to cope with some of these difficulties. Programming techniques can take account of limitations of capacity or other structural features of an operation. There are, of course, the perennial problems of joint costs and division of returns among joint products. The importance of the joint-cost problem in marketing led to the development of the techniques of distribution of cost analysis.

There is another fundamental limitation on marginal analysis which is of special concern to marketing. That is the fact that it is possible to approach the margin in many different ways. Thus, in an earlier example a seller was pictured as having the alternatives of extending his territory so long as he could absorb the increased delivery costs or of intensifying promotion so long as he could absorb the increased sales costs. The theoretical answer is that a businessman should approach the margin in both of these ways or in any other ways that are open. The difficulty is that correct allocation becomes extremely complex when action is open in various directions and imposes a heavy burden on either business judgment or mathematical analysis. The allocation problem cannot be analyzed in terms of simple continuous functions when there is a choice of direction in approaching the margin. There is also the serious risk that the businessman is not even aware of some of the possible directions and may be missing his best opportunity in choosing among the directions in which he can allocate efforts or products.

Assorting. The fourth type of sorting, which has been designated as "assorting," has already been discussed in a preliminary way in the chapter on consumer behavior. It was pointed out that the function of the household purchasing agent is to build up use combinations in anticipation of patterns of behavior the family desires to follow. Here, as in the case of the industrial purchaser, the assortment may be regarded as a set of supplies, each consisting of one or more units of a particular type of goods. Each of these supplies is matched against a possible use, while the assortment as a whole represents the purchasing agent's best judgment as to the pattern of use. Some of the supplies in the assortment are simple complements of each other—as, for example, the collection of ingredients needed in baking a cake. The balance within the assortment as a whole goes beyond the relation of simple complementarity. Some of the products in the assortment may be used every day or may be consumed quickly and have to be replaced. Others are there only because of the outside possibility that the occasion for use will arise. A balanced assortment is one in which the last unit of each supply makes the same contribution to the potency of the assortment. In applying this principle to a household assortment, the difficulty arises that many of its constituent supplies consist of a single unit. Nevertheless, in a balanced assortment the cost of this unit will have been carefully weighed against other possible uses of the money, in relation to the criteria of the urgency and probability of the anticipated occasions of use.

It has already been suggested that assortments and problems of creating balanced assortments are encountered at various points in the economy and not merely in the household. Retailers, standing next to the consumer in the channels of trade, are especially conscious of the need for balanced assortments. The assortment carried by a retailer does not correspond to the assortment owned by any single household among his customers. The retail assortment is designed to provide a satisfactory range of choice for a class of customers served by his store. However, the same principle applies as to being guided by preparation for future contingencies. In this case the events anticipated with varying degrees of probability are purchases by customers of the store. In some lines of trade, such as groceries, many items are stocked with little risk because of the repeat demands of customers. In other lines, such as style goods, the risks are high, with an increasing premium on good judgment as to what to stock. Perhaps one of the most hazardous lines of retailing is that represented by the bookshop. When a book is expected to be a hit, the publisher is obliged to ration the supply. Unless the retailer gets a good initial supply, he is likely to lose out on many sales. If he overestimates his demand or the publisher has overestimated the salability of the book, the retailer will be left with remainders which are hard to move at any price.

A fundamental issue concerning retail stocks is that of breadth of line versus depth of line. A broad line provides a choice among a wide range of products, many of them having basically different purposes. A broad line may attempt to reflect a way of life or a conception of contemporary life for a particular class of customers. It is no longer possible for even the largest stores to carry all of the types of goods which are offered to consumers. The entire range of goods available to consumers in a given economy might be designated as the "cultural inventory." The goods carried by any one store or purchased by any one consumer necessarily constitute only a selection from this cultural inventory.

There are other types of stores which carry a relatively narrow line, such as linens or photographic supplies, but provide a depth of assortment for the buyer with a special interest in this field. The narrow-line store attempts to give the consumer a more precise fit for particular requirements, while the broad-line store attempts to give him greater scope in satisfying all his requirements. Good retail assortments help to minimize the amount of consumer effort that must be expended in searching for desired items. Shopping is also facilitated through advertising sponsored by both the retailer and the manufacturer. These aspects of marketing will be treated more fully in discussing the evolution of the market transaction. The special problems of the wholesaler in maintaining effective assortments will be discussed in the next section, which deals with the various aspects of sorting which constitute marketing.

SORTING AND THE DEVELOPMENT OF INTERMEDIARIES

An advanced marketing economy is characterized by intermediary sellers who intervene between the original source of supply and the ultimate consumer. These middlemen include retailers and wholesalers and many specialized types of merchants, brokers, and sales agents. The present view is that the number and character of these intermediaries is determined primarily by the requirements of sorting and by the opportunity to effect economies by suitable sorting arrangements. This chapter so far has dealt with the various types of sorting and the characteristic problem of each type. The present section will show their application in the channels of trade in minimizing the various elements of marketing cost. The development of intermediate sorting will be traced from a hypothetical beginning in a primitive society.

Decentralized Exchange. In a primitive culture, most of the goods used within a household are produced by the members of the household. The term "produce" should be interpreted broadly enough here to include not only fabrication but also the collection of natural objects not already in the possession of someone else. At an early stage in the development of economic activities, it is found that some of the needs of a household or a tribe can be met more efficiently by exchange than by production. One family might be more skillful in making pots and another in making baskets. The first might be able to make two pots and the second two baskets faster than either could make one of each. If both families produce a surplus of the article they can make best and then engage in exchange, both may get better-quality goods at lower cost.

This is a very elementary example of the advantage of specialization in production and of the way specialization is promoted through exchange. The purpose here is to show why exchange takes place through intermediaries and to consider the additional advantages which are gained through the development of middlemen and their alignment into marketing channels. To that end, we may picture a slightly more complex exchange economy consisting of five households. Each is producing a surplus of some article used by all five. These articles might be pots, baskets, knives, hoes, and hats. In each case a surplus of four units is produced, and these units are then exchanged with the other households to obtain needed articles. Ten separate exchanges would be required, in accordance with the simple mathematical fact that a pair of households could be chosen in just ten ways from a total of five households.

Centralized Exchange. Now suppose that this pattern of decentralized exchange is replaced by a central market. All come together at an appointed place on the second Thursday in April, each bringing his surplus. This may be a time when they are coming together anyway to celebrate the spring festival of their rain god. The exchange is accomplished with greater convenience by bringing all five traders together at the same time and place, rather than having individuals seek each other out to conclude each transaction.

Only five trips are required instead of ten. Each participant has his surplus in readiness for exchange. This may not always be true in the case of decentralized exchange. When the potmaker visits the basketmaker to offer his wares, there may not be any finished baskets on hand and ready for exchange. Thus, it might require more than ten trips to complete the distribution of goods. In a primitive culture, the goods and the parties to the transaction must be brought together at the same time and place in order that exchange may occur. The example given shows how much more easily this is accomplished through a central market. Here in its most elementary form is the creation of time and place utility, a concept which is generally associated with marketing. Time utility and place utility have held little interest for the general economist but deserve a more intensive analysis from the viewpoint of the marketing economist. That which is accomplished through the central market is a decrease in the cost of creating these utilities. From the marketing viewpoint, nothing has utility unless it is present at the right time and place for use. The process of creating these necessary conditions for utility can be more or less efficient just as much as the process of production.

The Intermediary. The next step in the evolution of exchange is for the market to be operated by an individual who may be called a dealer. The five producers now engage in exchange with the dealer rather than with each other. The basketmaker, for example, trades his surplus to the dealer and receives from him the items he requires to replenish his assortment. He may acquire a pot, a knife, a hoe, and a hat in a single transaction rather than through four separate transactions with the respective producers of these articles. In this way he saves time either to make more baskets or to devote to other pursuits. Possibly he will make six baskets instead of five, and the dealer will retain one basket in payment for his services.

Our simplified model of exchange now embraces what has been called "possession utility" as well as time and place utility. Effort is involved in the act of exchange itself. The dealer has created possession utility by bringing about the transfer of goods from producer to consumer with less effort than would be involved in direct trading. Economic analysis of the factors in price equilibrium generally rests on the assumption that exchange transactions are costless. Marketing analysis directed toward an understanding of trade channels must begin with a recognition of the costs involved in the creation of time, place, and possession utility. It must be emphasized again that it is a highly artificial procedure to distinguish these separate aspects of utility or to regard them as the product of marketing effort. An alternative formulation is to interpret the above example as illustrating the economy in the cost of contact achieved through intermediaries. This is accomplished by reducing the number of transactions involved in creating complete assortments for every household.

The Ratio of Advantage of Intermediary Exchange. The saving might not be very important in the example given of a primitive economy consisting of only five producers. Cutting the number of transactions in half might not make a perceptible increase in productivity, and trading with each other might be valued in itself as a congenial form of social intercourse. The number of transactions necessary to carry out decentralized exchange is $\frac{n(n-1)}{2}$, where n is the number of producers and each makes only one article. Since the number of transactions required is only n if the central market is operated by a dealer, the ratio of advantage is $\frac{n-1}{2}$. Thus, if the number of producers is raised from 5 to 25, the ratio of advantage in favor of an intermediary increases from 2 to 12. With 125 producers the ratio of advantage is 62. The figure 125 is a tiny fraction of the number of articles which must be produced to maintain satisfactory assortments in the hands of all of the consuming units in our complex modern culture. Even at this preliminary level of analysis, the ratio of advantage in favor of intermediary exchange is overwhelming. Exchange arises out of considerations of efficiency in production. Exchange through intermediaries arises out of considerations of efficiency in exchange itself.

Intermediaries can increase the efficiency of exchange even when the producers and consumers under consideration are located in the same compact community. The advantages are greatest when large distances intervene. Place utility takes on new aspects when the potmaker and the basketmaker are hundreds or even thousands of miles apart. When buyer and seller are so far apart, one or the other must take the initiative in closing the gap; one of them must call on the other if they are to negotiate face to face. One side or the other must assume the cost of moving the goods; transportation and communication systems arise to bridge the distance. The railroads and trucking companies are, in effect, new types of specialized intermediaries serving buyer and seller more cheaply than they could serve themselves. It was no less an authority than Alfred Marshall who said that economic progress consists largely in finding better methods for marketing at a distance. The number of intervening marketing agencies tends to go up as distance increases. Many eastern companies who sell directly to wholesalers in other parts of the country sell through manufacturers' agents on the Pacific coast. This type of arrangement was even more common in the past but has been dropped in some instances as communication with the Pacific region has improved. Distance, for the present purpose, is not to be measured in miles but in terms of the time and cost involved in communication and transportation. In this sense there are points 300 miles inland in China which are further away from Shanghai than is San Francisco. Tariffs and the formalities of customs clearance are also a form of distance. As a result, specialized import and export firms in addition to other types of intermediaries commonly enter into foreign trade.

Specialized Intermediaries. Production and consumption may also be separated widely in time. The wheat crop which is harvested in June is destined to be consumed as bread or other foodstuffs over a period of a year or more thereafter. To bridge this gap in time is to create utility for both producer and consumer. One wishes to be paid as soon as the crop is harvested. The other wants bread as needed, without having to maintain a stock of wheat in the meantime. Specialized intermediaries, such as grain elevators and warehouses, enter the picture and help to create time utility through storage. Banks, insurance companies, and other specialized institutions help to minimize the costs and the risks of owning goods in the period between production and consumption. Retailers and wholesalers create time utility simply by holding stocks of goods available to be drawn upon by buyers. Without these facilities the only course open to the buyer would be to place an order with the producer and wait until the article could be produced and delivered. To be able to obtain the article at once instead of waiting is the essence of time utility. Another way of creating time utility is by selling on credit either to consumers or to other types of buyers. Through the installment purchase of an automobile, for example, the consumer is able to begin enjoying the use of the car long before it would be possible for him to pay for it in full. An automobile used partly for business, or other items entering into a further stage of productions, may help to raise the money needed for purchasing the product. Thus the production good in question starts creating value for both the maker and the user without waiting for the time when the user can pay cash for it.

TECHNOLOGICAL DISTANCE AND THE DISCREPANCY OF ASSORTMENTS

Producer and consumer are often a long way apart not only in time and space but also in other ways. A product has very different meanings for its producer and for the ultimate consumer buyer. The consumer judges the product in relation to anticipated patterns of behavior and considers how it will fit in with other products he expects to use. If the product is a mechanical refrigerator, it must fit into the space available for it in his kitchen or pantry and be equipped to utilize the supply of electricity or domestic gas. If the product is a tie, the wearer does not want the color to clash with the colors of his other clothing. The specifications of the ideal product from the consumer viewpoint are determined by use requirements, including the requirement of not detracting from the value in use of other items already in the assortment.

Association of Goods. The goods that a producer has for sale are the expression of his skills and resources. Ideal specifications from his viewpoint would be those which made most effective use of his plant capacity and of the available labor and raw materials. If he makes more than one product, his stock of finished goods may be regarded as an assortment in the sense that it constitutes a supply with diverse characteristics. In some cases the separate items will be quite unrelated from the viewpoint of the uses they serve. They may have nothing in common except that they were produced from the same materials or by similar processes. Two items may be linked even more closely, one being a primary product and the other a by-product. In any case it is a wholly different thing for goods to be found together because of convenience in production as compared to an assortment of goods that are all complementary in use.

The most convenient or constructive association of goods changes at each stage in the flow of merchandise from producer to consumer. This fact has been generalized as the "discrepancy of assortments." Goods are associated for transportation because of physical handling characteristics and common origin and destination. Goods are associated for storage in terms of the length of time they are to be stored and the conditions needed to preserve them. Between the producer's stock of finished goods and the assortment in the hands of the consumer, there may be other stocks or assortments maintained by retailers and wholesalers. The composition of these intermediate stocks is determined by the requirements of the functions performed.

The discrepancy of assortments places severe limitations on vertical integration of marketing agencies. A retail grocer typically relies on different wholesale sources for meat, produce, and packaged groceries. The requirements for storage, handling, and other aspects of the wholesale function are quite different in these three product fields. The retailer may provide the consumer who wants to buy peaches with a choice of fresh, canned, or frozen. Yet the routes by which the three items reached the grocery store would normally be quite different at both the wholesale and the production levels. If it were not for the discrepancy of assortments, marketing channels might be more frequently integrated from top to bottom. Most fundamental of these discrepancies is that between producer stocks and consumer assortments. The product appears in a very different setting at these two levels and may be said to belong to the technology of production at one stage and the technology of use at the other. In addition to distance in time and space, marketing channels serve to bridge the technological gap (which may be regarded as a third form of distance between production and consumption).

Intermediate Sorting. The ultimate in intermediate sorting is seen in the freight classification yard. Trains of cars arrive over various routes. These trains are broken up and recombined according to the routes over which they will depart. Let us assume a simplified case in which five railroads come into the same terminal point. There are five production centers on each line or twenty-five in all. A train coming in over route A consists of one hundred loaded cars. Twenty cars are picked up at each production center on route A, each destined for one of the centers on other lines. The same volume of freight originates on each of the other routes. Each of the production centers ships and receives twenty carloads of freight. Yet, because of re-sorting at the central interchange, the entire movement of five hundred cars is completed by each of the five trains making a round trip over its own line. Note that there are no two cars for which both origin and destination coincide. Great improvements are currently being made in the operation of classification yards through application of automatic controls to this sorting process.

THE ECONOMIES OF INTERMEDIATE SORTING

To summarize the case presented so far, intermediaries arise in the process of exchange because they can increase the efficiency of the process. The justification for the middleman rests on specialized skill in a variety of activities and particularly in various aspects of sorting. The principle of the discrepancy of assortments explains why the successive stages in marketing are so commonly operated as independent agencies. While economists assume for certain purposes that exchange is costless, transactions occupy time and utilize resources in the real world. Intermediary traders are needed in the creation of time, place, and possession utility because transactions can be carried out at lower costs through them than through direct exchange. In our modern economy, the distribution network makes possible specialized mass production on the one hand and the satisfaction of the differentiated tastes of consumers on the other. The terminal warehouses in a seaport perform a similar sorting function. The trucking industry has developed interchange depots for the re-sorting of freight in a manner similar to the classification yard.

Contact. Intermediate sorting brings about economies in the handling of transactions in the physical movement of goods and in the costs of storage and finance. It tends to minimize certain risks but to create others, thus leading to special efforts to control risks or to shift them to others. This discussion will be concerned primarily with the merchant wholesaler, since his operations are the most typical of intermediate sorting among all marketing agencies. His place in the scheme of things is based directly on the inherent advantages of intermediate sorting. He is always potentially in competition with both his suppliers and his customers. Unless he can bring about substantial savings in the cost of contact, they will dispense with his services and deal with each other directly.

The inherent advantage of the intermediate sort can be shown by a simple example. Suppose the case to be taken is that of a limited area in which producers and retailers are in close proximity, so that delivery from factory to store would be readily feasible. Suppose further that there are only ten producers in the industry under investigation and ten retailers distributing their products in the area. The possible advantages of an intermediary are apparent even in this compact market territory. Making use of an intermediary, the requirements of the retailers for a given operating period could be supplied by means of twenty transactions. The wholesaler would make one purchase from each of the ten producers and make one sale to each of the ten retailers. Without the intermediary, one hundred transactions would be required. That is to say that each of the ten manufacturers would have to make a sale to each of the ten retailers. When the wholesaler is dealing with hundreds of suppliers on one side and hundreds of retailers on the other, the economies of the intermediate sort are compounded. Thus, if the producers and retailers involved number one thousand each, direct distribution would require five hundred times as many transactions as distribution through wholesalers, all other things being equal.

Item Flow. The illustration as outlined assumes that all of the customers buy all of the products handled. This condition is desirable but is not always fully realized in wholesaling. The condition tends to hold in some lines of wholesaling, such as drugs and groceries. It is less true in a line such as electrical goods, in which the same wholesaler may handle everything from pole-line hardware, sold to public utilities, to radio tubes, sold to radio dealers. The justification for such a situation sometimes lies in the fact that the wholesaler is serving one or more manufacturers producing very broad lines and selling various products to quite distinct lines of trade. As a general principle, it might be said that products need to have some kinship, either in production or in retailing, to justify throwing them together at the wholesale level. As an extreme example, there would appear to be little occasion for the same wholesaler to handle both drugs and jewelry. Certainly there are very few cases either of suppliers who produce both or of retailers who would be selling both to the consumer. To combine the two lines in wholesaling does not fit into a rational sorting process, since they neither start together nor end together.

A well-balanced wholesale stock would be one in which all of the customers bought a large proportion of the items handled. If some of the items stocked are not purchased regularly by at least an important group of customers, then their presence in the inventory would have to be justified on other grounds. A wholesaler might carry certain items as an accommodation to favored customers who were large purchasers of other items. The extent of activity on products carried in stock is reflected by what may be called "item flow." This figure is obtained by counting the number of times each product is ordered during the year and taking the total for all products. In some wholesale trades, this figure is called "the total number of invoice lines." Item flow tends to vary directly with the number of products, the number of customers, and the frequency with which customers order the products carried. The following equation is an attempt to set up a yardstick which might serve for comparison among various lines of wholesaling:

$$\frac{\text{Item flow}}{\text{Number of suppliers} + \text{number of customers}} = \text{Index of sorting balance}$$

The higher this ratio, the more favorable the situation for a wholesaler acting as an intermediary between producers and retailers. Item flow is really a measure of the individual transactions that might be required if producers and retailers were obliged to deal with each other directly. It might be argued that there would be some exaggeration of the sorting advantage for those cases in which the original supplier sold more than one item. This is offset by the fact that a detailed sorting operation would have to be set up in each of these establishments if the wholesaler were not used. On the other side of the picture is the amount of time and effort that would be expended by suppliers and retailers merely in locating each other if there were no wholesaler. Thus the proposed index probably understates rather than overstates the advantage of the intermediate sort.

The index of sorting balance might be low for one of several reasons. Only a few products might be involved, as in the case of the distribution of passenger automobiles. This would cut down the item flow, which may be regarded as the result of a multiplication in which the number of products is one of the factors. Limitation of the number of products lends itself to direct distribution by the producer. Item flow would similarly be reduced if the second factor were small—namely, the number of customers. A case in point would be that in which the prospective customers were a few large chain or department stores. Limitation of the number of customers lends itself to direct buying by these customers. The third factor in item flow is the frequency of purchase of the average product by the average customer. If this factor is small, it may mean that the proposed wholesaling operation embraces too many products and customers with no relation to each other. This situation would call for breaking the operation down into more specialized units, each selecting its products and customers so that every product is bought by most of its customers. There is, in fact, a constant reshuffling of wholesale units and product-customer combinations in a dynamic economy. It is believed that these changes generally move in the direction of maximizing the index of sorting balance.

Location Pattern. The preceding analysis deals with the fundamental economies of the intermediate sort as a way of accomplishing contact between numerous producers and numerous consumers. These economies would hold whether there was only a single wholesale unit serving the entire United States or a separate warehouse in every community. The second basic problem is to determine the most efficient location pattern for a line of wholesale trade. This may be regarded mathematically as the problem of minimizing the total cost of transportation and handling in the movement of goods from producer to retailer. Movement in large quantities is generally more economical than movement in small quantities. The main outlines of a location pattern for a line of wholesale trade might be worked out by mapping the routes along which bulk movement is feasible for the major part of the goods to be handled by the trade. If transportation charges were the only factor, there might commonly be several stages in which the most economical method of transportation for the quantities involved were utilized at each stage. Offsetting the advantage of multiple stages is the cost of handling in and out of storage space from one vehicle to another at each stage. Thus the point of balance is the one which will minimize the sum of transportation costs and handling costs. The analysis of these cost factors is practical for given wholesale centers or products and is theoretically feasible for an entire wholesale trade serving the United States.

Operations research has been employed in recent years in solving problems of warehouse location. One of the earliest cases reported dealt with the pattern of warehouse location for a distributor of petroleum products in Canada. An ingenious method was employed for dividing the entire geographical area covered into a grid and then developing from the grid the type of matrix employed in linear programming. Variations of these techniques have recently been discussed in the *Journal of Marketing* in connection with a warehousing problem in New England. Both of these cases pertain to branch warehouses owned and operated by a single company. The same principles would apply in selection among independent units such as public warehouses or wholesale merchants. The manufacturer selecting wholesale outlets must employ either business judgment or mathematical analysis in balancing the advantages of car-lot shipments to wholesalers against prompt service of the wholesaler to the retailer.

Storage Capacity. A third basic problem of wholesaling is that of the amount of storage capacity which should be present in a line of wholesale trade. This problem must be considered from two viewpoints, the first of which is the requirement of space for adequate working stocks. The wholesale house should have enough of each item so that there is only a negligible chance of running out before the stock can be replenished. Back orders are costly, and sales are lost by everyone from the retailer on back because of inability to meet consumer demand. A broader approach to the determination of storage requirements rests on an examination of the time lag between production and consumption caused by seasonality and other factors. From this viewpoint the correct capacity in wholesale establishments is the amount which will minimize the total storage requirements of producer, wholesaler, and retailer.

The wholesaler serves a variety of producers and retailers whose seasonal peaks may vary. Thus, storage capacity in wholesale houses, over and above that required for adequate working stocks, can operate to smoothe out the level of space utilization and to moderate peak requirements. Without the wholesaler, each producer and retailer would have to provide for the peak requirements for storage of each product. If the producer sold directly to the retailer, there would be times in which sales were slow and stocks piled up with the producer, and other times when retailers were buying everything they could get and being confronted with peak storage requirements. The presence of an intermediary maintaining ample working stocks in itself tends to regularize the flow and avoid duplication of storage facilities by producers and retailers.

Goods Handling. Finally, there is the problem of the efficient handling of goods within the wholesale warehouse itself. As car-lot shipments are received in a modern warehouse, they are unloaded by mechanical equipment and placed in dead storage. Smaller amounts of each item are transferred as needed to the assembly floor. The activity taking place on the assembly line is a pure example of assorting. To fill a customer's order is to assemble an assortment of goods as specified from the various supplies on the floor. Much thought and engineering skill have been devoted to increasing the efficiency of this sorting operation. Goods are arranged along the assembly line so as to minimize the number of steps required in filling an order. Only minimum working quantities of each item face the assembly line, in order to keep the line as short as possible. Items which are ordered most frequently are kept nearest the shipping dock. Consideration may also be given to the weight of products so that, instead of minimizing steps, the warehouse planner is going somewhat farther and attempting to minimize step-pounds.

Information Handling. The sorting operations of a wholesale warehouse involve the movement of information as well as the movement of goods. In a streamlined modern warehouse, this flow of information is handled by punch cards which pass through mechanical sorters as a means of inventory control and through printing tabulators which produce the invoices mailed to the customers. Continuous improvements are being made through analytical study of this process of moving and sorting information. The handling of goods and the handling of information must be closely geared to each other for either to attain maximum efficiency. Electronic computers and control devices open up new possibilities for data sorting which will bring still further changes in wholesaling. In particular, goods at several locations may enter into a single process of sorting under an integrated network of electrical controls.

Sorting Balance. Each of the separate attempts to promote a type of efficiency through intermediate sorting is an illustration of what would be called "suboptimization" in operations research. That is to say that each is an attempt to find the best answer with respect to one phase of the total operation. In practice, something less than the optimum result might have to be accepted with respect to sorting balance, warehouse location, storage facilities, or internal handling in order to achieve an efficient pattern for the operation as a whole. Many such decisions must rest on business judgment because they transcend the possibilities of any precise method of calculation yet available. A common-sense approach would be to pick the element which represented the greatest potential variability in the total costs of marketing and to deal with it first. Having established an optimum for the most important element, the business planner would then try to get the best result for the other elements, subject to the decisions which had already been made. Another method would be to work out an optimum solution for each element and then consider which of these solutions would suffer least through adaptation to the others.

While the analysis of sorting problems is the key to technical progress, the marketing manager is always obliged to remember that he is dealing with people rather than machines. Thus the problem of obtaining co-operation enters into any decision concerning the right number of distributors. Copeland has pointed out that the number of wholesale distributors for a product should represent a point of balance between two policy considerations. On the one hand, the number should be large enough to give adequate sales coverage of all retail outlets. On the other hand, it should be small enough so that the potential volume for each distributor gives him a real incentive to push the product.

RISKS ASSOCIATED WITH INTERMEDIATE SORTING

It should be clear from the foregoing discussion that intermediate sorting inevitably leads to the development of marketing channels. In addition to cost reduction, these marketing structures also minimize some of the hazards of distribution. The consumer who has guessed wrong about future needs and failed to balance out his assortment correctly can quickly remedy his mistake in any trading center. Usually, he can gain access to the item he needs in a near-by retail store, with only a few hours' delay at the most. The retailer's assortment is in turn backed up by wholesale stocks not far away. Information, as well as goods, is available at each level, eliminating much of the uncertainty about sources of supply which would prevail in the absence of channels.

On the other hand, there are some types of marketing risks which remain and which are introduced into the system through the very fact that goods and information must pass through stages in a channel. As a part of the movement toward more efficient methods in marketing, there are various attempts by marketing agencies to cope with risk. The general strategies for dealing with risk include (1) the shifting of risk, (2) the pooling or hedging of risk, and (3) the elimination of risk through control of the operating situation.

Avoiding Risk by Shifting or Hedging. Attempts to avoid risk by shifting it to others are a common feature of marketing channels.

Retailers demand various guarantees as to salability of a new product. Manufacturers sometimes attempt to load up their distributors with surplus stock when they anticipate a change in the market, either in declining demand or in the advent of new products which will make the old ones obsolete. In the case of some farm products, the nature of government price supports has enabled the distribution trades to avoid marketing risks that were formerly incident to the business.

Hedging marketing risk by offsetting purchase and sale transactions is a traditional feature in the marketing of certain basic commodities. The wholesaler and retailer succeed to some extent in spreading risk over the wide range of products they carry. Violent price fluctuations, product obsolescence, or other marketing hazards are not likely to affect all commodity lines at once.

Eliminating Risk by Control. Of still greater importance in its impact on marketing channels is the attempt to eliminate risk by controlling all the critical factors in an operating situation. The critical factors affecting the operations of one marketing agency often lie outside the immediate domain of its executive management. The behavior of the firm's suppliers or customers may have the deciding influence on the outcome of a marketing program. A large manufacturer faced with the risk of having an expensive promotional program fall flat may undertake to give direction to the efforts of his distributors and dealers. Even though he is convinced that his customers would profit from conforming to the plan, he is not content to assume that they will do so on grounds of rational self-interest. The advantages to the customer have to be pointed out, and he usually needs to be given instructions as to what to do about it. Only when someone in the marketing channel takes responsibility for co-ordination can it be expected that anything more than routine operations will be carried out effectively.

Risks Involved in Control. The initiative in the co-ordination of marketing effort is commonly exercised by a large firm dealing with a number of smaller firms. The large firm has the greater incentive to minimize risk and usually the greater resources for developing an effective plan. The attempt of a large firm to control the actions of small firms is likely to be viewed with suspicion by regulatory agencies, whatever the justification from an operating standpoint. Attempts of a manufacturer to utilize different types of retailers and wholesalers in accordance with the facilities they offer often lead to charges of discrimination. There have no doubt been serious abuses in the past, and legislation such as the Robinson-Patman Act has made sellers more conscious of their responsibilities to the intermediate agencies which serve them. Many firms welcomed this law at the time as an aid in withdrawing from admittedly unsound practices in which they had become involved.

Equally difficult problems as to control and risk arise when co-ordination is attempted by a large buyer. This buyer may be a chain-store organization, a manufacturer buying materials and component parts, or a governmental agency. The buyer sometimes prescribes product standards, production methods, procedures in handling transactions, and even the margin of net profit for the supplier. While many regard these conditions as onerous, quite a few accept them as the price of security. Actually, such complete reliance on a single large customer does not eliminate risk so much as transforming its character. There is still the risk of being cut off for unsatisfactory performance. There is also the risk that the volume of sales of the large buyer—and hence his purchases—will decline, and that the small supplier has meanwhile lost the flexibility needed in adjusting to changing markets.

SYMBOLIC LOGIC AND THE ANALYSIS OF SORTING

Since sorting has its qualitative as well as quantitative aspects, its strict theoretical analysis will require something beyond the quantitative tools of mathematics. The term "theory" has been used in a less formal sense in this book, being intended to make a more immediate contribution to an improved perspective for marketing practice. The purpose of this section is to explore briefly the possibilities for developing a formal theory of sorting as applied to marketing processes. The formal theory should be consistent with the treatment of allocation by economic theorists, but should embrace all four aspects of sorting. To begin with, it might concentrate on the qualitative aspects of sorting, which have largely been neglected by economics.

Formal Theory. Symbolic logic and related fields such as set theory and Boolean algebra would appear to offer the best place to start. Structural problems such as the design of electrical circuits have been solved by such methods. Set theory is the foundation of topology, which deals with aspects of space such as connectedness which are not concerned with distance or measure. Topology in turn has been used by Lewin and others in exploring the motivational and problem-solving aspects of human behavior. The concept of closure in set theory is somewhat analogous to the way the concept is applied in this book to operating systems and the assortments of goods.

Symbolic logic, like other branches of mathematics, is essentially nothing more than a method for manipulating symbols. The marketing theorist who considers its application should not expect too much from it. Logic in itself will not enrich his conceptual grasp, but it can be useful in the step-by-step testing and extension of a conceptual scheme. The very attempt to define marketing concepts precisely enough to permit logical treatment should lead to greater understanding. Once meanings have been defined for the symbols to be used, logical analysis is a means of exploring the relations between the concepts for which they stand.

The technique for the construction of formal theories has been explained and exemplified by Woodger. It starts with the acceptance of the symbols and the rules of inference which are the basis of logic. The logical symbols represent a few simple English words such as "and," "or not," and expressions such as "if, then" and "if and only if." The next step is to decide on the additional primitives or basic ideas to be represented in the system. These primitives represent various entities or relationships which pertain to the particular subject matter. Thus Woodger, in developing a formal theory of biology, introduced a sign for "cell." He also used the sign P to represent the relationship "part of" and the sign T to represent the relationship "antecedent in time."

Application in Marketing. In developing a formal theory of marketing, one might first define the various kinds of collections which have been mentioned in this book—namely, conglomerations, supplies, and assortments. Each new term would be defined in relation to other terms whenever possible. Thus a necessary condition for a collection to be an assortment is that it contain two or more supplies. This is not a sufficient condition and would not distinguish an assortment which has some degree of potency from the standpoint of the individual or group possessing it. The theory would therefore be obliged to devise some means of indicating that a collection possessed potency. This might be accomplished by such a simple method as identifying it in relation to its possessors. Thus the notion Ai might stand for the assortment of goods in the possession of the household i. Assuming that the actual assortment might be depleted at any given time, a bar could be placed in this fashion, $\bar{A}i$, to designate the assortment that the household$_i$ was attempting to maintain. The use of two bars, $\bar{\bar{A}}_i$, could be taken to represent the ideal assortment which would make the household feel reasonably secure in relation to the contingencies presently foreseen. By means of these symbols, a fairly precise meaning could be given to an increase in the potency of an assortment. Also the items which the household is most likely to acquire could be designated as the complement in $\bar{\bar{A}}_i$ of A_i. The items most likely to be bought immediately would be represented by the complement in $\bar{A}_i$ of A_i. Extensions of this terminology could relate household assortment to the cultural inventory or to retail store stocks. Some simple examples of the use of such logical statements about sorting and about marketing will appear in Chapter IX.

The formal theory would require some symbols pertaining to exchange. For instance, there might be a sign to indicate that two items were exchangeable for each other in the sense that both assortments affected would be as potent or more potent than before the exchange. A rather natural choice for this symbol would be like this: $\simeq$. This is one of the signs of the Zodiac and is called Libra, or the balance, thus suggesting that the entities on either side of the sign in some sense have equal weight. The resemblance to the equals sign is obvious. Exchangeability would be what is called in logic "an equivalence relationship" and would have the qualities of being reflexive, transitive, and symmetrical. This discussion is only intended to illustrate the process of building up a logical vocabulary and analytical framework suitable for a formal theory of marketing.

SELECTED REFERENCES

ZIPF, GEORGE K. *Human Behavior and the Principle of Least Effort.* Cambridge, Mass.: Addison-Wesley Press, 1949.

SHOVE, G. F. "The Representative Firm and Increasing Returns," *Economic Journal,* March, 1930, pp. 94–116.

CRAIG, DAVID R., and GABLER, WERNER. "The Competitive Struggle for Market Control," in *Marketing in Our American Economy.* Vol. 209 of *The Annals of the American Academy of Political and Social Science.* Philadelphia: American Academy of Political and Social Science, May, 1940.

HOVDE, HOWARD T. (special ed.). "Wholesaling in Our American Economy," in *Journal of Marketing,* supplementary issue, September, 1949; Vol. XIV, No. 2, pp. 84–107.

TARSKI, ALFRED. *Introduction to Logic.* New York: Oxford University Press, 1946.

The book by George Zipf interprets a number of phenomena in terms of the matching of tools against jobs to be done. Zipf was originally a linguist but here tries to show the application of his principle of least effort to economic activity.

The earliest treatment of sorting as an economic function is apparently in the cited article by Shove. He recognized the problem of heterogeneity on both the demand side and the supply side of the market.

Craig and Gabler employed the concept of discrepancy of assortments to explain the development of marketing channels. The present author first presented his own views concerning the function of sorting and applied them to the economics of wholesaling in the volume cited, edited by Hovde.

This chapter has suggested that symbolic logic may provide the means for a mathematical treatment of sorting and related processes. The book by Tarski is a simple introduction to the subject.

Chapter VIII

ALLOCATION AND MARKET VALUES

Exchange can be interpreted as a dual process of allocation, with both buyers and sellers attempting to utilize their resources to best advantage. Out of all of these allocations affecting a product comes a consensus of judgments concerning its market value.

Marginal analysis is applicable to many aspects of economic allocation. Development of these methods has attempted to meet and overcome a series of obstacles in the use of the marginal principle. Some of these developments are discussed, and examples are given of applications to various types of management problems.

The second half of the chapter adopts a problem approach to price policy. The problems considered are divided among those in which management makes a passive adjustment to market changes and those in which it takes the initiative in aggressive marketing programs. The concept of an integrating price structure is presented as a means for attaining effective market prices.

MARGINAL ANALYSIS AND ALLOCATION

The preceding chapter began with a discussion of four aspects of the general process of sorting. Two of these are of relatively minor importance for the present discussion, while the other two are of major importance. Sorting out a conglomeration into more homogeneous supplies is an essential step in many types of marketing but is of purely technical significance. The same thing may be said for accumulation, by which small supplies of a particular material or type of good are brought together to form a larger supply.

The types of sorting with genuine significance for economic and marketing theory are assorting and allocation. The primary emphasis in the last chapter was on assorting or the building-up of assortments. From one viewpoint the whole economic process which takes place through the market can be interpreted as the creation and replenishment of assortments. Goods of various types are brought together into an assortment to serve the needs of an organized behavior system.

Goods in use derive their value from the way in which they fit in with other goods to form an assortment adequate to meet all the occasions of use facing the group which holds possession of the assortment. The statement that consumption is the end and aim of all economic activity might be rephrased to say that the ultimate objective is to create or maintain assortments of goods in the hands of households. The household as an operating system draws upon supplies of various types which are either present in its own assortment or in the inventories of conveniently located retailers. Similarly, every business firm participating in marketing maintains an inventory or assortment to sustain its operations and to enable it to produce a surplus of one kind or another. The point is obvious for retailers and wholesalers where the assortments are subclasses of the goods entering into the assortments of consumers in the market areas which these retailers and wholesalers are serving. In the case of the manufacturer the assortment consists of equipment, raw materials, and the finished goods inventory which he maintains for the purpose of serving his customers.

It is also possible to interpret the flow of economic activity in terms of allocation, which is the type of sorting most directly opposed to the building-up of assortments. Allocation is the breaking-down of a homogeneous supply. Economic theory has devoted much more attention to allocation than to assorting. Marketing theory cannot afford to ignore either of these fundamental processes. The marketing specialist should make use of the tested tools of economic analysis. Economic analysis bears a close association with what has sometimes been called the fundamental economic postulate. This postulate is that economic activity consists in allocating scarce resources so as to obtain the optimum result in terms of ends desired by the individual or the firm. The investigation of the process of allocation is fundamental to an understanding of market values. Thus, this line of analysis becomes part of an adequate marketing perspective, particularly with respect to the determination of prices and the solution of problems of pricing policy.

The Principle of Marginality. The basic procedure of the economist can be designated as marginal analysis, although it takes diverse forms varying with the kind of allocation which is under consideration. The principle of marginality common to all these situations starts with an individual in possession of scarce resources and confronted with the problem of making a rational use of them in relation to his objectives. The scarce resources may be the individual's own physical labor, raw materials out of which he will fashion some product, or money with which he will buy what he needs in the market. Marginal considerations help to determine the amount of resources to be allocated to a given purpose. There is a gradual decline in the amount of value or satisfaction which can be anticipated from each additional unit. Marginal returns finally diminish to a point beyond which it is not rational to allocate further units. The additional return is not worth the extra effort or the using-up of further raw materials which could be devoted to other purposes or conserved to meet some future occasion.

In most practical situations there are two or more different purposes for which resources may be used, and the principle of marginality guides the allocation of resources to these various uses. The principle of marginality is sometimes stated as allocating resources among two or more uses, so that the last units allocated to each use will produce the same return. Thus the household purchasing agent, in choosing among two or more types of goods, is presumed to allocate money to each type of good so as to derive the same amount of satisfaction from the last dollar expended for each good. Similarly, an individual living by his own efforts in an isolated environment might distribute his efforts among his various requirements in order to produce a balanced assortment of goods. According to the principle of marginality, the last unit of each supply in his assortment should have the same utility for him as the last unit in every other supply.

It will be noted that the application of the principle of marginality assumes that there is homogeneity in the supply to be allocated. Homogeneity is essential, at least in the sense that a common unit of measurement is required for allocation. In the examples that have been given, the supply to be allocated is consumer income in one case and human effort in another. In the management of a business enterprise an executive must assign resources of diverse character to various operating units or to separate functions to be performed. Operating units within the organization are rival claimants for man power, raw materials, and many types of equipment. In allocating these resources, he can think in terms of physical units so long as he is dealing with a single homogeneous supply. When he is confronted with allocation problems which transcend these limits, he is obliged to make use of some common yardstick such as money value. To this extent he is compelled to ignore structure and differentiation, even though they may enter in fundamental ways into the actual techniques of operation. Some economists would hold that any decision which could not be made in terms of marginal principles would lie in the field of technology rather than economics. The somewhat broader perspective required for marketing practice is obliged to take account of qualitative differences. Progress should lie in the direction of recognizing that allocation and assorting are alternative concepts for interpreting the same flow of economic processes.

The Process of Dual Allocation.   Prices emerge in the market place from the dual process of allocation carried on simultaneously by the buyer and the seller. The buyer is engaged in allocating available funds to obtain goods of the kind and quantity needed to maintain his assortment. The seller is engaged in allocating goods to those markets or those buyers from which he can expect the greatest return. Frequently, he may have to sell to several markets in order to dispose of his output. In that case, he will presumably distribute his output among markets, so that he will receive the same marginal return from the last unit sold in each market. Returns from various markets are influenced both by demand and by cost factors. One market may absorb only half as many units at the going price as another market. Similarly, the cost of serving two markets may be different. Thus the seller may allocate a larger part of his supply to the market which he can serve most economically. In fact, he may continue to allocate units to the market which he can serve more cheaply until he reaches the point where the price he can realize for additional units gives him no greater return than he can obtain in the next most costly market.

The process of dual allocation taking place in the market results in a balancing of judgments among many buyers and sellers. The economic theory of equilibrium price rests on the assumption that a large number of buyers and sellers are present in the market. Each buyer has many alternative sources for the same product as well as a variety of products to which he can allocate his funds. Each seller has the choice of many individual buyers and geographical markets to which he can allocate his goods in trying to obtain the maximum return. The assumption of large numbers is held to be essential to the continuous and effective adjustment of supply and demand. When supply increases, the movement of additional units to market is facilitated if they are held by a large number of sellers. When demand increases, the competitive bids of numerous buyers can stimulate producers to build up supplies to meet the demand.

The application of the marginal principle takes place in a parallel way on the two sides of the market. There is a difference in terminology and in detailed application. As it applies to decisions by the buyer, marginality is expressed in the concept of marginal utility. The seller, on the other hand, is motivated by considerations of marginal productivity in creating goods for the market and by considerations of marginal revenue in allocating his output to various buyers in the market. The rational basis of allocation is identical for all of these situations. Thus, market values as expressed in prices can truly be said to rest on a consensus of many judgments expressed through the process of dual allocation.

Marginal Utility and Marginal Costs. The classical version of marginal analysis reached its culmination in the writings of Alfred Marshall. The willingness of consumers to allocate income to a commodity at various prices was expressed by a demand curve. This curve reflected the fact that some units of the product could be sold at relatively high prices but that progressively lower prices were needed to move additional units. The market price of the product tended to be determined by what consumers would pay for the marginal unit—in other words, the last unit of the product which sellers wished to sell.

The willingness of producers to allocate resources to a product was expressed by a cost curve. This curve was first developed for industries obviously affected by diminishing returns. In agriculture, for example, it was evident that such costs as labor on a per-unit basis would rise as less and less fertile land was called into cultivation. Costs per unit would be low for a moderate supply and would rise steadily thereafter. The return even to the producers with the lowest costs would tend to be determined by the price which would barely enable the highest-cost producer to stay in business.

The process of dual allocation in accordance with this model tended to result in an equilibrium price in which marginal utility for consumers was equated with marginal revenue for suppliers. If consumer demand were greater than the supply which would be attracted at the going price, the price would tend to rise until it would just cover the cost of the last unit needed to meet effective demand. If supply became greater than existing demand, prices would decrease until the final unit of supply offered had just sufficient utility to attract a buyer. Similar adjustments, but in the reverse direction, would occur if demand or supply should decline.

Despite the essential validity of this analysis, it ran into some theoretical and practical difficulties. The subsequent history of economic analysis has sought in various ways to overcome these difficulties of marginal analysis. A primary difficulty on the demand side is the problem of measuring marginal utility. One way of meeting this obstacle will be discussed shortly. Two major obstacles on the supply side have been the falling cost curve and the factor of overhead costs. These two aspects of cost do not bring about fatal flaws in marginal analysis but, oddly enough, tend to offset each other, at least to the extent that both are associated with mass-production industry.

By a falling cost curve the economist means one which portrays a situation in which costs per unit go down instead of up as output increases. Faced with increasing returns rather than decreasing returns, the economist has no assurance that the cost curve will intersect the demand curve and thus indicate a determinate point of equilibrium. It was feared that the only path toward equilibrium under increasing returns was for one supplier to gobble up all the others and then to set a price which would maximize monopoly profits.

The fundamental significance of overhead costs was first established by J. M. Clark. The central idea of his work on the subject can be simply stated, but only a limited consideration of its impact is pertinent in this context. The idea is that to the extent that costs are regarded as overhead and not dependent on the number of units sold, it is impossible to know at the beginning of an operating period what sales and hence costs per unit will turn out to be at the end of the period. How can the businessman apply marginal considerations if he must set his price at a time when he has only imperfect knowledge either of the number of units he can sell or of what it will cost him to produce these units? The uncertainty arising from the factor of overhead costs creates the problem, but it also contains the germ of a solution.

The businessman will normally take any available steps to reduce uncertainty. His attempts to reduce uncertainty with respect to sales volume are expressed primarily through selling and advertising. The greater the risk that his production costs will be high because of the overhead cost of unused capacity, the greater his incentive to make outlays for selling costs to obtain sales at or near capacity. If one of several large competitors increases his selling costs, others will generally be obliged to follow. Thus, when production costs and marketing costs are added together, the cost curve is usually rising rather than falling, whatever the economies of mass production. The principle of diminishing returns is restored, and marginal analysis is fully applicable.

Clark was among the first to perceive that the sales function has genuine economic significance, as well as taking the lead in posing the problem of overhead costs. Selling creates value, according to one of his early essays, by increasing consumer knowledge and hence market adjustment. Competition in the performance of this function can result in a sharply rising cost curve, and differential advantage in this direction does not necessarily belong to the competitor with the lowest production costs. In a typical mass-production industry the cost curve may first be falling because of economies of scale but may later rise because of competitive selling costs.

INDIFFERENCE CURVES AND SUBSTITUTABILITY

There are some difficulties confronting marginal analysis on the demand side paralleling those which have just been considered with respect to costs. One is the problem of measuring utility as it is assumed to influence consumer choice. Pareto suggested a device for analyzing consumer preference which has been further developed by Hicks, Allen, and others. In this approach the classic demand curve is replaced by a family of indifference curves. The assumption that utility can be quantified is discarded, and greater flexibility and convenience are attained for some types of economic analysis.

Indifference curves reflect a pattern of preferences as among the various commodities available. They are charted on co-ordinate paper in the same way as demand curves, but the axes no longer represent price and quantity for the same product. Instead, units of one product are charted on one axis and units of another product on the other. In the real world the consumer must choose among a multitude of commodities, but the principles involved can be illustrated graphically by the two-commodity case.

Indifference curves are concave upward or convex toward the point of origin. Each point on the curve represents a combination of the two products which is equally acceptable to the buyer. It is assumed that he will give up some part of his supply of one product for additional units of the other. The positions near the center of the curve represent a degree of balance between moderate amounts of each product. Moving along the curve away from the center, it will take increasing amounts of product B to compensate for the loss of each unit of A or vice versa. This feature of an indifference curve would appear to be a true reflection of consumer psychology in buying goods to build or replenish an assortment.

The guiding principle expressed through indifference curves is not marginal utility but marginal substitutability. One product is accepted as a substitute for the other but at different ratios at different positions on the curve. Price in this analysis becomes the ratio at which one product can be exchanged for the other in the market. On the chart it is represented by a diagonal line tangent to the indifference curve. There are many subtleties of analysis growing out of these developments which it is not appropriate to review here. Our primary interest is in the application of marginal substitutability to practical marketing problems. Often a marketing analysis can appropriately take the form of a study of substitution between one product and those which are directly competitive with it. Such an analysis is directed toward determining the rate at which substitution will take place under various assumed conditions.

To complete the parallel to the more traditional type of demand and supply curves, reference should be made to a type of curve which has been utilized in economics and linear programming. This is a way of charting all possible production programs for a plant capable of producing two products. It has been called the "transformation curve," but might equally well be called the "feasibility curve." Again the two axes represent quantities of each product, and the points on the curve represent feasible combinations of the products in total output. This time the curve is convex upward. This means that moving away from the center there is a declining rate in the increased production of product A at the expense of product B, or vice versa. The principle of marginal substitutability is applicable to outputs as well as to inputs. Feasibility curves together with indifference curves provide a model of economic action in a two-commodity world with many practical applications.

The effectiveness of marginal principles has sometimes been called in question because of imperfect divisibility of products and because of the inertia of the established habits on both sides of the market. Neither of these considerations represents a serious limitation for the mass of buyers and sellers as compared to the actions of single individuals. It is true that a single consumer, for example, must buy a complete refrigerator or automobile on any given occasion and is not free to consider all of the many possibilities which could be plotted on an indifference curve, such as one and a half refrigerators and three quarters of an automobile. The principle of marginality applies nevertheless to decisions made by consumers as a whole. They may expand their purchases of automobiles at the expense of refrigerators, or vice versa, because of price advantage in one direction or the other. Consumers vary as to the urgency of their needs for automobiles and refrigerators. While each individually might make an either-or choice, the total effect is to give the proper weight to the need for each product in relation to its relative price. Similarly, it is not essential that all buyers and sellers react with complete flexibility in order that the market should adjust to changes in supply and demand. It is only necessary that some substantial group of consumers should respond to an increased supply or that an adequate segment of production facilities should be mobilized to take care of increases in demand. Thus the principle of marginality is a sound expression of balancing forces at work in the market as a whole, even though the application may not always be clear in analyzing the actions of a single individual.

SOME APPLICATIONS OF MARGINAL ANALYSIS

Consultants in marketing and economics have demonstrated on many occasions that marginal analysis can contribute to executive judgment both in problems of price policy and in problems involving efficiency of operations. Several examples from the experience of a single consulting firm will serve to illustrate the point. It is not contended that all such problems of management can be solved in this way, but only that marginal analysis is a powerful tool with wide application to marketing problems.

One case in which marginal analysis was used for price determination was in setting up a schedule of rates for a public utility selling natural gas both to domestic and to industrial consumers. Empirical demand curves were established and used in conjunction with information concerning the cost structure at various levels of operation. It was necessary, of course, to construct separate demand curves for each type of use, since the factors affecting demand were so different among the various uses. Gas for industrial interruptible use differs from gas for domestic use. Even within the latter field, there is an important difference in consumer reaction to price for gas for household heating as compared to other domestic uses.

In order to develop an empirical demand curve for gas for domestic use in a single city, figures were compiled and analyzed from a number of cities. The main purpose in analyzing these data was to determine how consumers reacted at various price levels and thus to find a way of picking the most favorable price in the city under consideration. Obviously, it was not possible to make direct comparisons between price and quantity consumed from one city to another. Several important statistical corrections had to be made to put the data on a comparable basis. One correction was based on the differences in the prices of fuel oil in the various cities, on the assumption that this is the fuel with which gas competes most directly. Another correction had to be made for what the gas industry calls the "degree of saturation." This is the percentage of all families with gas connections in their homes who are using gas for heating. Obviously, in a city in which this percentage already approached 100 per cent, there would be little room for increasing the number using gas for heating in response to a price reduction.

The utility business is in a preferred position for the use of empirical demand curves, since data on price and quantities consumed are generally available because of public-utility regulations. The possibilities for using similar methods vary greatly among various product groups. Information is relatively plentiful on basic raw materials and particularly on agricultural commodities. The situation is not so favorable for manufacturers' products; and comparisons from one product to another, even in the same class, become difficult because of distinctive product features. The development of empirical demand curves is often possible, however, by various survey and experimental methods. Consumers can be asked to compare or rank various products according to value, including the one for which a price is to be determined. Sometimes a price problem can be solved without going all the way to the development of a demand curve. It may be enough to find out how conscious the consumer is of price or price differences in a given field. It is also possible by such methods to make reliable judgments as to how large a price reduction would have to be in order to get a response from the consumer. While some of these methods stop short of enabling the market analyst to determine an optimum price, they at least enable him to approach it more closely by successive approximations.

Use of Surveys and Experiments. A number of pricing problems have been satisfactorily resolved by such survey and experimental methods, which take their departure from the principle of marginality even when they do not apply it in a precise and formal way. This type of approach has been applied to such varied products as canned foods, synthetic detergents, and fountain pens. In the case of competition among differentiated products the analytical objective can sometimes be narrowed down to setting a price on the specific feature of the product which is presumed to give it some superiority over other products in its group. This technique has been applied to both consumer and industrial products. Survey procedures are devised to determine what it costs to perform the same functions by existing methods and to place some measure on the added satisfactions which might be derived through the improved product. Such a survey takes the direct form of a study in substitution leading to a conclusion concerning the rate at which the new product can be expected to replace existing products under various assumptions as to price and promotional expenditures.

Marginal analysis has also been applied to a variety of problems concerned with productivity in marketing. Such studies usually start from some measure of a potential market, area by area. A multiple-correlation analysis is then undertaken to measure the relative effect of various kinds of selling effort on the relation between actual sales and potential sales. One such study was made for a pharmaceutical manufacturer whose sales efforts consisted primarily of promotional calls by detail men. The study showed very wide differences in the value of calls on druggists, physicians, and hospitals. Management was able to change the allocation of effort with very favorable results. In another case, management was concerned about the value of its newspaper advertising as compared to other media. The study revealed a great disparity in results for this particular situation from advertising placed in newspapers in small towns and in metropolitan areas. These differences in marginal returns led to a shift away from newspapers in one type of city and from other advertising media into newspapers in the other type of city. The distribution of sales and advertising effort by city size is a basic problem for many marketing organizations. There are marked differences as to the advertising media available and also as to the cost per thousand of people reached.

There may be factors in the historical development of a company which cause it to be relatively strong in one type of market or another. Something more than executive hunch is needed in determining where the emphasis should be in the next stage of expansion. One recent study utilizing multiple correlation indicated that the company could profitably make a substantial addition to its sales force in metropolitan areas of over one million population. In fact, the marginal increment per man in these larger markets was calculated to be greater than the average sales per man in smaller markets. The same study showed just the reverse situation with respect to media advertising and indicated the need for strengthening the advertising program in the smaller markets. One way of stating the position of this company with respect to its marketing effort is that it had been concentrating its advertising in major cities but not backing up the advertising with sufficient man power to gain the full advantage of the demand created.

Many marketing organizations now have the established practice of testing various forms of marketing effort on a small scale before applying them on a nation-wide basis. When well planned, such tests can give a valid picture of the marginal increment to sales or profits which can be expected from various marketing programs. If they are not well done, these procedures can be very misleading. To employ them successfully requires a knowledge of scientific principles of experimental design on the one hand and of market conditions on the other. A market test may fail because it is based on a faulty sample or because it makes no provision for experimental controls. It can also fail on account of an inadequate knowledge of buying habits, leading to a misinterpretation of sales figures during the test period.

The classical work on the development of empirical demand curves is *The Theory and Measurement of Demand,* by Henry Shultz. This study was entirely concerned with agricultural products. Demand equations were developed, showing the quantity of the products which could be expected to move at various prices. On this basis, it was possible to calculate other relationships such as the degree of elasticity of demand or the rate at which quantities purchased increased as price declined.

A similar basic reference on the development of empirical cost curves is *Cost Behavior and Price Policy,* by Joel Dean. Statistical correlation techniques were employed to show variations in cost at various levels of output. These studies were made for several types of manufacturing plants and also for marketing organizations such as chain stores. The development of empirical cost curves is obviously more difficult with respect to marketing costs than production costs. Nevertheless, some of the studies already mentioned represent some progress in plotting the functional relationships between advertising or total sales effort on the one hand and sales volume on the other.

The techniques of distribution cost analysis developed over the past thirty years represent a still more intensive search for functional relationships for the guidance of marketing operations. The established techniques make it possible to give separate consideration to the cost of handling different types of goods or selling various classes of customers. Progress in this field has been impeded in part by the tremendous volume of numerical computation which such studies require. The application of distribution cost analysis should now be accelerated through the use of electronic computers. The relation to marginal analysis appears at a number of points. Distribution cost analysis has enabled management to get rid of unprofitable business in several ways. It has been found that orders below a certain size will not repay the cost of a sales call; as a result, minimum order limits have been established. Some firms, such as wholesalers, have found that they were covering too much territory and have been able to increase their profits by dropping all customers beyond an economical service radius. Other limitations designed to implement marginal considerations have been adopted pertaining to minimum rates of turnover, percentages of gross profit, and the number of varieties or styles of goods offered in particular classifications.

BEYOND MARGINAL ANALYSIS

Valuable as marginal analysis can be in dealing with management problems, it falls short with respect to certain crucial decisions facing the executive. The difficulty is that in any operating situation it is possible to approach the margin in a variety of ways. Thus, certain key decisions must sometimes be made on other grounds before marginal analysis can be applied. At first thought, it might appear that approaching the margin on various fronts would present no basic stumbling block for marginal analysis. Since the principle of marginality pertains to allocation, it might seem to offer a guidepost for allocating resources or effort in all possible directions. That is certainly true, for example, if the executive is considering the allocation of sales effort to trade territories or to classes of customers. A more fundamental issue is at stake, however, in speaking of the possibility of approaching the margin in a variety of ways.

Some routes toward marginal returns are qualitatively and functionally different, and are to some extent in direct conflict with each other. Most fundamentally, the question often faces the executive as to whether he should attempt to expand his sales and profits by reducing prices or by increasing costs. No adequate way exists of laying out these two considerations on the same continuous scale. In fact, if prices are reduced substantially, this obviously tends to limit the gross revenues out of which increases in either production or marketing costs could be made. Similarly, if there are major commitments for improving the product or expanding an advertising campaign, it may not be possible simultaneously to make a reduction in selling price. Economic analysis, of course, assumes an intensive study of costs and potential returns before making decisions on price and promotion policy. Nevertheless, for any differentiated product, no such figures could completely determine the kind of marketing program to be followed. That is to say that, given any set of figures concerning demand and costs, several different programs might be equally consistent with these facts.

One program might call for trying to get the widest possible market immediately by manufacturing a simplified and low-priced version of the particular product. Another program might be directed toward a more selective and higher income market, at least in the early stages, and envision a higher level of production and marketing costs consistent with this sales objective. The choice between these two programs would depend on the judgment of executives concerning a number of factors beyond those ordinarily visualized by marginal analysis. Most fundamentally, there would be his point of view as to how markets develop for his type of products and how consumers judge values in this type of purchase.

Choice between Marketing Programs. The choice between types of marketing programs is so critical that there are numerous instances in which a continuation of a product or even the survival of a company has depended on making the right choice. Sometimes a company continues to behave as if its market were for a high-quality and high-priced product long after basic market conditions have changed. A well-known manufacturer of hats almost went out of business several years ago by pursuing such a policy. The conclusion was finally reached that men in general wanted to buy more hats but were not willing to put so much into a single hat as formerly. The company cut its average price in two and modified its production costs accordingly. The new models, which would have been considered inferior products by the company's earlier standards, were readily accepted by consumers; and the sales trend began to move steadily upward once more.

An example on the other side is that of a large chain drug organization which brought out aspirin to sell at a price about half that of the established advertised brands. The product languished on the shelves for several years and was about to be withdrawn. An investigation then disclosed the fact that consumers did not have confidence in the product as being genuine aspirin with so great a price differential. The president of the company concluded that it would take millions of dollars to convince his customers that this aspirin was as good as any other. Yet, he did not see how he could obtain that kind of advertising funds from the revenue generated at the very low prices at which the product was offered. The resulting policy decision was to move the price up to where it was about 80 per cent rather than 50 per cent of the price of other brands. At this figure there was some money available for advertising, and consumers were now willing to believe that it was a good product. As a result of this change of policy, the product very quickly established itself as a large-volume item on a profitable basis. While there was no change in the character of the product in this particular instance, there have been others where a company had to make product improvements in order to gain a foothold, even though the price was correspondingly increased.

Basic decisions about price and product are necessarily made at the very beginning of a marketing program, but it can never be assumed that the issue is settled once and for all. The same kind of choice in varying degree is always potentially present as long as a product is on the market. Management is often obliged to weigh the advantages of price appeal on the one hand as compared to quality and advertising pressure on the other. In the type of investigation that might be undertaken to assist management with such decisions, marginal analysis can be helpful but is frequently not decisive.

The Form of a Price Cut. The application of marginal analysis under conditions of pure competition is presumed to leave little choice to the individual as to the manner in which he will approach the margin. In practice, there is often a considerable area of discretion, leaving room for strategic choices of the type which has just been discussed. In the examples given, the choice to be made was between price reduction and cost increases. To a lesser degree, there are choices to be made with respect to price alone or with respect to costs alone which are beyond the practical reach of marginal analysis.

This type of difficulty in pricing is present particularly in the development of a price structure. A manufacturer generally wants his product to move to consumers at the lowest possible average price. It does not always appear that the best way to achieve this result is by setting the lowest possible price in sales to trade buyers. In fact, manufacturers sometimes make drastic cuts in their own prices with no perceptible or at least immediate effect on the prices paid by consumers. There are various ways of cutting prices which may be very different in their ultimate effect. A discriminatory cut in favor of the large buyer will frequently induce him to cut prices sharply to obtain a differential advantage. Others are then obliged to meet his selling prices to neutralize this competitive advantage. Such devices are still utilized, even though somewhat restricted under the Robinson-Patman Act.

Some price cuts to trade buyers are really regarded as allowances for marketing services which the buyer is expected to perform. The effect of such an allowance is quite different if the seller takes appropriate steps to make sure that he gets the desired service. If he does, it may help to build volume at the retail level and thus encourage retailers eventually to accept a narrower margin on the product. If he does not, the reduction may simply go to swell the profits of the trade buyer and have no effect on price paid or volume purchased by consumers.

The price reduction would have the same impact on the manufacturer's gross margin per unit, regardless of its form; but its effect on consumers, and hence on the manufacturer's revenues, could vary from plan to plan. Marginal analysis applies to elements which can somehow be reduced to a common quantitative basis. When this cannot be done, there are key management decisions which lie beyond the reach of the marginal approach.

The Form of Cost Increases. On the cost side the most obvious distinction is between production costs and marketing costs. When management decides that it will seek incremental sales and profits through raising its costs, it still has the problem of which type of expenditure will be most effective. In one case it might spend additional money on improving the product. In another case the increased expenditure might be directed toward increasing consumer knowledge or acceptance of the product. Frequently, the best strategy might lie in a combination of the two. In some degree, production costs and marketing costs are substitutable for each other in their effect on the revenues of the seller. In other respects they are complementary, and each type of effort is necessary to give full effect to the other. A fabricated product, no matter how excellent, cannot be expected to sell itself. A sales campaign, no matter how clever, cannot win a permanent place in the market for an inferior product. In practice, it may still be possible to apply marginal analysis in a modified way, using the previously existing program as a bench mark. Consideration may then be given to the incremental effect of product improvement on the one hand or intensified promotion on the other, considering them as alternative departures from the basic program.

The same considerations apply in viewing marketing expenditures alone. Various forms of effort may be regarded either as substitutes or as complements for each other. Advertising in some situations may largely eliminate the need for personal salesmen. In other cases, advertising would be powerless alone but gives effective support to direct selling effort. The best rule for the analyst is to be prepared to use marginal analysis at the level and to the degree that appears feasible. Marketing decisions cannot always await the construction of an elegant and comprehensive model, but the range of application of more precise analytical tools is constantly being extended.

FURTHER GUIDEPOSTS FOR PRICING DECISIONS

Business price making involves decisions about several related dimensions of value and not about the level of price alone. It is not simply a matter of determining what the traffic will bear on the basis of the unique position enjoyed by the seller. Rather, the seller is obliged to design a "package" or "bundle" of utilities which he will offer to customers. This package design must be specified in terms of various optional features of the product, the services which will be offered along with the product, the price at which it will move into marketing channels, and sometimes the prices governing the movement of the product at each stage within the channel. The sponsor of a fabricated product tries to find some rational basis for determining what this package will contain, and all elements of the design must remain fluid until the final decision is made. This is quite a different situation from that of the raw materials producer, who may have less freedom of choice either about his product or about his price.

One road toward rationality in designing and offering a bundle of utilities is to select the various components in such a way as to maximize gross sales revenue. In other words, the best package from the seller's viewpoint is the most salable one as measured by gross revenue. When the package is first offered, there is no certainty that it will yield a profit. The one sure thing is that it cannot be profitable if it does not sell. Once the product is on the market, other considerations arise which favor the continuance of maximum sales volume as a major policy goal. To strive for anything less is to face serious hazards as to the maintenance or improvement of market position and hence with respect to long-run profits. It is true that profits also depend on costs; but the businessman is faced with the task of designing a cost structure, and that offers choices and perplexities of its own. He may decide to let the product have time to establish itself through word-of-mouth advertising, meanwhile economizing on sales costs. On the other hand, he may choose to gamble on a comprehensive promotional campaign in the hope of getting his production costs down more rapidly.

Because of the complexities of decision making, both with respect to maximizing sales and minimizing costs, it is believed that management is obliged in most cases to attack each problem separately. That is to say that the first problem is to maximize sales and the second problem is to minimize or control costs so as to earn a profit on sales. This view is not difficult to reconcile with the economic doctrine that the businessman will price his products so as to maximize net revenue. The prevailing conception of the cost structure for manufactured products is such that there is no difference between maximizing gross revenue and maximizing net revenue so far as price is concerned.

Assuming that all costs of the seller were regarded as sunk or overhead costs, at the time a product is offered for sale, then obviously he wants to get the greatest possible number of dollars in return for the products he gives up. To maximize his gross return would mean that he will maximize net return. More typically, the seller regards only a part of his costs as overhead or fixed costs. Other costs, including selling costs, are usually budgeted as a stated percentage of the expected volume of sales. If the expected sales are realized, the margin between sales and variable costs will cover overhead and leave a satisfactory profit. Under this formula net profit would again be maximized at the price which would yield maximum gross revenue.

As the seller is confronted with decisions affecting price, these decisions are likely to be related to profits in one of two ways. In one case, he may be trying to improve his present profit showing if it is below the target level. In the other case, he may be endeavoring to maintain current profits if they are running at a satisfactory rate. There are several elements which may enter into his choice of a target rate of profits. The notion that there is a fair or just return for a given type of operation is by no means lacking in business thinking. Without resort to ethical considerations, it may often be possible to explain the target rate of short-run profits as the highest rate which is deemed to be consistent with other goals such as survival, growth, and long-run earnings.

The businessman seldom has occasion to take action all at once on all of the factors which might affect his operating results. Most of the time he operates on the assumption that the majority of these factors are in working adjustment with the market, and that he can focus attention on those factors which seem likely to get out of line. Sometimes price is the factor which is subject to market pressure, and corrective adjustment must be taken to defend the competitive position of the firm. At less frequent intervals the businessman may initiate broad programs of action in which a number of factors, including price, must be considered. In the latter case the businessman may be regarded as launching an offensive and weighing in advance every feature of the projected campaign.

Whether he takes an offensive or defensive position, the seller is faced with the necessity for one decision after another; and many of these decisions may pertain to price. If he can improve his position or at least maintain it, he is doing all that he can do in the majority of instances to maximize his long-run profits. Each time he is called upon to make a decision, he utilizes certain facts, or his understanding of the facts, in making a judgment. Marketing research and economic analysis can reduce the risk that these judgments will be in error.

Some typical situations calling for pricing decisions will be discussed. The six cases covered are all of major importance but do not constitute an exhaustive list. The discussion of these situations is meant to illustrate the principle of defining the pricing problem as narrowly as possible in each instance in order to determine how analysis can be helpful in improving the quality of business judgments. Three of these situations will be typical cases in which the businessman has to respond to developments in the market. The other three cases will be instances in which the businessman takes the initiative in an effort to control or modify market factors.

PROBLEMS OF RESPONSE TO THE MARKET

Response to Increased Volume. One of the situations in a growing economy which poses pricing problems to the businessman is an increase in his sales volume. Very often the first requirement is to determine whether this increase in sales reflects a genuine growth in demand. If a product is sold through trade channels, there are various things which can happen to create an exaggerated appearance of increased demand. For example, a product may be broadening its coverage in trade channels; and a part of the increased sales volume may represent purchases by retailers and wholesalers for the purpose of setting up minimum stocks. When the businessman enjoys an increase in sales, he must make a judgment as to whether he is merely filling pipe lines or whether a new level of demand will presently be established.

More generally, there is a variety of conditions affecting changes in trade inventories which complicate short-range analysis of demand. The largest marketing information service in the world provides manufacturers with periodical reports on how their products are moving to the consumer in drug and grocery stores. This movement is often quite different from the trend in the manufacturer's own sales. Another complication encountered in periods of shortage is the possibility of consumer hoarding. One product which was already enjoying rapid growth in sales showed a distinct upturn at the time of the outbreak of war in Korea. A special study was conducted which eliminated consumer hoarding as a significant factor in this situation. Investigation was essential to establish this fact, since hoarding was going on with respect to some related products.

Having satisfied himself as to the basic trend in demand, the businessman may be confronted with decisions as to price and related factors. His present volume may already be up to his productive capacity, but the evidence may or may not indicate a potential future volume beyond present capacity. The pricing problem will be formulated differently according to this judgment concerning the future outlook. If volume is expected to stabilize at the level of present capacity, there will be a strong tendency to leave price unchanged. In many cases, this will be the choice that involves the least risk. There may be a strong incentive to reduce prices, however, if there is some indication that new competition is about to enter the field. The amount of the reduction will rest on the balancing of the two considerations of a price low enough to keep competition out and high enough to return a profit.

In some instances an outlook for continued capacity production may provide an incentive for increasing prices. This is most likely to be true when there is an inflationary pressure on productive capacity in the entire economy. This situation is likely to be complicated by other factors affecting price decisions, such as increasing cost of labor and raw materials. The characteristic growth situation in the American economy is that in which the businessman is confident that future demand will outrun present capacity and undertakes to meet this eventuality. Analysis is likely to start with a determination of how large an addition should be made to capacity and when the new capacity can be ready to supply demand. Related decisions will be made with respect to cost of production and with respect to price.

In a given industry, there are likely to be several different ways of organizing production, each appropriate to a particular scale of operation. Some of these methods may require a large investment in new equipment. Whether such an investment will be made will depend on judgments as to how far the present upward trend in demand can be projected. It will also depend on judgments as to the lower prices which may be feasible at a new scale of operation and as to the extent to which new markets may be opened up by lower prices. Having reached conclusions on these complex and difficult issues, the businessman may finally be confronted with a decision as to action concerning prices in the immediate future. There may be a strong incentive to reduce prices immediately to the level which will become economically feasible at the proposed new scale of operation. This decision would rest on the judgment that an immediate price decrease will accelerate the increase in demand and thus reduce the length of time in which the new plant might have to be operated at less than capacity. The timing of this price reduction would usually be related to the timing of plant completion, although it might precede it by some months.

Response to Increased Competition. The businessman's response to increased competition is a situation of some special interest to the economist. This is one of the cases in which the process of making price decisions may bear some direct resemblance to the marginal analysis whereby the incremental revenue from the last unit sold is equated to the incremental costs of this unit. Without such competitive pressure and with sales maintained at a comfortable volume, the businessman may be fairly selective as to the orders accepted. There are various ways of eliminating less desirable orders, such as distributing only through specified trade channels or setting minimum quantities below which an order will not be accepted. A relatively high price may also be used as a deliberate means of limiting volume to that which can be produced with present plant capacity.

As competition increases, the businessman may make less use of all of these methods of order selection. If competition obtains some of the more desirable business, the original supplier of a product may be obliged to maintain his volume by accepting marginal business. With competition of moderate intensity, he may extend his business in these new directions to about the point indicated by marginal analysis. When competition becomes more severe, such marginal considerations will be cast aside; and prices will be cut still further. The businessman may then attempt to hold the line at the break-even or no-profit point on his whole volume, rather than at the point at which he makes no profit on the marginal unit.

Even this line of defense will be abandoned when business conditions are generally adverse. A business may be operated at a loss for months or even years on end, usually with the hope that conditions will be restored which will permit profitable operations again. This is a common manifestation of the fact that the expectation of long-run profits, rather than short-run profits, controls such decisions as continuing to operate rather than liquidating.

A differentiated product tends to go through a competitive history with several distinguishable stages. At first, it may stand alone as the only product which will meet certain specialized use requirements. At least for some limited classes of users, there is no immediate competition. Their choice in the market is whether to buy this product or not, rather than choosing between it and other products. A product in this position is referred to as a "specialty" in trade terminology.

As demand for a product grows, competitors are likely to enter the field with products which closely simulate the original product or which deviate from it in minor features. The degree of interchangeability among these products is a factor sometimes entering into price decisions. The product may eventually be classed as a staple and thus be responsive to price changes on any product in the interchangeable group. There are other classes of products subject to a never-ending struggle to maintain distinctiveness. That is a phase of aggressive marketing strategy which will be discussed later.

An apparent increase in competition is often reviewed very critically before deciding on a price response. It may turn out to be a passing phase rather than a permanent shift. The new entrant may not be able to continue to supply the product at his initial price and may either raise the price or withdraw from the field. On the other hand, the newcomer may be so strong and aggressive as to discourage any hope of meeting his prices. In many actual cases the original suppliers decide to ignore cut-price competition and to divide among them the business that is still available at the old level.

Response to Increased Direct Costs. Questions as to price changes are often posed by increases in direct costs, such as for labor and materials. These cost factors are frequently tied directly to price in the processes of bargaining and negotiation. This tendency is particularly marked at times when the government is attempting to maintain ceilings on both wages and prices. To the extent that the government permits a piercing of wage ceilings, it is likely to be confronted with a demand from industry for a corresponding increase in prices. Cost and price, as in a recent steel-industry case, become the subject of a complicated three-way negotiation involving labor, industry, and the public. In trying to find a workable solution, the government may contend that industry can absorb the wage increase with no decrease in its dollar profits. To some critics, industry may seem unreasonable in insisting on retaining its target rate of profits. Industry counters this argument by emphasizing its need for funds for dividends and expansion of plant capacity. Actually, there is no escape from bargaining as a primary procedure in such instances because of the nature of the criteria written into the legislation itself. The fact that industry insists on consideration of its full costs under these circumstances is not inconsistent with a different approach to price making in a free market.

The manufacturer has a stake in the price at which his product is sold to the consumer, since that price affects the number of units he can sell. The total spread between this price and manufacturing costs is divided in some proportion between the manufacturer and his wholesalers and retailers. The margins allowed to wholesalers and retailers usually bear some relation to normal or average costs of doing business. The manufacturer may allow more than average costs if he desires some special services from the distributing trades. He may allow less than average costs if his product is so well established that the trade has to handle it anyway. Sometimes the question of whether a particular function will be performed by the manufacturer or an intermediary is subject to negotiation, and appropriate differences in price are discussed in terms of the cost of the function. Not only individual bargaining but processes resembling collective bargaining go on in distribution channels, and cost factors are generally present in these price-making discussions.

The businessman who is subject to cost changes which are beyond his control is severely limited in applying any formula for maximizing net earnings over costs. The assumption that he is exploiting the market is unreal if he would quickly be obliged to pass on the increase in margin in higher labor costs. In fact, the traditional assumption that the businessman is attempting to maximize short-run profits does not carry the analyst very far in evaluating the individual's response to market changes. The businessman is confronted with market pressures which require him to make a choice among a limited number of possibilities. He attempts to emerge from each crisis in turn with the best result that is available to him under the circumstances.

PRICING PROBLEMS OF THE MARKETING INITIATIVE

Introduction of a New Product.   One of the most interesting pricing situations is that which arises when a new product is introduced to the market. Price research, formal or informal, has been widely used in such situations. It is scarcely possible to set up a formal demand curve at this stage, since there is no effective demand for the new product as such. Obviously, consumers cannot demand the specified product until they know that it exists and know what its specific use properties are. With respect to a product which has not yet been marketed, the appropriate concept is that of latent demand. That is to say that it is possible to make some analytical judgments in advance concerning the demand that will develop after the product is placed on the market. At this stage, it would be futile to attempt to relate demand to price. If the marketing program is successful, the number of units sold will expand over a period of time in relation to the success of promotional programs.

Meanwhile, the businessman is forced to make some decision about the initial offering price if he is to market the product at all. One approach to an initial price is what has been called the "full-cost principle." That means offering the new product at a price which will cover all estimated costs plus a target rate of net earnings. This basis for pricing a new product seems to be employed in the great majority of cases.

The initial price may be subject to many adjustments thereafter as information is accumulated, both about actual costs and about effective demand. In a sense, it may be said that offering any new product at a stated price is inevitably a step in informal pricing research. Sometimes the experimental character of the introductory program is recognized more explicitly, restricting it to a limited market area. The virtue of any initial price may be judged partly on the basis of whether it is a good instrument of pricing research. It may not be possible to sell a new product at a price representing full cost plus the target rate of earnings, but it is obviously worth-while to find out.

A price fairly high up in the possible price range is likely to be an advantageous starting point. It will be easier to reduce it later on than to raise it. Also, it may be taken as a crude bench mark by which the businessman can distinguish the core of his market from the fringe. In other words, it provides valuable marketing information if he can identify the consumers who are willing and able to pay for the product on a full-cost basis. He needs to know not merely how many such consumers there are, but what kind of people they are. This information will assist him in orienting his promotional efforts.

Various rule-of-thumb methods have been used for estimating the cost of growth and including it as one of the elements in a full-cost pricing formula. The consumers who make up the core of the market because of their greater-than-average need for the product or special interest in it are in effect asked to pay for the cost of remolding the habits of other consumers, so that the product can attain a volume adequate for mass production. The core consumers benefit along with others from the lower prices which usually go into effect when mass production is achieved.

Studies partaking of the nature of psychological experiments have been able to throw light on price as a separate factor in the marketing of a new product. These studies lead to the development of what might be called a "relative revenue curve." That is to say that it is possible to chart the percentage of potential consumers who will enter the market at each price, all other things being equal. Assuming that costs are completely flexible, the manufacturer is then able to develop product specifications which will permit him to offer a product at the most favorable point along this relative revenue curve. That is the point which will produce the greatest volume of sales from any given number of potential buyers. The absolute size of the market will depend on additional factors such as the amount spent for promotion.

Accelerating the Expansion of Demand.   Once the use of a new product has been established, compelling reasons may develop for endeavoring to accelerate the growth of demand. One consideration is to establish its base as broadly as possible before competition can enter the field. A somewhat more fundamental view is to consider that every fabricated product has a limited life span and will probably eventually be replaced by something better. The sponsor of such a product needs to maximize its sales during the limited period that constitutes its best opportunity. That is his only assurance of achieving a satisfactory return on product research and the other costs of introducing a new product. It is also a safeguard with respect to the investment in plant, which may be only partially recoverable before the original product becomes obsolete. These comments refer to the type of situation in which the product is highly distinctive and is not directly interchangeable with a well-defined group of competitive products. In such a case the businessman can plan for full exploitation of the product over its presumptive life cycle, subject only to the hazard of technical developments which may render the product obsolete even more quickly.

Much of what has been said with respect to the introduction of a new product is pertinent here also. There is a greater opportunity to determine the effectiveness of price reduction as a means for increasing demand once the initial job of consumer education has been accomplished. Price reduction can move large quantities of a product in the middle stages of its history if the conception of its value has been well implanted in the early stages. Issues arise during this period as to the balance between promotion and price appeal as inducements to buy. The extent to which prices can be reduced is limited by judgments as to the amount of revenue which must be retained to finance promotional campaigns. Certain minimum marketing costs are inherent in selling the product at all. Further discretionary sales expenditures are related to the goals which have been set up as to growth in demand. If the businessman aspires to have his product show a very rapid rate of growth, he can only achieve it by taking business away from other suppliers. Beyond a certain level of volume, his selling costs will increase rapidly for any incremental additions to volume.

These considerations are vital in any effort to assist the businessman in pricing his products for rapid market expansion. Further complications arise if the product is in a relatively competitive field. Marked increase in volume may be available only through an increase in market share for the business initiating the marketing program.

Competitors are also closely watching their shares of the market and may be ready to take immediate counteraction if their position in the market is affected.

That is one reason why the drive for an increased market share so often takes the form of product improvements. This is an indirect price reduction, involving giving more for the same money rather than offering a product of the same specifications for less money. This type of attack is more difficult to counter by direct price reduction. It may give the businessman who has taken the initiative the advantage over a considerable period of time while his competitors are putting into effect appropriate answers.

There are other elements of strategy in seeking an increased market share which may be considered by the price analyst. Widening a price differential is sometimes a matter of good timing. One way to accomplish it is by simply refraining from making an increase when prices are generally on the way up. Success in establishing a differential in this way is more likely than in leading the downward movement in a period of price decline.

Installing Cost-Control Measures. For the businessman who is assured of a stable or upward trend in demand for his products, one way to increase his profits is by cutting costs. Some roads to cost reduction do not involve pricing but only internal efficiency. The elimination of waste depends on the development of measures of productivity and the evaluation of each segment of a sales operation against these yardsticks. Advertising, in particular, has come in for increasingly critical scrutiny. Improved means are constantly being devised for assuring adequate return from advertising dollars. This type of cost-control program is related to pricing because it may be an essential preliminary to price reduction. Having achieved economies that would mean greater return at the old prices, the businessman has the option of retaining these earnings or passing the savings along to stimulate sales.

There are other types of cost-control measures which are more directly related to price. These measures pertain especially to procedures in purchasing materials and supplies. Whatever a purchaser undertakes in the way of a concerted program to bring down the cost of his purchases obviously reacts on the pricing practices of the sellers who are supplying him. Large distributing organizations have gone quite far with such practices. In many instances, they have helped a small supplier to reorganize his entire operation, so that he could supply a needed product at a lower cost and still make a profit. There have been some refreshing examples of labor unions which have assisted employers in reducing production cost per unit, so that these plants might continue to compete and thus provide employment. Leaders among industrial purchasing agents have sponsored a general program for standardizing and simplifying staple products. Sometimes a product has special features which are no longer needed or which are not needed for the application the purchaser wishes to make. These features can possibly be eliminated without affecting the usefulness of a product, while achieving a lower price level to the advantage of both buyer and seller.

Distribution cost analysis has been applied in many instances to the problems of firms selling a multiple-product line. The accounting methods which have been used in allocating joint costs have been well justified in terms of the results obtained. The steps taken on the basis of these results have generally been those of dropping the items shown to be unprofitable and concentrating more sales attention on profitable items. An alternative use of the cost and profit results would be to make adjustments in price to equalize the net profit obtained on each item. There are some obvious limits to this procedure, since certain items may have to be carried as a service to trade customers even though cost analysis shows consistent losses. Important results for business might be obtained by a combination of cost and price analysis.

Integrating Price Structures. From the viewpoint of marketing action or the orderly flow of goods and services, a system of prices is needed which will maintain this flow. Such prices might be called effective or integrating prices. No judgment is implied as to profit accruing to either buyer or seller or as to the desirability of the transactions in the long run. Effective prices are simply those which cause transactions to happen or which do not interfere with a flow of transactions already established.

In special cases the effective price would correspond to the theoretical concept of an equilibrium price. There are various requirements for equilibrium which are not essential for prices to be effective. These include strict standardization of accompanying services. Competitive equilibrium also assumes that there are so many buyers and sellers that no individual can have a perceptible influence on either side of the market. Every buyer is a free agent engaged in the purchase of goods rather than acting as a purveyor of distribution services to suppliers. All buyers have ready access to the numerous sellers in the market, and vice versa.

The remarkable fact is that there are very few market situations in which all of these conditions apply, and yet goods continue to move in ever-increasing volume. The conditions for effective prices, therefore, are obviously much less stringent than the conditions for competitive equilibrium prices. Yet it by no means follows that any system of prices will serve as well as any other. The marketing executive is faced with major problems in determining effective prices, even though these are not the theoretical problems of price equilibrium.

An effective system of prices can usually be described as a price structure. It not only states a price level but defines price relationships between various grades or models, between geographic areas, or between stages in the distribution process, and takes account of the costs of various services which may or may not accompany the sale of the product. An integrating price structure is one which brings all of these elements together in a workable pattern. This conception is different from equilibrium price, defined as a level which equates a large and homogeneous supply with a large and homogeneous demand. An integrating price structure must bring together many diverse and heterogeneous elements and place them in effective relationship to each other.

An integrating price structure generally represents a compromise between the factors of power and operating efficiency in marketing channels. A system of prices will not move goods if one or more participants in the channel refuses to co-operate on the stated terms. The marketing process will just as surely grind to a halt if the bundle of utilities delivered to the ultimate consumer is unacceptable. The marketing channel may have to become more efficient in order to satisfy consumers, but the rewards to the various participants must be adequate for the channel to hold together as an operating system.

For any given type of product a normal price structure tends to develop which is effective in promoting the flow of goods. A study made some years ago showed that there were at least one hundred and forty different ways of making prices on electrical products alone. Fuse plugs were priced in an entirely different way from electric motors or transmission cable. Each price structure took account of the major variables in the distribution of the given product. An offer of one of these products in terms of the price structure customarily used for one of the others would be completely unintelligible to buyers. Transmission cable, for example, is priced on the basis of a whole series of engineering formulas; and building the price is almost as technical a task as building the cable itself. Fuse plugs have a price structure allowing discounts for wholesalers and dealers, while motors are one of the few products with a price structure built up with multipliers which are the reverse of discounts. All of these differences arise out of differences in the product or in the methods of marketing it. Similarly, the price structure for fertilizers gives central emphasis to the cost of transportation, while the cost of freight is ignored or absorbed by the manufacturer on such high-priced packaged goods as perfumes.

Among the other aspects of structure are those involving the geographical spread of the market or of the producers. Special methods of pricing are characteristic of heavy commodities for which freight is a large percentage of delivered cost. Whatever the commodity, the price structure includes a statement concerning the method and terms of delivery and whether transportation charges are to be borne by the buyer or seller. There are also elements of price structure which pertain to the successive steps in the distribution channel, the stage at which various services are to be performed, and both normal discounts and special allowances pertaining to each stage. In many fields a price quotation is not regarded as complete unless the price structure contains a suggested price at which the product will sell to the consumer as well as the trade prices at each level behind the consumer.

Product, price, and service all enter into the design of a bundle of utilities to be offered the consumer. Yet price, in a sense, is the final element which closes the deal and makes due allowances for all of the other elements. Price is the most flexible of these dimensions and can be varied to offset any changes in the pattern of product specifications and services. Designing a price structure which integrates all these elements and allows the goods to move is a major step in the marketing of any product. The structure is sometimes built up by taking production cost as a base and estimating all the additional costs and payments for services which will be required in reaching the consumer. To an increasing extent, price structures are created by the reverse process of starting with an optimum combination of product, price, and service at the consumer level and moving backward to calculate what is going to be required at each level to produce the final result. Sometimes a product may have to be radically redesigned or new methods of production developed in order to meet the end requirement. In any case a price structure actually is a structure relating price, product, and services and setting up differentials in recognition of the major variables entering into transactions.

There are some principles of design which can be generalized from good practice in the building of price structures. One is to conform to the customs and terminology of the trade unless there are specific reasons for departing from it. A normal structure has emerged out of the balancing of many judgments to reach something which is generally acceptable to both buyer and seller. When the price structure represents a distinct departure from existing practice, it should be regarded as only one element of many which must all work harmoniously in a marketing plan. If a price structure, for example, allows more than the average compensation to the retailer, it should be accompanied by an effective drive to call this fact to his attention and make him aware of what the seller expects in return. If some customary feature is omitted from the price structure, a case must be made as to why this is justifiable in the nature of the product or of the marketing plan.

An initial price structure should always be designed with the probable course of future developments in mind. Thus, introducing a product at an abnormally low price to get a foothold may be a mistake if it is expected to compete with products of the highest quality later on. An initial arrangement with one channel of trade can become the source of serious conflict and difficulties when the product is offered to other channels. It is quite customary to offer specialty products at a higher price in the beginning than the seller expects to obtain later on. At the high price, it may attract just those customers who need or want it most and who are likely to have a successful experience in using it. Their patronage may give the seller the encouragement and the means to expand his volume. With greater volume of production, he may be able to expand his sales by reducing price. There are related problems in the selection of product features. The product may be so highly specialized as to satisfy very precisely the needs of a limited number of customers. If so, it will probably have to remain a high-priced product as compared to a design which will meet the needs of many more people once they are ready for it.

SELECTED REFERENCES

NOURSE, EDWIN G. *Price Making in a Democracy.* Washington, D.C.: Brookings Institution, 1944.

SAMUELSON, PAUL A. *Foundations of Economic Analysis.* Cambridge, Mass.: Harvard University Press, 1947.

ALLEN, R. D. G. *Mathematical Analysis for Economists.* London: Macmillan & Co., 1938.

HICKS, J. R. *Value and Capital.* Oxford: Clarendon Press, 1939.

AMERICAN ECONOMIC ASSOCIATION. *Survey of Contemporary Economics.* Vol. 1, Philadelphia: Blakiston Co., 1948. Vol. 2, Homewood, Ill.: Richard D. Irwin, Inc., 1952.

The literature concerning marginal analysis is enormous, since this is a central theme of economic theory. There is also an expanding contemporary literature dealing with specific pricing problems from the businessman's viewpoint or discussing price-making procedures as observed in marketing operations. The book by Nourse is one example of the latter type of treatment.

Samuelson discusses the general concept of maximizing behavior and shows that allocation is analytically identical in many different types of situations. Allen has participated in the refinement and application of indifference-curve analysis. The book cited is a convenient handbook of mathematical techniques useful in economics and marketing. The special importance of the book by Hicks in the present connection resides partly in his analysis of complementary as compared with competitive economic relations.

Some of the essays in the survey volumes sponsored by the American Economic Association provide a summary of contemporary thinking on marginal analysis and market values.

Chapter IX

ADVERTISING AND THE CAPACITY
TO CONSUME

Markets can be expanded either by reducing price so that consumers can buy more or by taking steps to make consumers want more. These general strategies for market expansion correspond with the two aspects of complete competition pertaining to price and product. On the product side the attempt to make consumers want more can take the form of product changes or innovations. It can also take the form of advertising and promotional campaigns designed to change consumer attitudes toward a product or even to change their preferred patterns of behavior. The potential response of the market to promotion might be designated as "plasticity," just as the response of the market to price competition is called "elasticity of demand."

There are a number of theories about advertising and the way it works. Some of these theories hold that advertising makes its impact by conveying information, but most recognize that persuasion is an essential part of its function. There are many variations in the persuasive theory of advertising with respect to the relative importance of rational and irrational appeals and the interaction of information and persuasion. The present view suggests that the consumer should be approached primarily as a problem solver who must first be convinced that he has a problem and then that the product offered will facilitate a solution. Attempts to expand the market through promotion raise questions as to limitations on the capacity to consume. A consumption choice, as compared to a buying choice, arises from these limitations rather than from the scarcity of goods. The term "hedonomics" is suggested for a projected empirical science of consumption choice.

THE MARKETABILITY OF PRODUCTS

The thousands of products now on the market are only a part of those which have been introduced to the public on the assumption that they would sell. All of the products which have been introduced are only a small selection among the infinite array of possible products. The domain of all possible products might be represented as a space of many dimensions, each dimension representing varying degrees of some product quality. Any location in this product space would represent some combination of properties or features. All the products which have ever been designed or marketed would account for only a scattered distribution of points within this infinite product space. Many of these points would occur in clusters, indicating that there were relatively minor differences among them. Clusters would grow up because of a recognition of consumer demand for a given combination of properties. The dispersion within the cluster would reflect the attempts of various producers to outguess each other in providing just the right combination of qualities. Some of the points would be almost identical because of outright imitation of a successful producer by others.

Also in the product space there would be great open regions, indicating that no products with certain combinations of properties had ever been designed. Some of these regions would be empty because of general conviction that no consumer would desire a product of this character. Other empty regions would reflect gaps in the necessary technology for producing a product, even though it might be of high utility once it was made available. In still other cases a region in product space might remain empty because the possible users were so few as to offer no commercial incentive to make and market a product of that character.

It would be a great convenience to product designers, of course, if the potential desires of each consumer might be represented by a point in such a product space. Given a cluster of such points, the designer would have the task of making the most of this concentration of demand. He would initially like to find the one point or combination of qualities which could gain acceptance from the greatest number of people. It would greatly simplify his production problem if he had to make only one model. Yet, any point he chose would be relatively close to some of the points representing individual requirements and would leave the others further away. One designer might introduce several models initially in the attempt to forestall competition. Another might prefer to take his chances with a single model in the hope of establishing a large volume and making his position relatively secure by low price. He might decide that some of the desirable features were regarded as essential by only a few of his prospects and save costs by eliminating these features.

The launching of products designed for a given use always invokes a choice among attributes, including price, and hence a choice among risks. Assuming some variation in individual tastes and requirements, any decision concerning the package to be offered will mean that some prospective users are relatively well pleased, while others must accept an approximation of their needs or go without. In some product fields, of course, the prospective users may not have been able to define their needs before some product is available for inspection. Once they have seen it or tried it, some may find it unsatisfactory in certain respects and begin to demand the same basic product with certain changes or adjustments. Some may find it satisfactory but not worth the initial price to them. It may be possible to reach some of these prospects later when they have reassessed the utility of the product or when an increased volume of production has made it possible to reduce the price.

Both product research and market research might be regarded as explorations of product space, looking for the clusters of points representing concentrations of consumer requirements and determining how they are to be exploited. Once a product is on the market, active selling and advertising are methods used in searching for customers. Before the product has been designed, there is the more intangible and difficult search for groups of consumers who desire or could be made to desire a particular product. This search is an exploration of both technological and psychological matters. An attempt is being made to probe the latent desires of consumers while experimental designs are being created and tested in the laboratory. At one time there was greater reliance on intuition, and both the product idea and the estimate of consumer demand might stem from an individual's hunch. More orderly procedures are common today, and in some firms there is a fully co-ordinated program of technical and market research directed toward continuing exploration of new products or new features.

The process of establishing new products in the market will now be viewed from the standpoint of both the producer and the consumer. On the one side is the business firm attempting to expand its sales through product-line diversification. On the other side is the consuming unit reacting to a proposed innovation and deciding its fate by either accepting it into a pattern of life or refusing it. The businessman turns to innovation as one solution for his problems of growth and profits. The innovation will stand or fall according to whether it can help solve the problems of consumers.

Classification of Goods.   From its earliest beginnings, there has been a need in marketing theory to develop classifications of goods which would help to account for differences in the way they are marketed and in their characteristic price structures. Copeland of Harvard and Parlin of the Curtis Publishing Company appear to share the credit for the first use of the three-way classification into convenience, shopping, and specialty goods. An improvement was introduced by Leo Aspinwall in his use of the terms "red," "orange," and "yellow" goods. He tried to arrange all goods on a scale according to their marketing characteristics and used colors from the spectrum to indicate position on the scale. Cigarettes are an illustration of what he means by red goods and pianos of yellow goods. His system has been criticized because it represents an attempt to combine seven different factors and raises serious questions as to whether these factors are truly independent and how they are to be weighted. For the present author the one factor which seems fundamental to the classification is frequency of sale. Red, orange, and yellow essentially represent points on the scale from high frequency to low frequency.

Another concept due to Aspinwall is what he calls his "parallel systems theory." He contends that there are certain channels and methods of distribution which pertain to the movement of red goods and sharply contrasting methods which pertain to yellow goods. One virtue of this conceptual framework is that it can allow for the fact that an article may be yellow when it is first introduced and gradually move across the marketing spectrum through orange until it ends up in the red portion of the scale. In other words, a product may change from low frequency to high frequency; and corresponding changes in marketing channels and in the price structure may follow.

The Segmentation of Markets.   This conception of the marketing characteristics of goods is related to the changing opportunities for segmentation in the market. Red goods generally serve large segments and yellow goods smaller segments. High frequency of sale results in part from the fact that a large number of customers are satisfied with the identical product. A time may come in the history of the product when its volume is great enough to encourage the process of differentiating it into several product variations, each of which meets the needs of some smaller segment of the market more precisely than did the original product sold to all segments. Each of these product variations is of relatively low frequency of sales and may go all the way back to the yellow end of Aspinwall's scale. As sales of these separate items pick up, they move again toward the red end. Frequency of sale is affected not only by the number of customers who buy the product, but by the frequency of purchase by the average customer. The latter factor varies greatly by products. A consumer may buy a favorite food as often as once a week but a new automobile only once in several years.

Low frequency of purchase tends to be associated with great durability in the product and with high price per unit. The buyer of an
automobile is buying a means of transportation which will serve him
for a long time. It is a little like buying thousands of bus or trolley rides
in advance. The consumer is buying a large stock of transportation
utility at one time rather than buying one ride at a time. The nature
of the product obliges the consumer to purchase in this way.

For that reason the stock of utilities in the consumer's assortment
represented by durable goods varies much more widely than do other
stocks, such as food products. The consumer is taking a greater risk
in buying durable goods. Since he has to buy a large stock of utility
at one time, he is gambling at the time of purchase that he will not
have a greater need for something else before this stock is exhausted.
He is also taking a greater risk with regard to future prices and the
possibility that the item he has bought will be rendered obsolete by
improved models.

The seller of durable goods adopts policies designed to moderate
some of these risks for his consumers, particularly with respect to price
changes. The price of a durable goods item tends to come down gradually, but does not change so fast as the drop in production costs.
The major part of the fruits of increasing efficiency tends to be passed
on in the form of product improvements. Because of the hazards of
buying durable goods, the market tends to dry up when consumer
income falls off. At this stage in the business cycle the market could
not be restored by price cuts because the consumer does not want to
make commitments so far ahead as is represented by major purchases.
On the other hand, at the peak of prosperity the optimism of the consumer may result in making commitments too far ahead, with a conse-
quent collapse in the market for durable goods.

Factors in Product Diversification.   Another important difference
among products for similar uses is the relative amount of labor content
incorporated in them. There is a general trend toward putting a higher
labor content into the product and cutting down on the amount of
labor required from the user. Thus, cake mix has a higher labor content
than regular flour which the housewife has to mix with other ingredients to make a cake. A ready-made cake has still higher labor
content. Price naturally goes up with the labor content because of
the additional utility for the consumer. Price may also become less
flexible because the product carried to a further stage is usually a more
complex mix of ingredients and of services. Variations in the costs of
these elements tend to offset each other. Thus, regular flour is very

responsive to the price of wheat; but cake mix is much less so, because it contains ingredients such as eggs and shortening with prices which move quite independently of wheat.

In addition to these product characteristics which affect the price structure in various ways, there are problems of reconciling product features among themselves. For example, automobile tires may be constructed so as to place the emphasis on safety, comfort, or style. All of these characteristics are interesting to consumers, but their relative importance varies from one customer to another. The manufacturer must decide on a compromise among these considerations at a given price or else convince consumers that they should pay a high enough price to cover all three to the fullest extent. The compromise does not apply only to the actual physical product, but to relative emphasis in promotion.

The seller is not always able to decide on the features of a product without giving consideration to other products in his line. All of the products in a related group may be regarded as a complex market-offering satisfying a broader segment of demand than any one product. The features of these several products need to be so related as to give the best over-all market coverage. From time to time the firm may give consideration to further diversification of its product line as a means of increasing its total volume. Diversification is to be regarded as one of several alternatives, including more intensive promotion of its present line. Diversification may merely mean added coverage of the same field of use, or it may mean entry into entirely new fields of use. When this is so, the cost of entry and anticipated profit should represent at least as favorable an outlook as would be expected if the firm directed additional effort toward increasing its efficiency or market share in its present field. The costs and profit expectations associated with entry into new fields should be weighed against the costs and expectations associated with expanding the sales of the present line. In the perspective of a well-considered growth plan, diversification of the product line can be regarded as one of the alternatives available for achieving sales and profit objectives.

The process of product-line diversification can be considered in three successive stages, each with a place for research and analysis. First is the need for a clear conception of what the product line as a whole should be like as a result of diversification. Investigation at this broad level is for the purpose of getting a sense of direction and developing a general program and policy. It means determining what places are to be filled in the product line before looking for specific products.

The other two stages are product screening and product introduction. Much time and trouble will be saved in these later stages if policy is firmly established in the beginning.

Restrictions on Product-Line Expansion. In this initial stage the company's long-run goals and objectives should be given primary consideration. What kind of a product line the company wants to have depends on what kind of a company it wants to be. The decision to expand the product line is usually associated with a desire to expand the company's operations, but often much remains to be determined as to the direction of expansion. A new product which is not compatible with the rest of the line is likely to create more problems than it solves. Incompatibility may arise with respect to either the marketing characteristics of a product or its production requirements, or with respect to the capacity and preferences of management itself.

A new product which seems to have promise may sometimes have to be rejected because it is incompatible with the successful sale of the present line. A good example is the case of the drug manufacturer producing prescription specialties; he runs the risk of adverse reactions from physicians or the drug trade if he takes on another type of item. The manufacturer of a prestige product may lose position if he sells a cheaper version of the same product. The product may be one that takes the company into new channels of trade or which confronts it with difficult and unfamiliar marketing problems. A new product might seem attractive because it could readily be produced in the company's existing plant and yet be a dangerous venture because of incompatibility on the marketing side.

Another approach to new product possibilities is to start from the market and add products because they serve end uses similar to those of existing products or because they can be distributed through the same channels of trade. It may turn out that such products are incompatible with present production methods. Superficial consideration might indicate that they would utilize excess capacity. Efficient production may require substantial additions to plant or use of present equipment in a way that conflicts with the production requirements of the existing line. On the whole, starting with the market to fill out a product line is less hazardous than starting with the objective of utilizing excess production capacity. If the sale of a product appears to be assured, management can generally find a way to make it. However, the cost of making it might turn out to be prohibitive; or analysis might disclose barriers related to patents, capital requirements, raw materials, or labor.

For the most part, these broad tests for acceptance or rejection may be regarded as relative rather than absolute. If it has been decided that product diversification is mandatory, the analytical job is to arrange the available opportunities on a scale of relative values. There may be serious obstacles in exploiting even the best opportunity. Whether these obstacles can be overcome depends on the capacity and preferences of management. A program which points toward sweeping changes on either the marketing or the production side may be incompatible with the existing management situation. What started out to be a problem of product-line diversification may become a question of executive man power and organization. In any case, extension of the product line needs to be viewed in the perspective of capacity to sell, capacity to produce, and management's capacity to organize for change.

CONSUMER REACTION TO PRODUCT INNOVATION

The process of innovation in product design, production methods, and economic organization has been discussed by Schumpeter, Barnett, and others. Less attention has been given to the process of acceptance of innovation by consumers. The general problem of how culture patterns change is, of course, a central topic for anthropology. One conclusion of the anthropologist is that any new culture trait available to a group must make its way in terms of fitting into the existing pattern and usually in the face of substantial resistance against any change at all. In marketing, much that is discussed under the general heading of motivation research is actually a study of the whole psychological process by which new products or product variations can gain acceptance by consumers.

The degree of novelty in a so-called "innovation" can vary from an almost imperceptible variation in a product to a startling and unmistakable break with the past. Toothpaste with a new ingredient more effective in whitening teeth would be an example of the first. Firearms when first offered to the American Indian would illustrate the second. An attempt to define innovation will be useful here as a means of identifying the types or degree of change to which the consumer may be asked to react.

The goods presently owned or used by any society or group might be called its "cultural inventory." Assuming a very simple inventory for purposes of illustration, it might be designated by the twenty-four letters $a \ldots x$. Each person in the group would hold an assortment of goods A_i which would constitute a subset of $a \ldots x$. This assortment serves to equip the individual for future action and is related to the principle contingencies he can foresee as requiring action. Each person may be aware of other items in the inventory a . . . x not included in the subset i but acceptable in case of need. The items he already holds plus these known and acceptable items might be given the symbol $\bar{A}_i$ and described as the extended subset. For an item to qualify as part of the cultural inventory $\bar{\bar{A}}_i$ consisting of the items a . . . x, it should be included in the basic assortment of more than one person. To qualify as an accepted innovation, it should represent an addition to a . . . x and not merely an addition to the subset or extended subset of a single individual. Cultural innovation is, on the other hand, the cumulative effect of the psychological reactions of individuals.

Eight different purchase situations will now be specified, some of which move in the direction of innovation. Symbols will be used in an attempt to make these formulations as precise as possible. The sign $\rightarrow$, as used here, may be read "implies that." The first letter in each statement represents the item purchased. Thus the first shorthand statement below means that the purchase of x implies or was brought about by the fact that the stock of x in the subset i was depleted.

OCCASIONS FOR PURCHASE

1. $x \rightarrow x$ depleted (custom or special need)
2. $w \rightarrow x$ palled (variety)
3. $y \rightarrow x$ failed (improved product)
4. $z \rightarrow x$ incomplete (simple complement)
5. $y \rightarrow$ extended subset $\bar{A}_i$ incomplete (preparing for new contingency)
6. $y + z \rightarrow$ extended subset $\bar{A}_i$ incomplete (new contingency requiring complementary products)
7. $y_D \rightarrow y$ is not a member of subsets $_{jkl}$ (desire for distinction)
8. $y_C \rightarrow y$ is a member of subsets $_{jkl}$ (desire for conformity)

The advantage of such formulations is that they provide a sharp contrast between the essential elements of one situation and another. The relation of each occasion of purchase to innovation will now be discussed.

Purchases Involving Innovation. Obviously, the first two occasions are not innovative at all. In the first instance the individual has been using x and replenishes his stock when he runs out of x. In the second case, he gets tired of x, at least temporarily, and replaces it with w, which is already part of the cultural inventory a . . . x. Conceivably, the desire for variety could sometimes help to support a true innovation. One of the borderline cases would be fashion goods. A simple desire for variety as compared to seeking distinction would be better illustrated by a switch from strawberries to peaches or from white potatoes to sweet potatoes.

The next four items in the list are clearly related to innovation. In case 3 a new product is tried because the product now used for the same purpose has proved unsatisfactory. In case 4 a supplementary product is used in the hope of making the original product work better. Simple illustrations would be the use of a new grade of gasoline on the one hand and the use of a petroleum additive on the other. In either case the end remains the same, and the innovation lies in endeavoring to improve the means.

The next two cases, 5 and 6, imply some reshaping of the ends sought by the individual. In these cases, he is willing to try something outside the inventory $a \ldots x$ and therefore outside that part of the inventory which is familiar to him, namely, the extended subset $\bar{A}_i$. The two cases differ in relative complexity, since in case 5 the individual is asked to accept a single new product, while in case 6 the innovation consists in using two new products in conjunction. It may be assumed that the inventory $a \ldots x$ contains all of the items which members of this society regard as necessary to meet the needs for future action as now contemplated. To accept items outside $a \ldots x$ is equivalent to recognizing contingencies which were previously overlooked or neglected.

The last two cases, 7 and 8, have an important bearing on the acceptance of innovation but reflect socially involved motivations rather than technical requirements. The subscripts D and C refer to tendencies to be different or conform and characterize the type of person who is purchasing y in each case. For the consumption leader, y has an extra appeal if no one else yet has it because it contributes to his prestige. In the case of a technically new product, he may be the first to try it because he has most knowledge of the special field. The follower may be moved by prestige feelings in buying a new product to match what others may already have. He may also feel safer in buying a product which others have found satisfactory, even though he is not able to evaluate its technical properties. Leaders and followers are essential elements in the dynamics of demand. This does not necessarily mean a sharp division of the population into two groups, since some may lead in one class of products and some in another.

Factors in Product Acceptance. It is now time to turn to another aspect of innovation—namely, the features on the product side which enable it to gain acceptance and to persist as an item in the cultural inventory. There is a useful analogy here to the filling of ecological niches by animal species. The modern theory of evolution holds that species arise in response to opportunity. Mutations occur and are selected for survival according to whether they fit into the existing pattern. Many variations fail because they do not fit in or because they are not large enough or significant enough to challenge the present incumbents of the ecological network.

The ecology of products is radically different in character, since products are not organisms but instrumentalities which may affect the survival or satisfaction of human organisms. They do not survive by laws of natural selection, but are selected for survival because they find a place in human minds and living patterns. Because the principles of selection are psychological, they depend both on perception of differences in the product itself and on any claims made on behalf of the product as to function and performance. Either product characteristics or claims on behalf of the product create favorable expectations and can cause the product to be accepted permanently if expectations are realized.

Both the product and the product claims must meet some minimal requirements for acceptance. The difference between the new product offered and the established product must be discernible, identifiable, and reproducible. To say that the difference must be discernible is to say that the innovation must be different enough to make a difference to the user. The innovation must be identifiable if the first purchase is to lead to further purchases by the same individual or by others. A current violation of this principle is the action of a leading detergent manufacturer in bringing out two new products with significantly different qualities. Neither product can make a separate place for itself, since the color and design of the two packages are identical and the moderate difference in package size is easily overlooked by the consumer. The condition of reproducibility is also essential to repeat sales. That means ability to make additional units which are not noticeably different from the first. Lack of effective quality control has killed more than one innovation which might otherwise have been accepted.

Acceptance of Product Claims. The conditions of acceptance are even more complicated with respect to product claims. Ideally, a claim should be meaningful, plausible, and verifiable; but each of these requirements in turn must be further analyzed. This is true even in the simpler case in which it is claimed that the new product is a better means for effecting an end that is already recognized. The complexities of gaining acceptance are all the greater if the innovator claims that he is offering a means for serving an end or solving a problem of which the consumer was previously unaware. Each of the requirements for a product claim will be discussed, beginning with the requirement that it be meaningful.

A product claim for a new product is an offer to solve a problem for the prospective purchaser. A problem arising from a state of urgency is complicated by uncertainty. The meaning of a product claim is compounded of three elements: the urgency of the contingency the product is designed to meet, the probability of this event occurring, and doubt or reservation as to the utility of the product in meeting this contingency.

Plausibility of claims rests on various grounds. First is pure credulity, which is the willingness to believe what is pleasant to believe. This is a human failing which was sometimes exploited outrageously before the days of the Pure Food and Drug Administration.

Another ground of belief is authority. The discriminating consumer is in a large degree the one who exercises critical judgment in the choice of authorities as compared to direct judgment of product claims. A third ground of belief is scientific proof or what appears to be scientific evidence. There is a growing tendency to seek scientific foundations for claims.

If a new product under consideration by consumers is a more or less direct replacement for something previously known, the item being replaced may serve as a yardstick for evaluating the new one. If a test or demonstration serves to verify the claims for the product, it may be assumed that there is a favorable net change over what has been used before after taking account of several factors. The value of the product in use may be enhanced by a positive change in performance. The enhancement of value may be increased or decreased by what happens on the cost side. Cost is measured not only by price or investment in the new assets, but by expenditure of effort. A change in the time or labor required to use the product may be either favorable or unfavorable. There is also the issue of how much skill is required in the use of the product. There are various ways in which these factors might add up to a net favorable change. For example, an innovation might involve only a moderate improvement in performance and some increase in cost, but might involve a substantial decrease in labor and in the skill required to use the product. The introduction of Bisquick during the depression would be a good example.

If a product is a radical innovation in the sense that consumers have nothing with which to compare it directly, verification must be related to expectations as created by claims and by the general attitude toward claims. This is not essentially different from the other situation except that, in the case of a recognizable replacement, claims are somewhat tied down by the previous product.

Acceptance by Type of Innovative Situation. With this background, it is now possible to consider the requirements for acceptance in relation to the principal types of innovative situations, particularly the four cases, 3 to 6, in the previous list. As already pointed out, cases 3 and 4 can usually be regarded as offering an improvement in means, while 5 and 6 involve the recognition of new ends or new problems to be solved. Cases 4 and 6 also involve the relationship between complementary products as contrasted with the cases with which they are paired, which are 3 and 5, respectively.

In case 3, involving simple product improvement, the need for a discernible difference is especially acute. There is no point in making a change from the customary product unless something is to be gained thereby. Reproducibility is also important. For example, the individual cannot readily switch to a kind of food encountered in a foreign country unless it is obtainable at home. Claims would be meaningful primarily in terms of utility, since the urgency and probability are already established. Plausibility would not be a major problem, since the individual dissatisfied with the present product might be predisposed to believe in the possibility of a better one. Evidence of superiority would usually have to rest on some factual evidence, since the consumer is well acquainted with the existing product. Verifiability of claims would doubtless emphasize money costs as well as improvement in performance. Laborsaving and simplicity, requiring less skill, are also verifiable attributes likely to be alleged in presenting a product improvement.

Case 4 is not meant to bracket all of the many kinds of complementary relations. It specifically excludes the necessary complement, such as gasoline for use with an automobile. Case 4 pertains rather to the case where a basic product might work by itself, but would work better with the complement. The adding of a water softener to a soap would be an example. Identifiability is especially important to relate the use of the product to its basic purpose. Claims would also make a greater attempt to convince the consumer of a high probability of the occasion of need. Performance improvement would be emphasized, and the sponsor would doubtlessly rely heavily on the authority of previous users or recognized specialists to substantiate the improvement in performance.

The distinguishing feature of cases 5 and 6 would be the primary reliance on product claims, since the products themselves would be unfamiliar. To make these claims meaningful, the sponsor would have to make out a strong case for both the urgency and the probability of the occasions of use. To do this, he would call on both available authority and scientific evidence. The net advantage under verifiability would be likely to reside mainly in performance, in the sense of a satisfactory solution of a new problem measured by the expectations which had been aroused. The consumer might have to acquire new skills and would certainly be using time not previously used for the same purpose.

The complementary product offered in case 6 might be either a necessary complement or a facilitating complement. In either case, it would complicate the decision to be made by the consumer and would be more likely to require additional skills. It is likely that many innovations in the future will be of this type, in which the innovation consists of more than one product to be accepted at the same time. A new appliance and a product to go with it would be typical. Sometimes the consumable product and the instrument for using it can be combined in an applicator package. If the two are separate, the two product sponsors may still combine their efforts to gain acceptance for the innovation. Until recently, one of the obstacles to the acceptance of automatic dishwashers has been the lack of a washing compound regarded as fully satisfactory for the purpose. The manufacturer who is sure that he has developed one will have a real stake in promoting the sale of dishwashers and will doubtlessly engage in such activities as demonstrating their successful use to consumers.

Human culture has been extremely conservative throughout the long period studied by anthropologists, beginning with the Old Stone Age. Innovations have come more rapidly since the invention of agriculture in about 6000 B.C. The subsequent period accounts for about one per cent of the period of man on earth. One per cent of this period in turn takes us back eighty years, or about to the time of the invention of the telephone. Life has changed hardly at all during that period in some primitive cultures which still survive. The enormous potentialities for change provided by advancing technology have been partially realized and exemplified by the acceptance of innovation in the United States.

The rate of change and the differences in the rate between communities and between nations pose some of the gravest contemporary problems of social philosophy and public policy. Technical assistance programs in undeveloped countries have encountered resistance to change as a major problem. In some of the more successful programs, strategies for gaining acceptance for innovation have played an important part. The two most powerful nations in the world present a striking contrast in policies toward innovation in consumer goods. In the United States, economic freedom implies the freedom of the consumer to accept innovation and the freedom of many individuals to promote innovation. These promoters of change include the sponsors of new products and their advertising agencies. Other groups promote innovation on a broader scale by advocating their particular vision of a contemporary way of life. Leading stores and stylists, editors of fashion and service magazines, and many public leaders and educators participate in this generalized propaganda for innovation.

In analyzing the innovative process, it must be recognized that services are part of the complex of substitutable and complementary goods along with products. Very frequently, the consumer is confronted with the choice of spending money for a product or a service. A householder who has found the care of his lawn too great a burden may either buy a power lawn mower or hire a service company which provides its own tools. The available services develop through successive innovations as products develop. What has been said about product innovation generally applies to services, except that the term "assortment" must be used in a broader and somewhat figurative way. The customer of a service organization has a claim on the use of its facilities, which may therefore be regarded as indirect extensions of his assortment.

The most satisfactory starting point here, as in the consideration of price and product, is analysis of what is to be offered to the ultimate consumer. This is a bundle of utilities consisting of various product features and accompanying services offered at a price. Market planning can well start with this picture of what is to be offered to consumers, treating services occurring farther back in the channel as instrumentalities for accomplishing this goal. The services offered the consumer may be classified as related to the effective use of goods, to the transfer of goods, and to the original selection of goods.

Services related to the effective use of goods are mainly concerned with matching them more closely to the individual's needs. An obvious illustration is the fitting and alteration of clothing, by which a limited number of sizes in the retailer's stock are made to fit a much greater variation as to the human figure. Another example is the service of installation commonly provided with major household appliances. Contrary tendencies are at work here, one toward designing the conventional appliance so that it merely needs to be plugged in and the other toward greater use of built-in appliances which can only be installed by skilled mechanics. Another service is that of keeping an appliance in working order, which is usually the responsibility of the seller during some initial warranty period. Later the user will have to pay for repair services, but it is the duration and character of the warranty which enters into the design of the bundle of facilities offered in the original sale. Finally, there is the service of demonstration and instruction in the use of the product. The more complex and diverse the products on the market, the greater the consumer's need for some expert guidance in using them. In the last analysis, what the consumer is buying is not a product, but some anticipated level of product performance. In only a few cases, such as the automobile, has responsibility for learning to use it passed to the consumer; and even here the retailer takes pains to explain any new features of his model.

Services related to the transfer of goods include credit, packaging, and delivery. The emphasis with respect to such services has shifted from time to time in various lines of trade. A generation ago the credit and delivery store was dominant in the grocery trade, but it is relatively insignificant today. The introduction of perishable products formerly sold in separate outlets, the general availability of family automobiles, and the rising level of consumer income have helped to produce this change. In other lines of retailing, both credit and delivery services are major elements in the transaction. Some products could not be hauled in the family car or conveniently loaded at downtown stores. Many are so high in price that the consumer cannot conveniently pay for them at the time of purchase. In some sales, such as real estate, there are special transfer services such as title search. Also, there are special arrangements, as in the case of automobiles, to certify ownership.

Services related to the selection of goods include display of merchandise, service or counsel by salesclerks, advertising, and the distribution of catalogs. All of these services are of mixed character, since they are partially designed to influence the choice of the consumer in a direction that is profitable to the store. Nevertheless, shoppers do require help in the process of selection; and many repose confidence in retailers to give them the help they need. Others turn to sources of help they consider more objective, such as buyers' guides. The seller tries to meet this need in various ways, such as the fitting rooms provided in apparel stores, the listening booths in record shops, and swatches of cloth which can be carried home for matching with various furnishings. All of these devices pertain to the transmission of information as compared to the transfer or use of goods.

ALTERNATIVE THEORIES OF ADVERTISING

Advertising and promotion are generally associated with product competition rather than with price competition. In fact, some of the critics of advertising would hold that the primary aim of the advertiser is to avoid direct price comparisons and hence to escape the rigors of competition. This view ignores the fact that a large share of advertising dollars is spent by retailers, and price is usually the main feature of retail advertising. Indeed the typical weekly advertisement by a supermarket is nothing more than a price list. Thus, it appears that advertising is essential to effective price competition in modern markets rather than being inimical to competition.

Advertising in one of its aspects is simply an economical means of transmitting information. Consumers cannot respond to prices unless they know what the prices are. Complete reliance on visits to retail stores would often be an excessively costly way of obtaining the needed information. These considerations hold with even greater force with respect to special features of a product. The consumer must be informed about these features in order to take them into account in a buying decision. Advertising can make price competition more effective, but product competition of the intensity known today simply could not exist without it.

A fairly satisfactory theory of advertising could be evolved based on its informational aspect only. The flow of information is obviously vital to the flow of goods. Much information about price and product is general in nature rather than applying to a single transaction. Information of general application can be transmitted through mass media far more cheaply than through individualized messages. It is wholly natural that the seller should take responsibility for transmitting this information, since he is the only one in full possession of the data, since he should be able to make a valid judgment as to who wants it, and since he has a clear incentive for bearing the cost of transmission.

The informational theory of advertising raises some issues as to the capacity of consumers to receive and react to information. There are limits on the time and attention which the consumer will give to advertising messages and on the ability to retain a message long enough to act upon it. There are conditions which determine awareness and receptivity, such as some previous knowledge of the product advertised or a sense of urgency concerning the need it is intended to serve. It is a well-attested psychological fact that a message is picked up and understood much more readily if the recipient is expecting it. An informational theory can take account of the efforts of the buyer to acquire information as well as the efforts of the seller to transmit it. At the beginning of a shopping trip or in the preshopping consideration of a need to be filled, the buyer may be searching primarily for information. The degree of knowledge increases as the shopper responds to advertising, merchandise displays, or other sources of information. A sale takes place when the consumer feels sufficiently well informed to make a choice.

Advertising as Persuasion. The informational theory is not wholly adequate, since advertising is concerned with persuasion as well as information. Advertising experts are inveterate theorists, and most advertising is sold on the basis of some theory of how it works. Practically all of these theories hold that advertising does not merely inform the consumer but motivates him by transforming his attitudes and eventually his way of life. An interpretation of advertising and selling as persuasion raises issues about the plasticity of consumers— that is, their potentiality for being remolded and responding in a new way thereafter. The term "plasticity" suggests an enduring change as compared to the immediate but transient response designated by the term "elasticity of demand." Making consumers change their minds is a costly process and scarcely worth-while for the advertiser unless the effect carries over beyond a single transaction.

Habit and Impulse. While most advertising theories count on the plastic quality of human desire, they differ as to the mechanism by which the transformation of attitudes takes place. There has been much emphasis over the years on the irrational factors of habit and impulse. The stress on habit came first and was directly associated in its origins with Watsonian behaviorism. Just as the training of a child was conceived as a process of inculcating habits, so the advertiser attempted to instill in consumers the habit of using his product. Under this view the power of advertising lay in constant repetition, first to create buying habits and then to maintain them.

Advertising copy and illustration showed the sponsor's product in pleasurable surroundings and through repetition built up an association between the product and established sources of satisfaction. The application of the principle of the conditioned reflex was almost as transparent as in the case of Pavlov's dogs. The objective was to give the brand name of the product the status of a psychological cue which would trigger buying action whenever it was encountered in the retail store. The bond between stimulus and response was termed "brand loyalty." If it had been carefully and solidly built, it became relatively invulnerable to competitive attack. This type of advertising result was doubtless approximated in many cases so long as the competitive products were not backed by equally intensive campaigns. The inculcation of buying habits by means of repetition is not so simple when a number of equally determined advertisers are striving for the same result. Brand loyalty turns out to be highly perishable, and each brand must gain many new users to offset its losses to others.

The effort to induce consumers to try a product is a major goal of promotional strategy in highly competitive markets. The spotlight tends to shift from the buying habit to the buying impulse. The advertiser comes to rely on the irrational power of emotional drives to break through established patterns and give the new product a chance to be heard. This view of advertising draws nourishment from the Freudian type of psychology. A product gains acceptance because it serves as a vehicle for expressing an urge that has been frustrated or suppressed. Products, according to this theory, are preferred because of symbolic values and only incidentally because of their utility. One product fails because it arouses guilt feelings, and another succeeds because it provides release for unconscious desires.

This theory is appealing to the advertiser seeking differential advantage. It offers the hope that he may discover the secret springs of motivation which remain hidden to his competitors. His knowledge leads to subtleties of copy appeal with greater emotional impact than the mere repetition of utilitarian claims or pleasant associations.

Both of these views of how advertising works favor the exploitation of irrational or nonrational aspects of consumer behavior. Those who count on buying habits are attempting to instill preferences which will be impervious to rational appeals. Arrayed against the *status quo* are those who find in irrational impulse the means for establishing a foothold in the market. There are elements of truth in both viewpoints, but they tend to ignore or confuse the essential rationality underlying consumer decisions in the market place. While the consumer is a creature of habit and impulse, he is also a problem solver.

ADVERTISING AND CONSUMER PROBLEMS

If the consumer is basically a problem solver, there should be a place for the kind of advertising which attempts to help him with his problems. Advertising may use emotional appeals in motivating the consumer to try a product, but there is no assurance that he will continue to use it unless its utility can be demonstrated. A buying habit fits within the broad pattern of rationality, representing a routine method of serving a need, so long as the product functions satisfactorily. Even the clamor of competitive claims may serve the rational end of matching segments of supply and demand, assuming that there are genuine differences in consumer requirements within a given product field.

Most products most of the time are sold on the basis of rational utility. Housewives buy food to feed their families and with an eye for a balanced diet. Appliances are bought to make life easier and home furnishings to make the home attractive and comfortable. Transportation needs are basic in the purchase of automobiles, although cravings for prestige may influence the price that many are willing to pay for extra features and for horsepower that is not strictly necessary. It is in classes of products where there is little perceptible difference among brands that the greatest reliance is placed on irrational appeals. The arts of mass persuasion are lavished on cigarettes, cosmetics, and beverages. It is a bit ironic that all of the Freudian psychology and television talent used in stimulating the sale of cigarettes should end by putting more money in the hands of the tax collector than in those of the tobacco grower. But even here the manufacturers pay tribute to the essential rationality of the consumer by the desperate attempts to differentiate their products in the hope of showing enhanced utility.

Needs versus Wants. The problem-solving aspect of consumer behavior is somewhat obscured in an economy of relative abundance. The idea is generally accepted in the advertising fraternity that we live in a stimulated economy and that the present high level of production cannot be maintained without active promotion. Some writers in marketing have attempted to crystallize this issue by contrasting needs and wants. They are inclined to limit needs to absolute necessities without which life could hardly be sustained and then to say that it is the business of marketing organizations to sell wants rather than needs. This formulation of the issue is rather unfortunate, since it implies making and selling products which nobody needs and provides ammunition for critics who feel that active selling is an unsound element in the economy.

There is no deficiency of consumer needs anywhere in the world, including the United States. Some needs appear more urgent than others, such as enough food to sustain life from day to day; but people need much more than the bare essentials of food, clothing, and shelter. They need whatever protection foresight can provide against the hazards and disasters which threaten to disrupt the preferred pattern of life. In a world of change, they need the means for adjusting and improving the pattern of life rather than being gradually overwhelmed by circumstance. The opportunities of life are so varied, the dangers which beset it so uncertain, that people will always need more things than they possess.

It is wants that are lacking, not needs. To need something is to be dependent upon it as an essential factor in maintaining or enhancing a way of life. The individual is not always conscious of his needs. To want a product is to recognize it explicitly as a means of meeting a situation which is regarded as both probable and important. Marketing creates wants by making consumers aware of needs and by identifying specific products as means of meeting these needs. It would be absurd to spend money to get consumers to want a product which would cause corns and bunions, on the ground that no such preparation was needed. Even if by some perverse psychology a few eccentrics could be made to want such a product, the chances of putting over a product for removing corns and bunions would be far greater.

Marketing assuredly deals with the creation of wants, but it starts with the principle that wants spring from needs and are not something alien to be set off in opposition to needs. The transformation of needs into wants is a difficult process and a challenge to marketing skill. The process varies according to the underlying need and the nature of the product recommended for meeting it. One kind of need is relatively trivial but almost certain to occur. A case in point would be the need of a confirmed smoker to light his next cigarette. At the other extreme would be the prospects that one's house would catch fire. This event is not very likely to happen in the average case, but it would create a situation of extreme urgency if it did. Need situations vary both as to their probability and their importance, and there are endless combinations of these two dimensions of need. A person may fail to want something he needs either because he underestimates its probability or because he does not appreciate its importance. Creative selling works on one factor or both to turn the need into a want.

The second phase in conversion is turning a generalized want into wanting a specific product. That means convincing the consumer that the product is an acceptable means for satisfying the need. The consumer must know what a product will do in order to want it. Even so basic a marketing fact has often been ignored. If there are several products which will serve the same purpose, demand for any one of them will depend on letting consumers know their special merits. The core of the market for a product will consist of just those consumers who have the greatest appreciation of these features. How far beyond the core of the market to go in active promotion is one of the basic issues in designing a marketing program. Suppose a product has three positive advantages over competitive products. The effort to cultivate demand may center on consumers who want all three, or it may be directed to a more inclusive group who want one feature which is regarded as the most essential advantage in use.

Confidence on the part of the prospect that he can use the product successfully is also a requisite for demand. The same product will not always please both the amateur and the expert. One camera may be too complicated for the beginner. Another may lack the refinements that the experienced camera fan insists upon. Many consumer products go through a cycle of design, moving at one stage toward technical refinements and at another stage tending toward sturdiness and simplicity of operation. Amateurs usually offer the biggest market because in most fields of use there are more of them. Those with some specialized knowledge and experience very often provide a place to get started with a new type of product. It is important to retain their good will indefinitely, even though sales later on are made largely to the general market. Step by step, the amateur also must be educated to the most effective use of the product. Part of the marketing job is to inculcate user skills among buyers through demonstration and instruction. For sound and continuous development of a market, it is not enough to claim that a product will fill a need. It is in the seller's interest to see that the product is used in such a way that the need is adequately served.

The right price is also a factor in turning a need into a want. A product must not only find a place in the pattern of life but must bear some reasonable relationship to the family budget. That does not mean that the initial price must bring the product within the reach of every family that needs it. Rather, it should be priced for maximum gross revenue, so that funds will be available with which to do the kind of selling which will turn need into want. Here is where the distinction between a need and a want is really significant. As that transformation takes place, sales can be expanded by steadily lowering the price. Every family has a limited budget with which to meet a multitude of wants. It is reasonable for it to spend its money so as to satisfy the most desirable pattern of wants.

The doctrine of wants, not needs, represents the opposite extreme from another notion that is equally fallacious and even more widespread. That is the idea that if the producer has designed something that people really need, all he has to do is make it and demand will take care of itself. This might be called the "better mousetrap theory," to name it after an old story erroneously attributed to Emerson. Marketing effort is essential no matter how beneficial the product. Launching any new product is a complex co-operative project in which consumers, producers, and distributors must participate. Enough consumers must want the product to make it feasible to place it in distribution. The product must be placed in distribution, so that consumers who want it can get it. It must be promoted effectively, so that consumers are willing to try it and retailers are willing to stock it. Money must be spent for advertising and selling, but the product must sell to produce the dollars to cover selling expenses. A good marketing program can cut through this maze and co-ordinate efforts at the various stages, so that the product begins an orderly flow to the consumer.

Sales versus Customers.   Another issue often discussed in marketing circles is that of making sales versus making customers. On the one hand, there is the possibility of putting all possible pressure on one sales transaction after another, hoping thereby to maximize total sales for any stated operating period, such as a month or a year. In contrast, there is the view that what every business needs is loyal customers who will regard it as their regular source of supply and will individually account for a number of sales in succession. The relative emphasis on these two points of view naturally varies with such considerations as the character of the product. Many products are sold in such small units that it is only repeat business over a considerable period of time which could offset the cost of inducing a customer to make the first purchase. By contrast, there are products which the individual uses only once in a lifetime, so that there is no element of repeat purchases to consider. Marketing practices are greatly influenced by these considerations, as might be illustrated by toothpaste and cigarettes on the one hand and wedding rings or caskets on the other.

There is an increasing tendency in most lines of business to regard every sale as having a bearing on future sales, regardless of how durable the product is or how infrequently it is purchased. Even though the particular individual may never buy again, his satisfaction with his purchase may influence others in his immediate circle. Very few marketing organizations can afford to proceed as if they had no interest beyond the immediate sale. Possible cases would be the sale of doubtful mining stock or the house-to-house peddling of gadgets which would not stand the test of actual use. In such cases the salesman hopes to make a killing the first time round and has no intention of coming back. For all legitimate and continuing marketing operations the policy position on making sales versus making customers necessarily leans toward the latter side.

The issue of making sales versus making customers is not concerned merely with the tools of marketing such as selling and advertising. Customers for many products are made through education and experience and through contact with the product in use in other households. It would take time for a product to become an accepted part of the culture relying only on these tendencies which do not involve marketing initiative. Often it is constructive to regard the problem of marketing policy as that of determining how much the firm can afford to spend in accelerating these trends. Marketing effort alone cannot create demand unless the other factors are favorable. What it may be able to do is to speed up the process, so that individual consumers might begin to buy the product from one to five years earlier than would have been the case without marketing effort. That degree of acceleration can be very important in a dynamic economy. It can have great value to the firm that designed and introduced the product by establishing a substantial lead over prospective competition. It may mean the difference between success and failure in establishing a position at all, because new developments and other ways of accomplishing the same purpose have taken the market before the product gets a foothold. The fundamental decision for the policy maker might be characterized as determining the extent to which expenditures for speeding up the growth of demand should pay off for the seller.

Demand Creation versus Sales Economy. Another issue of comparable importance with that of needs versus wants and individual sales versus customers is the issue of demand creation versus sales economy. This issue is particularly important in determining the aim and character of the company's advertising program as part of its total selling effort. Advertising may be justified in one situation as a means of making customers which the product would not have otherwise. It may be justified in other situations as a more economical way of reaching customers as compared with personal selling. These possibilities have been discussed in an earlier chapter, showing how preselling helps to reduce actual sales transactions to routine. At the same time, this preselling or prenegotiation is performed on a relatively low cost basis through mass media as compared to having missionary salesmen call on customers before they enter the retail store. Some very large users of advertising say that their only reason for using it is that it is cheaper than any alternative method of accomplishing their sales objectives.

Economy in selling, as in any other economic activity, may have a dual impact. On the one hand the seller may change his goal but simply accomplish the result through a smaller expenditure. On the other hand the fact that he has an efficient instrument available may encourage him to raise the goal and spend an even greater sum of money, but in the anticipation of greater accomplishment.

In organizational terms, these substantive issues may be reduced to the question of relative emphasis upon advertising and selling in the marketing mix. Since this is an issue which affects the basic structure of the organization, it cannot ordinarily be left as an open issue. An effective marketing program will necessarily tend to make one instrument primary and the other secondary. Advertising can be regarded as a means of giving background support to salesmen and making their job easier even while recognizing that the product must be moved by personal selling in the last analysis. There are other cases in which advertising may be regarded as the fundamental means of creating demand while salesmen do nothing more than take orders and reap the harvest which advertising has produced.

NATURE OF CONSUMPTION CHOICE

A new type of investigation and analysis dealing more directly with consumption itself is urgently needed, in the hope of determining the conditions under which our capacity to consume can expand as fast as the potential increase in productive capacity. At present, there is not even a name for such a field of study, although it is the concept of such a field which is represented by recent discussions and pioneer efforts in basic research and marketing. The word "economics," interestingly enough, is a very appropriate designation for that aspect of consumer behavior which it covers—that is, consumer buying. The two parts of the word, "eco" and "nomics," are derived from two Greek words. The first part of the word is Greek for "house" or "household"; the second part of the word can be freely translated as "management." Thus the whole word means "household or estate management." The household manager attempts to be prepared for the types of occasions which involve consumption by the various members of the household. In a free-enterprise economy, she draws upon the market place to replenish or extend her inventory of goods which prepare the household to meet the expectations of its members. The economist, for the most part, has been concerned about the factors which would determine the price at which a product would be purchased. Both the economist and the marketing specialist have shown relatively little concern for what happens to the goods after they reach the household. Many books and articles in the field of marketing use the term "consumption," but it should usually be understood that what is actually implied by the word is consumer buying.

Many, indeed, would deny that the difference has any significance for economics and marketing. The individual, whether regarded as a consumer or a consumer buyer, is confronted by the fact of scarcity; the important question is how he uses the available means to satisfy his desires in the presence of scarcity. It might be said that if the condition of scarcity were removed, there would be no economic problem, since each individual could choose to consume any kind or quantity of goods. The point of this discussion is to insist that there is another range of choices which are fundamental for consumption and eventually for marketing, even though they may lie outside the field of economics as concerned with scarcity.

There are many practical situations in which the consumer is obliged to make a choice even in the midst of abundance. There are some limitations on our capacity to consume which would still exist if all restrictions on the supply of goods were removed. Economics is presumed to deal with supply and demand but actually is concerned almost wholly with the problem of supply. The concept of demand in economic analysis is concerned primarily with the consumer buyer making a choice in the presence of scarcity. To analyze demand for its own sake would be to explore the problems of choice which affect consumption in the midst of abundance.

Some simple and obvious examples should suffice to illustrate the point. Suppose that an individual visits a free library in order to get a book to read. In addition, suppose that the library has more than one hundred thousand volumes and that at least several thousand of these are of potential interest to the particular reader. He may have a difficult or even painful choice to make, since he can obviously read only a few of these books during any given borrowing period. The viewer sitting before his television set may find that the two programs he is most anxious to see occur at precisely the same time. An individual or a family

planning a vacation is more likely to be troubled by the fact that there
are so many places to which they want to go than by facing a lack of
alternatives. Even so simple a consumption situation as ordering a meal
in a restaurant poses problems of choice, since the patron can consume
only one of the meals offered on that occasion. The problem of leisure
time for many people is not the lack of entertainment resources but the
problem of choosing among a range of activities, all attractive, such as
golf, dancing, swimming, going to a show or concert, or staying at home
with a good book. Anyone's personal experience will yield examples of
difficulties which can arise when two or more people are involved and
try to agree on how to spend the evening.

Possibly it might appear that this area of consumption choice is
not the business of the economist or the marketing specialist. The
economist in particular often tries to dodge these difficulties by saying
that it is his job to deal with the efficient use of resources, and with
satisfying wants once he is provided with a schedule of what is wanted.
He might say that consumption choices, in the sense that the term is
used here, are in the realm of personal taste and are the proper
study of ethics, esthetics, and psychology. This easy way out is scarcely
available to the marketing man once he assumes responsibility for
creating or stimulating demand. He is then obliged to look at a whole
new set of factors pertaining to the act of consumption and not related to the scarcity of goods as means for satisfying desires. A very
sketchy preliminary discussion of this new field of study will be presented here.

The basic characteristic of a consumption choice as compared to a
consumer buyer choice is that the need for choice does not arise from
the scarcity of goods. All the goods to be used in satisfying conflicting desires are presumed to be available in this choice situation.
The problem of management for the individual in this predicament
is not that of making the best use of scarce resources but of meeting
other requirements of selection in the midst of abundance. The necessity for choice arises from limitations on our capacity for enjoyment,
which are as real as the restrictions on supply. Capacity for enjoyment
is limited through lack of sensitivity or experience, through lack of
time or energy for pleasurable activities, and through confusion or
uncertainty as to relative values.

Management of capacity for pleasure in order to fill one's time
with satisfactions might be called "hedonomics," which is a construction from Greek roots directly parallel to "economics." This is the
ultimate application of management skill to the extent that the

individual is motivated by the pursuit of happiness. It poses some problems which are beyond solution either by the individual alone or with the prodding of outsiders such as the sponsor of advertised products. The appreciation of music is limited for the tone-deaf, or of painting for the color-blind. Appreciation of a play or a football game is not very penetrating in the case of a person who is seeing one for the first time. Limitations of time and energy can be overcome to some extent by the lifelong movement toward symbolic experience, which has already been discussed. Otherwise, enhanced satisfaction rests on skillful personal management of time and energy.

A primary application for advertising is in helping the individual to overcome his confusion and uncertainty as to relative values. Advertising messages can help to persuade him that a given activity is really the best one for him and that he has chosen this activity in its most agreeable form relative to other variations. It can provide him with the kind of background knowledge about his chosen pursuit which will aid him in justifying this pursuit to himself and others. It can help him relate this activity to other aspects of his style of living and to his more fundamental life objectives.

There are two contrasting psychological types with respect to the pursuit of pleasure which must be recognized in any attempt at stimulation or guidance from the outside. These are not pure types, of course, but occur in various shadings and combinations. They appear under various designations in the history of esthetics. Perhaps the most suggestive designations are those employed by Nietzsche to characterize this contrast in pleasure seeking. One type he called "Apollonian," the person who finds pleasure in creating or experiencing an orderly pattern with its aspects of unity, balance, and symmetry. The other type is the "Dionysian," the person who drives toward self-expression by breaking through all patterns and who values intensity of experience to the point that his pleasures verge on the orgiastic.

For the present purpose, these types might be labeled the "pattern maker" and the "pattern breaker." There is a tendency for the first to be more strongly conditioned by his social environment than the latter. In his eagerness to conform, he may yet be uncertain about the norms for the group with which he seeks alignment. Similarly, the pattern breaker is often troubled as to whether his impulsive deviation truly represents the direction in which he should depart from the norms imposed by the group. Most individuals have some mixture of these two orientations. They are held in uneasy balance, like the tendencies toward monostasy and systasy observed in enterprise competition. Here lie some of the deeper problems confronting the individual in the pursuit of happiness. At present the utility of selling and advertising is limited to problems of the consumer buyer. They may yet gain greater skill and effectiveness in relation to the problems of the consumer as consumer.

In considering a sicence yet to be born which has here been called "hedonomics," we can scarcely do more than speculate on the type of analytical models and experimental research which the field may require. A useful starting point might be to regard the time of the subject as divided into some arbitrary units, such as fifteen-minute periods for analyzing a week's activities. Longer intervals might be appropriate if a life history were being studied. The most desirable pattern of life, either in general or for a given type of individual, might then be visualized as a series of time units filled with a sequence of experiences. Possible experiences would be regarded as amounting to a very large and yet finite number.

Given a weekly record of this sort for any individual, several characteristics might be expected in a series which represented a happy experience on the whole. Some experience types would be repeated frequently, while others would occur only once during the period recorded. Some rhythm or cycle might be observed in the repetitive experiences. Among those occurring only once would be some which the subject had experienced before but which followed a longer cycle of repetition. Some might occur at random in the sense that the time of their appearance was not under the control of the subject. The element of surprise might be an important factor in the satisfaction they produced.

Some experiences might be regarded as new by the subject. Determining what constituted novelty in experience would be a major problem for the science of hedonomics. In some cases the experience might be analyzable into elements which had previously appeared in a different combination. In other cases the whole experience might seem so novel as to represent a break with the past. It would doubtless be found that subjects varied greatly as to their acceptance of radical novelty as a source of pleasure. For some, it might be found that the shock of change or even intervals of pain increased the intensity of subsequent intervals of enjoyment.

The kind of research required to record such behavior sequences might resemble that carried out by Gesell and his associates on infant behavior. That is to say that it would be a most detailed and exhaustive type of observation which could only be carried out by someone who was accepted as a part of the individual's environment. For longer time spans a somewhat less exhaustive record might be compiled by the subject on a diary basis. Even longer-range procedures would be needed for recording and analyzing the maturing of taste or the shift toward symbolic experience which has already been discussed.

The suggested field of study may seem somewhat remote from the pressing marketing problems of today. Advertising and selling certainly have room for improvement in the more limited role of contributing to problem solving by the consumer buyer. The time is not far distant, however, when marketing must achieve a deeper insight into consumption choice if promotional techniques are to make their fullest contribution to market expansion.

ADVERTISING AND MARGINAL ANALYSIS

There have been some attempts to bring advertising within the framework of marginal analysis and thus to bridge the analytical gap between price and promotion mentioned in the last chapter. Chamberlin suggested that the effect of advertising was to move the demand curve upward and to the right. This means that consumers are induced to place a greater value on the product and that more units can therefore be sold at any given price. The advertiser will then make more money if the additional revenue he obtains is greater than the additional cost of the advertising. If the advertiser were to utilize formal analysis, he would presumably have to consider a whole set of demand curves representing the outcome of various levels of advertising expenditures, and would have to consider the corresponding cost curves to determine the optimum combination and hence decide how much to spend for advertising.

While this type of analysis would be difficult, it would not be theoretically impossible under the terms stated. What removes it from the realm of practical reality is that the advertiser would be obliged to analyze some complex risk functions as well as cost functions. Thus the contemplated level of advertising expenditure might have either the expected effect on sales or a zero effect. If badly executed, the advertising program might even have an adverse effect on sales. A moderate level of expenditure might not be adequate to make any impression on the consumer, while twice as much money might have a decided effect. Thus, over a certain range of expenditure, the risk might decrease as the amount increased; but formal evaluation of this risk function in advance would be practically impossible.

There are other ways to conceive of advertising within the framework of marginal analysis, suggested by the way in which advertising appears to have operated in some actual cases. Often it is only after a product has become widely known through advertising that the producer can sell it at a low price. With the assurance of large demand, he can cut the price and reap the advantages of economies in large-scale production. At an earlier point, it might have been futile to reduce the price in order to reach low-income families. They still would not buy it because they did not recognize the need for it or possibly even know of its existence. The earlier situation was as if the demand curve terminated at a point representing a maximum number of units which could be sold to the existing market. The effect of advertising under these circumstances might be described as extending the demand curve downward to the right, making it feasible for the seller to consider a price in this lower range.

Another difficulty in the formal analysis of expectations from advertising involves the distinction between substitutability and complementarity. One aim of advertising is to persuade consumers that they should substitute the advertised product for some other product they have been using or might use. But advertising can also operate to enhance the complementary demand for a product. The aim is to persuade the consumer that it is necessary to buy the advertised product in order to get full satisfaction out of something the consumer already owns or is using. Where the advertiser can capitalize on a complementary relationship, he may get larger results in proportion to the amount expended. On the other hand, he may face peculiar limitations and risks concerning his potential market. His market will expand only if the market for the other product expands. If the other product is rendered obsolete by an innovation, the advertiser's product may also be wiped out. Thus, while complementary relations may help a product to gain a foothold, marketing strategy may be directed later toward establishing its market position independently.

It takes time for advertising results to accrue and to find ways of evaluating its impact. The approach to determining the right amount or the right kind of advertising must continue to rely in part on trial and error or successive approximations to the optimum program. Meanwhile, the optimum requirements are also subject to continuous change in relation to competition and the stage of market development. Progress in the application of analytical methods should be encouraged, but the most successful models will recognize the time dimension. Advertising is intricately involved in the processes of growth, both as an instrument of expansion and as an activity which itself is continuously transformed by the dynamics of the free market.

SELECTED REFERENCES

SCHUMPETER, JOSEPH A. *Capitalism, Socialism and Democracy.* New York: Harper & Bros., 1942.

BARNETT, H. G. *Innovation.* New York: McGraw-Hill Book Co., Inc., 1953.

BORDEN, NEIL H. *Economic Effects of Advertising.* Chicago: Richard D. Irwin, Inc., 1944.

NATIONAL RESOURCES BOARD. *Consumer Purchases Survey.* Washington, D.C., 1935–36.

HALL, CALVIN S. *Primer of Freudian Psychology.* Cleveland: World Publishing Co., 1954.

SNYGG, DONALD and COMBS, ARTHUR W. *Individual Behavior.* New York: Harper & Bros., 1949.

ASPINWALL, LEO. *Cost and Profit Outlook.* Philadelphia: Alderson & Sessions, July, August, September, October, 1956.

Among economists, Schumpeter is perhaps the best-known student of innovation; he assigned it a place of key importance in economic theory. Barnett is an anthropologist whose background for an analysis of innovation derives from a study of culture change in primitive societies.

Borden's massive treatise is still the definitive work on the economics of advertising. It contains important implications for theory, even though the author assumed that his task was primarily the critical and empirical evaluation of a major aspect of marketing.

The *Consumer Purchases Survey* provided the most comprehensive view of consumption patterns yet available and showed how they vary by such factors as family income.

The two references on psychology are included for their relevance to the concept of market plasticity. Hall's book is a simple summary of Freud's basic ideas. Snygg and Combs have been mentioned before in connection with their development of the concept of the phenomenal self.

Leo Aspinwall is one of the most creative thinkers in marketing theory. His ideas on the marketing characteristics of goods have been utilized in this chapter.

Chapter X

THE EVOLUTION OF THE MARKET TRANSACTION

Every transaction in the market place is an attempt to match a segment of demand with an appropriate segment of supply. Matching is facilitated through the various aspects of sorting, but it is effectuated through market transactions. Matching would remain on an elementary and localized level if every transaction were between the original producer and the ultimate consumer. The intermediate steps of sorting result in great economies with respect to the number and character of transactions required in the matching process. Economies also arise through the gradual evolution of the transaction itself.

The main line of progress with respect to the nature of the transaction lies in reducing it to routine or at least routinizing some of its features. Routine transactions may be regarded as implicit negotiations because they usually take place within a framework established by a fully negotiated transaction. Many individual transactions must still be fully negotiated because of their strategic importance. Negotiation in some lines of trade is a distinct specialization, separated from the physical handling of goods and thus promoting the development of greater skill and efficiency. There are other routes to increased transactional efficiency, such as separating the transfer of goods and the transfer of title.

THE INVENTION OF EXCHANGE

The development of exchange was as big a step in the history of civilization as the first use of tools by primitive man. The problems of mutual confidence and of valuation of goods to be exchanged were as difficult to solve as the development of technical methods in production. In learning to engage in market transactions, primitive man had to deal with other men and often with strangers. He was working in a social situation which was uncertain and explosive until patterns of action began to develop. By contrast, the toolmaker could work in solitude, gradually perfecting his art by trial and error. Hence, it seems altogether reasonable to describe the development of exchange as a great invention which helped to start primitive man on the road to civilization.

In order to understand the later developments of transactional efficiency, it is worth-while to consider some of the obstacles which had to be overcome and some of the primitive roots out of which the process of exchange was developed. Reference was made in a previous chapter to contravalence or the concept that men exercise power against each other. In a primitive environment, everything strange is likely to appear hostile. In the face of competition for the use of scarce resources, the first primitive reaction is likely to be that of obstructing attempts of competitors to use these resources. Warfare was probably antecedent to commerce throughout the primitive world.

The first examples of goods moving from the hands of one group to another were not exchange transactions but were entirely one-sided. Such movement of goods would have been the result of war in the first instance. Loot was exacted by the victor; and later, tribute was levied annually on a people held in subjection. Out of such rudimentary beginnings came political instruments such as taxation and treaties. The tribes or the individuals who were subjected to tribute or taxation no doubt got something in return, if it was nothing more than the imposition of a stable order and defense against tribes which lay outside the realm. Another type of one-way movement of goods occurred in connection with religious ceremonies and sacrifices. The animals and other products which were brought to the temples for sacrifice also helped to maintain subsistence for the priesthood.

Exchange of Gifts. The next step along the path of progress was doubtless the exchange of gifts. This practice came to be an essential adjunct of travel and diplomacy. The traveler carried gifts with him and received hospitality in return. Tribes which had long engaged in the custom of propitiating the gods through gifts eventually learned to improve relations with each other through the exchange of gifts. Anthropologists have described a strange custom existing in a group of islands in the South Seas. Two types of objects are used as gifts, one a variety of sea shell and the other a semiprecious stone. One of these objects circulates in the islands in a clockwise direction, and the other circulates in a counterclockwise direction. At each stage, individuals meet and engage in exchange, thus facilitating the circular flow of these products. This circular flow of gifts does not appear to serve any utilitarian function, but simply to help maintain contact and good relations among the people in the islands.

In other primitive customs, there is a movement of goods connected with marriage. One form is that of bride purchase, in which the groom must give goods to his prospective father-in-law in exchange for his bride. Another form is the dowry, in which the father of the bride is expected to provide the means for the young couple to start their household. In other cases, there is an exchange of gifts connected with marriage or with other social occasions. One of the strangest of these customs is the potlatch, practiced by Indian tribes in the Pacific Northwest. Goods are used in the potlatch as a means of display and as part of the competitive battle for personal prestige. A potlatch is actually a party at which a chief makes a great show of his wealth and power by giving away goods or in some cases destroying them. The chiefs who have been entertained at the potlatch are expected to return the invitation and try to outdo the first chief by the magnificence of their hospitality and their generosity. The potlatch has some relation to modern commerce both in its competitive aspect and in the degree to which it stimulates production, even though a large part of the output is not used for economic purposes.

Barter. All of these primitive practices were part of the slow process by which men learned to deal with each other. Genuine exchange does not emerge until the stage of barter. Neighboring tribes with different raw materials or with distinctive skills learned gradually to trade with each other. Primitive trade eventually spread over a very wide geographic area. For example, jade tools and ornaments of very early origin have been found in areas far removed from any natural source of this material. In ancient and medieval times, trade routes developed for the exchange of goods or materials produced at locations hundreds or even thousands of miles apart. For example, there is a fascinating chapter in the history of early commerce having to do with the movement of amber from the Baltic regions down to the cities of Greece and Rome. This material was attractive and very easily worked, and the more advanced communities were willing to echange various handicraft products for it. Roman exploration and conquest in western Europe resulted in a similar flow of trade with the copper-mining regions of Spain and the tin-mining regions of Great Britain.

It was a long hard road from tribute and the exchange of gifts to the first appearance of organized markets. A more orderly type of transaction grew up along with the development of market organization. A very important facilitating step was the development of a monetary medium of exchange. One of the first needs was for a standard measure of value. These standards of value were rather cumbersome in the beginning, as illustrated by the word "pecuniary." It is derived from the Latin word for "cattle," which were once used as the basis for calculating relative values. The idea of a light and convenient token of value to be used in exchange was a somewhat later development. Modern commerce, first facilitated by currency, has of course developed far beyond that stage and now makes use of varied instruments such as checks, drafts, and letters of credit.

FULLY NEGOTIATED TRANSACTIONS

One of the most important distinctions to be drawn is between fully negotiated transactions and routine transactions. This distinction is similar to that made by Commons between strategic and routine transactions. Fully negotiated transactions are those required to deal with the unique or nonrecurring situation and are effected by a small and temporarily organized group consisting of the agents of both parties. The fully negotiated transaction is strategic in the sense that it sets the conditions which may govern a number of subsequent transactions. For example, a manufacturer may negotiate a contract with a large chain-store organization. Thereafter the movement of goods to the individual stores belonging to the chain takes place on a more routine basis, but subject to the conditions established in the fully negotiated contract. Reference has already been made to the fact that one way of achieving efficiency in transactions is by reducing the transactions or their component elements to routine insofar as that is possible. Before discussing the various ways in which the routinization of transactions is accomplished, it is well to consider what is involved in a negotiated transaction. Various conditions are necessary in order that negotiation may take place, and there are some inherent limitations which control the outcome of a negotiation once it is under way. Negotiation techniques have been discussed in an earlier chapter. The main purpose here is to characterize the fully negotiated transaction as a background for discussing the problem of transactional efficiency. Some portions of this chapter may seem repetitive in relation to Chapter V. The emphasis here, however, is on types of transactions rather than on negotiation as an aspect of behavior systems.

Seminegotiated Transactions. Sometimes the seller offers a standard bundle of utilities at a stated price, and the details of this package are not subject to modification. Nevertheless, this might still be a fully negotiated transaction because of the amount of money involved or the importance of the purchase to the consumer. Major consumer purchases such as homes, automobiles, appliances, and life insurance policies tend to conform to this pattern. Even in this type of transaction the representative of the seller has some room for true negotiation. He may have authority to grant some concession from the stated price in order to clinch a sale. He may undertake to have certain alterations made in the product or to carry back to his principal the requirements specified by the buyer, such as the renovation of a house to put it in satisfactory condition for occupancy.

It has been stated that fully negotiated transactions sometimes set up the conditions for routine transactions which are to follow. There are many business transactions where this is not the case. These usually involve the sale of major assets rather than the movement of goods through the channels of trade. Fully negotiated transactions of this type might involve the transfer of a major piece of equipment or the sale of an entire plant. This type of transaction also arises in the merger of firms or the acquisition of one firm by another. Such transactions are pertinent to marketing primarily because marketing considerations are usually invoked in evaluating the plant or business which is offered for sale. In a negotiation of this type the character of the negotiating group as an organized behavior system becomes quite clear. All of the participants in such a negotiation have an important stake in arriving at a deal to which their principals on either side can agree. One side or the other may be represented by a broker, whose compensation is contingent on the deal taking place.

In all fully negotiated transactions the participants may be regarded as collaborating to produce an integrated price structure which can cause the transaction to happen. In those cases in which a prefabricated bargain is offered by one party to the other, this central task of negotiation is shifted to the organization which worked out the deal. In these cases the construction of an integrated price structure becomes a matter of internal negotiation inside that organization. The interests of the customer are then likely to be represented by the sales department or by others inside the organization who undertake to advocate the customer's interest and who insist that certain conditions will have to be met if the customer is to accept the proffered deal.

THE ROUTINIZATION OF TRANSACTIONS

Reducing transactions to routine is as basic a means• for achieving economy in marketing as the use of intermediate sorting. In fact, it is hard to separate the two principles of marketing efficiency, since each reacts upon the other and each is a part of the continuing search for greater efficiency in marketing. In order to reduce any operation to routine, it must be highly repetitive in nature. Transaction routines apply to classes of transactions that are judged to be essentially similar in their purposes and in the means of carrying them out. To divide transactions into similar groups so that routines can be applied is in itself an act of sorting performed by management. A recognition of classes of transactions which can be performed in a generally similar way becomes the basis for setting up such intermediaries as wholesalers and brokers. There are, however, a number of other aspects to the routinization of transactions; and it is the purpose of this section to discuss these methods. Routines are essential when a large volume of transactions must be carried out within a very limited period of time. Elaborate institutional arrangements have been developed to permit the handling of a large volume of transactions of similar character. Prime examples are afforded by both the stock exchange and the commodity exchanges. Transactions involving millions of dollars may be effected almost instantaneously by the passing of a few words or even by the use of hand signals. It must be recognized, however, that such routine transactions occur within the framework of an elaborate set of regulations governing all the traders on the exchange and the conduct of transactions. The individual trader must hold a seat on the exchange and must fulfill some rigorous qualifications in order to be admitted. His fellow traders are prepared to deal with him on the basis of code signals because he has been fully investigated and they have confidence in his financial responsibility and the reliability of his word. All of the rules and regulations of the exchange and all of the commitments made by the individual traders are implicit in each of their transactions, even though they occur in an instant of time. This is an apt illustration of the elements of negotiation which are implicit in routine transactions.

Types of Routine. The various commodity exchanges are believed to serve the economic function of bringing about a stable relationship between supply and demand. It is important to recognize that this stabilizing effect takes place within an institutional framework which has been especially devised for the purpose. There is no magic as to numbers among buyers and sellers which guarantees market stability. The tendency toward equilibrium prices could not manifest itself except through man-made facilities for communication and integration between all parties on both sides of the market. Thus, even in those products which are assumed to be most fully characterized by equilibrium prices, there is an integrating structure which relates supply and demand. This structure does not have to be negotiated separately for each transaction but is imbedded in rules which apply to a number of transactions. The rules on the exchange cover many things, such as trading on margin, short sales, and brokerage fees. These rules can be changed from time to time; and new rules, when adopted, represent the consensus of the traders on the exchange or of its governing body. This occasional modification of rules as a result of discussion is in effect a form of negotiation. Sometimes rules may be imposed upon the exchanges by the government. In that case, there is a still broader negotiating framework involved, including discussions in Congress and appearances before congressional committees by various parties who have an interest in the proposed legislation.

Improvements in Routines. There are many opportunities for improving routines in sales of products to consumers. One outstanding development in this direction, at least in the grocery field, has been the almost universal adoption of self-service. Not only do customers assemble their own orders, but they also serve themselves in a rather uniform way and pass out by the same checkout stations. Reduction of the transaction to routine is fairly complete so far as store personnel is concerned. Most of the visible personnel in a busy supermarket are occupied at the checkout counters checking off the items purchased, receiving payment and making change, and packaging the goods for convenient removal from the store. By reducing the final transaction to routine, it is possible to routinize all of the preceding steps in store operation. Personnel not engaged at the checkout counters is busy with such operations as replenishing the shelves from which the customers have removed merchandise. Behind the scenes, there may be a team of meatcutters cutting and packaging meat for open display.

In the absence of clerk service to customers, routine methods have been found to provide the information needed by customers in making their selections. All packages are now price-marked for the convenience of the customer and of the clerk at the checkout counter. Large display signs in the store indicate the general location of types of merchandise that the consumer may wish to buy. Many packaged products have labels carrying information provided by the manufacturer as to how to use the product in order to get the best results. In other retail lines, such as department stores, all merchandise generally carries price tags; and many items carry informative labels provided either by the manufacturer or by the retail store to tell the customer about the quality of the product and about its uses. It is believed that much more must happen to improve the routine of selling in lines other than groceries. Retail salespeople constitute a relatively low-paid occupational group. It will not be economically feasible to make a great improvement in the compensation of retail personnel unless means are found for putting their efforts to better and more productive use. There are many new possibilities, some of them already going on in an experimental way, for increasing the volume of goods which can be moved effectively by a given number of retail salesmen. Meanwhile the use of vending machines continues to increase, and more and more products are being adapted to sale by this method. The mechanization of selling in retail stores does not seem likely to follow this direction. Stores have been tried which were really nothing more than collections of vending machines for a variety of products, but without great success. Progress is more likely to lie in the direction of mechanizing aspects of the selling process, such as the display and demonstration of merchandise. Many visual aids, including television, will no doubt be applied; and electronic control devices will be used in quickly locating the merchandise the customer wants and in making sure that inventories are replenished.

The greatest single step in routinizing consumer transactions so far has been in the application of mass advertising. Individual transactions do not have to be negotiated on the spot because the consumer has been presold on the product before entering the store. In the case of such products as cigarettes, it has been possible to create the kind of brand following which makes selling truly automatic. In other classes of products, preselling cannot accomplish quite such a marked result. At the very least, it may help the consumer to feel reasonably well informed on a number of competitive makes, thus narrowing down the scope of the negotiation at the time of the retail purchase. Competitive advertising of refrigerators, for example, may have called attention to special features in each of several brands. The consumer has an opportunity to check these features when she sees the product on display in the retail store. Negotiation tends to be reduced to an evaluation of how much the special features may be worth in the individual purchase as compared to a more streamlined model. Thus, what Aspinwall called "orange goods" (see Chapter VI) tend to be moved through what might be designated as partially negotiated transactions. Even this stage represents a great step forward in the economy of distribution as compared to a full-fledged discussion of all features of the product between the consumer and the retailer.

One important aspect of routinization of transactions is in the handling of the credit phase of the operation. A customer of a department store in effect negotiates concerning the privilege of buying on credit, and all transactions thereafter are governed by that agreement so long as the customer's credit remains good. The distribution of charge plates to the customers of department stores is an obvious effort to routinize the credit transaction still further. In recent years the use of charge plates has been extended to cover groups of small stores located in a single business center. Thus the cost of credit investigation and collections is shared by all of the stores, some of which could not afford to sell on credit if they had to bear these costs alone. In lieu of consumer credit, some stores administer lay-away plans by which customers are allowed to make their selections and call for the merchandise when they are ready to pay for it. Installment credit is another widespread routine for handling payment when the customer is not able to pay cash.

Ordinary open-credit accounts, when administered through effective routines, may actually represent a saving to both the store and the consumer in time and effort. It is easier to make and to receive periodic payments by check than to receive cash payments on each of the transactions that might be involved over a period of time.

One of the great opportunities for the routinization of transactions pertains to transactions between the retailer and the wholesale warehouse. In fact, there is wisdom in the definition of a chain-store organization as a wholesale warehouse with an assured group of customers. Having an assured group of customers, of course, eliminates an element of risk; but it also contributes to the routinization of transactions. Usually, the retail stores make requisitions on standard forms which list the whole inventory carried in the warehouse. In some cases, these forms are arranged so as to correspond to the arrangement of goods along the assembly line in the warehouse. Thus the processes of order assembly and of charging out goods to the stores are reduced to effective routines. This kind of operation is not restricted to relations between chain-store units and their central warehouse. Many modern efficient wholesale warehouses, particularly in the grocery field, have adopted similar devices for co-ordinating orders from retail customers with operations taking place within the warehouse.

A regular method for checking on credit standings is even more necessary at this level than in dealing with the consumer, since it would be inconvenient and costly to make all sales to retailers on a cash basis. Not only does each wholesaler have his own credit manager, but special credit services have grown up to fit this need. Keeping intact the fabric of business confidence as to credit on one side and as to quality of goods on the other is an essential background for establishing and maintaining effective and cost-reducing routines. Thus, quality control, no less than credit investigation or mass advertising, is an important means toward the routinization of transactions at all levels. Quality control can give some assurance that goods will be uniform and that they will really meet the needs of the buyer. Under the best of circumstances, there will be a flow of complaints from consumers to retailer and from retailers back to their suppliers. Good routines in handling complaints are not only important in themselves but also help to maintain the atmosphere of confidence which must support the other established routines.

Problems of Routines. A number of special problems in the routinization of transactions arise in selling durable goods to consumers or in selling equipment to industry. The problem of payment on such major items has been met in part by the development of installment credit and the growth of special finance companies to help finance installment payments on such purchases as automobiles. Another characteristic feature of automobile retailing is the trade-in allowance. The automobile is the only manufactured product on which a well-integrated secondhand market has developed. The individual who owns an automobile and trades it in for a new one may be said to be increasing his stock of utilities so far as personal transportation is concerned. In other words, what he is buying on that occasion is not a complete new automobile but the difference between the utility remaining in his old car and the full utility represented by the new car. The present annual sales of automobiles could not have been developed without the use of trade-in allowances.

While the existence of a secondhand market facilitates the movement of new cars, it also creates some special problems for the automobile industry. On the average, every sale of a new car to one consumer involves the purchase of used cars by two other consumers. The industry has attempted to induce new-car buyers to put repurchase on a regular schedule, taking on a new car every two or three years and disposing of the old one. This is an ingenious attempt to routinize transactions in a field of major importance for the stability of the entire economy. An attempt at routinization can scarcely hope for more than moderate success in the purchase of a product involving so much money. If there were a loss of confidence among new-car buyers because of a business recession, most of them would be able to prolong the use of their present cars by as much as two or three years. Thus, automobile sales are especially sensitive to business trends; and, because of the size of the industry, any uncertainty as to its sales is a point of vulnerability for the whole economy. To get new-car buyers to place their purchases on a more or less routine cycle is equivalent to inducing them to recognize what they are paying out annually for personal transportation and to allow for it in their household budgets.

Routinization by Lease. One way to accomplish this change in consumer psychology would be to rent automobiles on service contracts rather than selling them. An increasing number of consumers are being supplied with automobiles in this way, with all costs of maintaining the cars in working condition being handled by the supplier under the service contract. This method involves not only another approach to the routinization of transactions but also the separation of use and ownership. Technically, what the consumer wants from the product is its utility, although there is also an intangible value in pride of ownership. The satisfaction in the use of the product might well be greater when it is obtained on a lease basis and the supplier must compete by trying to keep all of his customers fully satisfied.

There is no real novelty in this type of development for automobiles, and it is not clear how far it could reasonably be extended to other types of household goods such as furniture and appliances. The principle is not new because it is so widely applied in the case of dwellings. Homes may be rented completely furnished, which is the principal avenue by which furniture and appliances might be provided on a rental basis. The subject is introduced here as representing another direction in which the market might be expanded or the cost of marketing lowered by decreasing the consumer's investment and thus making it easier to reduce this type of transaction to routine. For the foreseeable future the leasing arrangement is likely to serve as an alternative, with an appeal to a limited class of consumers rather than as the chief reliance of consumers in satisfying their needs for durable goods.

Industrial selling is quite a different matter, and lease arrangements are likely to meet an expanding need in the use of equipment of many kinds. There are large companies using many automobiles or trucks which obtain all of these automobiles under lease arrangements. There are some tax incentives for the use of rental fleets, but there are also good operating reasons in turning all problems such as maintenance and insurance over to the specialists represented by the staff of the supplier. Some firms own their own fleets of trucks but nevertheless have all of their tires provided on lease contracts. The rental service replaces or repairs the tires as needed and charges for them on a mileage basis.

There are some types of business equipment which are provided on a rental basis, such as punch-card tabulating equipment and some of the new electronic computers. There must certainly be a substantial saving in the cost of negotiation as compared to selling all such equipment outright. There are two conditions with respect to tabulating equipment which appear to favor this type of arrangement. One is the rapid technical progress which is being made in the field. The other is the relative ease with which the cost of using such equipment can be justified as part of a current operating budget. There should be many opportunities for this type of arrangement in industrial selling wherever these two conditions exist. It is obviously more difficult to routinize transactions involving the sale of industrial equipment than those involving consumer goods. It is for this reason that the rental basis of providing equipment seems particularly hopeful as a means for routinizing transactions in the industrial field.

Routinization by Service Guarantee. Another factor which is related to routinization in the purchase of durable goods is the service guarantee. The guarantee for an initial period serves a purpose similar to quality control in maintaining customer confidence. In the case of equipment the user is interested in performance and is often greatly inconvenienced when service is interrupted. The high cost of service and repair can come to be a major obstacle in the sale of various classes of durable goods. For example, the owner of a moderately priced watch may find it is more economical to buy a new watch than to get the old one repaired. To reduce transactions of this type to routine would require a substantial change in present attitudes of consumers. With the progress of automation, it may be increasingly true that many products can be turned out so cheaply in mass production that it will not pay to repair substantial damage to a unit already in use. Visitors from Europe are sometimes shocked by the graveyards of old automobiles that they observe in various places around the country. Of course, much of the steel in these junked automobiles finds its way back to the blast furnaces; and some of it eventually shows up again in new automobiles.

Routinization by Prepackaging. One of the more obvious methods for routinizing transactions which has not been mentioned so far is that of prepackaging many types of consumer goods. The package provides a predetermined amount of the particular product, thus limiting discussion of the amount to the size of the package or the number of packages to be purchased at one time. It also, of course, eliminates the labor of weighing and packaging the product at the time of purchase. Some products are provided in returnable containers, so that the handling of empty bottles becomes a further step in routinizing transactions. Milk and beer and soft drinks are all handled in this way, but there has also been an increasing use of one-way containers for all of these products. The one-way container is a still further step toward routinization, so long as the economy as a whole is not confronted by a problem of conservation of materials. Even so, it is probably more efficient for wastepaper or other packaging materials to be collected by specialized agencies and to be sent back to the mill than it is to have empty containers moving back through the retailer to the producer.

SEPARATION OF GOODS AND TITLE

It is sometimes convenient analytically to distinguish between the movement of goods through the channels of trade and the movement of the title to goods. In most transactions, both goods and the title to goods are involved. There are many variations in this pattern, particularly in the area of wholesale trade. The conventional wholesale merchant handles both the goods and the title to the goods. That is to say that he buys merchandise from suppliers and takes possession of it, storing it in his own warehouse until each case is sold and passed on to his retail customers. Unless there is some good reason for separating the aspects of physical possession and ownership of the merchandise, the routinization of transactions is facilitated by keeping them both in the same hands. The wholesaler who sells goods to the retailers is assumed in most cases to have these goods on hand for immediate delivery after the sale is made. It would be an unnecessary complication if the retailer had to buy goods from one firm and look to another firm for the actual delivery of the merchandise to his store.

It is not always true, however, that goods and title move most efficiently in the same channel. Thus the separation of channels may become a basic source of economies in marketing, closely related to those which have been stressed so far, such as the use of intermediate sorting and the routinizing of transactions. It is essential, of course, that the use of separate channels for the movement of goods and for the transfer of title should not interfere with unified responsibility for the completion of the transaction. Thus, in those cases in which the two phases of marketing are separated, one of the two firms on the supply side takes major responsibility and is the one upon whom the customer primarily relies for the satisfaction of his requirements. There are a number of ways in which the separation of goods and title can take place. Four specialized types of intermediary or of intermediary transactions will be described where each separation occurs.

Consignment Selling. One such separation is represented by consignment selling, in which the intermediary takes possession of the goods but does not take title. This deviation does not affect the character of the transaction with the customer of the intermediary, since he still collects from his customers as well as delivering the goods. The purpose of consignment selling is to relieve the intermediary from the cost of investing in the merchandise and thus avoiding risk, particularly in connection with the introduction of products which so far do not have an established market demand. Consignment selling has also been used for the special purpose of enabling the original producer to maintain control over selling policies—as, for example, the resale price at which the merchandise will be sold. The value of consignment selling with respect to the effectiveness of marketing lies primarily in the direction of getting goods on the market more quickly than might be possible if it were necessary to make an outright sale to wholesalers or retailers who were not yet convinced of the salability of the products.

Wholesalers without Stocks. A special type of intermediary which has been growing rapidly in the past few years is the wholesaler who does not carry stocks. This type of wholesale merchant takes title to the goods but does not take possession. In other words, he is involved in the financing of the movement of goods but not in physical handling. Wholesalers without stocks are now found in a number of fields. Typical of the commodities handled in this way are products such as lumber and coal which the retail dealer is prepared to buy in carload lots. The wholesaler arranges the transaction, but the goods are shipped directly from the manufacturer to the retailer. Nothing would be gained by the maintenance of wholesale stocks when the goods can be sold in such large volume. The reader might wonder whether the wholesaler serves any economic function at all under these circumstances. Aside from finance, which has already been mentioned, he serves the very important function of negotiation with both the retailer and the supplier. Even though the producer ships in carload lots, he is relieved of the necessity of maintaining the kind of sales force which could sell on a car-lot basis or the kind of credit service which would be involved in selling to numerous retail dealers, many of them located hundreds or thousands of miles away from his place of business.

The Broker. Another type of intermediary who serves an important function in such fields as groceries is the broker. The broker does not take either title or possession of the goods he is selling. His function is strictly that of contact and negotiation. The strength of a good broker lies in the standing he enjoys with wholesalers and chain-store organizations in his territory. The economy he provides for the manufacturer rests on the fact that he represents several different lines. The cost of a call by a broker's salesman can really be divided among his various customers.

The Commission Merchant. Another type of intermediary who operates on somewhat the same basis as the broker is known as a commission merchant. The commission merchant differs from the broker in that he takes possession of the goods, which are in his care and custody until sold. Nevertheless, he is authorized by his principal to negotiate the transfer of title, so that the operations of the commission merchant are quite similar to consignment selling. Commission merchants have played an especially important part in agricultural marketing and have handled a large proportion of the livestock which is shipped to terminal markets. The routinization of transactions of this type involves special problems of grading and the regulation of terminal markets by government agencies.

SPECIAL PROBLEMS OF TRANSFER

Some types of transactions involve special transfer problems, such as valuation, contact, and physical movement. Internal transactions taking place within a single firm and international transactions which involve movement from one country to another are worthy of a brief review because of the light they throw on these problems of transfer.

Internal Transactions. Internal transactions are increasingly important in major industrial firms. A large chemical company, for example, may have a volume of transactions going on between its various divisions equal to a significant fraction of all transactions with external customers or suppliers. The biggest single problem posed by the internal transaction is the problem of valuation. In some cases the transfers are made at prices which are supposed to reflect the costs to the originating division. In other cases, transfers are made at what are presumed to be market prices or the same prices at which the product would be sold to external customers. If the various divisions are held individually responsible for profits on their operations, neither of the policies mentioned will be wholly satisfactory to both sides. The first policy of transfer at cost assumes that the originating division was fortunate to recover its cost on this part of its volume and that the main job of further manufacture and external marketing still remains to be performed by the division on the receiving end.

The second policy would proceed on the assumption that the main job of creating utility has been performed by the originating division and that the second division should be able to compete with external customers in any further enhancement of the utility of the product or of the total output of the company. On the whole, the latter theory is nearer the mark; but external prices may not be altogether fair to the receiving division. There is good reason to believe that the internal customer can be served more economically than an external customer. Certainly the cost of negotiation should be less, although there is still a large amount of explicit or implicit negotiation with respect to internal transfers. It should be possible to schedule deliveries to an internal customer in a way that will even out the production load of the originating division. Reference has already been made to the advantages accruing in the operation of a chain-store warehouse through the fact that the warehouse has an assured list of customers consisting of the retail units of the chain.

The problem of valuation is inescapable in transfers between organizations which are individually held responsible for making a profit even though they may be under the same ownership. In some companies the chief executive or executive committee finds itself occupied frequently in adjudicating problems which arise in connection with internal transfers. The best answer would seem to lie in the direction of setting up a standard procedure for negotiation between divisions, with someone who exercises central authority stepping in only when the divisions are not able to reach an agreement. Transfers between divisions should exemplify the principle already described that fully negotiated transactions set the pattern for a series of routine transactions which are to follow. Perhaps these contracts should come up for reconsideration on a regular schedule, just as in dealings with external customers. It should be possible to regularize the process of renegotiation to a greater extent than in dealing with external customers. That is to say that there should be a general understanding of points to be covered in every negotiated transaction and of the criteria to be used in resolving disagreements. It might be possible in the internal situation to set up a standard negotiation procedure and require all negotiations between divisions to follow this pattern.

All the problems of maintaining an orderly flow of goods can arise in the internal situation. There can be serious disputes over quality control, for example; and it often appears essential for the receiving division to make some independent check over and above the quality control measures undertaken by the originating division. Just as in external transactions, the end result should be an integrating price structure which covers all aspects of product specification, services to be performed on either side, and the terms and conditions governing the transfer. In addition, there are broader policy questions which may be essential topics of negotiation, just as in the relationships between independent firms. There is the question of whether the originating division is to be the sole source of supply for the receiving division for a given product or whether the receiving division is to be authorized to buy outside when it can buy on a more favorable basis. One policy might reflect a greater emphasis on a regular and orderly flow of supplies to the receiving division, while the other is aimed toward getting the lowest possible price, whatever the source.

Another policy issue which arises is whether internal or external customers should be favored by the originating division or whether an effort should be made to treat them on the same basis. If the originating division is held responsible for earning a profit on its investment, it will be inclined to resolve this issue in a way that seems most favorable to the long-run interests of the division. Management, on the other hand, may have reason to enforce a policy of equal treatment for internal and external customers for the sake of good trade relations on the one hand and good internal morale on the other. Without such a policy the tendency to discriminate can be carried pretty far. For example, an originating division which has developed a new product may be reluctant to offer this product to its internal customer until it has first been offered to external customers. The originating division may be very sensitive about having another division of the company enter into active competition with external customers, pointing to the hazard of causing external customers to look to other sources.

International Transactions. International transactions are in a sense at the opposite extreme from internal transactions. That is to say that the two parties to a transaction, instead of being part of a single firm, are separated not only by distance but also by international boundaries and trade barriers. The governments of the two countries as well as the companies involved in effect become parties to the transactions. The participation of the governments is always implicit, but sometimes it is very direct and obvious. The flow of trade between two countries may be initiated by a trade agreement between the two governments which constitutes a fully negotiated transaction. But detailed negotiations then take place between customers and suppliers on either side. Finally, the more routine and continuous flow of goods takes place within this double framework of negotiation. Because of government involvement in international trade, detailed techniques of trading are necessarily concerned with clearances such as customs inspection, enforcement of import quotas, and the granting of export licenses.

Problems of valuation are especially difficult in the international sphere. This difficulty arises in part from a lack of a universally accepted medium of exchange. It is no longer possible for a transaction to be concerned largely with goods and services, but equal attention must be given to the means of payment. Historically, it has always been difficult to maintain a balanced relationship among the currencies of the various countries of the world. The money which serves so well as a medium of exchange within the boundaries of a single country serves less well on the international plane because its use becomes complicated by involvement with other monetary functions. The currency of a country represents a reservoir of value and reflects the accumulated assets and productive capacity of the country. Thus the value of currencies relative to each other changes for reasons which are not related to the flow of products in the channels of marketing. As long as these forces are reflected in the valuation of currency, the various currencies of the world serve very imperfectly as a medium of exchange for facilitating the flow of goods. Free trade in the classical sense among separate nations must always remain a dream unless some answer is found to this problem concerning the medium of exchange. It is true that trade is impeded by other barriers imposed by the various nations. It is also true that these restrictions are in part at least an attempt to cope with the problems created by the fact that the available medium of exchange is defective.

Some aspects of this problem of exchange are reflected by the technical phrase "the terms of trade." It is recognized that the terms of trade can deteriorate or improve from the viewpoint of one country in considering its trade relations with other countries. The author suggests the hypothesis that there is an ever-present tendency for the terms of trade to deteriorate from the viewpoint of raw materials countries in their dealings with countries whose exports are primarily finished goods. This hypothesis is consistent with the conception mentioned in an earlier chapter that goods in a sense have zero utility until they are fabricated in usable form and placed in the hands of the ultimate user. They accumulate market value along the way in anticipation of their final value in use. The further back the product is in the marketing channel, the less the value, and the greater the risk that it will never achieve utility in the sense of being placed in ultimate use. Something like the deterioration in the terms of trade seems to be involved in the chronic farm problem in the United States, with farmers, as producers of raw materials, tending to suffer a cumulative disadvantage in trading with other sectors of the economy.

The urgency to dispose of raw materials more often than not exceeds the urgency of industrial consumers to buy. Today the countries engaged primarily in the export of raw materials tend to be the smaller countries with less advanced economic development. Because of their urgency to sell, they are likely to engage in cut-throat competition for the markets provided by large customer countries. An example is the competition among the so-called "coffee republics" of Latin America for the market of the United States. For years these excesses of economic competition were a significant factor in the political instability of these republics. Our own State Department finally organized and operated what was in effect a coffee cartel in the hope of contributing to political stability and reducing the frequency of revolutionary outbreaks. While our government has generally taken a vigorous stand against cartels in statements of public policy, it was obliged to turn to this device when confronted by apparently insoluble practical problems.

Problems of contact and market development can also lead to the creation of special trading organizations. Such problems are characteristic of firms in an advanced economy like that of the United States in attempting to sell to small countries such as many in Latin America. The size of each individual market has not always justified the kind of sales organization and representation on the part of individual companies that they might maintain city by city in the United States. Some of these countries are smaller in population than leading American cities. The low level of consumer income and the amount of educational work to be done in developing markets for modern products in these countries increases the problem of contact still further. Trading companies can be established under a special act exempting American companies from antitrust action when they work together in the field of export trade. Thus, they are jointly able to maintain adequate sales representation in the various countries to which they sell. American firms are said to produce 60 per cent of all consumer goods and to consume most of these at home rather than selling them through export channels. Thus the relatively small scale of the export market, particularly when considered country by country with all of the trade clearances pertaining to each of these countries, is an obstacle to serious and sustained effort on the part of American exporters.

Aside from these special problems of valuation and contact, all of the normal problems involved in physical movement and the transfer of title are aggravated when trade takes place across international frontiers. There are special problems of physical handling and rigorous requirements for packaging to preserve the merchandise from the various hazards of rough treatment and salt water along the journey. Problems pertaining to quality and style represent special barriers in the development of export business. Esthetic tastes differ country by country, and most other countries have not moved so far as the United States in the direction of uniformity and standardization of products and perhaps give greater weight to individuality and the workmanship of skilled craftsmen. Sometimes, stylists and quality control experts from the consuming country must intervene at the stage of production in the producing country in order to assure that a product will be acceptable to the market. There are in the United States, as in other countries, firms engaged in the import business which sometimes try to give such guidance to their sources of supply in foreign countries. The imposition of new types of intermediaries in international trade as compared with domestic business was brought about in part by the special problems of negotiation and contact involved in international transactions.

REACTION AGAINST ROUTINES

With the emphasis which has been placed on the value of routines in reducing the cost of transactions, it would not be fair to close this chapter without acknowledging that there is often a sharp reaction against routine and that routinization can indeed be carried too far in some types of transactions. It is believed that customers grow restive and dissatisfied in many retail stores today because of the impression that they are being "processed" or put through routines to suit the store's convenience rather than their own. Emphasis on pleasing the customer is likely to decline in special types of retail institutions such as government stores or company commissaries. A few years ago the Russian newspaper, *Pravda,* was extremely critical of the attitude of Russian retail clerks toward customers. The American consumer needs only to go back to the days of wartime shortages to remember instances when he was treated in a similar brusque fashion by retail salespeople.

Customers grow impatient with routines, particularly when they feel that they are seeking service to meet emergency requirements. Some customers are particularly demanding and expect to be given favored treatment over anyone else in the store whenever they appear. There are other occasions requiring special handling of the products purchased in which consumers are likely to become impatient with established routines. The large retail store is a massive and complicated operation. It is sometimes difficult to arrange deviations from normal procedures. The customers who call up to cancel their orders may later be faced with all the extra bother of sending the merchandise back, sometimes becoming embroiled in lengthy correspondence with the store before receiving the proper credit to their accounts. Mass handling of goods and people will always have its weaknesses no matter how efficiently designed, and these weaknesses offer opportunity for retailers of special types to meet the desires of the more demanding customers. Thus, there continues to be substantial demand for custom-made goods, particularly in apparel, but applying to many other fields as well. Consumers, of course, differ as to what they would classify as routine purchases. Some are willing to buy one product on a relatively routine basis, while others would demand special service on that product but adjust themselves to routines on some other products.

Buyer Reactions. One new but rapidly growing type of retailing is the so-called "merchandise club" plan. This is really a mail-order operation in which one woman acts as an agent for the firm in securing orders from her friends or neighbors. However, she is not called an agent but is designated as a "club secretary." She induces other people to join the club in the sense of ordering a minimum amount of merchandise, helps them in making their selections from the catalog provided by the company, handles the weekly collections from all of the club members, and forwards the money to the company.

A detailed investigation of this type of operation led to the conclusion that its greatest strength lay in restoring a social atmosphere to purchasing transactions. The customer in this case was dealing with someone who was personally interested in her problems and who enjoyed going through the catalog with her and discussing various possible selections. The appeal of this plan appears to be especially strong with low-income families, where the housewife probably has been accustomed to deal with mass merchandisers and has not enjoyed the deferential and flattering treatment accorded to customers in the more exclusive shops. The prices at which the club plans offer merchandise are no lower than those for the same merchandise in the regular retail outlets and frequently somewhat higher. The housewife who serves as club secretary is performing a retail function which imposes a considerable burden of time and effort. She accepts a lower rate of compensation than would be represented by the normal margins of retail stores; furthermore, she is willing to be paid in merchandise rather than in cash. Thus the only explanation for the vitality and the rapid growth of this kind of operation seems to lie in the fact that it puts buying back in a central place in the social lives of the people involved. In a simpler economy the social aspect of marketing tends to be very much in evidence. Purchasing appears to be a congenial activity for many people. The strain and stress of getting to big stores and abiding by their routines seems to have had an unfavorable impact on this pleasurable aspect of buying.

Seller Reactions.   Sometimes there is a reaction against routines on the part of the seller. The manufacturer may be uneasy about his product being handled in a purely routine fashion by retailers and wholesalers, for fear that it will not realize its full possibilities in the market. Special sales on the part of retailers and special merchandising programs devised by suppliers are intended to create more than usual interest in the sale of merchandise and thus to overcome the inertia inherent in routine handling. A very able sales manager for a drug manufacturer once put in words what he considered the ideal situation for a manufacturer selling packaged products through drug stores. He said that he would like to have his products sold on a stable and routine basis throughout most of the year so long as he could arrange to have "all hell break loose" about four times during the year. This was an expression of a desire for special treatment and special attention from the channels of trade at recurrent intervals to provide assurance that everything possible was being done in developing the market for his product at retail.

One of the difficulties about resale price maintenance admitted even by its advocates is the fact that it tends to take the excitement out of merchandising. The retail drug field seems relatively tame and inactive in merchandising effort today as compared with the period before the fair-trade laws went into effect. Some of the transactions negotiated by the supplier in the course of the year are directed at purposes such as those suggested by the sales manager quoted above, and special inducements are given to wholesalers and retailers to break away from established routine at least for the duration of a special sales event. This effort to obtain special sales attention is in no way contrary to the fundamental principle that established routines should apply in moving the bulk of the volume on any commodity that is purchased regularly by the consumer.

Conflicts between Buyer and Seller.   Another difficulty is the conflict of routines which may arise between buyer and seller when each has his own ideas of how transactions can be routinized to suit his convenience. A big company may attempt to impose its own routines on both its suppliers and its customers. Its purchasing department prefers certain ways of handling transactions and requires its suppliers to abide by these routines if they want to do business with the company. At the same time, its sales department may similarly have its own preferences for handling transactions and may attempt to prescribe the procedure for dealing with its customers. These considerations involve the design of working forms such as purchase orders and sales invoices. If a company is fortunate enough to standardize these forms either in purchasing or in sales, it facilitates the establishment of standard routines within the company for processing orders and merchandise moving either inward or outward. The company which is too small to dominate its relations either with suppliers or with customers has to adapt itself to their procedures. There is a substantial element of cost involved in making this adjustment. Where large companies are on both sides of the transaction, there may be considerable conflict as to the method for handling transactions between them. In fact, the determination of routines for handling transactions which are satisfactory to both sides is likely to be one of the major subjects of a fully negotiated transaction when a large supplier and a large customer are dealing with each other.

Changes in the Character of Transactions. Aside from the deliberate deviation from routine on the part of either the buyer or the seller, there may be a tendency for routines to break down because the character of transactions has been undergoing a change. Routines set up to handle orders of a certain average size may no longer serve so well if there has been a sharp decline in the average size of the transaction. Routines may have been established on the assumption that most customers want to have the merchandise delivered, while as a matter of fact the majority have come to prefer to call for the merchandise themselves. Under one set of circumstances a manufacturer's salesman may call on his customers only once every three months. As circumstances in the trade undergo changes, it may be necessary to call as often as once a week.

Routines which are no longer appropriate may begin to break down under the stress of change. One signal that a breakdown may be imminent is the increasing number of instances in which some departure from routine seems to be required. The growing proportion of orders requiring special handling in a wholesale house as compared to those moving through the regular routine can well be interpreted as a sign that the time has come for a basic revision of routines which are better adapted to the new situation. So far as internal routines are concerned, this adjustment can be made through action taken by the company's management. If the routine pertains to the method of handling external transactions, it is clear that a new basis will have to be negotiated with customers or suppliers; and this process of renegotiation may occupy a considerable period of time.

In adopting new routines for customer transactions, a firm is faced with the fact that there are many variations among its customers and an important minority may still prefer the old methods, even though the requirements of the vast majority seem to indicate the necessity for revising routines. These considerations do not conflict with the desirability for good routines in general. The conclusion rather is that routines must be kept up to date in order to serve their basic purpose of reducing the cost of transactions and that occasional revision is necessary in order that they may perform that function.

THE LOCUS OF THE TRANSACTION

There is still another possibility open to functional analysis in trying to find means to reduce the cost of transactions or to make them more effective. That is to give analytical consideration to the question of where the transaction is located in time and space. Too frequently, marketing concepts seem to imply that the market exists in a single instant of time and that buyers and sellers are dealing with each other face to face in carrying out market transactions. Actually, there are some difficult analytical problems in deciding just where the market is located or when a transaction begins or is completed. From the viewpoint of functional analysis, these considerations as to the dimensions of time and space may open the way to new methods of increasing the efficiency of market transactions.

Suppose that two firms are located a thousand miles apart and one buys goods from the other. Where does this transaction take place? Does it occur at the seller's place of business or at the buyer's place of business? This is not a trivial question; it has real significance for considerations of geographical competition. When both buyers and sellers are spread over a wide geographical area and freight makes up a considerable part of the delivered cost of the product, some judgment must be made as to the geographical point at which the forces of competition are brought into focus.

Where the Transaction Takes Place.   It was this problem of the location of the market which was one of the underlying issues in the famous basing-point case in the steel industry. The effort of the government to compel the steel mills to quote prices at the mill plus freight equivalent to a determination that the transaction took place in he producing center where the sellers were located. The contrary policy of complete freight absorption is in effect on many small packaged products. Quoting prices on this basis is equivalent to a determination that the market exists and the transaction takes place at the buyer's

place of business. In the early stages of the controversy over steel prices
one government economist defended a modified basing-point system a
representing a fair compromise between the two extremes and amou
ing to a determination that the market was located and the transacti
took place at a hypothetical point somewhere between the locatio
of the buyer and the seller. Under the multiple basing-point syster
steel prices were equalized at a number of selected points; and a pri
was quoted to the customer based on this point plus freight from t
basing-point to his place of business. The government contended th
the basing-point system charged some customers unfairly with phanto
freight and contributed to excessive concentration in steel productic
The fact seems to have been overlooked that a small-scale steel indus
requiring shipment from one plant to another, as the various sta
in manufacturing proceeded, might result in a great increase in i
freight costs. It might also increase the cost of steel production as co.
pared with integrated mills by making it necessary to reheat the st
at each stage in the production process.

Where the Consumer Takes Possession.   In considering the lo
of the transaction, account may be taken separately of where the neg
tiation takes place and where the consumer takes possession of the goo
These two aspects of the transaction do not always occur at the sar
place, although they usually occur together unless there is good reas
to separate them. In most lines of retailing, both negotiation of the s
and transfer of possession to the consumer occur in the retail sto
In the purchase of furniture, appliances, and many department st
lines, the sale is usually concluded in the store; but the customer actua
takes possession when the goods are delivered to his home. Most typica
in transactions taking place in the wholesale trade, the sale is negotia
at the customer's place of business. Title or responsibility for the go
passes to the customer at the point when the merchandise is turned o
to a common carrier. If the merchandise is damaged in transit or is
layed in delivery, the customer has recourse against the transportati
company. There are some lines of retail trade, particularly in style goo
in which buyers regularly visit the wholesale markets to make
selections. The sales negotiation in these instances takes place a
seller's offices, but the physical transfer of goods may be handled
same way as in other wholesale lines.

There is a considerable volume of consumer buying in which
negotiation and taking possession of the goods occur at the consumer's
home rather than at the retailer's place of business. House-to-house

selling is still a recognized channel of distribution. A few years ago
it was said that about one third of the sterling flatware bought by
nsumers was being sold by house-to-house methods. Hosiery and a
riety of household necessities have been marketed in this way for
any years. At one time it was much more prevalent for urban house-
ves to have most of their food supplies delivered to the home. Dairy
d bakery products are the main examples of food products which are
till handled in this way to a substantial degree. At one time the actual
rchase was made at the home for important classifications of food
oducts such as fresh fruits and vegetables. Even packaged groceries
re sold some years ago from trucks which constituted traveling
ocery stores and which drove into neighborhoods and made sales to
usewives on the spot. The original experiments were well received but
were discouraged by legislation prompted by the conventional type of
tail grocer. It is somewhat doubtful whether the same kind of opera-
n could establish itself today when family automobiles are almost
versal and many large stores with ample parking space are available.

Locus of the Transaction in Time.   The problem of when a
nsaction occurs can be considered in terms of its beginning and its
termination and also in terms of the transfer of possession as compared
the transfer of title. In many transactions, possession and title are
nsferred at the same time. When this is not true, it might be reason-
e to assume that the transaction is completed by either the transfer
possession or the transfer of title, whichever is later. In major sales
olving the use of credit, such as homes and automobiles, the transac-
n might not be completed even then. The buyer takes possession of
he house or the car and receives a formal title, which nevertheless is of
rovisional nature until the last payment has been made. Only then
is title clear and free and no longer subject to the possibility of re-
session by the seller. It is even more difficult to say when a transac-
begins. If a deal is finally concluded, with both title and possession
sing to the buyer, it is possible to start with this accomplished result
and work backward. In other words, the beginning of the transaction
ght be identified with the first contact with the buyer and seller which
lly led to the completed transaction. The first contact might have
n a casual shopping call or a request for information. Many such
ial contacts never result in completed transactions. There are oc-
ons when a buyer and seller may go through protracted negotiations
and be on the verge of closing a deal several times and in the end fail to
reach an agreement. In such encounters, many of the same activities

occur which make up market transactions; but they can scarcely be described as transactions unless they finally result in the movement of goods or services.

New Possibilities for Transactional Efficiency. Consideration the locus of the transaction might open up new avenues for devisi novel methods of distribution. These new possibilities would pert both to the geographical dispersion of the market and to differences time preferences between the buyer and the seller. The time may come when two-way television and other electronic developments will mak it possible to conclude many transactions without either buyer or sell leaving his regular location. Many transactions today, of course, a concluded by mail or by telephone. The use of television would mak it possible to show samples without bringing the customer into th presence of the merchandise. Further developments in communication might make it possible for an intermediary such as a wholesaler withou stocks to hold a three-way conversation with a supplier and a custome concerning such purchases as carload shipments of coal or lumber.

The difference in time preferences of buyers and sellers has bee partially resolved by the mechanism of credit selling. During the wa years, when there was a scarcity of automobiles and many other types of durable goods, the disparity of time preferences ran in the other direction, with many individuals unable to get delivery of goods ev though they might be able to pay cash. The late Rolf Nugent devise a plan whereby customers could receive substantial discounts by makin advance payments for durable goods and at the same time establishin a priority as to delivery date. This idea received considerable publicity at the time under the name of the Nugent Plan. Under the boom con-ditions and with the high levels of consumer income which have pr vailed in the postwar years, there has apparently been little demand f the use of such a device in marketing. Dr. Nugent did not regard device as merely a wartime expedient but believed that it could be u in peacetime to stabilize the economy and to regularize the rate o production of durable goods. He once related an incident of a conver-sation with John Maynard Keynes in which the British economist told him that if he had developed his theories in the United States, he woul have been compelled to give the regularization of the buying of c sumer durable goods a central place in his theories concerning the bus ness cycle.

One of the goals of every business concern is to develop a steady flow of business from individual transactions. Quite possibly, new develop-ments in marketing will arise from a study of the transactional flow as compared with further analysis of the individual transaction. Many firms during wartime found it relatively easy and agreeable to do business, since they were steadily engaged in capacity production to fill the apparently insatiable needs of government purchasing agencies. Many businessmen whose first love is production would prefer some such arrangement in peacetime rather than face the uncertainties of the market. In normal business, opportunities of that kind lie primarily in supplying the needs of great merchandising organizations such as the mail-order houses and the chain stores. There are also cases in industrial marketing where a company of moderate size sells its entire output either to one firm or to as few as five or six customer firms.

The really important achievement is to establish that type of transactional flow in the face of market uncertainties. Various devices have been used for this purpose, and others may yet be developed. Some of these might resemble the long-term contracts for continuous supply which are frequently observed in industrial markets, but adapting the same principle to the needs of consumers. Consumers are already familiar with supply contracts, as in the purchase of fuel oil or the various household utilities. The fuel oil dealer undertakes to keep his customers supplied without waiting for orders from them and bills them periodically.

In recent years there has been some use of this type of supply contract to provide household services such as household cleaning or window washing. These services have developed because of the scarcity of domestic help. Through greater specialization the employees of such services are able to provide a greater economic product for the customer and to obtain higher compensations for themselves. Similar arrangements with respect to repair services will be increasingly needed because of the number of appliances in the average household and the problem of keeping them all in continuous service. Eventually the consumer may be able to contract for such services on the assumption of preventive maintenance rather than waiting for a breakdown to occur and suffering the resulting inconvenience.

Another problem in regularizing transactional flow results from the recurrent peaks of sales on either a weekly or a seasonal basis. Types of retailing such as the jewelry business which reach a high peak during the Christmas season have endeavored to find means of supporting their sales during the remainder of the year. The department store field seems to have adjusted itself to living with its seasonal peaks. Some feel that their operations might be much more efficient if their volume were spread more evenly throughout the year. Others hold that the excitement of Christmas shopping produces additional business which the stores would not be able to obtain by any other means. The reasonable conclusion might be that the peaks could be moderated somewhat but could never be entirely eliminated.

SELECTED REFERENCES

COMMONS, JOHN R. *Legal Foundations of Capitalism.* New York: Macmillan Co., 1924.

ALEXANDER, R. S., SURFACE, S. M. and ALDERSON, WROE. *Marketing.* 3d ed. Boston: Ginn & Co., 1953.

LONGMAN, DONALD R., and SCHIFF, MICHAEL. *Practical Distribution Cost Analysis.* Homewood, Ill.: Richard D. Irwin, Inc., 1955.

MAYNARD, H. H., and BECKMAN, J. N. *Principles of Marketing.* 5th ed. New York: Ronald Press, 1952.

There has been relatively little analysis of the exchange transaction, despite the fact that it is the basic unit of marketing activity. Commons sensed its importance more than any other economist. The analysis of the transaction is a major topic both in the reference cited here and in his *Institutional Economics.* He was the first to draw the distinction between routine and other transactions which is employed in this chapter.

Students of distribution cost analysis were obliged to recognize the fundamental importance of the transaction and to try to determine the relative weight of commodity characteristics and customer characteristics to transactional cost. This subject is discussed in Alexander, Surface, and Alderson, and more recently and comprehensively by Donald Longman and Schiff. Maynard and Beckman give some attention to the geographical locus of the transaction, as well as to its position in time.

Chapter XI

DYNAMICS OF MARKET ORGANIZATION

The organization of the market is dynamic because of inherent factors quite aside from response to changes in supply and demand. The concept of a free market implies freedom to organize. Firms do not confine their competition to operations within the market but strive competitively to influence the organization of the market in their own interest. To the extent that competition centers on market organization, change is inevitable.

Units in a behavior system, such as firms in a marketing channel, experience a combination of independence and interdependence. There is an ever-present tension between the desire to stand apart and the urge to stand together. There is the further complication that two systems of behavior may be relatively conformable or nonconformable quite aside from the attitude of the two parties toward working together.

Following a discussion of these dynamic tensions, the resulting concepts are applied to some major aspects of market organization. These include marketing channels, trading centers, and interregional and international trade. Inherent organizational tensions serve to explain changes in structure or the re-sorting of functions by areas or among organized behavior systems.

EVALUATION OF DYNAMIC PRINCIPLES

The various types of behavior systems in marketing change over time and thereby bring about changes in the organization of the market itself. Intensive consideration has already been given to the dynamics of the individual marketing firm and the way that it reacts with its environment. This chapter will consider the dynamics of other types of behavior systems in marketing, such as the marketing channel, the trading center, and the national or international market. Each of these types of behavior systems will be discussed in turn, but first it is necessary to review some of the dynamic principles which might apply in the development of these behavior systems in relation to the organization of the market as a whole.

Several formulations of dynamic principles have been introduced in preceding chapters. Our present concern is the search for a central principle which either embraces all of the others or can be regarded as of overriding importance in the interpretation of dynamic market organization. Functional analysis does not hesitate to use a variety of principles or of perspectives in illuminating practical problems. It is true, however, that science in any field tends to progress toward the identification of a relatively few principles of interpretation which can at least serve to establish the logical relationship among the various perspectives. This preference for a relatively simple and well-integrated conceptual scheme is sometimes called "the principle of parsimoney." This section represents a moderate attempt to proceed in accordance with the principle of parsimony in treating the problem of the changing organization of markets.

Group Drive Based on Individual Expectations. One set of dynamic concepts which are basic to the whole approach to marketing theory presented here starts with the group drive based on individual expectations. The capacity of an organization results from mobilizing the energies of all the individuals who expect to share in the output produced by the organization. In order to share in the output, the individual has to have status in the organization. In order to be sure about the extent of his share, he must have an established and well-defined status. There is a hierarchy of positions within an organization, so that individuals compete for status. In their competition for status, each of these individuals is acting in accordance with the power principle. Without status in some organized group, the individual's efforts are usually without avail in trying to achieve his personal objectives. Hence, status is the first and underlying objective which the individual must hold in mind if he is to attain more specific goals. The dynamic drive of the individual organization participating in marketing rests on this complex of factors centering in status expectations.

Drive toward Growth. Another set of dynamic principles was introduced in discussing the relationship of the marketing firm to its environment. Growth is a normal goal of a marketing organization and often an essential requirement for the maintenance of individual expectations and hence of group solidarity. At the same time, growth creates strains and tensions both within the organization and in the relation of the organization to its environment. Externally, marketing firms are always in competition with other marketing firms. They do not compete merely by homogeneous groups, but each is trying to find its own individual niche within the market. In discussing competition, the concept of differential advantage was introduced. The very essence of competition is the attempt to find some distinctive feature which will set a firm off from all of its competitors. Thus, even if firms within a given industry were considered to be identical at the start, the very processes of competition would move in the direction of differentiation and hence heterogeneity.

Drive toward Closure. Other concepts which can be used in explaining market changes are the varying degrees of uncertainty in closed and open systems and the drive toward closure which appears to be present in all systems of action. The marketing executive exercises relatively effective control within his own sales organization, but his actions are subject to greater risk in dealing with his marketing channels and still greater hazards in making plans for influencing the actions of consumers. All problem solving in marketing or any other field of action may be defined as coping with uncertainty and reducing the risks of action to tolerable limits. Every behavior system is open for such purposes as replacing or increasing its membership when needed, but must be closed in a structural sense to provide complete circuits for effective action. The drive for closure carries us a step closer to the central principle we are seeking. The drive for status, fundamental as it is, is not sufficient to explain the creation of behavior systems; rather, it throws light on the persistence of those which already exist.

Drive to Expand in a Single Direction. The peculiar rhythm of competitive development was discussed and the apparent alternation between periods of rapid but unbalanced growth and periods of readjustment by which balance is restored. Just as in animal evolution, it appears that developments with a definite direction can become established and then seem to have a self-perpetuating momentum. This drive to expand in a single direction can be manifested at various levels in the market. It is manifested in some instances in the rapid spread of a new fad among consumers or a new type of operation among retail stores. At a broader level, it can be observed in the drive of the whole economy toward greater specialization at one time and the predominance of integration and mergers at another.

Proliferation of Opportunity. A closely related concept is that of the proliferation of opportunity. The appearance of a new firm or of a new type of operation does not foreclose opportunity for others in a free market. It often tends to open up new dimensions of opportunity. The three primary aspects of proliferation, as discussed in an earlier chapter, were simulation, deviation, and complementation. Simulation is clearly related to the biological notion of hypertrophy. In other words, hypertrophy might be defined as a condition in which the appearance of a new type of operation immediately produces a whole swarm of simulants which continue to be propagated until the movement has obviously gone too far. The opportunity to compete by taking away some of the prospective business of an established firm by deviating in some respects from the pattern it has established is clearly in line with the pursuit of differential advantage. The opportunity to establish a new firm or a new operation to complement those that are already in the market is a manifestation of the drive toward closure. In this case the new firm comes into existence precisely because of the need for completing a system of action or for balancing the structure by adding a missing link. The innovator must have the insight to see this opportunity and the confidence to develop it. At the same time, it is fair to say that conditions are prepared for his entry into the field by the unsatisfied needs and the excessive uncertainties of existing organizations.

Behavioral Drift and Pathology of Organization. Finally, there are the concepts of behavioral drift and of the pathology of organization. According to these principles, organizations are inherently vulnerable to change because fixed patterns of behavior cannot be expected to persist indefinitely. Individuals may drift away from these patterns quite unconsciously, and the most conservative behavior system may turn into something different over a period of time. An operating system consisting of human beings and the patterns of behavior which they follow by tacit consent turns into something else simply through the processes of use. The pathology of organization is important in this connection primarily as creating mutations in behavior patterns which can become the basis of selection for organized behavior in the future.

Competition in the Drive to Organize. Taking these various concepts into account, it appears possible to interpret the dynamics of market organization in terms of a simple extension of the theory of competition presented in Chapter IV. The individual or the firm does not merely compete within a system of action; it is also engaged in the attempt to create and maintain a system of action. The system of action the individual is trying to create is naturally of such a character that he can operate to advantage within its framework. This result is of great advantage to the individual or to the firm if it can be achieved. As a result, there is very keen competition in the effort to establish or control organized behavior systems.

Status and Competition. The competitive attempt to design and bring into being a behavior system according to one's own preferences is the keenest form of competition and the one which shapes the course of development in market organization. This extension of a functionalist theory of competition is quite consistent with the emphasis on expectations derived from status. The more vigorous individuals within a group do not merely accept status conferred by their associates, but take the lead in creating a status structure from which they may gain further advantage.

These attitudes with respect to status and competition are the attitudes of self-assertive individuals who have confidence in their own ability to rise within the status structure or to dominate the marketing system they are attempting to create. It might be said that the kind of competition described is the competition of leaders for followers. Within the marketing system, it is the competition for suppliers to get customers to abide by the plans that they have developed; or it is the competition among large buyers to persuade suppliers to co-operate in accordance with the policies which they have adopted. The highest form of differential advantage is the advantage which an aggressive marketing organization may obtain over its competitors in securing co-operation from its customers or its suppliers. Just as in the simpler forms of differential advantage, there is no assurance of holding on to such a competitive edge permanently. There is a direct challenge to competitors to find an effective counterstrategy. Thus, marketing institutions and processes change because aggressive market leadership finds ways of making it appear to the advantage of others to accept these changes.

Free competition is not confined to freedom for operating within the existing marketing structure. Freedom also involves the privilege of organizing the market in a way that is considered advantageous to the individual or the firm taking the initiative. Freedom to organize the market is quite generally confused with monopoly power. Freedom to organize is not monopolistic so long as it is exercised by a number of competitors each of whom is eager to offset any differential advantage obtained by the others. Administrators concerned with antitrust enforcement have used tests of market structure as indicating the existence of monopoly. They infer that the ideal market is one completely without structure, or at least one in which structure cannot be influenced by the participants. Other students of antitrust enforcement have insisted that tests of actual behavior are to be preferred to tests of market structure. This distinction is not so sharp as it perhaps appeared at one time, if one of the major forms of behavior is that of imparting structure and organization to marketing systems.

Monostasy and Systasy. The theory of monopolistic competition is part of the foundation for the general viewpoint presented here. The term "monopolistic competition" has sometimes appeared rather unfortunate, even to its originator, Professor Chamberlin. It seems to imply that competition is not genuine but involves many of the abuses formerly attributed to monopoly. In fact, some critics of modern business would argue that all attempts to organize the market are monopolistic, however essential they might appear for orderly marketing. The real meaning of the term is that while business firms are truly competitive, they compete from the vantage point of unique positions in the market. Each is earnestly trying to maintain its established position or to expand this position by finding new dimensions of differential advantage through which it can invade the established positions of other firms. The term "monopolist" means "single seller." The firms engaged in monopolistic competition are not single sellers in the sense that any one of them has exclusive control of the sole means for satisfying a particular segment of consumer demand.

Instead of trying to build on the term "monopoly," a fresh start can be made in the present context, using a term which would characterize the phenomenon of standing alone or apart in the market. Such a word can be created from Greek roots in the same way that the word "monopoly" was obtained. This term would be "monostasy." Monostasy would be the condition of occupying a unique position that was in some respects unlike any other in the market or in the given organized behavior system. The term would also have the secondary meaning of making an active effort to stand alone or to carve out a unique position for the individual or the firm. A companion term could be created in similar fashion to signify "standing together." This word is "systasy." This term would refer to the relationship between or among the individuals or firms making up the components of an action system. Again the term might be given the secondary meaning of "a tendency to stand together or to seek support from the other components making up the system."

The paradox of human activity is that both monostasy and systasy are desirable states for most of the participants. In a free society and in a free market, everyone desires to stand alone, to maintain some degree of independence and some freedom from interference or invasion from without. The same individual is usually aware of the help he needs from others in achieving his objectives. He necessarily desires the state of being bound together with others in an effective operating system. His desire for systasy rests on assumptions concerning his participation in the output to be produced by the operating system. A well-adjusted individual generally recognizes that he must serve as the instrumentality for fulfilling the goals of others if he, in turn, is to receive satisfaction through the group effort. Nevertheless, strong-minded individuals may be very confident that they know what is good for the group as a whole. Assuming that there are two or more such individuals in a system, they will enter into an active competition to determine and dominate the pattern of action.

In a complex structure, there is always a problem of attaining adequate co-ordination by one means or another. Inside a business firm of moderate size the co-ordinating function may be carried out by a single executive, with little interference from rivals. It is not always the person who is presumed to be in official control who determines the details of behavior patterns. He often finds it easier to let subordinates do things in their own way so long as they get the stated result accomplished and stay within prescribed limits as to time and budget. Thus the struggle to control the pattern of behavior can take place, within limits, between superior and subordinates. It is a constant aspect of interaction in all situations where individuals or firms must work together and where there is no formal agreement giving one authority over the other.

The dynamics of market organization rest on these competitive attempts at co-ordination. The balance of power may shift from time to time between supplier and customer, each trying to set the pattern for his transactions with the other. Thus, even those who are co-operating with each other may be competing for control. A supplier who is not able to get his wholesalers and retailers to conform to the pattern of action he prefers may be able to find others who are willing to work with him in his own way. If adequate alternatives do not exist, he may take active steps to bring them into being. Every business firm appears eager to see active competition at adjacent levels, however lukewarm it might be about competition at its own level. The competitive drive at each level to secure a desired form of co-operation contributes to the maintenance of active competition at other levels. The term "competitive articulation," rather than the term "monopolistic competition," might be used to characterize what transpires in dynamic markets.

Degree of Conformability. Some additional concepts must be introduced to complete the picture of the balance between monostasy and systasy in the competitive drive to organize the market. Assume that the directing heads of two separate organizations have cast the die in favor of working together. They are then confronted with the technical problem of conforming their operations to each other. Sometimes, they fit together hand in glove, given only the will to co-operate. Sometimes, it turns out that they can be conformed only with the greatest difficulty, however eager one or both sides may be to make the attempt. The degree of conformability is an objective operating fact. When it is low, it places severe restrictions on the tendency toward systasy. Even when the degree of conformability is high, the extent to which the two organizations work together is limited by the tendency toward monostasy.

Reference was made previously to the discrepancy of assortments which helps to account for the fact that the successive steps in distribution channels remain independent. The conformability or lack of it between two operations embraces the discrepancy of assortments but is a still broader concept. Two organizations handling precisely the same assortment of products might still be nonconformable because of other aspects of their operations. For example, a cash-and-carry wholesaler would not be a satisfactory source of supply for a retailer who wished to buy on credit. On the contrary, there might be a marked discrepancy of assortments between two organizations; but insofar as they were concerned with the same class of products, their operations might be highly conformable.

The Dichotomy of Attraction and Repulsion.   Monostasy and systasy on the one hand and degree of conformability on the other may be bracketed under the dichotomy of attraction and repulsion. In explaining the tendency of two firms to work together, systasy may be regarded as the subjective factor and conformability as the objective factor. Similarly, monostasy and lack of conformability are the corresponding factors which tend to hold two firms apart. Attraction and repulsion may sometimes be treated in a blanket way, but this manner of speaking is subject to confusion through false analogy with physical forces. Distinction between the subjective and objective factors lends itself to a clearer perspective.

Assume that the operations of two firms are highly conformable and that they are actually working together. While both sides agree that cooperation is essential, one has taken the lead in getting together or plays the dominant role in guiding their common activities. The concepts of dominance and submission have been employed by sociologists in analyzing social structure. From the standpoint of monopoly theory, economists are suspicious of any degree of dominance, whether accomplished through force or through persuasion. In the present view the avoidance of any element of dominance in market organization is neither a necessary nor a feasible requirement for a free market. It is not feasible because dealings between any two groups, or even between two economists, can almost never be so delicately balanced as to eliminate all traces of dominance. The condition is not necessary so long as the submissive partner has the option of withdrawing whenever he concludes that the arrangement is no longer worth what it costs, including the indignity of submission as one of the costs. The urge toward monostasy motivates the submissive as well as the dominant. Many new businesses arise from the excessive exercise of dominance within existing firms. Highly prized customer-supplier relations are frequently broken in reaction against dominance on one side or the other.

THE DEVELOPMENT OF MARKETING CHANNELS

It was pointed out in a previous chapter that intermediate agencies such as wholesalers and retailers arise because it is impractical in many cases for the producer to sell directly to the consumer. Great advantages for the economic system as a whole can be produced by the processes of intermediate sorting. Yet, this form of organization does not emerge automatically because of the inherent efficiencies. The gradual emergence of channels and their step-by-step improvement result from the driving force of individual buyers or sellers who are undertaking to gain differential advantage thereby. Since there are many agencies engaged in distribution and each puts forward some effort to co-ordinate the neighboring stages in distribution, it is not practical to discuss this drive toward market organization from the standpoint of every type of participant. Attempts to organize or control distribution channels will first be considered briefly from the standpoint of sellers in general and then from the standpoint of the buyer.

There are many kinds of sellers interested in the sale of a product to the ultimate consumer, some sellers attempting to control the channels of distribution by economic means and some by political activity. There have been a number of investigations and a substantial amount of legislation conceived from the viewpoint of the American farmer, in the hope of shortening the route from the farm to the consumer's table and thus increasing the farmer's share of the consumer's dollar. Our interest here is primarily in economic methods of control that lie within the scope of the individual firm. The case of the manufacturer selling consumer goods can be taken as illustrative of the problems facing sellers in general in trying to control distribution channels. The seller has to find means of moving his goods to thousands of consumers, most of whom he will never see and who are generally dispersed over a wide geographical area or even the whole United States.

Selecting an Appropriate Channel. The first task is the selection of an appropriate channel for the particular class of goods. The term "channel" is somewhat deceptive in itself, since it suggests a clearly marked route which is already established. Selection of a market channel is not like making a choice between two or more highways which connect two principal cities. From the manufacturer's viewpoint, it would be more accurate to speak of selecting the area through which he is going to try to cut a channel. The particular product may be readily classified as a packaged drug, but that does not mean that there is a free and open passage already available through drug wholesalers and retail drugstores. Both the wholesaler and the retailer must be induced to carry the new product, and it is usually necessary to prove that it is in their interest to do so. One type of drug product might find its way into these intermediate agencies because it has been endorsed by the medical profession. Another might break through the initial trade resistance because of an advertising campaign which caused consumers to ask for it in retail stores and the retailers in turn to order it from their wholesalers.

In a third type of situation, the seller might offer the wholesaler and retailer a sufficiently attractive introductory deal to induce them to give the product a trial run. If the manufacturer already has other products going through the same channels, this may simplify his problem on the new product in some respects and complicate it in others. It may be easier to get the trade to stock the product as an addition to an established line. On the other hand, the manufacturer may be entering a new competitive field with this particular product; and it may be regarded as inconsistent with the character of his existing line. Thus a drug manufacturer who has specialized in the so-called "ethical specialties" soon runs into a road block when he develops a packaged product to be sold over the counter rather than by prescription only. In many cases, manufacturers of products of this type have had to drop them because of unexpected difficulties in achieving distribution.

Selection of channels does not end with determining a line of trade whose co-operation will be sought in moving a product. It is not sufficient to decide that a product should be sold through department stores; co-operation must be sought from individual stores reaching the type of customers who are most likely to be interested in the product. The appliance manufacturer naturally turns to appliance distributors to give him distribution of his product, market by market. It is not always possible to obtain suitable distributors, and the most desirable ones may be engaged already in the distribution of a competitive product. Other types of wholesalers get drawn into appliance distribution by the manufacturer who cannot find representation among distributors already established in the market. If the product is successful, the character of the distributor's business may change until he becomes essentially an appliance distributor and pulls out of his other lines. In many cases, distributors or dealers become established with the support and encouragement of a manufacturer. New-automobile dealers may be appointed from among retailers of used cars and operators of service stations, or drawn from quite unrelated lines.

Adding Additional Channels. Once a product line is established in a single channel, the manufacturer may attempt to add additional channels. A product formerly sold only in drugstores may move into grocery stores, or a hardware item may move into variety stores. Even though the original channel may be the best single route to the market, the manufacturer may not be satisfied with the volume which this channel produces. He may add a second or even a third channel for the sake of the marginal increment to sales. Quite often, there are two distinct types of channels engaged in moving a given product. On the one hand, there is a relatively specialized type of distributor and dealer who can be expected to give special attention and priority to this class of products. On the other hand, there may be another type of store, perhaps much more numerous than the first type, which provides broad availability of the product to consumers everywhere. Individually, this second type of channel may account for only moderate store volume; it may not add very much to the development of new demand through skillful presentation at the point of sale. The total volume through this channel may be considerable, however, and may represent, to a large extent, sales which would not be expected to accrue through the primary channel.

Problems Encountered with Multiple Channels. When a manufacturer reaches the stage of using two or more distinct channels of trade, he is confronted with the possibility of conflict which can threaten the orderly flow of his goods to market. The two channels may have quite different structures of marketing cost, so that margins that are adequate for one are not attractive to the other. Services may be demanded from the manufacturer in one channel which prove to be of no consequence in the other. The channel which was first to handle a manufacturer's product is likely to develop a sense of vested interest and to regard any sales made in the other channel as an encroachment. The sales organization which is selling through multiple channels generally directs a substantial part of its effort toward maintaining good relations with each type of distributor or dealer handling its goods.

Channels may become obsolescent because of changes in the way that consumers like to buy. The crossroads country store was largely eliminated by good roads and automobiles, enabling rural consumers to go to the larger towns to do their shopping. Separate meat and bakery shops are much less common today because of the tendency of the consumer to want to buy all food products in a single store. A channel may also become obsolescent from the standpoint of a single manufacturer. Prepared baby foods provide one illustration of products originally introduced through drug stores which today are sold very largely through the grocery trade. Occasions may arise when the manufacturer is engaged not merely in adding a channel but in making a fundamental shift to a more appropriate channel from one which has become obsolescent. In such a shift, he has the doubly difficult problem of soliciting cooperation in the new channel and at the same time trying to cope with adverse reactions from the older channel. A major shift between channels may be as large an operation as establishing satisfactory distribution through a single channel in the first instance.

Firms engaged in industrial marketing sometimes regard the plants which buy from them as intermediaries through which they are reaching the ultimate consumer. A large manufacturer making raw materials may be an active force toward putting many small manufacturers in business to produce fabricated products based on these materials. Sometimes the sense of common interest is so great that the manufacturer of the raw materials engages in substantial advertising or market research programs to help his customers dispose of their consumer products. This relationship is often complicated by the fact that the original manufacturer is also fabricating consumer products. Thus, he has two channels to reach the market—one through his own sales organization and one through independent fabricators. His problems of maintaining harmony between these diverse channels pose difficulties similar to those encountered in dealing with two quite independent channels.

The Power of Market Organization of Channels. The contribution of the buyer to market organization is probably older than any serious attempts of the seller to organize the market. Men went looking for materials and articles which they could use before it ever occurred to them to make them or before the technical arts for this purpose were adequately developed. In the early stages of travel and exploration, men saw things they wanted to use in the hands of other men as well as in the state of nature. The most primitive impulse was, no doubt, to seize the desired items by force. Later on the practice of acquiring these items through trade originated by some such steps as those that were traced in the last chapter. Thus the competition among buyers to organize the market arose directly out of the primitive competition for goods, which only gradually came to be manifested within an ordered institutional framework. In this sense the competition among buyers is more fundamental than the competition among sellers.

The great commercial revolution which preceded the industrial revolution was due primarily to the enterprise of merchant adventurers who had an assured market among the wealthy classes of their respective nations, but who exercised great initiative and daring in seeking out the products of far places which could be brought home and sold to these customers. The silks and spices of the East and copper and tin out of the West were brought into the great centers of ancient culture through efforts of such buyers rather than through the efforts of sellers undertaking to dispose of their products.

Today the initiative has passed to the seller to a large extent, but this never could have happened except for the gradual development of elaborate marketing facilities. Some students of marketing feel that it would be beneficial if the balance of power could be restored to the buyer. They argue that if control over marketing organizations remained essentially in the hands of retailers, there would be greater assurance of the right products being made, at prices which consumers could afford to pay, simply because the retailer is more closely in touch with the consumer market. The advocates of this position evidently have in mind the great modern department store as the prototype of a retail operation. If all retailing were in the hands of such units, there is little question that the balance of power in control over the market would rest in the hands of the retailer. There is one great advantage of reposing the initiative in the hands of the seller, including such original suppliers as manufacturers and farm co-operatives. The competitive struggle for markets has unquestionably greatly speeded up the rate of innovation, both in products and in methods of distribution.

While retailers stand closest to the consumer in the channels of distribution, many products which are extremely successful today would never have come on the market if it had been left to the initiative of either the consumer or the retailer to demand them. The consumer cannot demand a product which does not now exist unless he has the imagination to visualize and to design a workable model. Innovation takes place because a producer with an idea can by-pass the retailer and find out on a sampling basis whether consumers are likely to accept his product and what features are important in its design. The great majority of new products go into stores today because a producer has designed them and has developed evidence that consumers will accept them. It is only in relatively minor product variations, such as style features, that retail stores typically take the initiative in reflecting developments of consumer demand back to the producer. One can grant that the balance of power should rest with the buyer in terms of ultimate decision as to the goods which should move through the channels of trade. The power of decision does not necessarily carry with it the power of initiative. The author agrees that a buyer's market may be sounder for the economy as a whole than a seller's market. The term "buyer's market," however, implies nothing more than a sufficient degree of waiting power to enable the buyer to make a judicious choice. Through the exercise of waiting power, buyers can exercise a selective influence upon the organizing efforts of the seller. Nevertheless, freedom to organize the market is available to buyers as well as sellers and in some cases has been exercised very effectively.

The outstanding examples of market organization from the buyer's side of the market is that of the great mail-order houses and some of the leading department stores. In the industrial field, many such examples are found in which the buyer has set the pattern in dealings with his supplier, developing elaborate procurement procedures for raw materials and component parts. The large buyer often administers a system of product standards and quality control. Not all of his suppliers are large producing companies with their own quality-control laboratories. For some products, such as foods and drugs, there are public bodies which police the maintenance of quality control and enforce the giving of full measure in packaged products. For other products, it is more difficult to formulate or to administer universal standards, so that the supplier's primary concern is to meet the standards prescribed by his major customers. In the case of the industrial buyer, standards and specifications are often peculiarly his own. A raw material may need special qualities to work to best advantage in his plant processes. A component part naturally has to be designed to fit into the final assembly manufactured by the buyer and must meet stated tolerances in order to serve the purposes of mass production.

Sometimes the large buyer goes so far as to control the internal operations of his suppliers. He finds that a small manufacturer cannot produce at the low prices he requires until his plant has been subjected to study and reorganization by engineering experts. In many instances the buyer has been the source of the engineering talent and has made the acceptance of such help one of the conditions of a supply contract. The results have often been quite profitable for the small supplier, since prices are computed on the basis of all costs plus a fixed percentage of profit. He has often done much better on this basis than when his costs and his market position have fluctuated and caused current profits to be uncertain. The special virtue of buyer's initiative in market organization lies in getting prices down. This can be wholly constructive from the standpoint of maintaining a continuous flow of goods if it is coupled with the kind of help just described in reducing costs.

The buyer can be an important influence in maintaining competition at stages farther back in the marketing process. The buyer does this in part by attempting to maintain multiple sources, especially for raw materials. Even though there might be some transactional economy in buying from a single source, a large chemical firm, for example, usually prefers to buy from two or three sources, partly as a means of providing greater assurance of delivery in case one of the sources should fail or be interrupted. Sometimes, this division of business among sources is made in a completely arbitrary fashion—as, for example, dividing the volume in roughly equal parts among the sources used. The buyer may also cause new organizations to be established for the specific purpose of providing him with the goods he needs. New mines or timberlands may be opened and farm co-operatives established primarily to supply the requirements of a single large industrial buyer.

Farther on in the channel, the power of market organization is exercised by such means as bidding for exclusive distribution contracts or for favorable price arrangements. The rivalry of buyers such as large department stores in attempting to secure exclusive franchises for the distribution of a product in their cities provides an example of competitive attempts to organize the market as compared with direct competition in the ordinary sense. The attempt to induce price discrimination has been somewhat lessened as a result of the Robinson-Patman Act. In some cases a large buyer will not sign a contract unless he has the assurance of the seller that he is not being favored by illegal discrimination. This is because the law makes a buyer equally guilty with the seller in cases of price discrimination. However, there is nothing to prevent the buyer from pointing out special advantages or cost savings which he can offer the seller. Price differentials are within the law if the difference in price is no greater than the difference in the cost to the seller.

Continual Change in Marketing Channels.   Because of these competitive attempts from either side to organize the market, the marketing channels are in a continual state of flux. New types of marketing firms and marketing arrangements appear, and old ones pass out of existence. When the new type of operation becomes firmly established, there is a tendency for its position to become stabilized so that it accounts for a fixed percentage of the total volume of business thereafter. This tendency toward stabilization of market share has occurred with respect to chain stores in each of the major fields in which they have developed. Once they became established in the grocery field, the chains did approximately one third of the total volume of business, year after year. In the drug field, their stabilized share of volume turned out to be around 25 per cent. In a few trades the volume of business is handled almost entirely by chains. One example is the variety store; but here the whole concept of the fixed-price, limited-variety store as originated by Woolworth started off as a chain operation almost from the very first. Here it is the independents who have entered to claim a small share of the volume originally in the hands of the chain. The general effect of these progressive changes in market organization is to move from less effective to more effective forms of organization. This is roughly the reverse of the notion that markets were relatively perfect at one time and that efforts of individuals to escape from competition led to various forms of market imperfection. An effective market is not quite the same thing as a perfect market. Effective market organization is essential to maintain the orderly flow of products from producer to consumer.

In competing for the favorable response of the same buyer, two sellers proclaim the merits of their respective products and the accompanying services. Each is trying to enlist the particular buyer as part of the system of action he is attempting to construct. The buyer may realize that he must work with one or the other in order to meet some of his requirements. Not only do the sellers place a competitive check on each other by their respective offers, but either may run into resistance if he goes too far in dictating the terms of the arrangement because of the desire of the customer to stand alone as an independent entity. The balance between monostasy and systasy is constantly shifting with respect to any given organization. The degree of conformability may change with respect to any pair of firms, making it easier or more difficult for them to work together. The competitive attempt to organize the market is always in opposition to the tendency of channels to become fixed and static. The over-all trend is not toward monopolistic dominance and control, but toward more effective markets and marketing channels through the endless quest for differential structural advantages.

FACTORS IN THE DEVELOPMENT OF TRADING CENTERS

A trading center is a behavior system in quite a different sense than a firm or a marketing channel. It obviously lacks the unified control of the single marketing firm. It is even looser in structure than the marketing channel, which is held together by voluntary co-ordination. The firms making up a trading center may be competitive or complementary in the relations among themselves and might each be able to discharge their functions with little or no formal contact with others in the trading center. What makes the group a behavior system is that its members function as a unit in providing a service of supply to consumers. The group competes against other trading centers which are alternative sources of supply for these consumers. Joint operation internally and joint competition against the outside are none the less real in the absence of formal co-ordination.

Sometimes a trading center exhibits a self-conscious unity, at least with respect to outside competition. Retailers contribute to a joint promotional campaign aside from any advertising undertaken individually. They may collaborate in a common scheme of Christmas lighting and decoration. They may provide special attractions to draw crowds to the center at Christmas or at other seasons of the year. In some cases, such groups collaborate on credit and delivery services. In a few instances, stores have jointly supported a market survey or continuing informational and merchandising services. The newer trend toward planned shopping centers quite often reflects the initiative of a landlord or promoter. Usually, he will have lined up some of his major tenants before he starts to build, so that at least part of the retailers who will occupy the center become involved in planning it. Despite these examples, formal co-operation is still exceptional and is quite incidental to the day-to-day functioning of the trading center.

Monostasy and Systasy in Choosing a Location. The most basic factor which makes the trading center an organized behavior system is geography. Together, the retail stores in the group occupy an area which is favorably located with respect to access by shoppers. Location is a differential advantage shared by the whole group and provides the basis for joint opportunity. Factors determining the number and distribution of trading centers will be discussed a little later. Before turning to this aspect of the subject, our basic concepts of dynamics must be reconsidered in geographical terms. This will lead to some conclusions concerning functional allocation of activities within the land area occupied by the trading center.

Monostasy and systasy are in evidence here, just as in the product-line policy of the manufacturer or in efforts to co-ordinate trade channels. Retailers choose to stand alone or stand together, first of all, with respect to location. The individual who wishes to open any type of retail store from groceries to jewelry has the option of choosing an isolated location where he will have no competitors near-by, or of selecting a site in a well-established trading center. He is making a choice between two sets of costs and risks. In the first instance, he runs the risk that his operation will never reach the break-even volume or accepts the costs of extra effort involved in attracting customers to this out-of-the-way location. If he locates in the established center, the total volume is greater; but he has to compete for a share of it with stores already established in the center or with stores which may locate there later. His rent and other operating costs are higher from the start, but there is also less risk regarding his expectations of volume. The fundamental issue facing him is whether to try to build an independent position for himself or to accept a share in something larger than he can build alone. In this instance the universal tension between monostasy and systasy is expressed primarily in geographic terms.

Conformability in Choosing a Location. Conformability is a major factor in the development of trading centers. In this connection the degree of conformability refers to whether two activities react positively or negatively when carried on in close proximity. A fish market and an exclusive dress shop would not make good neighbors. A quality jewelry store and other specialty shops handling china or fine table linens are readily conformable within the same block. The stores which locate at the same center have made the decision to stand together, but some who choose such locations may not be readily conformable to other activities in the center. Among the established stores, there may be one or several institutions which set the tone, to which others must willingly conform or else be subject to some pressure either to withdraw or to change the character of their operations.

The retailer who chooses to locate in a trading center may still gain some advantage through judicious selection of the individual site. There are gradations of location value within a center of any size. Many activities may be conformable within the total area of a major trading center which would not react favorably as next-door neighbors. Every retailer in the center depends on the shopping traffic generated by the center, and many of the stores play a measurable part in generating this traffic. Some of the dominant institutions spend advertising money to draw consumers to the center. Consumers attracted by this advertising may end up buying in neighboring stores, just as the manufacturer who advertises his product is in some degree creating business for similar competitive products.

Functional Allocation; Attraction and Repulsion. The resolution of these forces tends to take the form of functional allocation within the center. Attraction and repulsion between various types of activity shape the geographical arrangement of stores to facilitate the effective functioning of the center as a whole. An intensive study of the central business district of Philadelphia showed the clear predominance of one type of institution or another in the various functional areas making up the central district. Large retail stores generated traffic which nourished small service establishments. Large service establishments, such as hotels, theaters, and public institutions, generated traffic which supported small retail stores. Factories and warehouses were conformable to each other but not to major retailing or consumer services. The pattern of functional allocation does not stay put, since the increasing size of any center forces a continual re-sorting of functions by area. Factories and warehouses leave the center as the value of central space and the needs of retail and service establishments increase. Presently, some aspects of retailing begin to decentralize also. Finally, some general offices, which generate traffic but draw no special advantage from it, move to suburban locations. There remain activities which can do better at a central location, but these activities tend to become more and more specialized.

Some students of urban development see the disappearance of nucleated cities and visualize urban growth in the future along radically different lines. One school holds that the nucleated city has grown so large that it can no longer function effectively and that it is bound to break down into a series of cells, all more or less self-contained and lying adjacent to each other. This is in effect a prediction that modern cities will fall apart and be replaced by what amounts to clusters of small towns. Another idea is that the future development of cities will take the form of a web or network spreading out along the highways which now connect the major cities. The reasoning behind this point of view is that automobile transportation has become so essential to urban living that all development will be arranged so as to provide the most convenient access for traffic. At the opposite extreme are some geographers who expect nucleation to take place on a much broader scale than that represented by our present metropolitan centers. They contend that for some planning purposes the whole east coast area, extending from Boston down to Norfolk, Virginia, should be regarded as a single urban region with New York as its center. They see the need for full integration of this region in terms of transportation and various aspects of government. They assume that there will be a functional sorting-out of activities within this urban region in accordance with the distance from the center.

The author believes that we will make the nucleated city work, because we have no alternative except to make it work. Any attempts to break it down into smaller cells or to ribbons along the highways cannot succeed, because they do not eliminate the fundamental fact of centrality. The center of an urban concentration always has special value for some types of activities, arising from the simple fact that it is potentially the most accessible spot for all of the population throughout the area. However, it is doubtful whether any one simple pattern of growth can be relied upon to predict what will happen to metropolitan centers in the next twenty-five or fifty years. The pattern of development may be modified in the future because of far different conditions as to transportation and the extent of specialization which has developed in urban activities.

The relationship between trade and traffic is ambivalent, involving both attraction and repulsion. The central area offers superior convenience for so many activities as to exercise a strong attraction both on firms seeking locations and on consumers looking for goods or services. The very response to this force of attraction creates congestion and other unpleasant conditions in the central city which thereupon tend to drive away activity, including some of the activities contributing to congestion in the first instance. So far as retail trade is concerned, the trend seems to be toward a moderate rate of growth downtown, while much larger percentage increases are occurring in suburban shopping areas. Both with respect to retailing and with respect to office activity, it can be expected that there will be a continuous process of sorting-out activities and their functional allocation to the center or the periphery, according to where they can operate to the greatest advantage. Smaller places will tend to follow the same course of development that the large cities of today passed through at an earlier period. The larger cities, as they continue to grow, will constantly be breaking new ground in the development of suitable functional patterns.

Struggle for Control of Market Organization. The struggle to control market organization goes on continuously in major trading centers. The battle lines may be drawn in various ways, but most typically they represent a struggle between the downtown stores and the new shopping centers on the periphery. There is always a group of powerful interests who are concerned with maintaining the development of activities at the center of the city. This generally includes the large department stores and major specialty shops, although many of the big stores are making their adjustment to decentralization by opening branch stores. The transportation companies are vitally concerned with maintaining the daily flow of traffic to and from the center of the city which results from shopping and from office activity. In most major cities the public transportation companies appear to be fighting a losing battle. The volume of traffic is static or is even beginning to decline, though costs continue to mount at an alarming rate. More and more commuters turn to the use of their own automobiles, but it is not clear that any major city can maintain the integrity of the downtown area without the services of public transportation. The income of newspapers depends on the maintenance of downtown activities, since the major metropolitan newspapers may be regarded on the business side as functioning primarily as an advertising medium used by the large stores to induce people to come downtown to buy. The newspapers, of course, need not suffer if the large stores, through gradual decentralization, can turn into a form of local chain. Any retail organization with a city-wide appeal can still use newspapers effectively as an advertising medium. Meanwhile the outlying centers are competing with increasing effectiveness by setting up planned combinations of retail stores and by providing parking space which is not available downtown. In an earlier day, decentralization took place on a trial-and-error basis, with one small store after another attempting to establish itself in the suburban area until success finally crowned the efforts of a few.

So far as consumer appeal is concerned, the underlying forces in this battle are convenience versus breadth of assortment. For products of very frequent purchase, convenience tends to win and lead to retailing at dispersed locations. For products where problems of selection are paramount, retailing will still tend to concentrate at the center of the city in order to provide an adequate breadth of assortment.

Origin of Trading Centers. Prosperous trading centers are often associated with a high level of activity in the immediate area. Thus, some of the great trading centers of ancient times developed in the rich agricultural valleys of the Nile, the Euphrates, and the Ganges. The point of intersection between trading routes at which a variety of materials were available also came in time to be a natural location for the fabrication of finished products, which could then move out over the various trade routes. Sometimes the local development helping to sustain the trading center was in mining or lumbering. This happened more rarely than in the case of cities with good agricultural background because of the tendency of extractive industries to work themselves out and to have to move on to new locations. Some of the early trading nations developed more because of the lack of opportunity in other directions than because of the richness of their resources. Thus the ancient Phoenicians were first settled on a rather barren seacoast, but they became great sailors and made their way in the world primarily through the development of Mediterranean trade.

Within a relatively homogeneous national market like the United States, major centers tend to be dispersed geographically. Thus, in some areas, there are cities which have enjoyed a development as trading centers which is out of proportion to the level of local activities. The cities of Atlanta and Dallas enjoyed much of their early development through the advantages of their location as distribution centers for the Southeast and the Southwest, respectively. Among the obvious factors which can be observed in the development of trading centers are the advantages of the early start. Once a place has begun to grow, it attracts other activity and in a sense forecloses the possibility that similar centers will spring up near-by. As opposed to the advantage of the early start, there are continuous shifts in population and activity which tend to upset or modify the original pattern. An obvious example is the fact that Philadelphia was once the largest city in the United States but has since been surpassed, first by New York and later by Chicago and Los Angeles.

Competition between Trading Centers. Next to the question of how trading centers start is that of how the division of trade among competing centers is determined. The marketing field has given considerable attention to this question both for its intrinsic interest and because of the need of the marketing organizations to decide on the best pattern for covering the market. One early formulation is known as "Reilly's law of retail gravitation." Reilly believed that the devision of trade between two neighboring centers would vary directly as the population of the centers and vary inversely as the square of the distance between them. Empirical investigation by such students as Converse suggested the need for revision in this law. Converse believes that under some circumstances, distance will be less important and population more important in deciding the division of trade than this formula suggests. He found in some cases that the cube of the distance rather than the square of the distance produced a formula that was more in accord with the observed facts.

Naturally, any such principle as to the division of trade has to be qualified in terms of the type of goods. The frequency of purchase of so-called "convenience goods" sets rather narrow limits as to how far consumers will travel to buy them. One of the most effective studies of this problem consisted of a series of regional surveys in the state of Iowa. Here it was found that the attraction of a city increased in proportion to its size up to a radius of ten miles, but at that point the trend stopped abruptly in the case of convenience goods such as groceries and drugs. With respect to more occasional purchases, particularly those involving larger amounts of money or factors of style and durability, the ten-mile limit did not hold. As a matter of fact, the drawing radius for apparel and furniture continued to increase with the size of the city, many consumers traveling fifty to sixty miles to buy in the largest cities involved in the study—namely, Des Moines and Omaha. If this study had covered the whole United States rather than a single state, it is probable that the drawing radius would have continued to increase indefinitely with respect to some limited categories of goods bought by a few consumers of high income or specialized interest. Thus, New York City continues to be the market town for the whole country, both at retail and wholesale, for some limited classifications of merchandise.

Something approaching the dimensions of a revolution in marketing occurred during the last twenty-five years through the almost universal use of automobiles. The impact of this new form of transportation was especially marked in rural areas. At one time a large part of the farm population depended on crossroad centers of only a few hundred people for most of the merchandise they bought. Today, many of these little centers have disappeared except as the location of stores of the pure convenience type, such as filling stations and small food stores. A study made a few years ago showed that most farm families throughout the United States were doing a substantial part of their shopping in trading centers of twenty-five thousand population or more. A city of that size is large enough to be genuinely urban in the character of its retail facilities and in the range of merchandise offered.

The Trading Center as a Consumption Center. Major cities are centers of consumption as well as of production and marketing. Reavis Cox has suggested that this consuming function is almost as basic in explaining the character of modern cities as their productive functions. The city is a consuming center not only for its residents but also for transients. The large cities draw people from the outside not only to transact business but to reside for various periods of time, for purposes of sightseeing or for enjoyment of the many forms of recreation offered by metropolitan centers. Thus, wealthy families from the South or West may move into New York for a week or several weeks during the opera or theatrical season. The great hotels and famous restaurants of a large city are not merely conveniences for the traveler but sources of satisfaction in themselves. On its recreational side a large city may draw people from a great distance or from foreign countries to an even greater extent than from its own immediate area. Not long ago a study was made in downtown Philadelphia of the place of residence of persons attending motion-picture theaters throughout a given week. There were more transients in town attending downtown theaters from New York and Washington than from some of the near-by suburbs. As a matter of fact, during the period covered, a larger percentage of the movie-goers in Philadelphia were residents of Europe than of the near-by county seat of Norristown. Thus, this small town seems to have a remarkable power to resist the attraction of the near-by large city in some respects, even though it may succumb to it in others.

INTERREGIONAL AND INTERNATIONAL TRADE

A national economy is an organized behavior system for the purposes of marketing theory partly because of internal integration linking all parts of the market. It is also an organized system in relation to other national economies because of government policy with respect to international trade. Nations exhibit tendencies toward monostasy and systasy in making trade policy. A measure of national self-sufficiency is an almost universal goal. No nation can achieve it completely; each is concerned about trade relations with other countries but would like to mold these relations to its own advantage. Two friendly nations which favor trade with each other may still have difficulty in conforming their marketing requirements. Either the lack of a truly functional linkage or excessive dominance on one side may cause a breaking-down of attempts to establish trade.

The marketing flow among regions in the United States bears some resemblance to international trade. A region is not an organized behavior system to the same degree because of the very limited extent to which marketing policy can be exercised on behalf of a region. There is an implicit unity resting on geographical isolation and on the distinctiveness of regional products. Both business groups and marketing theorists have given some attention to the special problems of such peripheral regions as New England, the Southeast, and the Far West.

Geographical and Technological Differentiation. Ricardo developed the doctrine of comparative advantage to explain the origin of international trade and to provide the basis for sound policy in trade among nations. Reduced to its simple essence, the doctrine of comparative advantage said that each country would tend to specialize on those activities for which its costs were relatively low and to exchange its surplus with other countries which were similarly concentrating on those phases of production which they could perform most efficiently.

A country might be quite capable of producing both product A and product B. Nevertheless, it might be so much more efficient in the manufacture of product A that its business and its workers would tend to concentrate in that field, gradually drawing resources out of the production of product B and exchanging the excess of product A for product B originating in another country. The doctrine of comparative advantage was part of the struggle for free international trade which was going on at the time that Ricardo was writing in England. Ricardo's theory was designated as "the doctrine of comparative costs" and was obliged to take account of the cost of transportation, which was one of the factors encountered in the high specialization of production among various countries. In some respects, it was a rather stark doctrine, implying that a country might be left with relatively inferior types of industries as the only ones in which it would not suffer a severe handicap as compared with other countries.

Ricardo's doctrine of comparative advantage supplements the earlier emphasis by Adam Smith on division of labor and specialization within a particular economy. It emphasizes geographical differentiation as compared to differentiation along technological or product lines. The ideas of J. M. Clark concerning the economics of differential advantage were discussed in the chapter on competition. This view is a generalization of all types of economic advantage, whether based on geographical location or on technological skill. Usually there are elements of both present in any concrete situation; but there are real problems of choice for marketing management concerning which of these dimensions of advantage to emphasize in building marketing position.

Choice between Geographical and Technological Advantages. The end and aim of economic activity is to satisfy consumer needs as precisely as possible and at the same time to minimize the cost or the amount of effort required. The problem of marketing policy posed by geographical versus technological differentiation involves the three elements of production costs, marketing costs (including transportation), and the degree of satisfaction provided for the consumer through getting as nearly as possible the exact style and type of product desired. The problem can be simplified by holding production costs constant and assuming two different plants, each turning out a single product of the same general character and each producing the same number of units at the same unit cost. One plant produces a relatively simple model of the particular product, which can be used by a great many people, but which fits the needs of most of these people only in an approximate way. The product produced by the second plant is much more specialized but meets the needs of a small segment of the total market much more accurately than the first product. The sales manager of the first plant can presumably find all of the customers he needs to consume his product within a relatively small radius of the plant, so long as there are no competing products which satisfy the various segments of the market with greater precision. The sales manager of the second plant would have to sell his product over a much wider area in order to find enough consumers of the type for whom it was specifically designed. Under this formulation the cost of transportation involved in going further afield can be set off against the extra utility which the product has for the limited segment of the population which buys it. If the incremental value of the more specialized product is equal to or greater than the cost of transportation, specialization in production would tend to develop along the lines of product differentiation. If the incremental advantage is less than the added cost of transportation, it may be expected that the predominant type of differentiation would be by geographical area.

Another way of posing the problem of choice between two lines of specialization is to assume that the production of a firm in the beginning is limited both in geographical extent and in the range of needs which can be filled by a highly specialized product. The question can then be posed as a choice between two possible lines of sales expansion for the future. The company might continue to make a single specialized product but might market it over a wider and wider area. On the other hand, it might stick to its original geographical area but bring out more models and styles to reach the various segments of the market within its limited territory. It would choose the first course if the increase in costs of marketing and transportation were relatively slight as a percentage of the total cost, thus providing the greater prospect of marginal return through expansion in that direction. If its production facilities and methods were relatively flexible, it might choose to bring out an increasingly broader line for distribution within its limited territory by breaking down its production schedule into smaller lot sizes in order to produce a greater variety of models. Dependence on mass production and skill in mass marketing would tend to push the firm toward greater geographical expansion. Dependence on skilled labor rather than assembly-line methods in production, and dependence on personal contact as compared with mass advertising in marketing, would push the firm toward more intensive development within its own region.

In the American market the general tendency appears to have been to push the distribution of many consumer products in the direction of full national coverage. The reasons for this would appear to lie in considerations affecting both production and marketing methods. It is clear that moving from a single territory toward national distribution can be accomplished with little change in production methods. It may also involve the least change in selling methods and, aside from transportation, the smallest increment to marketing costs. Once a method of selling a standardized product to a particular class of people has been developed, the same pattern merely has to be repeated in other areas in order to sell the product to the same class of people elsewhere. In increasing the breadth of the product line, on the contrary, the seller is confronted with a new type of marketing problem, both because he is appealing to a different type of consumer and because he may have to go into new types of retail stores to reach them. It is only on the class of products for which transportation cost is a major factor in the price the consumer has to pay that the producer is still compelled to operate within a relatively limited geographical area. The distance away from his headquarters at which sales become marginal because of the increasing cost of transportation will depend in part, of course, on the extent to which he encounters local competition as he moves into these areas. There are cases in which a product is in national distribution but the extent of use tends to thin out in moving away from the production areas. A case in point is Douglas fir plywood, which is indeed consumed throughout the United States but with per capita sales substantially larger in the Pacific coast states, where the product originates, than in other parts of the country.

The existence of national advertising media and their relative economy is one of the considerations which tends to favor national distribution. The influence of the advertising agent is, on the whole, in the direction of moving toward national distribution as compared to local or regional distribution. The general emphasis on the national market in the United States is represented by the phrase "going national." It is generally assumed that for most thriving organizations which began in a limited area, the time will come in the history of the firm when it is appropriate for it to go national. There are some cases, however, in which it is necessary to operate on a national scale from the beginning. Thus a product which was manufactured for use with automatic washing machines had to be sold on a national basis from the first if it was to receive the support of the washing machine manufacturer who was already operating on a national scale. Attempting to distribute on a national basis is a manifestation of the competitive drive to organize the market. In fact, the national market as an organized entity may be regarded as the result of this drive.

Moving into Foreign Trade.   Once a firm is national in scope, further differentiation is likely to occur mainly along product lines The firm often has the option of moving into foreign trade at this stage. The American market continues to be so much more attractive for the average manufacturer of consumer goods that he is likely to turn to product-line diversification before he becomes interested in export business. There are some types of products marketed on a national scale for which further intensification of market coverage looks in the direction of decentralizing plants to give better service to local markets. The production of paper containers is a good example. Some of the leading firms in this field consist of a chain of plants located in all of the principal markets, with each plant operated by essentially autonomous management. In the course of its history a large national firm may have at one time emphasized product-line diversification and at another time geographical extension or intensification of coverage.

On the other side is the drive for self-sufficiency on the part of nations or regions. The so-called "underdeveloped" countries are all eager to promote industrial development of their own rather than importing their finished products from the more advanced countries. At the other extreme are countries like the United States and Russia with the largest and most diversified endowment of natural resources. Both of these countries continue to express their native isolationism in one way or another. Being more nearly free than any other nations from dependence on the outside world, there is a body of national sentiment in both cases which would like to make this independence complete.

The International Drive toward Self-Sufficiency.   Each country would like to have its cake and eat it too, in the sense of developing a completely independent economy to the extent that that is feasible and still being able to obtain the items which it lacks through international trade. There is an obvious similarity here to the concepts of monostasy and systasy, introduced in an earlier section. On the one hand, each individual unit of production, such as a firm or even an entire nation, wants to stand alone and to enjoy a sense of security in not being dependent upon others. At the same time, there is the need to stand together or to feel security of status within a larger system in order to obtain those goods and services which it cannot produce for itself.

The dynamics of trade between nations or regions arises in part from the different stages of development among the various nations. What the underdeveloped countries want most of all is the means to promote and accelerate their development. What they would like to import from the more advanced nations is not so much their consumer products as the plant equipment and technical know-how which would enable them to get along without imports of consumer goods. What the more advanced nations want is assured sources of supply of such raw materials as are needed to round out the basis of their own manufacturing production. On the one side, there is the constant attempt to acquire production capacity as the road to independence. On the other side, there is the attempt to become independent of raw materials supplies by developing synthetic substitute materials or by exploiting domestic resources more fully. Striking examples of the effort to become independent of outside sources of raw materials include the development by Germany of synthetic fertilizers from atmospheric nitrogen and the development of synthetic rubber in the United States. Here the drive toward market organization is the drive of each country to organize its own economy according to a pattern of self-sufficiency. At the same time, each is attempting competitively to organize its external trade with other nations to its own advantage. The advanced nations such as the United States are in the more paradoxical position because they are pointing toward freeing themselves of dependence on either the finished goods or the raw materials of other countries. At the same time, they would like to obtain foreign markets for their own surplus production both of raw materials and of finished products.

The twentieth century has moved a long way from the ideals of free trade which were accepted to some extent in the nineteenth century. The competitive attempts to control international trade by each country to its own advantage have led to a chaotic tangle of tariffs, import quotas, export licenses, and exchange limitations. Each country is trying to outguess the other in economic strategy, which is really a form of economic warfare running counter to the general need for the interchange of goods and services along lines which will promote efficiency for the whole world economy. Unfortunately, many of the restrictions imposed on the free flow of goods do not represent anyone's conception of the true national interest. In many cases a tariff or import restriction is imposed at the instigation of a small group most directly affected by competition from foreign sources. What emerges is not truly a national policy but the projection of the policies of numerous interested groups relying upon the central power of the government to enforce their point of view.

There can be no clear-cut or one-sided decision in a debate concerning self-sufficiency versus international trade. The political uncertainties of our day cause most nations to give some weight to the prospect of military threat. In purely economic terms, there is reason to believe that some measure of balance, area by area, is necessary in order to achieve a constructive equilibrium in the world as a whole. Each country has the problem of keeping its entire working force employed and productive, and it may have to turn to its second-best and third-best opportunity to accomplish this result, even though this may run contrary to the principle of comparative advantage. While it may mean making goods which theoretically could be produced more efficiently in another country, the comparison may be unrealistic if there is no better opportunity for local employment or if the terms of trade continue to be adverse on the products which a country must export to obtain goods from other countries.

The Interregional Drive toward Self-Sufficiency. Whatever the justification of the drive for self-sufficiency among independent nations, these tendencies certainly deserve critical scrutiny in considering the various regions within the United States. An amazing number of trade barriers have been erected among the states which have the same motivation as protective tariffs levied against the products of foreign countries. Great ingenuity has been displayed in finding means of favoring local products as against out-of-state products. Each state, of course, fully expects to be able to sell its own products without restrictions in other states, in spite of the barriers which it imposes at home. In addition to barriers against out-of-state products, there is a steady flood of state legislation erected against out-of-state organizations, such as chain stores, which may establish branch operations within the state. Aside from legislation, there are promotional and publicity campaigns not only by states, but even by individual communities, exalting the virtues of patronizing home industry. Some of the government bodies concerned with the regulation of commerce seem to favor local over national marketing operations, on the assumption that local business would be more competitive simply because it was on a smaller scale. The intensity of competition could actually be reduced by restricting business to local operations, since each small firm would be competing only with those in its own territory and not with the many small firms of the same type across the country. Certainly the hope of reducing the intensity of competition is the precise objective of state legislation and other local movements to protect home industry.

The Effect on Market Organization. Despite all these attempts at Balkanizing the American market, the effect on market organization has been relatively small. Much more fundamental has been the steady tendency for both population and industrial activity to become more closely adjusted to the distribution of national resources and economic opportunity. A leveling-up has been proceeding in the American market which is gradually moderating some of the differences which formerly prevailed. For a number of years the greatest growth in population has been in the Far West, which had long been sparsely settled. There are obvious limitations to the number of people who can sustain life in the mountain and desert areas. The extremes of population density among the major regions of the country can be moderated but not eliminated. This redistribution of population is made possible in part by new technology and developing uses for raw materials which once had no economic value. There is also a tendency for new developments as to sources of power to facilitate the dispersion of industrial activity. These tendencies, both with respect to sources of power and with respect to the use of raw materials, can be observed on the international scale as well as among regions of the United States.

SELECTED REFERENCES

BOULDING, KENNETH E. *The Organizational Revolution.* New York: Harper & Bros., 1953.

KNAUTH, OSWALD W. *Managerial Enterprise.* New York: W. W. Norton, 1948.

SCHRECKER, PAUL. *Work and History.* Princeton: Princeton University Press, 1948.

CONVERSE, P. D., and HUEGY, H. W. *Principles of Marketing.* 5th ed. Prentice-Hall, Inc., 1952.

CLEWETT, RICHARD N. (ed.). *Marketing Channels for Manufactured Products.* Homewood, Ill.: Richard D. Irwin, Inc., 1954.

Boulding contends, in the reference cited, that a vast increase in the power to organize is the most remarkable characteristic of modern times. This generalization obviously applies to competitive attempts to organize the market.

Knauth describes the efforts of the executive to organize a system of action within which he can operate. In marketing, this organizing effort necessarily extends beyond the confines of a single firm.

Professor Schrecker's field is the philosophy of history. In this book, he shows how social forms and organizations are necessarily modified through the very act of making use of them.

Converse has concentrated his research efforts on the trading center and has suggested a number of principles pertaining to its organization.

The volume edited by Clewett presents a view of the development of marketing channels, both in general and for specific industries.

Part III

EXECUTIVE ACTION IN MARKETING

The culmination of marketing theory is in demonstrating its value as perspective for marketing practice. The management of a marketing operation is first considered in terms of positive control over resources to meet predetermined goals. The principles of management suggested take account of the fact that every operating system is necessarily a structure of power and communication. Next, the element of uncertainty is introduced, together with various approaches to problem solving in reducing uncertainty. Problem solving as an operation employs insight, systematic calculation, and selective exploration. The discussion of market planning shows how planning can become a technical and scientific procedure which can be delegated to staff specialists. Finally, the marketing viewpoint is shown to offer a constructive approach to management policy as a whole and to the reconciliation of management goals and public policy.

The term "action," as contrasted with behavior, is intended to suggest decision in activity guided by deliberate and self-conscious rationality. Parts I and II are intended to develop a perspective on market behavior, and Part III shows how this knowledge may be applied through principles of executive action. Among these is the power principle, which is implicit in all organized behavior but is made an explicit rule of action for the executive through management policies, planning, and problem solving. The role of the marketing executive is examined in its various aspects of creating and directing a system of action and reconciling its struggle for survival and growth with the broader aims of the community.

Chapter XII

MANAGEMENT OF MARKETING OPERATIONS

Sales results are the function of organized marketing effort applied to market opportunity. Management of marketing operations should begin with this fundamental equation. Both opportunity and effort can be segmented in various ways to facilitate effective matching.

Mobilization of the striking power of the marketing organization is considered at various levels, beginning with an analysis of the executive function. The management of line and staff activites is discussed, as well as the reasons for the decentralization of one and the centralization of the other. Principles are suggested to govern the deployment of man power according ot the type of marketing operation.

The problem of budgeting is treated in terms of the special difficulties of the advertising budget. The negotiative approach is recommended, whereby the budget becomes the occasion for reviewing the sales and advertising plans and for formalizing the commitments as to performance on the one hand and resources available for use in meeting these objectives on the other. The top executive undertakes to bring about an effective integration of the power structure and the operating structure; he seeks to blend current efficiency with adequate preparation for greater opportunity tomorrow.

OPPORTUNITY AND EFFORT

The two sides of the market have been traditionally described as "demand" and "supply." From the standpoint of a marketing organization attempting to achieve its objectives in the market place, there appear to be distinct advantages in substituting the terms "opportunity" and "effort." These terms refer to the same thing as demand and supply, but they reflect a more dynamic view of the relationship as seen by the marketing organization itself. The term "opportunity" is more specific and more narrowly defined than the broad concept of "demand." It means demand for the particular products or services that the individual firm is prepared to provide. The correspondence to the concept of the ecological niche, which has been discussed in earlier chapters, is obvious.

It would be possible to generalize the term "opportunity" and refer to the opportunity for a group of firms making up an industry. In using the term "opportunity" in a broader sense, however, it should be kept in mind that even within a single industry a group of firms does not really face homogeneous demand, but that the total opportunity is the combination of the related and yet separate opportunities for individual firms. If the opportunity for all the firms were truly and completely homogeneous, then the Marxian principle of capitalistic accumulation might apply in the long run, so that this entire segment of demand would come to be served by a single firm. If there is no difference in requirements within the field served by the industry, then there is nothing to prevent the entire market from being taken over by the most efficient firm, particularly in the presence of modern technology.

The term "effort" designates the activities which a firm puts forth to serve its market. While it pertains to supply, it is a more dynamic concept than supply because it relates to a set of activities rather than to a quantity of goods. This is one of the key points at which the present view is trying to press beyond traditional theory in order that marketing may be understood in terms of the functional analysis of behavior systems. Demand can be satisfied even though the goods demanded are not in existence at that particular instant. What is needed on the supply side is not products but capacity to produce. It is only an arbitrary analytical device to suggest that market equilibrium can be understood as a balance between goods wanted and goods available at a particular instant. In an organized economy, what is involved is a steady flow of goods to market in anticipation of the demands of consumers who will be ready to receive the goods when they get there.

The third major concept in this approach to the market is management or the skillful direction of effort in relation to an understanding of demand. This chapter will be devoted to the subject of market management and the way it functions in organizing marketing effort to make the most of the market opportunity. Having these three factors in mind, it is possible to set up what might be called the fundamental equation of marketing. For the individual marketing firm, sales results can be regarded as a function of organized marketing effort applied to market opportunity. Part III will largely be devoted to various aspects of this process of applying effort to opportunity. This opening chapter undertakes to present a broad view of the management process, starting with the chief executive of the firm and working down through the principal subordinates and various separate units through which the firm achieves its objectives. Thus the chapter will deal with the various subfunctions by which the organization carries out its general aim of maximizing sales results by applying effort to opportunity.

Segmentation of Opportunity and Effort. In matching opportunity with effort, management must start out by recognizing the elements of structure on either side of the equation. Both opportunity and effort must be broken down into significant segments in order to determine the best application of a type of effort to a phase of opportunity. This process begins logically with the evaluation of market opportunity. Evaluation of opportunity or sales potential is not quite the same thing as the measurement of demand. In the traditional view of the market, the analyst considers demand at a given instant of time and tries to determine what quantity of the specified product would move at various prices. He prefers, where possible, to develop a complete demand schedule which in effect indicates the volume of goods which would move at each possible price. In this approach to the measurement of demand, all other factors are held to be constant, with price alone determining the volume of business. Demand is not a single quantity but is characterized by the price-volume function.

In considering sales potential or market opportunity, the analyst is necessarily concerned with all dimensions of the bundle of utilities offered and with what is likely to happen over a period of time as well as at a given instant. Admittedly, the available tools for dealing with this more complex analytical problem are relatively crude; but the market analyst is necessarily more concerned with practical decisions than with the elegance of his analytical results. He is interested from the first in the potentialities for expansion and in the kind of effort that will be required to expand the market. He may divide the total opportunity into segments in various ways and look upon each segment as a unit which follows the laws of growth on its own account. He is interested in the kind of sales which will lead to future sales as well as to immediate profits. He must keep himself open to consider variations in product specifications and accompanying services as well as in prices. He must try to estimate potential at various levels of marketing effort rather than treating opportunity as something static which does not respond to effort. Admittedly, there is an element of circularity in estimating potential at various levels of effort in order to determine how much effort to apply in cultivating the potential. Actually, there is no escape from this circularity, since the essential problem is precisely that of finding the optimum level, after taking account of all factors affecting both opportunity and effort. The market analyst recognizes that there is no technique for identifying this level with absolute certainty. He pursues the more modest aim of trying to reach a reasonable approximation in the first instance and then moving closer and closer to the optimum by successive corrections. This is equivalent to saying that successful marketing has not outgrown the trial-and-error approach but is finding analytical methods increasingly helpful in improving the results of trial and error.

Major Differences in Market Opportunity. The market opportunity for an individual firm can be broken down in various ways. If the company is selling a consumer product, it can classify its ultimate consumers by age and sex, group them as users and nonusers of the product, or divide them into large users and small users. There are three ways of classifying consumers which seem to have almost universal application to all classes of products—namely, by region, by size of the place in which they live, and by family income level. Demand differs by region in accordance with such differences as climate and the racial background of people in the region. Texas and the other states of the west-south-central region offer the best market in the country for home air conditioning. New England and the north-central states provide a superior market for central heating. While these differences are obvious, climate has a pervasive effect on demand for all types of goods, resulting in important differences in sales potential for various types of food, clothing, and housing.

An interesting example of differences in demand due to racial background is provided by the type of coffee preferred in Louisiana. Because of the French ancestry of many people living in this state, they have become accustomed to drinking coffee to which chicory has been added. Even some of the national manufacturers of coffee package a different blend under the same brand name for shipment into the Gulf states. A similar example is that of the demand for flour in the southeastern states. There is still a strong preference in this area for hot breads, such as biscuits. Some leading millers use a greater proportion of soft wheat in flour to be shipped to these states to adapt the product to this prevailing use. The general tendency throughout the country is for differences in demand due to racial background to disappear. There is no longer a separate Italian, Jewish, or Negro market for products to the extent that there was only fifteen or twenty years ago. Nevertheless, regional differences will continue to be important because of climate and topography and long-established patterns of behavior arising from these geographical differences.

The second factor of size of place in which the consumer resides is correlated with important differences in demand, although these have been greatly moderated in recent decades. The farm market as a separate entity is gradually disappearing, except as it applies to farm machinery and other productive goods purchased by the farmer. In the area of consumer goods the farmer and his family are inclined increasingly to follow the same pattern of living as urban families. Nevertheless, important differences will remain between the pattern of life in the larger cities and in the small towns and rural areas. For example, the great majority of farm families today own and operate at least one automobile as a matter of practical necessity, while less than half of the families in New York City own an automobile. It was scarcely more than ten years ago that great differences existed between farm and city homes as to the use of electrical appliances. This difference is now being rapidly eliminated because of the vast expansion of rural electrification in the decade from 1940 to 1950. Even among the large cities, there are considerable differences in patterns of expenditure resulting from differences in the degree of congestion and in the availability of recreational facilities. Differences in types of stores are of decreasing importance, since the majority of consumers, including farm families, are now within driving distance of shopping centers which offer most of the products which can be purchased anywhere.

Family Income—the Key Factor. By far the most important of the general market factors is the level of family income. Family income, of course, affects both the total amount and the range of products which can be purchased. In the American economy, families quickly adapt their style of living to the new pattern as family income increases. There is a greater similarity in the pattern of life of families in a given income bracket throughout the United States than there would be among families in all cities of a given size or among all families living in a specified region of the country. There has been a marked tendency toward the leveling-up of income among various sections of the United States. The Southeast, which long has been the region of lowest per capita income, is also the region which has been showing the greatest percentage gain. There has, of course, been a tendency nationally toward the leveling of incomes because of progressive tax rates in the higher brackets. Thus, in certain respects the whole national market may be said to be moving toward greater uniformity and equality. There is an offsetting tendency, however, as average income increases to give the individual consumer or household a greater opportunity to express its own individual tastes and preferences through the goods it purchases.

Segmentation of the Industrial Market.   For firms selling to the industrial market, there are similar fundamental ways of breaking down the market opportunity. Region of the country is again important, not only because of climate but because of labor supply, raw materials, markets for end products, and other factors which are likely to affect the future of industrial customers located in each region. An especially important classification is, of course, type of business. Products can be sold to the chemical industry which would be of no interest to the textile industry, and vice versa. In this connection, however, the market analyst is confronted by the great difficulties of industrial classification, since many firms engage in a variety of activities. Standard classifications, such as those available through the Census Bureau, do not entirely meet the needs of the individual firm engaged in industrial selling. It is obliged to adapt such classifications to its own needs, combining the results of experience and field studies with information from public sources such as the Census Bureau.

Some products are sold to a great many different types of plants and others to a much smaller segment of industry. A study of the market for burlap and jute products some years ago revealed substantial demand among 110 separate industries for use either for packaging or as a component part of an end product. To determine the market for steam valves and fittings means trying to locate all types of plants in which there are steam lines. The relative importance of steam lines in productive processes varies greatly from one industry to another, being relatively high in chemical plants and food processing plants and relatively low or nonexistent in automobile factories and steel mills. Size of plant is an obvious indication of market potential, and figures on plant size are available through census data and other sources. Problems arise as to whether size of plant is to be measured by number of employees, value of output, or what the Census Bureau calls "value added by manufacture." The relevance of these various measures depends on the kind of product for which the market is being evaluated.

In both consumer goods and industrial goods, it is useful to distinguish between the core and the fringe of the prospective market. The core of the market consists of those potential buyers who are likely to have the greatest interest in the given product and who may be willing to pay the highest prices for it in the initial stages before it has attained the level of mass production. The core of the market offers the firm a place to get started and continues to be the foundation of its security in the market, no matter how great its sales expansion. Earlier chapters suggested that a solidly established core might enable a business to survive and make a successful readjustment during a period when it was losing at the fringes of its market. The main point here is the importance of the concepts of core and fringe in the initial evaluation of market opportunity. To distinguish the core of a market means to gather facts and make judgments about the interests and tastes of consumers. Classification by degree of interest in a particular product in relation to anticipated patterns of behavior is both more important and more difficult than any of the other classifications which have so far been suggested. This is subject, of course, to the ability of the consumer to indulge his preferences by the purchase of a product. The initial core of the market is likely to be found among families of average income or better, but the analysis needs to go much further in determining the characteristics of the families who will be most inclined to try the product in the beginning.

Types of Marketing Effort. The classification of effort for the purpose of matching effort against opportunity will be considered more briefly at this point, since it is involved throughout the remainder of this chapter. Possible types of marketing effort can be broken down into such categories as personal selling, advertising, and sales promotion. It is the province of management to determine the best combination of these ingredients, sometimes designated as the "marketing mix." These various types of marketing activities have both competitive and complementary relations with each other. That is to say that one can be substituted for the other to some extent, but one may also work better when it is supplemented by another form of effort. A major justification of large advertising budgets is that the use of advertising often reduces the amount of personal selling required and thus cuts down the total costs of marketing. It is seldom possible to move goods by means of advertising alone, but personal salesmen usually find that their job is made much easier when they are given substantial advertising support. Sales promotion covers a somewhat indefinite and intermediate area. As a matter of fact, the term is by no means uniformly defined in various marketing organizations. In general, it might be said that sales promotion lies somewhere between personal selling and advertising. It is usually designed to intensify sales pressure directed at some especially significant group, such as the trade or certain classes of consumers.

Phases of Effort Related to Marketing. There are other types of activities which must be regarded as part of a total marketing program, even though they may not be carried out through the sales organization. These activities include product development, sales development, and quality control. Product development and quality control have already been discussed in relation to the central marketing problem of offering an acceptable bundle of utilities and maintaining consumer confidence in the uniformity and quality of the product available. Sales development is a step between product development and regular selling. Product development undertakes to produce a combination of features in the product which consumers will buy at the stated price. It is carried on mainly in an engineering laboratory, utilizing information obtained through sales contacts and through market research. Sales development means learning how to sell the product or demonstrating that the product can be sold to customers who are sufficiently interested and by salesmen who are adequately informed as to the virtues of the product. Sales development may be directed toward rounding out the bundle of utilities by determining the services which must be offered along with the product in order to sell it successfully. It might also be regarded as a preliminary exploration of the core of the market as defined by market research. Sales development is not always recognized as a separate marketing activity; there is an increased tendency to set it apart, both in industrial selling and in the selling of some types of consumer products. Whether or not sales development is handled by a separate unit in an organization, management should be conscious of it as a stage in rounding out a marketing program. The regular sales force can perform to best advantage if there is a standard package to offer customers in which all aspects of product, price, and service are specified. This package or bundle of utilities can scarcely be considered complete until the task of sales development has been performed.

Marginal Productivity in Marketing Effort. The principle of marginal productivity can be applied in comparing various forms of marketing effort. For any given marketing organization, there are likely to be a number of ways of gaining ultimate consumers. Some of these methods may prove most effective for the organization and some of them less effective. Thus a supplier may feel obliged to sell his product both through drugstores and through grocery stores, but he may feel that drugstores are really the main channel so far as his product is concerned. Some organizations may rely primarily on personal selling backed up by advertising, while others assume that the main selling job is performed by advertising, so that the salesmen merely have to pick up the orders. A study was made some years ago for a firm which was marketing a low-sudsing detergent for use in automatic washing machines. At that time it was possible to obtain a reasonably good sample of consumers who had been sold the product by various methods, including advertising, distribution of free samples, and demonstration of the product at the time that the washing machine was installed. It was found that personal demonstration was the most effective method in terms of the number of dollars expended. It was also found that the number of instances in which an effective personal demonstration could be arranged was limited to only a part of the customers buying new machines. Even though this method was more effective than any other when it could be used, it did not provide a means of reaching the large number of prospects who already owned washing machines. Thus, in designing a marketing program, an organization may not be able to confine its efforts to its most effective methods. It will concentrate on the most effective method so far as possible, but will probably have to supplement it with its second-best and third-best methods in order to get optimum results. This can be very simply illustrated in the case of personal selling. The company may have one star salesman, who is more effective than any other. Nevertheless, it cannot afford to trust its future to the efforts of this one salesman, but will need to use other salesmen so long as each can produce some net return over cost.

Triangulation in the Control of Effort. The problem of matching marketing effort against opportunity is complicated by the fact that a considerable period of time must be taken into account in setting up marketing programs. It is not merely the state of the market today or the type and amount of effort required in its cultivation which management must consider. Both market potential and marketing effort change over time and must be kept in balance with each other as well as with the third factor of productive capacity. The attempt to keep these three factors in balance in market planning may be designated as "triangulation" and will be discussed more fully later. The term is meant to suggest a parallel to the process by which an engineer or an artillery officer might set his sights on a target and estimate how far away the target is and what it will take to reach it. Market potential five years ahead depends on various aspects of demand, but it also depends on the amount of marketing effort which will be expended meanwhile in developing demand. Plant capacity must be ready to satisfy demand, or the maximum volume of sales cannot be realized. Planning for many types of plants has to start a year to five years before the time that the plant will go into operation. Some estimate of future demand is the basis for justifying the planning and construction of a plant, whether this estimate is based on formal analysis or executive hunch. Once the commitment to build a plant has been made, it is essential that every reasonable effort be expended to make sure that, when the plant is completed, it can be operated at a reasonable percentage of capacity.

It is apparent that these three elements involved in triangulation are interrelated in several ways. Marketing effort cannot be justified unless there is some indication that a fair sales potential is available. The amount of this potential, on the other hand, depends in part on the effort expended. Similarly, plant capacity must be kept in line with the expected potential; but marketing effort may have to be stepped up in order to reach a satisfactory relationship between market potential and plant capacity. It appears certain that market potential will not be created by the simple expedient of building a plant, and that customers are not automatically available because a supplier stands willing and able to serve them. Similarly, the existence of potential demand does not automatically produce the supply to serve it unless someone has had the insight to foresee this demand and has been willing to take the risk of providing the necessary facilities. The key factor in triangulation might thus appear to be marketing effort, which is doubly linked to market potential on the one hand and plant capacity on the other.

Management is obliged to establish some priorities in the organization of marketing effort. The successive steps might not always occur in the same order, but a schedule of priorities is suggested which might be suited to many marketing situations. The first step in this schedule is defining or redefining opportunity. This is the attempt to qualify the particular opportunity which exists in the market in terms of the bundle of utilities which is most desired or which will lead to maximum volume. The second step is making sales forecasts or estimates of how the market opportunity can be expected to develop over a number of years ahead. The third step is the laying-out of the marketing program governing the expenditure of marketing effort. The program should be planned in a general way for a number of years ahead and in specific detail for the immediate operating period. The fourth step is production scheduling, by which the most efficient use of present production capacity can be made. The fifth step is investment planning, which undertakes to provide new capacity as needed. Additions to basic plant capacity necessarily proceed in stair-step fashion rather than by continuous increments in line with sales expansion. Production scheduling, together with minor engineering adjustments in production processes, can help smooth out the capacity function, so that the periods in which sales are catching up with additions to plant are relatively brief.

THE NATURE OF THE EXECUTIVE FUNCTION

The chief executive of a large corporation directs the use of company resources in the pursuit of company goals. His task differs in scale and complexity from that of the consumer, who uses individually owned resources or the resources of a single household. Departures from rationality are also of a somewhat different character. While the executive, as a human being, is partly a creature of impulse and habit, his failures to act rationally must be interpreted in the corporate setting. One type of departure might be called "subrationality." The executive might be performing in a way that was entirely acceptable at a lower level of responsibility or at an earlier stage in his company's history. The imperfection lies in not fully measuring up to the broader or more current requirements of his position. Another type of departure might be called "pseudorationality." That would designate the practice of adopting certain procedures because they looked rational or because they were used by other executives who were regarded as competent. Subrationality leans toward flying by the seat of the pants. Pseudorationality is often expressed in an addiction to reports, surveys, and control systems which never really become effective as management tools. Most major business executives occupy a sounder middle position and are constantly striving to adapt their behavior more effectively to the scope of their responsibilities.

Every normal person acts in order to achieve a range of satisfactions. In the prevailing pattern of life, many specialized means are required to obtain various kinds of satisfaction. A prudent person is necessarily engaged much of the time in acquiring such means rather than indulging in behavior expected to yield more direct and immediate satisfactions. Success in this instrumental type of behavior is in turn a source of satisfaction. As a goal of rational action, success outranks but does not supplant direct satisfaction. Still more fundamental is the goal of survival. The drive for success may be self-defeating, and hence irrational, if it involves too large a risk that the individual or the operation he directs will not survive.

The Power Principle in Executive Action. An overriding test is found in the power principle. The rational individual will act in such a way as to promote the power to act. Whatever he does today, he will not lose sight of the resources and facilities he will need in order to act tomorrow. The problem is complicated by the existence of multiple objectives, some of which may be in conflict. The individual also faces uncertainty as to the relative weight these objectives will have in the future and as to the feasibility of obtaining them.

Transferring this problem to the corporate setting, it becomes still more complex in terms of the responsibilities of the chief executive. The subordinates through whom he must work have their own individual and often divergent objectives. The interests of stockholders, labor, suppliers, and customers also enter into the puzzle. Uncertainties as to future requirements arise from changing demand, from changing technological possibilities, and from the shifting strategies of competitors. At worst the task of the chief executive is like driving a fractious or balky team up a mountain road in total darkness. The general aim is to reach the top in the face of severe hazards and in spite of wasted effort.

The first step toward coping with multiplicity of objectives is for the executive to identify himself as completely as possible with his company. That is to say that he must have achieved a state of mind in which his greatest satisfactions spring from the success of his company and in which his present conception of success for himself is wholly dependent upon the survival and prosperity of the company. To the extent that the executive succeeds in this identification, he will have a basis for evaluating individual objectives and for resolving conflict. He may listen to many proposals from subordinates but be guided in the last analysis by his own judgment as to whether they contribute to the welfare of the company. If he can follow such a line with clarity and consistency, it will tend to reduce uncertainty within the organization. The individual gains a better conception of what will promote his own stature in the company and feels more secure with respect to the actions of others who are competing for advancement.

The chief executive is aided in identification with the company because he stands in some degree above the struggle for status. He has reached the top of the present career ladder and generally is paid enough so that he cannot easily be induced to leave. There has been some speculation as to whether the salaried executive can be a true enterpriser if he is not a substantial owner. The basic question is still the degree of identification, which rests on many factors besides ownership. Indeed, many cases can be observed in which professional management identifies itself with the company more fully than the owners do. The owners may have a greater interest in other enterprises or may have reached the stage in their personal careers at which they would welcome a chance to retire from business.

Major Executive Functions. The functions of the chief executive will now be examined in greater detail. This search for standards of executive behavior will be guided by the postulate of rationality, and by such related considerations as the power principle and the corollary that rationality is a scarce resource and therefore must economize itself. The phases of executive action outlined hereafter may be designated as the organizing functions, the operating functions, and the symbolic functions of the chief executive.

Chester Barnard, a distinguished student of the executive function, has said that the head of a large company should not assume that he is running the organization. He should regard his role as that of keeping the organization tuned up, so that it can run itself. The operations of any great company are beyond the power of a single mind to comprehend. It would be an illusion for the man at the top to imagine that all of its essential operations could be activated by his decisions and commands. The more he attempted to operate in this fashion, the less effective his subordinates would become.

This statement of Barnard's expresses a philosophy but does not describe a procedure. The concept of keeping an organization tuned up involves a variety of possible activities. It might start with definite specifications of responsibilities at all levels and with some orderly procedure for evaluating performance. It might include frequent spot checks into various phases of the operation to determine how decisions were being made and to savor the quality of performance beyond what could be reflected by objective standards. In one phase of his daily activities the chief executive is consulting with his subordinates on problems they bring to him. Consistent with the Barnard philosophy, he would usually take the position that he was consulting with them on how to solve a problem rather than taking it on as his own. To an important degree, such consultation would be educational and intended to encourage the subordinate to take greater responsibility in coping with the next problem of the same type.

The Organizing Function.   This emphasis on maintaining the effectiveness of the organization would be unsound if conceived in purely static terms. In a growing business the chief executive is inevitably involved in organization planning. At least three versions of his organization structure must be present in his thinking. The current structure, the appropriate structure five years ahead, and one or more transition stages are important points of reference. To keep an organization tuned up is to keep it moving ahead. To change the specifications of a job in accordance with new requirements is one way of challenging the individual or the operating unit to meet new standards of performance.

The relationship between growth and organization structure deserves continuous attention from the chief executive. It is only through growth that he can hope to satisfy the aspirations of ambitious and competent men. But he must surround himself with associates of this type to promote the welfare of the company and give it some assurance of growth and profits. The executive must somehow set a pace which brings company objectives and individual objectives into balance. Mastery of many techniques for the management of men is implied in the deceptively simple phrase of keeping the organization "tuned up." The executive is promoting the power to act in placing primary emphasis on a healthy organization.

Operating Functions. To assert that the first concern of the chief executive is organization does not mean that he has no operating responsibilities. He is a part of the machine, as well as being the machinist who keeps it in working order. That is to say that the final essence of the executive function cannot be delegated but must always be exercised by an individual or executive committee at the top. These phases of executive action are related to company goals, commitment of resources, and assumption of major risks.

The executive leader must project an understanding of company goals and policies to the organization. That is true whether he originates policy or is simply transmitting it from a source such as a board of directors. Department heads must be guided by some vision of what the company is after. The translation of objectives into detailed programs necessarily occurs within each department. A department objective must in turn be transmitted to the second level and go through a further detailing of procedures. The eloquence and persuasiveness of the initial statement can have an impact all the way down.

To lead his organization in this way, the executive must be ahead, but not too far ahead, of the group. His vision of company growth or improved operation must be understood and accepted to be effective. His thinking may run far ahead of the program he puts in words. At some point in this advance, he is forced to recognize the limiting factor of communication and to concentrate on presentation. The ideal executive is a master of effective English who can express his vision in the kind of words which result in action.

Allocation of Resources. Another top function is the determination along broad lines of how company resources are to be used. No one short of the chief executive can evaluate the respective claims of production, marketing, finance, and engineering. While the executive usually comes out of one of these specialized fields, it is very important at this point that he identify himself with the total welfare of the company and not with any specialized phase of the operation. He may use staff assistants or outside consultants in screening proposed programs. He may require the proponent of a budget to justify it according to prescribed standards. The ultimate decision is his, since it could scarcely be reached by negotiation and compromise among departments.

Budget approval is a primary means for keeping the lines of authority taut. A departmental budget, when approved, should constitute a mutual commitment running between the department head and the head of the company. On one side it is a commitment of resources and on the other a pledge of performance. If changes in objectives or operating methods are desired, if the department is expected to expand its operations or improve its efficiency during the year, that understanding should be incorporated in the commitment. In return for the support he is given, the subordinate accepts standards of performance by which he will be judged at the end of the operating period. If the budget approved is less than requested, it is still fair to require a showing of how these resources will be used to the greatest advantage of the company.

The network of mutual commitments, with the chief executive at the center, relates back to the problem of keeping the organization tuned up. The greater the strength of these understandings, the less the temptation to form cliques and coalitions which result in internal conflict and wasted effort. If the chief executive fully identifies himself with company welfare, his subordinates are related to this broad objective through their commitments running to and from the top. A company with this structure can move rapidly and with great striking impact. It is democratic in the sense that a commitment is arrived at in a framework of negotiation and each man helps determine the bargain he will be bound by. It represents centralized authority, since all lines of commitment radiate from the top.

Evaluation of Risks. The third operating responsibility is the choice among major risks affecting the outlook for the company. Risk taking is implied in most of what has been said. Unavoidably, management takes chances on men, on marketing strategies, and on the allocation of resources. There are analytical methods available for measuring risks; and to the extent that they are applicable, they can be carried on at the staff level. The measurement of risk and the acceptance of risk remain separate and distinct.

Possibly a more telling distinction is between uncertainty and risk. The analyst and the executive may consider uncertainty together and arrive at the same evaluation. Risk enters only when something of value is at stake on an uncertain outcome. Risk is uncertainty weighted by the amount at stake. The top executive, if he truly identifies himself with the company, is peculiarly equipped to evaluate major risks. Both objective and subjective factors are involved. In making his calculations, he uses inputs of information which may be available to no one else. They include a vision of the future he may not be ready to disclose fully to others and his private reservations about the strength of the organization or of key individuals. Finally, there is an emotional or temperamental factor which enters legitimately into his decision—that is, how the proposed risk feels to him and whether he can bear it comfortably as compared with risks associated with alternative courses of action.

The risks which can most obviously be delegated are repetitive in character. They are subject to probability analysis and statistical control. The risks which gravitate to the top are nonrecurring and of larger magnitude. Management sets the tone and the rules for handling one type and deals with the other directly. At the same time, management attempts to minimize uncertainties arising within the organization itself. That is part of the significance of concentration on organization planning and on co-ordination through policy direction and budget approval. Rational leadership of a large company makes effective use of industrial power in coping with the uncertainties of the economic environment.

The Symbolic Function. The chief executive must stand as a symbol of the corporation as well as directing its operations. This symbolic role is inescapable and is in some respects the most difficult phase of leadership. The potency of an executive as a symbol does not depend entirely on rational grounds such as his personal competence. It can spring from family tradition or from the legend of success. The task for rationality is to understand the sources of symbolic power in the particular case and to use the symbolic role effectively for the benefit of the company. One characteristic of the ideal executive is skill in dealing with symbolic values both in his own person and as they affect other members of the organization.

The chief executive must regard himself as a primary instrument for the company's public relations program. A few executives have a natural flair in this field, but most need the guidance of professional counsel. There are several different groups whose good will should be cultivated. A stance which would please one group might antagonize another.

The symbolic role of the executive is exercised inside the company as well as outside. He has already attained that to which many others aspire. They obtain vicarious fulfillment through him, particularly if he has come up within the company. If he is truly admired by his subordinates, the desire to emulate him can be a powerful incentive to good performance. His point of view and his work habits are communicated by contagion rather than by precept and admonition. Loyalty to the company takes on a more concrete and stable form as loyalty to the man at the top. Belief in his leadership inspires confidence in the stability and prosperity of the company.

In addition to serving as a symbol himself, the chief executive is involved in the management of the power structure through the use of symbols. This is a field in which it is difficult to behave in a truly rational and effective manner. To mistake the symbols of power for power itself is usually self-defeating and hence irrational. Management seeks to maintain the operating structure of the organization in healthy condition. To do this, it must be concerned with the power structure and the symbols of power. Even though they are not identical, a break in the power structure through the neglect of symbolic values often imperils the operating structure.

The effective management of power and the symbols of power requires the chief executive to be sensitive to the career expectations of his subordinates. Every step upward is an occasion for evaluation and a new understanding of what is expected. The symbols of status are among the significant rewards which can be given in return. Similarly, when a man fails to achieve an expected preferment, he deserves to know why he failed. Otherwise, he may brood over the disappointment and impute sinister motives to others instead of facing his own problem.

To summarize the view of the executive function which has been presented here, it would appear that the chief executive must manage the operating structure which constitutes the organization and the power structure which is intimately related to it. In addition, he enters into these structures personally, both as an essential operating element and as a symbol. He is responsible for making the power of the organization effective. To do this, he must identify himself with the organization and apply the power principle which has been discussed from a corporate rather than a merely individual viewpoint.

STRUCTURE OF THE SALES ORGANIZATION

A sales organization is generally pictured as a structure built on the delegation of authority and responsibility at successive levels of operation. This structure provides a framework within which decisions are made and a set of channels carrying a stream of communication about actions which have been taken or which are proposed. Finally, a sales organization must contain within itself the means for renewal or replacement and the means for adaptation to growth and change.

One very helpful figure of speech is that which compares a sales organization to a fighting force. The salesmen in the field and in actual contact with the customers are often referred to as men on the firing line. It may be useful to carry this comparison a little further, since there are various ways in which a fighting force can be organized and each has its parallel in selling. Under some circumstances, an army appears to be most successful when it is scarcely more than a collection of guerilla bands. The guerilla fights best in rough country, adapting himself to the local situation as it develops and living mainly by his own wits and resourcefulness, with little direction from headquarters. Guerilla warfare is not necessarily on a small scale, since we have seen the development of huge armies of this type in modern times.

The parallel in selling includes cases in which the market has been very large relative to the size of the force employed. Market shifts were so rapid that it was difficult for central management to set up or administer any general plan of attack. When a salesman can knock on almost any door and get enough business to keep plants working to capacity, there is little incentive for careful planning or strict control of sales operations. Formal organization tends to be at the minimum, and the performance of the star salesman may be regarded in somewhat the same light as the legendary exploits of the individual guerilla fighter.

At the other extreme in military affairs is the highly mechanized modern army with a general staff and successive levels of field command. The man on the firing line depends on others behind the lines for his weapons and ammunition. He is expected to carry out his assigned task with fidelity and precision, but strategy is determined at the higher echelons. This is the kind of organization which develops for planning and executing a sustained attack against major obstacles in order to accomplish the most effective use of resources and man power.

The obvious parallel in marketing is the national sales organization which is trying to reach a sales volume representing something like the full potential for the company's products and to use its limited resources efficiently in the pursuit of these objectives. In planning this kind of sales organization, it is essential to keep in mind the requirements of both the top command and the men on the firing line. The top marketing executive needs effective control, reliable measures of performance, and flexibility in the deployment of his resources to attain his objectives. The man on the firing line is entitled to a clear statement of a well-conceived assignment. He also needs some discretion for seizing upon opportunity as it arises and for going beyond his literal instructions, so long as he acts in harmony with general plans.

Building an Organization Structure. Each sales organization occupies a unique position in the market. Many perplexing questions arise in shaping its structure and the flow of its decisions to match its special needs. No formula can fit every case, but there are some general principles which can be applied in designing an appropriate structure. In building or remodeling a sales organization, it seems well to start with the salesman in the field and the size and character of the sales force required for adequate contact with the company's customers. Next is the question of the level of supervision immediately above the salesmen and the grouping of sales territories into districts or branches for administrative purposes. The assignment of salesmen within the districts may be purely by territories or on some other basis, and the relative merits of methods of assignment will differ by companies or even by sections of the country for the same company. When this groundwork has been established, it is time to consider organizational requirements at headquarters. How many assistants should report to the top marketing executive? Should their work be divided on functional lines or on some other basis? What should be the nature of the staff units in the headquarters organization? Finally, there are the questions of the line of command between headquarters and the field and the proper relation of staff units to the line organization both at headquarters and in the field.

Major companies differ widely in the number of salesmen employed in relation to the volume of business. The number of men required is obviously affected by many factors, such as the type of products and the kinds of customers served. The economist's answer as to just how many salesmen a company should have is "just as many as it can use profitably." That rule may sound pretty trite, but it is certainly violated in hundreds of cases. Consulting experience suggests that the companies who do not have enough salesmen would outnumber those who have too many. There are some obvious reasons for this, including the analytical difficulties in determining the right number. Another problem is recruiting, training, and keeping men with adequate qualifications for doing the job. It is true that all aspects of sales management are related, but that only emphasizes the basic need for creating a sound organizational structure. Problems of personnel will be minimized by a structure which makes the best use of the available man power and which contributes as much as possible to good individual sales performance.

Planning Sales Coverage. To determine the number of men required, it is necessary to consider several degrees of intensity in sales coverage. The minimum degree of intensity is that which will provide calls on established customers with a frequency that is adequate simply from a service standpoint. This calculation usually should allow for some gradation of frequency by size or relative importance of customers. It must, of course, allow time for travel, for the planning of calls, for the organization of schedules, and for time actually spent with the customer. Higher degrees of intensity of sales coverage must be evaluated in relation to the company's objectives as to an accelerated growth trend and judgments as to the responsiveness of its market to sales and advertising. Theoretically, salesmen should be added until the last man who is beyond the training stage just manages to pay his way. Practically, there may be good reasons for stopping short of this point; but it is still important to know where the point is. Once the number of men has been settled, the next step is to delineate sales territories. This is a problem in economic geography, involving a consideration of such factors as travel cost and the distribution of customers and prospects. Laying out individual sales territories at this stage does not necessarily involve a commitment that salesmen will be assigned on a territorial basis. The purpose rather is to create some elementary building blocks which can be used in planning the structure of the sales organization. In working with a going organization, these building blocks already exist, although they may have to be modified substantially in the final organizational plan.

The first step in using sales territories as building blocks is to group them into sales districts. The size of a sales district should be no greater than a good district manager can control effectively. There are compelling arguments for simple and direct supervisory contact in the field. The district manager should be able to make frequent calls on his men in their territories and to talk with them directly when they show up at the district office. A salesman needs to know that there is one man to whom he can turn for an interpretation of policy or for counsel on a special problem. Setting up several levels of supervision in a district office tends to lengthen lines of communication to the point where they are cumbersome and ineffective. If a need is felt for more than one level of supervision over the salesmen in a district office, it can usually be taken as a symptom that the district is too large.

But while the individual district manager should not be given the opportunity to build up an empire of his own, it should be recognized that in most companies he occupies the key spot in the line organization. Whatever the superstructure of line and staff that is set above him, nothing should be taken away from his authority or his responsibility for performance in his own district.

The Basis of Sales Assignments.   The salesmen who report to the district manager may be assigned to territories, or they may be specialized along other lines. The principal possibilities are by territory, by product group, or by type of user industry. If the company is selling a long list of products to many types of customers, there is a strong argument for giving up straight territorial assignments in favor of one of the other two. The case for maintaining territorial assignments rests largely on the distance factor, with the two objectives of minimizing travel cost and recognizing the salesman's resistance to being on the road constantly. The cost factor can be easily overlooked if it is offset by economic factors on the other side. The bugaboo of excessive travel for the salesman may be overcome if it is recognized that his job is something else than the routine coverage of so many square miles every week. If his headquarters city has been properly chosen, and if there is an appropriate gradation in frequency of calls, he usually will not have to be away from home every night of the week. Add to this the further factor that selling of more than routine difficulty will require some time in the office for planning and preparation.

Once it has been decided that something else than the territorial basis is indicated, there is pretty sure to be a lively debate between the other two principles of assignment, by product or by type of customer. This conflict can be moderated when it is recognized that whether the choice is product groups or user industries, some recognition should be given to the other in the detailed classification. Thus, in determining which products should be grouped together and sold by the same salesmen, one criterion is whether they tend to be purchased by firms in similar lines of business or distributed through the same trade channels. Those who believe in an industry classification may insist that classifying customers by trade or industry is the only way that takes the market as it is and in its own terms. The catch in this proposition is that industrial classification does not consist of one simple and universally recognized set of categories. Firms may consider themselves to be part of the same industry because they make the same products, because their plant processes are similar, or because they use the same raw materials. The supplier is well justified in classifying firms from his own standpoint and grouping together those who have similar requirements for the products he supplies. In these terms, it may turn out that there is little difference between an industry classification and a product classification. When this is true, there are substantial advantages in describing the plan and making assignments to salesmen on the basis of product groups. It is easier for the sales department to deal with the production and development departments in these terms. It is easier for all concerned to keep a firm grasp on the broad outlines of a classification based on the company's own products rather than on an industry classification which is somewhat foreign to the daily experience of anyone except the salesmen themselves. There is always the possibility of supplementing product assignments by setting up a special task force to deal with an industry that is heavily concentrated regionally or that is in a phase of extremely rapid growth and development.

CO-ORDINATION OF LINE AND STAFF

The degree of separation of line and staff and the working relations between them are bound to differ at various stages in the history of a firm. It will possibly be clarifying to go back to the starting point of a one-man organization and consider what happens thereafter in the delegation of both line and staff activities. A single executive at the head of a small organization obviously combines the functions of line and staff. He not only makes all decisions concerning the commitment of resources, but he personally collects and considers such information as may be used in making these decisions. It has often been said that market analysis, of a type, goes on in every sales organization, even though the function is not formally recognized. The sales executive acts on the basis of some conception of the facts gained either from direct operating experience or, in the case of a major decision, from a special investigation such as a field trip or a study of government statistics. Our preliminary definition of the line and staff functions implies the dominance of line over staff. This dominance is not so clear when the functions are combined in the same individual. The effectiveness of the manager of a one-man company may depend as much on his propensity for gathering and weighing information as upon his willingness to take the risk of making definite decisions. On his staff side, he may be continuously preoccupied with plans and programs of a long-range character. He will consider the feasibility of long-range objectives in relation to his understanding of market opportunity and the competitive situation. He is acting as a line executive, on the other hand, when he determines upon trying to attain these objectives and when he commits resources from day to day in carrying out this program. Depending on his temperament and training, the executive in the one-man company might be convinced that his staff functions take precedence over his line functions. He might feel that the really difficult job was to define feasible objectives and to prescribe corresponding programs and standards of performance. Under this conception the line function would be relatively routine, consisting of a continuous series of operating decisions within the framework of the general plan. The contrary point of view is that the line function is more fundamental, since it is only the revenues produced by day-to-day operations which give the company its chance for survival and eventual achievement of long-range objectives.

Delegation in a Growing Organization. Turning to the next stage of growth, it is worth-while to take a look at the delegation of executive responsibility to subordinates as the company continues to expand. Both line responsibilities and staff responsibilities may be delegated, but the delegation of line functions has generally come first and has been carried substantially further. The reasons for delegation are quite different as between line and staff functions. Line responsibility is delegated because of the multiplicity of routine and repetitive decisions which must be made in carrying out major decisions. Obviously, the terms "major" and "minor" are relative and are measured by the extent of the commitments which can be made by any given executive as compared with his subordinates.

A further complication in a growing company is that many decisions must be made simultaneously and often in widely separated parts of the country. Suppose that a sales executive decides that several hundred leading customers must be notified of a change in model by personal visits on the morning of the same day. This is an action which he obviously cannot carry out himself. It is also likely to involve a number of minor decisions for district sales managers in touch with each local situation. It may be necessary, for example, to decide who should be notified in each company and which salesman should call on each of these individuals.

As in a military organization, a delegation of line authority in a corporate structure passes down to smaller and smaller units to the final level of supervision which is in direct and continuous contact with specific operating situations. There is a considerable tendency in line organizations toward administrative decentralization. That means putting greater authority to act at the end of the line. It amounts to encouraging action on the basis of the specific facts available at the operating level, subject to standards of performance and policy directives formulated higher up.

The reasons for delegating staff functions are quite different. The top executive's need for staff assistance does not grow out of the multiplicity of minor decisions but out of the complexity of major decisions. The time required to consider all the factors which might affect a major decision is often so great that the top executive could not possibly fit it into his schedule. In any case, he must spare himself the effort of gathering and analyzing the detailed evidence which must be used in evaluating these factors or in weighing the alternatives for action which he has before him. In this respect the staff man is an extension of the analytical powers of the top executive and is employed because there are not enough hours in the executive day. To a growing extent, however, the need for specialized staff goes further than that. It is increasingly recognized that the proper weighing of evidence requires scientific techniques for the handling of data which the top executive does not usually command. He is obliged to recognize limitations in the directions of marketing and economic research similar to those he must acknowledge with respect to the specialized skills he employs in engineering and chemical research.

Centralization versus Decentralization.   The point has already been made that the logic of line organization seems to move toward administrative decentralization. The fundamental requirements of staff activity probably tend in the opposite direction. The activities of analysis and planning in a company are likely to be more effective if they are well integrated. The determination of market potentials, for example, can be carried out more effectively if it is undertaken for the whole company by a single staff unit than if the potential for various regions is determined separately in each district office. Each market analyst employed by a district sales manager would have to be concerned about such factors as gross national product and would have to repeat much of the work in getting estimates for a single region that would be involved in making estimates for all regions.

Various staff activities impinge upon each other. Each staff unit deals with information, and the results reached by one unit may need to be tempered by information in possession of another. Thus, in his work on markets for new products, the market analyst would obviously benefit from contact with the product development department. He can scarcely work effectively on a problem of marketing efficiency without the co-operation of the accounting department. Similarly, his work may be vital to the solution of problems which are not strictly in the marketing field. Short-range market forecasts are of interest for production scheduling. Long-range market forecasts may be essential to investment planning in the treasurer's office.

The logic of centralization as it applies to staff activities works out differently at different stages of corporate history. If staff units at different levels are actually performing the same function, the one in the more centralized position is likely to win out. Other things being equal, such as the skill of the market analysts, the one in the central position should be able to get better answers because it has access to more information. It is also likely to find more opportunities for the application of its results.

The decentralization of line and the centralization of staff are bound to create problems of communication and mutual understanding. The line man may become convinced that he is doing the work which pays the bills, while the staff groups are luxuriating at the home office. The staff man, on the other hand, may become cynical about the ragged performance in the field, through which the effectiveness of the best calculated plans may be largely lost. The staff executive would be well advised to accept this problem of communication as his own, since his activities are generally newer and less understood within the company than the line function. More fundamentally, it might be said that the staff executive functions largely through communication. The results of his analysis and planning can only take effect to the extent that they are fully communicated and sympathetically received by the line executives who are expected to be guided by them. Frequent field trips and mailings should be standard practice. When something of major importance is to be communicated, the presentation deserves as careful consideration as the results themselves.

The level at which the staff unit should operate may be determined in part by its stated objectives. The same kind of activity may be carried on at more than one level if it is clearly understood that different objectives are sought. Market research can function very effectively within the sales department if the sales manager genuinely regards it as an essential tool for discharging his line responsibilities. Any staff units reporting to him should, of course, devote their energies to the types of analysis and planning which are directly related to his line responsibilities. A marketing research unit within a sales department sometimes finds that it is performing more and more work for executives outside the sales department. Such a situation clearly raises the issue of whether marketing research is properly placed. A very large company with a number of product divisions may find it necessary to have a marketing research unit in each division. The head of a product division may feel that the service he needs is too urgent or too highly specialized to depend on a central unit. In some cases the competitive rivalry among divisions is so great that the heads of the divisions insist on having self-contained staff units.

Placements of Staff Units.   There are two principal arguments for placing such staff units as marketing research directly under top management. This is indicated when the staff unit is used by management as a means of checking up on the operating divisions. If the measurement of sales efficiency is regarded as the major objective of marketing research, there is some question as to whether it can operate without bias within the sales department. The same consideration holds with respect to research as a measure of advertising effectiveness. Similarly, quality control may be regarded either as a check on production efficiency or as a tool of production management. Sometimes, this activity is carried on by two groups. A quality control group in the production department determines from day to day whether the output is being kept within prescribed quality limits. If the product is out of control, plant management is able to take immediate remedial action. Another quality control group reporting to top management may be pursuing longer-range objectives. Its job is to detect any trends reflecting fundamental difficulties in the maintenance of quality standards. It may from time to time re-examine the established standards and prescribe changes.

The other reason for placing staff activities at the top is to secure the necessary integration among staff activities. Top management may have to take into account findings of various types of specialists in reaching a decision. Top management undertakes to preserve a constructive balance between production and sales or between current stability and continued expansion. It is seldom possible to reduce a major decision purely to an issue of production, marketing, or investment policy. The more divergent the technical skills involved in staff work, the more essential it may be for top management to rely on a staff executive whose administrative responsibilities cover a range of staff units. Integration may simply bring together all of the various aspects of marketing, or it may extend to staff activities related to other departments. The top staff man is sometimes right at the top of the management pyramid. In some companies the chairman of the board is the co-ordinator of staff activities, while the president is the chief line executive.

These trends in corporate organizations have an important bearing on the careers open to specialists in marketing. Opportunity for this type of employment is steadily expanding as business moves toward line and staff organization. The path of advancement for the market analyst has been less clear in the past. Promotion to top management usually came about through advancement in successive stages of the line organization. Individuals performing staff assignments were likely to find that their position remained static over long periods of time. This situation is changing through increasing recognition of staff functions at the highest level of management.

MANAGEMENT FUNCTIONS OF THE ADVERTISING BUDGET

The work of budget preparation falls largely upon advertising specialists in advertising departments and advertising agencies. From the viewpoint of these specialists, it is not unnatural for the budget to be regarded primarily as a means for securing the annual authorization for advertising expenditures. It is their vehicle for selling management on spending as much or more than the amount spent in the previous year. This is no reflection on the sincerity of their conviction that they are serving the best interests of the company. If they did not believe in advertising, they would not be fully qualified for their jobs.

Management, indeed, wants to be persuaded that its advertising program is effective and that it is making adequate use of this instrument of survival and growth in competitive markets. It is clearly the prerogative of management to set the framework within which these discussions will take place. Persuasion within an orderly framework is essentially negotiation. Recognition that the budget-making procedure is basically a process of negotiation should put it in a better perspective than any of the attempts to reduce it to a mechanical formula.

Management is not a passive customer waiting to be sold. There are management functions to be served through budgeting if the initiative comes from the top. A full awareness of these functions should favor a more constructive outcome of the annual negotiation concerning advertising expenditures. This section will discuss several aspects of this functional or negotiational approach to budgeting.

Discussion of an annual budget provides a channel of communication concerning goals and the means of attaining them. It may be used by top management to communicate an understanding of company objectives and of what selling and advertising are expected to contribute. There is a great deal of lip service today for the so-called "objective and task" method of determining advertising expenditures. This doctrine often means little in practice, since the task cannot be defined in the absence of a clear statement of objectives. Management in some companies may prefer to have the advertising department present a budget based on its best guess as to what the objectives are. The program as presented can then be criticized in terms of the undisclosed objectives. Considering the amount of effort which goes into the preparation of a detailed budget, it is recommended that short-range objectives at least should be defined by management in advance of the budgeting procedure.

Company Goals and Advertising. The starting place for management in considering advertising is long-range objectives, whether these are fully disclosed or interpreted for the benefit of subordinates. These underlying objectives might be grouped under the headings of growth, profits, investment, and personnel development. More than advertising is involved in these objectives, but the preparation of the advertising budget provides the occasion for reviewing them in relation to the entire marketing program.

Sales growth is a basic goal for most companies which advertise. The desired rate of growth is dependent in part on management's estimate of competitive developments. Not only the rate of growth, but the direction of growth, may be a part of company goals. Management wishes to broaden its product line for the sake of stability, to make better use of projected additions to plant capacity, or to add items which will strengthen its position with its marketing channels. One of the uses of advertising is to accelerate favorable trends in demand. Bringing about changes in demand or adjusting to them as they occur are perhaps the most basic of all long-range company goals.

The goal of greater profits can be served either by increasing sales or by decreasing costs. Advertising is often more economical than other means of selling, as well as more effective. The total amount of distribution costs, including wholesale and retail margins, may be reduced through a shift to advertising. Profits are both the result of continuing growth and the necessary condition for further expansion. Management, upon occasion, does an admirable job of explaining its need for net revenue and the uses to which it will be put. An advertising program acquires greater point and urgency when it is visualized as a means of seeking these goals of growth and profits.

Next to producing adequate sales revenue, management is most concerned with finding investment dollars. Growth must be financed through retained earnings or new issues. Either way, advertising makes it easier to obtain the needed funds. Present stockholders are willing to see profits go into retained earnings rather than dividends if they foresee an appreciation of the company's equity values. New investors will buy the company's securities on a favorable basis if they appear to represent an attractive combination of risk and return over a period of years. There is some statistical evidence that advertising affects the market for securities as definitely as the market for products.

The future of a company depends in large measure on the quality of its personnel. The successful company must equal or excel its competitors in attracting good men and in holding them. Advertising which carries conviction as to the present and future strength of a company can facilitate recruitment. It can also help to maintain morale of existing staff and inspire loyal and competent performance. Dealers and distributors are often considered a part of the organization for this purpose. Advertising cannot be aimed primarily at the company's own personnel, but the influence on morale is a very important side effect to be considered in making a budget.

A variety of objectives should shape the advertising task. They must be weighed by management and assigned relative priorities. Otherwise, the advertising department is likely to define its own tasks in terms of short-run sales goals only. It can make its program sound very concrete and practical but may not be on the target in terms of a broader perspective. Disclosure of what management is really after does not provide an automatic solution for advertising problems, but it at least makes it possible to state them.

THE EXECUTIVE PARAGON

The ideal executive will promote a degree of routinization appropriate to each level in his organization and yet keep his own outlook flexible and attuned to change. He will apportion incentives to his subordinates in a way that will encourage both superior performance in their present tasks and active preparation for larger responsibilities. Yet he will act as if the overriding incentive for himself is the utmost success for his company. He will exercise caution in forthright or implied commitments to individuals and exact rigorous compliance with goals which have been accepted as feasible. He will project a humane and tolerant understanding of the firm as a social organization and yet never lose sight of its primary operating functions. The chief executive will constantly be matching his organization against the tasks and the trials of tomorrow. But he must interpret his vision of the future in a way that will stimulate maximum effort today. By keeping the lines of authority taut, he will maintain the healthy tensions of a vital and mobilized behavior system rather then permitting organized power to be frittered away through internal conflict.

Granted that this is a large order, its reward is the type of self-realization to be gained only from top executive responsibility. This role is not available to everyone in an organized society, and not all are qualified to discharge it. In a free society, there is reason to hope that those who accept the challenge are at least among the best qualified to meet it. They will be intuitive in recognizing opportunity but articulate in translating their insights into action. They will be bold in facing risks but curious about the facts and respectful of analytical judgments. The chapters which follow will discuss some of the management aids which are available to this paragon of executives. Let him who is conscious of his limitations be humble enough to welcome help and proud enough to aspire to the best.

SELECTED REFERENCES

BARNARD, CHESTER I. *The Functions of the Executive.* Cambridge, Mass.: Harvard University Press, 1945.

DRUCKER, PETER F. *Concept of the Corporation.* New York: John Day Co., 1946.

WHITEHEAD, T. NORTH. *Leadership in a Free Society.* Cambridge, Mass.: Harvard University Press, 1944.

TOSDAL, HARRY R. *Principles of Sales Management.* New York: McGraw-Hill Book Co., Inc., 1939.

DEAN, JOEL. *Managerial Economics.* New York: Prentice-Hall, Inc., 1951.

Perhaps the most exalted and at the same time most scholarly view of the executive function was that expounded by Chester Barnard. He was himself the successful head of a large corporation, and yet the president of the American Sociological Society once described him as one of the leading social theorists of his day.

Drucker and Whitehead have also written about business leadership in a way that recognized the social character of operating systems. Drucker has studied the corporation at close range as a management consultant. Whitehead's views reflect those of his preceptors at the Harvard Business School in combination with the organismic philosophy of his famous father.

Tosdal, also of the Business School, is a recognized authority on the executive function in marketing organizations.

Joel Dean's book, as its name implies, arrays the tools of economic analysis in relation to management problems.

Chapter XIII

THE SOLUTION OF MARKETING PROBLEMS

Problem solving is analyzed from three separate viewpoints designated as the procedural, the operational, and the functional. The responsible executive is most concerned with the function of producing answers. The master analyst to whom the problem is assigned shares the functional viewpoint, but his professional contribution is to think operationally about the problem-solving process. He endeavors to give the process an integrated form and structure within which his subordinates can apply detailed techniques and procedures.

As an operation, problem solving can be characterized as the application of insight, as systematic calculation, and as selective exploration. Ideally, these aspects are combined in an integrated operation but with the fundamental emphasis on insight. Puzzles are used for illustration, as a type of problem which can be precisely specified. The consideration of puzzles leads to some principles of problem solving with wide application.

The application of mathematical models to marketing problems is considered in a section on operations research. The problems treated in this section are arranged in four groups, according to an ascending level of uncertainty faced by management. While these new techniques are regarded as highly significant, the general treatment is founded on Singer's dictum that problems should determine methods and not methods problems.

SOME PRELIMINARY DEFINITIONS

The term "problem" and related terms will be defined in a variety of ways in the course of this discussion. In fact, the transformations from one definition of a term to another definition conceived from a new perspective will be one of the principal analytical devices employed. Since the end result sought is the most fruitful perspective on problem solving, one purpose of the discussion is to test alternative perspectives. The first set of definitions will be presented from the viewpoint of a person who will be called "the executive." An executive, for our present purpose, is not necessarily an officer of a company, although that would be an important example of the problem solvers this discussion is intended to serve. The executive is the one who has the problem or who is responsible for taking action in a problem situation.

A problem situation is one in which the executive hesitates to act because of uncertainty as to the relation of means and ends. Uncertainty may pertain to the best deployment of diverse means against plural ends, it may arise from a conflict of ends, or it may consist of doubt concerning the attainment of preferred ends with the means at hand.

A problem is the analytical task of finding the means for reducing uncertainty in the problem situation. Uncertainty may be reduced by providing information or a plan of action. In practice, success in precipitating action may be aided by persuasive presentation that will induce the executive to believe the information or accept the plan. It should be stressed, however, that the problem as such is the task calling for analysis, even though the analysis may result in the conclusion that what is needed is a persuasive presentation. After all, there is some parallel in the executive's need for conviction to the mathematician's need for proof or demonstration. Carnap's approach to the theory of probability, in which the probability ratio reflects the degree of confirmation of a theorem or a conclusion, might also be cited.

Puzzles are a subclass of problems which will be used from time to time in this chapter for purposes of illustration. Puzzle solving presents a parallel to the situation in practical problem solving as to the relationship between the solver and the person from whom he received the assignment. Puzzles have purely a social or recreational function, in which the analyst accepts the challenge of the assignment whether for the pleasure of exercising his analytical abilities or in order to demonstrate these abilities to the person who set the task. Puzzles can hardly be dismissed as a trivial aspect of human culture, since interest in puzzles goes back to ancient times and numerous important mathematical discoveries have grown out of a study of one type of puzzle or another. In this exploratory investigation, it has been useful to consider puzzles and problem solving from three separate points of view, which will be discussed in the following section.

These different approaches to the discussion of problem solving may be designated as the procedural, the operational, and the functional. By the procedural approach is meant that which attempts to formulate rules of procedure, to outline a series of steps, or to list some helpful hints as to where to begin when tackling any problem. The operational approach starts off with a re-examination of problem solving as a process and attempts to characterize it as an operation or a phase of human behavior. The functional approach begins with a consideration of the ends to be served in problem solving. That is to say that it is concerned first of all with the nature of a solution and the kind of a solution that may be required in various problem situations. There is actually no conflict among these three approaches, but all fit within a general theory of problem solving. Logically, the steps in this investigation might be to deal first with the functional approach and a general study of the nature of solutions, to move on to characterize the operation by which solutions are generally obtained, and finally to translate the operation into detailed procedures in order to arrive at concrete and definite rules to aid the practical problem solver. The course that will be followed in the current presentation is just the reverse, since it is felt that this exposition can proceed with greater clarity by moving from the procedural to the operational and finally to the functional perspectives.

THE PROCEDURAL APPROACH

Many good minds have set themselves the goal of coming up with a general procedure which would be applicable to a wide variety of problems. The names in this illustration record stretch all the way from Pappus, a Greek mathematician writing in about A.D. 300, to a modern mathematician named Polya, who published a book in 1945 called *How to Solve It.* One of the greatest names in this running discussion of procedure is associated with one of the simplest and most illuminating of the sets of rules for problem solving. René Descartes, in his *Discourse on Method,* lists the four principles which he had found basic in his mathematical investigations. These principles can be stated in a somewhat abridged form as follows: (1) Take a fresh look at the problem, banishing all preconceptions. (2) Divide the problem into its constituent parts. (3) Begin by examining the simplest parts or elements first. (4) Be sure not to leave anything out, either as to the elements enumerated or as to the steps in the solution.

The application of these principles can all be illustrated by reference to some well-known puzzles. The study of puzzles also suggests other rules for solution which were not made explicit by Descartes, but which have been treated by other authorities on the subject. First, there is the principle that the solver should banish all preconceptions or prejudices from his mind in order to see clearly what is involved in the particular problem. There are a number of puzzles in which the whole difficulty lies in the failure of the solver to clear his mind, letting certain unconscious preconceptions stand as the principal obstacles to solution. A case in point is the puzzle of the three missionaries and the three cannibals traveling together. The missionaries assume that they are safe as long as they do not leave one or two of their group outnumbered by two or three cannibals. They come to a river which they must cross, using a boat which will carry only two people. Someone must bring the boat back each time until all have crossed.

Any adult could solve this puzzle in a few seconds, if it were not for his assumption that the natural thing is to have only one person bring the boat back. There is one point in the solution at which two persons must bring the boat back to avoid a situation in which the missionaries are outnumbered on one side of the river or the other. A solution follows immediately, as soon as the solver sees this point—in other words, as soon as he drops the restriction he brought into the situation himself, which was not one of the original conditions as stated.

Another example is found in what will here be called the red-cap problem, for convenience of reference. In this problem, eight black checkers or counters are placed in a square formation, with three counters on each side. The solver is given seven red counters and assigned the task of placing caps on seven out of eight black counters. He is told that he must count four, touching a checker each time, and putting the cap on the fourth one. A checker which already has a cap can be counted as number two or three, but it cannot be counted as one and of course not as four. One common difficulty in getting started with a solution of this problem is that the solver starts out with the conception that the corners are significant. He is likely to begin by counting in such a way as to cap the four corners first. If he does, he will not be able to complete the solution. Actually, the corners do not constitute a significant structure with respect to this problem. The problem would be exactly the same if the black checkers were arranged in a circle or a loop. The red-cap problem will be referred to again, since it illustrates other principles besides the confusion arising from preconceptions residing in the mind of the solver.

Bacon versus Descartes.   Descartes was not the first to emphasize the need for getting rid of preconceptions. In fact, this was the main burden of the *Novum Organum,* written a few years earlier by his great contemporary, Sir Francis Bacon. Bacon was disgusted by the tenacity with which his contemporaries hung on to traditional ideas and theories. He proclaimed the necessity for making a clean start in science and called upon scientific workers to dispose of what he called their idols. He classified these in four groups, which he called "idols of the tribe, the den, the market, and the theatre." What he was symbolizing by these somewhat fanciful titles were errors arising from four sources: certain tendencies of the human mind, the peculiarities of the individual thinker, the conventional notions arising from social intercourse among men, and finally, the purely speculative spinning of theories as a kind of intellectual showmanship. Bacon deserved some attention even in this brief statement, since he is frequently credited with having been the forerunner of the modern scientific viewpoint. Actually, his repugnance to theories current in his day carried him much too far toward reliance on a mere collection of detailed facts. He was not in touch with the scientific achievements of his day, such as those of William Harvey and William Gilbert; and the procedure prescribed by him has not turned out to be the model for scientific method. In Bacon's defense, it might be said that he was before his time in several respects, including the fact that it was several years after his death when Pascal and Fermat began to establish the foundations of probability theory.

Returning to the *Discourse on Method* by Descartes, a puzzle may be used to illustrate his second and third principles of breaking the problem up into its constituent parts and then dealing first with the easiest parts. One pertinent puzzle is the type in which the solver is given a page showing the calculations in a problem of long division, except that all of the digits have been replaced by code letters. The problem is one of decoding, in which the solver must substitute a number for each letter. This problem should be considered as ten subordinate problems, since each digit must be identified and the characteristics which can be used in decoding are different for each digit. The rational solver will then consider which of the digits are easiest to identify and work on those first. It happens that zero is easiest of all, and that the digit one is next in ease of identification. Obviously, the remaining digits are easier to deal with after the first few have been identified. When ten digits are unknown, the possible arrangements in matching digits against code numbers is equal to the very large figure of ten factorial. As soon as one digit has been identified, the remaining possibilities are only one tenth as numerous, or nine factorial.

The fourth principle of not leaving out any of the possibilities can be illustrated by the coin-weighing problem, which has been studied in several variations. In one form the solver is told that he has twelve coins and a balance scale for weighing them. One of the coins is off-weight, and he is to find out in three weighings which one it is and whether it is too light or too heavy. In the correct solution the solver, in making his first weighing, puts four coins to one side and four in each pan of the balance scale. Given the conditions as stated, one of three things will happen. The arm of the scale on the left will go down, indicating that the spurious coin is on that side and is heavy or that it is on the other side and is light. The reverse situation may exist with the arm of the scale on the right going down. Finally, the two arms may balance, indicating that the spurious coin is among the four which were laid off to one side. A satisfactory solution requires the solver to follow out all of these possibilities at the first weighing and then similar possibilities which show up at the second and third weighings.

Detailed Techniques of Solution. One difficulty about the *Discourse on Method* is that it does not give either detailed directions or examples for carrying out the four principles with respect to various types of problems. Concerning the first principle, for example, clearing one's mind of all preconceptions is easier said than done. Considering the puzzles already described as illustrations, the solver would not accomplish this by a pious resolve to be open-minded. It will be remembered that in one case the solver was distracted by an element of structure that turned out not to be significant, and in the other case he imported restrictions into the situation which were not a part of the conditions of the problem. A simple device which is sometimes found helpful is that of making a check list and then examining it critically. In the red-cap problem, this list might include the fact that the arrangement of the eight black checkers had four corners, as well as the fact that together they formed a closed loop. As soon as the significance of these elements of structure became a conscious question, it would probably become apparent that the closed loop was an essential element of structure in relation to the nature of the problem, but that the corners were nonessential. It might be objected that formalized methods of this sort are out of proportion in dealing with a trivial problem such as a puzzle. The answer is, of course, that we are really not concerned with solving puzzles, but with any light that the consideration of this process will throw on more complicated practical problems.

There are several important principles not mentioned by Descartes which can also be illustrated by reference to puzzles. One of these is the principle of starting with the end to be achieved and working backward through a series of intermediate goals until the process finally links up with the initial problem situation as stated. The idea of working backward in problem solving goes back as far as the Greek mathematician already mentioned, but has also been stressed by several modern investigators. This principle can be illustrated by a number of puzzles, including the red-cap problem. If the solver will start out by putting all seven red counters in place, the first step in working backward will be to count from the one open space and take off one of the red caps which could have been reached by counting four from this point. The solver now has a second open space which he can utilize in the same fashion. He will have no difficulty in taking the red caps off one by one, whereas he might encounter great difficulty in the beginning in putting them on. This simple principle of working backward is used over and over in the development of a time schedule against a final deadline, in the apportionment of funds or resources within a fixed budget, and in many other practical marketing problems.

Preliminary Analysis of the Problem.   Another problem-solving principle is that of making a thorough analysis of the problem or the problem situation before attempting a solution. This principle is especially associated with the name of John Dewey, although other philosophers have attempted to develop it further, including F. C. S. Northrup. Dewey says that problem analysis is essential in order to set up hypotheses which can be tested by research. Northrup points out that there are many ways of setting up hypotheses, so that the researcher must have some means of avoiding those that are trivial and of reducing the number of significant hypotheses to manageable proportions. He stresses the importance of identifying the underlying factors or variables which must be handled in order to solve the problem. In marketing research the device of the pilot survey is often used for the purpose of identifying the significant variables as a basis for planning the full-scale study. In puzzle solving, this principle can be illustrated by a variety of puzzles which are similar in structure to the Koenigsberg bridge problem.

At the university city of Koenigsberg, there was an island in the middle of the river; there were seven bridges connecting the island and the mainland in a particular pattern. It was a tradition of the place that students out for a walk would try to direct their course so as to cross each bridge once, but only once, returning to the original starting place. Euler generalized this problem for all possible arrangements of the island, the mainland, and the bridges. He developed a formula by which it could be determined when a solution was possible and when it was not. The writer has accomplished the same thing for the red-cap problem, which has been mentioned several times before. Having solved the original problem as stated, he undertook to vary the two underlying factors—namely, the number of black checkers or stations in the arrangement and the number that must be counted before a red cap is placed. To state the resulting formula, let S represent the number of stations and C the number of the count. Then, among the infinite number of possible puzzles of this type, there will always be a solution when C minus 1 is prime to S. Thus, one problem-solving method is the investigation of general classes of problems or solutions.

THE OPERATIONAL APPROACH

The second approach is to begin by characterizing problem solving as an operation. The intent is to understand the process as a whole rather than attempting to identify rules of procedure. Hence, we must begin with the structure of the situation in which the problem arises and the relations between the executive with the problem and the analyst to whom he may delegate the responsibility for seeking a solution.

In terms of modern psychology a problem emerges into consciousness when the individual's adjustment to his environment is at stake. In business terms the executive is most likely to have a problem when his firm is entering an unfamiliar field or when its customary pattern of operation appears to be breaking down. In either case a problem is an issue requiring choice, in which the executive is uncertain about the outcome of his decision. He may decide many issues referred to him by his subordinates which scarcely impress him as being problems at all, because he is so confident he knows the right answer. At the other extreme are issues which occasion the gravest doubt and concern because his personal destiny or that of his company may be at stake.

Marketing problems are problems of action. Questions about the strength of a market have little meaning aside from a marketing operation which exists or could be created to cultivate the market. The marketing executive who makes a formal analytical assignment wants to know how to extend the scope of his operation or how to make it work better. He is usually seeking to increase its returns, to decrease its costs, or to devise a program which will give him a more favorable ratio between cost and return. All of these factors in the problem situation are imbued with risk. Returns may fall short of expectations, costs may exceed budget estimates, or a plan which seemed structurally sound may develop a fatal flaw.

An adequate statement of a marketing problem begins with the objectives to be achieved and the resources available for the purpose. There are times when it may appear inexpedient to reveal the company's precise objectives to the analyst. It must be realized in these cases that the analyst will inevitably be influenced by his best guess as to what the company is after. In no other way can he perform his function of determining what questions of fact must be answered in order to solve the problem of action. Starting from one or more possible plans of action, he must find out whether the conditions exist which will permit the plan to succeed. Every plan rests on explicit or implicit assumptions about the facts. It is the responsibility of the analyst to identify these assumptions, to test them through research, and, if necessary, to come up with a revised plan which fits the facts better. In any event, the end result of marketing research and counsel is the creation or evaluation of plans of action.

There may be many routes to a solution, depending on the temperament and training of the analyst and the viewpoint of the executive he is serving. Whatever methods are to be employed, the first concern on both sides should be for good communication. There is no substitute for an understanding with some formal structure. It should include a statement in writing of what the assignment is and how it is to be satisfied. But behind the formal agreement, there should be some genuine appreciation on either side for the way the other side functions. The analyst needs to be able to interpret his findings into the concrete situation faced by management. The executive should cultivate a tolerant understanding of the power of precise analytical techniques in searching for a solution.

The analyst must always work backward from the way he visualizes the use of his findings and recommendations. His report must be clear and convincing to the mind of the user. Once the executive who authorized the study has made up his own mind, he will usually need to motivate numerous associates or subordinates. A comprehensive answer to a marketing problem includes both a plan of action and persuasive reasons for its adoption. If several alternative courses of action were pictured in the beginning, a detailed comparative evaluation may be needed when the facts are all in to prove that the course selected is the right course.

The analyst who loses sight of the end result sometimes paints himself into a corner, using all of his facts merely to underscore the seriousness of the problem and leaving the implication that there is no way out. A more skillful analyst can often use the same data to point the way forward. Working backward from the end result has many advantages in planning a study. A report on a problem may not constitute a solution at all unless it is delivered on time. To meet a final deadline, intermediate deadlines must be established, allowing time before the presentation for analysis and review, before the analysis for collecting and tabulating data, and before data collection for planning and preliminary exploration.

The problem-solving process as a type of intellectual activity has been the preoccupation of scientists and philosophers through the ages. Elaborate theories have been propounded in support of one approach or another. Three factors are variously stressed, but the viewpoint here is that all three are essential to an adequate approach. These three factors are hunch, logic, and experiment. Somewhat more broadly, they may be designated as insight, calculation, and exploration.

Insight into Marketing Situations.   Solving a problem always means seeing a situation in a new way. If looking at the situation in the old way will still work, there is no problem. There are many occasions for action in everyday affairs which never become problems because we find the answer by direct perception. We see the latch on the gate and open it immediately. If it turned out to be a false latch placed there to deceive us, we might then act on a hunch that there was a spring release concealed in one of the hinges. Insight is the perception of possibilities in a situation which may not be apparent at first glance. A hunch often carries the further connotation of a belief that the first possibility which occurs to us is the correct one. Mature insight strives to make the list of possibilities exhaustive before starting the process of selection among them.

Sometimes insight appears to be a function of interest and attention. The analyst gets his first clue while making a careful examination of the situation or listening intently to the statement of the problem. No conscious analytical process may be involved but only a concentrated effort to be perceptive. The great asset at this stage is an open mind. The individual who has been living with the situation constantly may have been conditioned to see it in a way which blocks off the road to an answer.

Insight is sharpened and reinforced by experience. Familiarity with the common features of marketing operations sets the observer free to look for crucial differences. Experience provides a stock of somewhat similar situations in which working solutions are known to have been discovered. In this aspect of his work, the analyst becomes a channel of communication from firms which have successfully dealt with a problem to others which are facing it for the first time. Experience with a wide diversity of marketing situations imparts confidence that a solution can be found for the current one. Sometimes the analyst amply fulfills his role by confirming the validity of a solution that is already suspected. While he should reach his conclusions entirely independently, he should not hesitate to recommend the simple and obvious, if that is where his analysis leads him.

While experience enhances the skill of the problem solver, there is also the factor of native bent in that direction. A chess master has exceptional power to see patterns of relationship among pieces on a board. His special flair is usually evident before his formal training begins. A marketing specialist has a somewhat similar power to think in abstract terms of the essential relationships in a problem situation. It usually takes longer to achieve a semblance of mastery, since his materials are the needs and aspirations of people, the changing techniques of production and distribution, the arts of negotiation and persuasion. The pieces on his chess board do not passively obey his will. Each piece on the board has its own game to play, its own problem to solve. A marketing plan cannot succeed unless it challenges the assent of many participants.

Insight is often conceived to take the form of a flash of inspiration yielding a complete solution all at once. In practice the flash may come only after hours or even months of intense study. Nevertheless, it is felt that the most satisfactory view of problem solving is one that takes insight to be fundamental. Everything else that is done has the function of giving insight a chance to work. That is true of the most elaborate and precise forms of calculation. It is also true of observation and experiment as they are employed in marketing.

Insight, as the obvious etymology of the word suggests, is a kind of seeing. The training of artists demonstrates that people can be taught to see what is pertinent to the painting of a picture and what they may have completely missed before. Similarly, in problem solving, seeing depends in part on knowing what to look for. Trained insight helps the problem solver to look beyond apparent structure in the situation to that which may be more pertinent for a solution. Insight in action may be described as finding a parallel situation or an abstract model where the relations among elements are similar. In puzzle solving the first achievement of insight may be simply to classify the puzzle as to type or to recognize that it is similar in character and probably involves the same principle as one previously solved. This is not always an easy step because of the difference between apparent structure and pertinent structure. Many puzzles which appear superficially quite different are identical in their essential structure. This is true, for example, of several puzzles which involve tracing a prescribed figure without lifting the pen.

A number of figures can be identical topologically, even though they have a very different appearance. Insight may sometimes be scarcely more than recognition of a previous structure in a new situation if the analyst remembers the structure as it appeared in a previous puzzle or problem.

The Logic of Marketing Systems.   There is a wide-open opportunity for the use of analytical models in marketing. The term is relatively new in this field, but there is a rapidly growing interest and application. Broadly defined, models include a great variety of devices for ordering information or setting guideposts for planning. The two principal types which can be used in marketing are statistical models and operating models. A statistical model is a conceptual scheme applied to the interplay of variables in a marketing situation. It may involve the assumption that the sales of a product will vary in accordance with certain characteristics of the population or will change at a specified rate over time. A statistical model can be tested through survey techniques.

An operating model is a picture of the way that separate parts or a sequence of steps will work together in a system of action. In a sense the full solution of every marketing problem consists of a tested operating model. A partial test can be made by reference to the statistical facts, but that only establishes limits within which the model must work. Another test is to consider extreme cases which might arise to put a strain on the model in one direction or another. Above all, the analyst should make an imaginative effort to foresee the unintended consequences which may flow from the installation of a plan.

Considering the great complexity of the variables, it is not likely that problem solving in marketing can ever wholly be reduced to a systematic process of calculation. It is often helpful to formalize the problem, even though the calculations cannot be fully carried out. The effort to find a formal structure can serve as a powerful aid to insight. It may be regarded as a deliberate attempt to see the situation in a new way and one that is likely to suggest pertinent parallels with other situations. In the present state of the art, this may be described as one of the chief functions of formal methods. We are able to *see* through the problem because of an orderly effort to *work* through the problem.

Systematic calculation can be applied to various types of puzzles. Some can be reduced to problems in simple algebra or can otherwise be given mathematical formulation. In others the elements required for a solution can be deduced by strict logic from the given elements. Typical of this group of puzzles is one in which the solver is given the names of nine men making up a baseball team and is asked to say which man plays each position. The information available deals with relationships among the players. The most orderly way to solve this type of puzzle is to make up a nine-by-nine matrix with the names of positions on one stub and the names of the men on the other. Check marks should be placed in each of the eighty-one cells as the analysis proceeds. If Fred is the best friend of the left fielder, a negative check mark can be placed in the cell where "Fred" and "left fielder" cross. As soon as we deduce that Jim is the catcher, we put a positive check mark in the proper cell and a negative check mark in sixteen other cells, eight for "Jim" and eight for "catcher." Puzzles of this type, if carefully constructed, require vigorous thinking; but solution is assured if the solver makes no mistakes in checking the matrix.

Some types of puzzles have been subjected to exhaustive mathematical analysis. The solver familiar with this background would be able to solve any of these puzzles as positively and systematically as he would solve a pair of simultaneous equations. The mathematical treatment of various well-known puzzles is presented in *Mathematical Recreations and Essays,* by W. R. Ball. The author freely points out, however, that some types of puzzles have so far resisted the efforts of the mathematician; and among these are some which presumably can never be formulated in a strictly mathematical way.

The solver who tackled a puzzle without knowing that a general solution was available might still suspect that it could be solved by systematic calculation. He would be displaying insight if he devised a process for himself or if he was able to find a description of the needed process devised by someone else. In marketing problems the analyst is displaying insight when he identifies forms of systematic calculation which are applicable to the case. He may have made the principal contribution to the solution, even though he turns over the actual calculation to subordinates.

Insight is greatly aided by systematic calculation, but insight must determine what system of calculation is applicable or point the way toward devising a new one. Sometimes it is a useful exercise to set up a problem in mathematical form, even though the statistical values are not available for a strict solution. The equation or graph of a function provides a model which gives insight another chance to see the situation in a new way. It is to be assumed that ways will be found to cast more and more problems into mathematical form, including practical marketing problems. Whenever this is possible, problems can be assigned to technicians; and the master analyst can save his time for problems which call for the use of mature insight.

Selective Exploration. The third general view of problem solving as an operation is that which regards it as trial and error. One psychologist, Rignano, goes so far as to characterize thinking as trial and error carried out mentally. In any case, it is quite legitimate to regard all research and experiment as a phase of trial and error; and the solution of marketing problems often makes use of this tool. An experiment is a trial on a small scale as compared to the kind of trial which proceeds by making a decision in the large and having to stand by the consequences. A properly controlled experiment is a rational and organized use of trial and error. Sometimes trial and error in more sophisticated forms will yield a reliable result faster than the available forms of systematic calculation. An example would be the use of Monte Carlo methods in certain types of probability solutions.

The problem solver should admit in all humility that he is still dependent in large measure on simple trial and error. "Try it and see" is one way of finding out what will work when more elegant methods are not available. But while admitting the substance of the "fumble and search" approach, it is worth noting that there are some unfortunate implications in the term "trial and error" that should be overcome, if possible. In skillful hands the process is not so random as the term suggests. It is not merely a matter of feeling about in the hope that something will turn up. Psychologists have attempted to develop more suitable designations, such as the method of approximation and correction. According to this view the problem solver makes a provisional try and then comes closer and closer through successive approximations. This is precisely the theory of such a relatively modern method as linear programming. The term adopted here is "selective exploration." It is felt that the designation should be broad enough to cover observation and survey, as well as experiment.

Research techniques in general might be described as organized procedures for conducting selective exploration. Research attempts to secure valid information on stated questions, but it must also find ways of narrowing down the list of questions which are worth exploring on a given occasion. Market investigations often proceed in two or more stages in order to identify the key points to be investigated. There may be a series of interviews with executives of the client company to determine the operating assumptions which need to be checked. There may be a consumer clinic to make sure of uncovering all of the psychological variables which may possibly affect demand. The clinic may be followed by a pilot survey designed for the effective application of analysis of variance. This technique serves to identify the truly significant variables so that they can be the subject of measurement and analysis in the survey proper which absorbs most of the research funds. A rising proportion of marketing research funds is being spent in actual testing of marketing programs. To begin with, the previous use of a distribution method by another firm may constitute an adequate test if the facts can be obtained and properly evaluated. This type of information can be misleading unless the analyst is on the alert for hidden pitfalls in his own operation or for special circumstances which accounted for the earlier success. Many companies now try out programs in a few cities or a limited region before adopting them nationally. Some of these companies are learning the necessity of good experimental design if the results of these tests are to be taken as conclusive.

Aside from formal testing, all marketing research is tending to take on an experimental character. Readership interviews, consumer sampling of new products, and reactions to packages, trade-marks, and slogans are taking on the character of psychological experiments. That is to say that the researcher is not so much interested in the information conveyed by the answer as in the reactions of the respondent to the question and the way his reactions can be modified under experimental conditions. Questionnaires of this type may seem almost trivial to the uninitiated unless they realize that the results will be interpreted within an experimental framework.

In selective exploration, as in systematic calculation, there is to be found an important aid to insight. The new view of the situation which will lead on to a solution may burst upon the analyst in the midst of his explorations. Even if exploration could be completely exhaustive, it would take insight to recognize the solution when it turned up. Insight operates throughout the process, guiding exploration and accounting for its selective character. The subject of selective exploration has been discussed in terms of external studies of consumer markets. The same principles would hold for studies of industrial markets or internal studies of sales productivity and organization structure.

The Structure of the Problem Situation. The remainder of the discussion of problem solving as an operation will make use of a series of definitions drawn from a study of puzzles. The purpose of these definitions is to serve as operating models which may illuminate first one aspect and then another of the problem-solving process. The goal is either to arrive at a general description of the problem-solving operation or to discover distinct types which must be dealt with separately. The very broad but operationally empty definition of a puzzle might be stated as follows: A puzzle is an analytical task in which x is given and y is required. In the operational definitions to be used hereafter, the form will be abbreviated to a statement of what is given and what is required.

The first definition derived from a study of puzzles is as follows: Given two sets of elements, match one against the other under stated restrictions on the matching process. This statement is a reasonably good characterization of the process of solution for many types of puzzles. It holds for most of the puzzles which have been referred to as illustrations so far. It holds without too much straining for crossword puzzles, for the decoding of ciphers, for many puzzles performed with counters or requiring placements on a checkerboard, and for jigsaw puzzles if it is assumed that the essence of solution is matching the separate pieces against parts of the completed picture. It could probably be extended to nearly all puzzles by admitting abstract sets such as classes, rank positions, and relationships as one of the sets against which the other set is to be matched. This model has some attractions for the market analyst because so much of his work in solving marketing problems takes the form of matching two sets against each other, such as segments of opportunity and types of effort.

From a purely logical viewpoint, it may be better to use a model with only one set of elements and to prescribe a more general type of process than matching: Given a set of elements, place them in a required arrangement or relationship with stated restrictions on the ordering process. It is easier to conceive of a puzzle type such as anagrams in these terms. The letters forming a word are given; and the solver is asked to rearrange them into another word, usually with the restriction that the new word should have a stated meaning. In another type, called "word transformation," the solver changes one letter at a time to reach a required result, proceeding under the restrictions that the combination of letters at each stage shall constitute an English word and usually that the process should be accomplished in a certain number of steps.

Neither of these formulations takes explicit account of the type of puzzle or problem in which the solver must obtain additional information about a problem situation which is only partially specified. Definitions framed in these terms might lend themselves to the distinction between problems of knowledge and problems of action. Here is a pair of such definitions: (1) Given a state of affairs which is only partially specified, to specify it more completely. (2) Given an initial state of affairs, to specify the process of transformation leading to a desired state of affairs. The term "state of affairs" is broader than "set of elements" because it may embrace specified relationships among the elements. In many mathematical puzzles the solver is given certain elements and relationships which he is expected to use in such a way as to identify other elements or relationships. Other puzzles are more analogous to a problem of action in which the analyst is required to specify changes in the initial situation. In marketing, the initial problem situation is often a marketing operation that is not working satisfactorily; and the analyst is assigned the task of recommending a plan which will lead to improvement.

The one thing that all of these models have in common is the idea of order or structure as applied to a problem situation. A problem situation might now be redefined in these terms. A problem situation is one in which the executive doubts that he has an adequate knowledge of the structure of the situation, particularly as it affects possibilities for action. An attempt will now be made to characterize a solution in corresponding terms: Given an initial situation and a stated goal which may involve a transformation in the situation or be limited to the need for further knowledge, apply an organizing principle which will result in restructuring the situation and reaching the goal. The term "restructure" has to be broad enough here to include changes in the subject's knowledge of the structure.

Both the term "goal" and the term "organizing principle" are introduced here for the first time in this discussion. The term "goal" is broad enough to cover the required results of various types—as, for example, more adequate knowledge on the one hand or a change in the situation on the other. The term "organizing principle" is meant to embrace the central idea in any method of matching, ordering, or specifying. Most puzzles of real intellectual merit respond to an organizing principle. It is the means by which the solver succeeds in seeing the situation in a new way. The organizing principle is the starting point for restructuring the situation and is usually the key to the successful presentation whereby the executive is persuaded to accept the solution. The organizing principle may be something as simple as the principle of closure discussed by Gestalt psychologists. This is the inherent tendency to complete a figure or Gestalt that is presented in incomplete form. The attempt to accomplish closure is a powerful organizing principle in many practical problems. In planning communication systems in marketing, for example, the analyst is concerned to see that he is setting up closed loops. This illustration suggests that closure should mean "closed in terms of function." More broadly, an organizing principle should relate to the structure of the situation in terms of function. This point will be developed further in the next section.

THE FUNCTIONAL APPROACH

In discussing the functional approach, greater prominence will naturally be given to goals and to the resources available for use in attaining these goals. There are obstacles or limitations as well as resources to consider, and these correspond more or less to the restrictions which have to be observed by the puzzle solver. A model which will be useful at this stage of the discussion is one formulated in terms of an action field rather than a problem situation. Instead of applying only to crisis situations, such a model might give effect to the idea that action is always problematic in some sense, whether or not the executive is prepared to define an analytical task for a problem solver.

The functional approach must give careful attention to the nature of a solution as well as dealing with the character of the problem-solving process. In solving an individual problem, many authorities urge the analyst to begin with the solution and work backward. Perhaps the same principle is just as important in the more general treatment of problem solving—namely, working backward from what is regarded as a solution. One more definition of a problem will be presented because it seems especially useful in discussing certain aspects of solutions: Given an action field, examine its pertinent structure, including resources and limitations, to discover a path which will lead to a specified goal. What is meant by "pertinent structure" is that which is relevant to the process or operation under consideration. The word "path" can pertain to any marshalling of means to achieve a specified end. The figure of speech of a path through an action field is deliberately chosen as an effective model for bringing out certain general aspects of a solution. There are at least three criteria of a good solution which will be illustrated by reference to the analogous concept of a path.

The first test of a good solution or path is feasibility. When the analyst is assigned a problem, he may be confronted by several situations as to feasibility in either puzzles or practical affairs. Among the cases is that in which no path exists. One path, and one only, may exist. Perhaps there exists a finite number of paths, but still more than one. Finally, there may be an infinite number of paths. If no path exists in the case of a puzzle, a good solution is one that states that the trick cannot be done and tells why. In practical affairs, there is often a direct parallel, in which the analyst is forced to say, in the words of the old chestnut: "You cannot get there from here." Usually, that solution is not very acceptable, so that the analyst has to provide very specific evidence as to the lack of opportunity or the limitations of the resources and facilities the executive can command for pursuing the stated objective.

The more typical situation is one in which it can be assumed that at least one path exists. It is rare in marketing that there is only one possible way. If the problem is that of a going operation, its present program is one such way. The investigation would not be undertaken unless there was some reason to feel that there were one or more alternatives and that at least one of these might turn out to be better than the present program. If here is an infinite number of paths available, a solution may consist in showing that there is no problem after all. More likely, it will consist in developing some sort of decision function which will make it possible to select the optimum path or one which meets certain minimum standards. The preferred path may be the shortest path, the path which reaches its destination while avoiding certain hazardous areas along the way, or the path which leaves open until the last possible moment the choice between acceptable destinations.

The situation which is most nearly parallel in practical marketing problems is that in which a finite number of paths are open for reaching the goal. The task of the analyst is to be sure that he has listed all of the realistic possibilities and then to apply various criteria in selecting the one that is best or that may be regarded as among the better possibilities by certain standards. A simple example in puzzle solving would be a word transformation that was supposed to be accomplished in four steps. The analyst might first find a way of accomplishing the transformation, even though it took six or seven steps. He might then try to eliminate steps until he was able to get within the restriction. Market planning often starts with tentative programs, followed by an attempt at successive improvements.

A solution may not be an adequate basis for decision, even though it is intellectually acceptable to the executive. He may have to convince his associates or his board of directors in order to get them to make the commitments as to resources or co-operation which he feels will be needed for success. Thus, he may be disappointed in the proposed solution or its presentation because he does not think it can be sold to others, even though it is convincing to him. Other developments may have occurred since the assignment was made. Favorable events may have removed the pressure for an immediate decision, or unfavorable events may have made it necessary for the executive to turn his attention to even more crucial matters.

Some of these matters may seem to reach beyond the scope of

problem solving or the responsibilities of the analyst as analyst. Nevertheless, every professional analyst participates in some degree in defining his own responsibilities, and may seek either to restrict or to expand them in comparison with the conception in the mind of his client. In relation to the use and application of the results, he is at least entitled to take the position that he and his client are mutually responsible for formulating the assignment in a way that favors successful application of the results. One such step is to set up in advance criteria for interpretation of results, just as a puzzle solver might insist that there be a written answer on file before he starts. If there is a difference of opinion within an executive group, it is very helpful if each side will agree in advance as to the findings that will be accepted as decisive in one direction or another.

The Strategy of Problem Solving.   The preceding discussion of the functional approach and of the nature of solutions is not regarded as exhaustive or conclusive. For one thing, both the executive and the analyst function at various levels in relation to problems. This fact brings in elements of intellectual and operational strategy with respect to the problem-solving process, with a hierarchy of problems to be considered. One problem may be the choice of which problem to solve. A puzzle solver might be assigned two problems and told that he would win a prize of $10 if he solved problem A and of $50 if he solved problem B. He may be conceived as playing a sort of a game, in which he weighs the relative difficulty of the problems against the relative size of the rewards and then decides to take his chances on one route rather than the other. The businessman often is confronted with similar choices. If he chooses between two products to make and sell, he knows that there are distinct risks attached to each. He also knows that there will be a chain of problems to be solved after he has made his choice, so that his solution of the general problem might be interpreted as a decision to cope with one group of specific problems rather than others. This relationship of choice points is sometimes charted in the form of a tree. The choice made at the main fork determines which minor fork may present the next occasion for a decision and what limb the analyst will eventually have to climb out on.

The passage of time and continuing developments are often crucial. The retailer looking for a location, for example, may have to decide by a certain date or else eliminate some of the possibilities under consideration. In other situations, time works with the executive; and he has to judge the speed of favorable development which will open up a wider range of choice for him. Deciding to take the initiative or to wait out an opponent is a question of policy which can be made to depend on analysis rather than temperament.

The choice of methods of problem solving is often influenced by time considerations. An elegant method may be more intellectually satisfying and more certain to provide a complete solution. Less formal methods may get a practical and usable result much faster in some cases. In puzzle solving, the analyst can sometimes guess the answer after a little exploration and prove it by working backward. It might require a much longer time by precise mathematical formulation of the problem. In some practical situations a certain type of problem recurs over and over. In these cases a thorough investigation might be productive, leading to a method of systematic calculation for solving such problems in the future. If a problem occurs only rarely, it may be better economy of problem-solving talent to deal with it if and when it arises. In any case a major strategic consideration is to make the best application of the mature judgment and problem-solving ability of the executive or the senior analyst in relation to a succession of problems or a hierarchy of problems. Thus an executive may be making a sound decision when he decides to ignore a chronic problem for the time being. A factor in grand strategy is the decision as to which general view of problem solving to adopt. To hazard a recommendation at this stage, the common ground of the executive and the master analyst should be the functional approach. The master analyst, in turn, must be able to think in terms of an integrated operation. He must be able to communicate with his subordinates in both operational and procedural terms, even though he leaves the details of procedure to them and may be less skilled than they in some of these detailed techniques.

At the operational level a strategic choice may have to be made as to whether to emphasize insight, calculation, or exploration. Insight is most essential in dealing with the broadest problems. Systematic calculation may be developed, as previously indicated, to deal with recurrent problems in a narrower range. Exploration is especially important where the problem has not been fully formulated or where it is suspected that the real problem lies at a deeper level than that currently under consideration. Scarcely any major investigation of an urgent and well-defined problem can proceed without some elements of all three.

The scientist undertakes to investigate whole classes of problems, just as some mathematicians have exhaustively investigated classes of puzzles. Important elements of strategy arise in this connection as to choice of problems and methods of securing co-operation among specialists who can contribute to a solution. Practitioners of market research and operations research have some appreciation of how a group with diversified scientific backgrounds can contribute to the solution of a practical problem. As this interchange progresses, the practitioner should stimulate interest in investigating more general problems. The solutions he has devised in particular cases may be suitable in some cases as starting points for more general solutions. There is a strategy of interchange among the sciences and the practical arts.

OPERATIONS RESEARCH AND MANAGEMENT PROBLEMS

A new tool of problem solving, known as operations research, is exciting interest in many marketing managements. Some executives have been sufficiently convinced of the value of this new approach to set up operations research units within their firms. Others remain skeptical as to whether operations research really represents anything new or are genuinely perplexed as to its practical applications for them. The illustrations of the successful use of operations research which have come to their attention seem far removed from business operations. Many of the practitioners of these new techniques have had little contact with management problems. An attempt will be made here to place operations research in a perspective compatible with a management view of operating problems. The examples of potential application will largely pertain to the marketing function. The same plan of evaluation could be extended to problems of production and finance.

It has already been said that an executive with a problem is an individual responsible for decision and beset with uncertainty as to the course of action to follow. To solve a problem is to reduce uncertainty to a point that will permit a choice to be made. There are at least four levels of uncertainty which can readily be distinguished in characterizing management problems. Many of the new techniques associated with operations research can be sorted out in relation to these four types of uncertainty in management. What follows is not presented as an exhaustive review of operatioms research techniques. Rather, it is intended to show how some of its most characteristic methods can be utilized in the problem-solving or decision-making process. The elements of uncertainty in the four broad types of management problems pertain respectively to allocation of effort, control and co-ordination, information and contact, competitive strategy and value theory. Each of these areas and the applications of operations research will be discussed in turn.

Programming Marketing Activities. Allocating marketing effort is the same thing as selecting a marketing program. Like any other economic activity, marketing can be described in terms of inputs and outputs. The desired outputs are the sales of the company's products projected over the next operating period and are often set forth in a sales budget or schedule of market forecasts. The inputs are the various kinds of marketing effort, such as selling, advertising, and sales promotion. In discussing the programming problem, it is assumed that the market forecasts can be taken as reliable, despite the possible actions of competitors. Unexpected shifts in demand are also ruled out for the time being. A further assumption is that the program, once established, will be kept under effective control and produce results as anticipated.

The point is that the programming problem remains, even with all these favorable assumptions, and is often exceedingly difficult. The source of the difficulty is largely the complexity of the operating processes involved. That means that there is a large number of possible programs, and the analytical task of picking the right one is formidable. The most tangible achievements to date are in physical operations, such as warehousing, which are the aspects of marketing most closely resembling manufacturing. The warehouse expert controls costs by minimizing the movement of goods required in storage and order filling. One step in accomplishing this result is to arrange products along the assembly line in accordance with Zipf's principle of least effort. That is to say that the greater the number of pieces or pounds to be moved, the closer the item is kept to the loading dock. Operational analysis in warehousing produces other benefits beyond the proper positioning of products. It prepares the way for efficient use of mechanical handling equipment and for the functional design of warehouses.

Operational analysis is making headway in other aspects of marketing. Requirements as to the number and size of trucks for a delivery operation have been determined by balancing the cost of movement over the road against the cost of waiting time. Principles of layout for display in retail stores rest on a balancing of the traffic created by a product against its response to traffic created by other products. Some excellent work has been done, both theoretically and practically, on store location and urban land values; but the opportunity is wide open for the development of more precise optimization formulas in this field.

Marketing offers many opportunities for a developing aspect of operations reasearch known as "activity analysis" or "linear programming." No attempt will be made to describe these methods; it will only be explained in simple words what they are intended to do. Linear programming sets out to identify the most favorable among the feasible programs or ways of combining the possible activities or processes in a system of action. Starting with any given program, the method enables the analyst to find a more productive one if it exists, then a still better one, and so on. This may sound like no more than an advanced form of trial and error; but it is distinctly superior to informal trial and error, with no reliable means of weighing one plan against another.

There are serious computational difficulties in the more complicated programming problems. However, it frequently turns out to be an aid to insight to set up the problem in this form. In this connection an attempt to apply linear programming may revitalize some of the older and more conventional analytical procedures. Sales analysis and distribution cost analysis in skillful hands can still lead to marked improvements in marketing operations. They might acquire a new significance if regarded as means for obtaining the parameters needed for carrying out linear programming. It might equally well turn out that linear programming will provide a conceptual framework giving point and direction to the older types of analysis. Operations research, in its very nature, embraces any existing method that can help solve a problem rather than introducing a new one purely for the sake of technical virtuosity.

Control and Co-ordination in Marketing Systems. In the second class of problems, as in the first, the aim of the operations researcher is to find an appropriate optimization formula. That is to say that he is offering analytical help to management in minimizing costs, maximizing results, or identifying the best possible pattern of activities in a complex operation. The chief difference is that the discussion from here on must take account of further factors of uncertainty. In the first case, uncertainty for management was largely the result of complexity and not of contingency with respect to control of the problem situation. In this section, we drop the assumption that management is dealing with a well-oiled machine. The individuals or organization units involved in the operation are recognized to be semi-independent, but are susceptible to management. That is to say that they are willing to be co-ordinated to the extent that there is a common interest in results. The best means of control and co-ordination may become the key management problem.

The techniques of operations research can assist management in coping with uncertainty at this level as well as in programming and allocation. This particular phase of operational analysis is called "control and communication theory." In one of its versions, it has been given the name "cybernetics," which freely translated is "steersmanship." The mathematics of the field have been developed by such diverse specialists as neurologists and electrical engineers. But while cybernetics has made a substantial contribution to an understanding of servo-mechanisms and of the nervous system, applications to operating organizations are only in the beginning stages. A central principle of control is called "negative feedback." That means that when the operation moves beyond the control limits, the information is fed back along appropriate channels, so that corrective action can be taken.

In a co-operative setting, each individual performs a specialized function on the expectation that other individuals will be performing related functions and the total program will proceed in a satisfactory manner. The performance of each participant depends in part on his confidence in the performance of others. Often, one participant must have definite knowledge of the action of the other in order to proceed with his action. One may be responsible for initiation of action and another for detailed execution of the plan of action.

The elementary model of co-operation would consist of two participants, with the action of each conditioned in some degree by a feedback of information about actions taken by the other. The study of such models might be extended step by step to take account of larger co-operative systems. That type of model has already been employed in studies of the inventory problem. The co-ordination of any sequence of steps or the balancing of production and selling activities is a problem of this general character. After the parameters of control have been established by operations research, it may be possible to design electronic devices or other mechanical means to facilitate co-ordination.

Another type of study in this area is that directed toward improving an organization structure to permit more effective co-operation. One of the techniques of operations research is the operational experiment. This means setting up a probability model which has a structure paralleling an actual or potential operation and then putting it through an operating cycle. Thus, in a situation involving a waiting line of units to be serviced, the arrival of units on a random basis over time can be simulated by pulling numbers from a table of random numbers. The capacity required to maintain a given standard of service can be estimated in this way. Because of the relatively low cost of securing data by these so-called Monte Carlo methods, it is possible to try out several alternative patterns of operation on paper before putting any one plan to the final test of action. One of the side advantages of such a procedure is that of minimizing the number of adjustments which have to be made after a plan is put into effect and which can have a very adverse effect on morale. One important field of application would appear to be in the management of marketing channels. Any new policy may tend to favor one type of customer to the dissatisfaction of others, so that damage is done either by changing it or by attempting to hold the line. There is a high premium in such cases on being approximately right the first time, a result which might be achieved more readily by using operational models.

Search Theory and the Problem of Closure. Applications of operations research were first made on the assumption that the operation to be programmed was fully controlled. The assumption of control was then dropped to take account of cases in which the problem of control is crucial to the system of action. It is now time to drop the assumption that management is dealing initially with a closed system. The crucial problem then becomes that of achieving a sufficient degree of closure to permit an operation to be completed. A supplier searching for customers is able to market his goods only to the extent that he makes successful contact. A buyer searching for goods is similarly seeking to effect the closure in the system which is necessary to the continuity of the processes in which the goods are to be used. Problems of control and of programming may remain to be solved, but they are naturally subordinated in many cases to the primary problem of contact and closure.

The probability models required for this phase of operational analysis can be derived from what is known as "search theory." To do this, the analyst must proceed in terms of basic conceptions and not rely on superficial analogies. In physical terms, there is very little resemblance between a plane sweeping over miles of ocean looking for submarines and a consumer examining retail assortments looking for a dress. The basic similarity is that both must be guided by some sort of a priori estimates of the probabilities of finding what they want. These probability estimates may undergo change in the course of the search, but from moment to moment may affect decisions as to where to look and whether to break off the search or continue. Work now being done on consumer shopping behavior is making use of such probability models and appears to be yielding significant results. The study of actual shopping trips, in turn, has led to the development of psychological tests having the same probability structure as shopping. In these tests, it is possible to control and to modify the parameters and to gather data much more rapidly and economically than could be done through collecting further data on actual shopping trips.

In seeking to establish contact with customers, the marketing organization is trying to reduce uncertainty by achieving operating closure.

This function can be performed with greater assurance if the seller takes account of the dimensions of uncertainty confronting the buyer. One objective of every supplier is to induce a certain number of customers to buy with confidence and to regard him as their regular source of supply. At the same time the supplier who endeavors to expand his position in the market must attract some customers who are habitually buying from his competitors. To do this, he may undertake to plant doubts in their minds and may be said to be increasing the degree of uncertainty they experience. However, if he has a legitimate claim upon their attention, he may simply be making them aware of actual hazards in their situation and suggesting that his product can help solve their problems. There is no necessary conflict of interests here, since consumers, like persons playing any other economic role, may have to be made aware of problems before they can undertake to solve them. It is believed that operational analysis of this type can have an impact on many aspects of marketing, including advertising and retail assortments and display.

Problems of Competition and Conflict. Discussion so far has been limited to an operating system in which there is some community of interest among the participants. Operations research can also deal with situations involving conflict. Conflict may exist between organizations or within an organization. External conflict is typified by competition among large-scale enterprises. It is among large companies that management can conceive of marketing strategies and in turn must take account of the strategies of their competitors. An effective strategy often takes advantage of some special character of the firm which employs it and may be difficult to counter in precisely the same terms. Competitors may not have a good answer available and are only able to choose strategies which tend to minimize the degree of competitive injury suffered. A firm may be coerced to employ purely defensive means for some time, until it finally matures a plan of counterattack which makes use of its own natural advantages. In intensively competitive industries, there may be observed an ebb and flow of competitive advantage, not unlike a succession of military battles or campaigns.

The division of operations research which can provide models for this type of competition is game theory. In some games, there is a point of balance between the players representing the worst that can happen to the stronger competitor and the best that can be achieved by the weaker one. That kind of stable adjustment has been reached among large competitors in many instances. Game theory also provides models for competitive situations without this type of stability. Game theorists are working actively toward the construction of models which can simulate a greater range of competitive situations with greater fidelity. Some applications have already been made in business, and accelerated use can be expected as the theory progresses. There is no substitute for managerial experience and resourcefulness in devising or meeting competitive strategies, but an orderly framework for evaluating the possibilities could be useful to the sharpest competitors.

There are a number of economists and operations researchers who are attempting to cope with the conflict of values within an organization. Schemes have been devised for rating objectives and working toward a point of compromise by successive trials. Conflict of values affects many types of economic activities, starting with household purchases. There are doubtless many families lacking anything approaching a stable expenditure budget because of the lack of agreement on basic family goals. These tensions with respect to family requirements may often reflect still deeper tensions, including basic conflicts within the individual personality.

The resolution of conflicts can range over into the areas of ethics and psychiatry, but they are not thereby excluded from the interests of the operations researcher. He may properly take on the assignment of finding a procedure for resolving conflicts within an operating system, if that is the crucial problem which is interfering with productivity. Conflicts at one level of consideration are sometimes resolved by appealing to criteria pertaining to some broader level. Conflicting goals in a single organization unit may have to be resolved in terms of the aims of the whole organization. Conflict in short-range objectives may be reconsidered in terms of long-range objectives. Some conflicts cannot be resolved at all within the existing frame of reference. Management must decide when to fight and when to seek constructive compromise. The analysis of the factors involved in the conflict is therefore an appropriate topic for operations research.

One danger with respect to operations research is the tendency to stress specific techniques as its essence. It is easy to lose sight of the concept of problem solving as a unified operation and the ultimate function which it serves. It is understandable that individuals possessing technical virtuosity should be eager to find opportunities for using these new tools. From the marketing viewpoint the problem always comes first. The marketing executive and the marketing analyst are concerned with a specific field of action. They should be prepared to utilize any techniques which will lead to practical solutions. Neither operations research nor any other analytical techniques are to be regarded as ends in themselves but only as means toward finding better answers.

SELECTED REFERENCES

DESCARTES, RENÉ. *Discourse on Method.*

POLYA, GYORGY. *How to Solve it.* Princeton: Princeton University Press, 1945.

WERTHEIMER, MAX. *Productive Thinking.* New York: Harper & Bros., 1945.

HILGARD, ERNEST R. *Theories of Learning.* New York: Appleton-Century-Crofts, Inc., 1948.

CHURCHMAN, C. WEST. *Theory of Experimental Inference.* New York: Macmillan Co., 1948.

MORSE and KIMBALL. *Methods of Operations Research.* New York: Technology Press and John Wiley & Sons, Inc., 1951.

The essay by Descartes is a classic statement concerning problem-solving procedures. Descartes is a major figure in philosophy, science, and mathematics; his great accomplishments may have been due in part to his consciousness of the importance of method.

Polya is a contemporary mathematician who felt the need to give his students a general perspective on problem solving to supplement their training in specific mathematical techniques.

The Gestalt psychologists in general assert the primacy of insight in problem solving, and Wertheimer in particular is a vigorous advocate of this viewpoint.

Hilgard's book is broader than its title suggests. It has a good deal to say about problem solving, including an excellent analysis of selective exploration.

Churchman is a leading figure in the philosophy of science and an exponent of the functional approach in problem solving.

The Morse and Kimball book was the first to discuss operations research and is still a good introduction to the field.

Chapter XIV

PRINCIPLES OF MARKET
PLANNING

Market planning is emerging as an area of staff specialization parallel-ing the earlier recognition of marketing research in business. It is de-veloping its own body of scientific techniques, so that management can rely on an acceptable standard of performance from specialists assigned a planning problem. Planning is the art of designing marketing programs, but it is also a science insofar as the planner has an orderly procedure for testing his plans against the facts.

Some fundamental principles of programming are presented, as well as a discussion of devices which are designated as the major instruments of planning. Among these is the principle of postponement, useful in plan-ning the sequence of steps in a process. In addition to the design of a mar-keting program, there is the marketing approach to organization planning.

Progress in methods for advance testing of plans will assure the general adoption of a professional approach to planning. Steps in the develop-ment and testing of a marketing plan are compared with the evolution of a production process through the stages of laboratory demonstration, pilot plant operation, and full-scale commercial production. The improvement in planning techniques and in testing methods makes it increasingly possi-ble to separate detailed planning from the essence of the executive func-tion, which is decision making.

TIME, MONEY, AND EFFORT

Planning is the exercise of foresight. Most planning is the attempt to exercise such foresight with respect to the anticipated outputs of an organization so that the inputs can be utilized with maximum efficiency. The discussion of triangulation in Chapter XII suggested the relation-ship of planning to management. The core of the management func-tion is decision. However, the problem of decision is not always that of passing on a single clear-cut issue of policy or action. It becomes necessary to explore the structure of possible courses of action, in order that executive judgment may be brought to bear at the key points. A

414

situation could be imagined in which management operated merely as a decision center, with no attempt at planning. That would mean that management dealt with each exigency as it arose, without attempting to anticipate it. Actually, management at even the most primitive levels utilizes planning to deal with exigencies more effectively by anticipating them.

The Activity of Planning. In some organizations the top executive appears to spend a large part of his time in planning. It can be a serious mistake for the chief executive to become so involved in detailed planning as to obscure his still more fundamental function of decision making. Planning is a technique for effectuating decisions and should generally be regarded as a staff function which can be delegated. Planning is an instrumentality of management rather than the art of management itself. The fact that such a concept has been rather slow to take hold in business is perhaps due to the uncertainties of planning techniques. In the years ahead, techniques may become more definite and positive. Management may then be as ready to delegate the planning function as the fact-finding and analytical functions which are now largely assigned to staff units.

The preceding statement makes planning an activity which follows decision, but it can also function as a facilitating activity antecedent to decision. All plans, of course, are to be regarded as tentative or purely hypothetical until the decision has been made. In this hypothetical stage, in which planning is spelling out the structure of a possible course of action, it should leave room for executive choice. That is to say that the professional planner should usually come forward with two or more alternatives which might follow from differences in basic assumptions as to policy. It is not always possible for executive policy to be determined completely in advance. Only after reviewing the implications of alternative policies in terms of different courses of action can management make a wise choice in borderline cases. Once the decision has been made as to the general courses to follow, the function of planning is to develop the detailed procedure for putting the decision into effect. Many minor decisions are involved in working out a detailed program. The planner may be given authority in advance to make these decisions, or he may be expected to refer certain types of issues back to the chief executive as they emerge in the course of detailed planning.

Major Instruments of Planning. From a slightly different point of view, planning may be regarded as dealing with time, money, and effort. Money and effort represent inputs which must be considered by the planner, and time itself has some of the character of an input because of the limited amount of time which is usually available for putting into effect a proposed course of action. Time, money, and effort correspond respectively to three major instruments of planning: the schedule, the budget, and the program.

The orderly procedure in devising a schedule is to work backward from the terminal date. That is to say that taking a given date as the time at which the whole operation is to be completed, the planner looks first at the last stage of the operation and decides on a deadline when this phase must start in order that the operation may be completed on time. Similarly, he considers what must have happened before the final stage can start and thus works backward progressively through a whole series of deadlines. The validity of any schedule, of course, depends on the reliability of the terminal point toward which it is directed. This date may be fully determined by some obvious requirement. For example, if it is planned to have a new product ready for sale to consumers in the early fall, the stocking of retail stores must begin at some interval of time before the goods go on display. Similarly, if the goods are to be marketed through wholesale channels, they must be stocked by wholesalers some little time before retail stocks will be required.

A longer-range marketing schedule might be geared to the anticipated date for the completion of a new plant, which might be as much as two or three years ahead. Sometimes the terminal date established in connection with a marketing program is simply the latest possible date in the eyes of management with respect to action which competitors are expected to take. Thus, in introducing a new product, management has to make some judgment as to the extent of its technological lead over possible competitors. The advantage of being first on the market is considerable. If the firm enjoys a lead, it should make optimum use of the interval rather than allow its competitors to seize the initiative. All of these possibilities for establishing a terminal date should be explored, in order to determine whether the proposed course of action is one that can be undertaken at leisure or whether it must be greatly accelerated. If no such considerations apply, a definite date should still be set in terms of the judgment of management as to the period of time that will be required before the operation can be concluded. There are many situations in marketing, of course, in which no question of judgment is involved as to the terminal date. These are cases in which there is a fixed date by which it is necessary to comply with a legal regulation or with the terms of a contract.

The length of time required for each step in an operation is a central concern of planning. In many cases, there will be some basis in experience for judging the time needed for each phase. There is always a danger that the later and frequently most important stages will be slighted in planning because the first step can be visualized more clearly than those which are to follow. Just as in looking at a mountain range on the horizon, details of a future course of action are often hazy when seen at a distance. After adequate time has been allowed for each step, working backward from the terminal date, the total time allowed for each of the separate phases may add up to more than the period that is actually available. In these circumstances, time is clearly one of the scarce resources which must be dealt with in planning. Several trial runs may be needed in order to arrive at a correct allocation, just as in attempting to allocate any other scarce resource. In an effort to make the operation fit within the time available, one expedient is to search for possible shortcuts which can be applied to one phase or another. Another planning device is to consider whether any of the steps can run concurrently instead of being finished before another stage can begin. This decision must rest on a close analysis as to which steps are really necessary antecedents to steps which will be taken later. A schedule becomes, in effect, a multilevel schedule by separating out those sequences of events which are linked in this fashion and setting up a separate allocation of time for each of these sequences. The first stage in the action sequence is the development of the plan itself. It has been shown in many cases that adequate time for planning is the best way to economize in the use of time later on. If planning is to achieve this type of economy, it must work with well-established planning techniques and procedures. It is too late to start inventing planning techniques when it is already time to get started on a major planning assignment.

The budget is the means of balancing various forms of effort and weighing them against each other by the common yardstick of their money cost. The budget is also the means of relating expenditure to current income or to capital assets which the company is prepared to draw upon to meet an emergency. The importance of the budget as a means of control and communication by the top executive and those who will carry out his instructions has already been discussed and illustrated in terms of the advertising budget.

The term "program" applies to the specification of steps to be taken to reach the desired objectives. The program should cover the marketing mix or, in other words, the proportion in which various types of marketing effort are to be blended. It should embody the detailed instructions or policy rules which will govern the application of effort. The program says what is to be done, the schedule specifies when it is to be done, and the budget covers the allocation of resources for carrying out the program. Planning is to be distinguished from the executive decision by which the program is adopted as the means of accomplishing company goals. It can be distinguished also from the broad policy considerations which established these goals in the beginning, or from specific performance at each level of responsibility in the organization by which the program is carried out.

THE PLANNING PROCESS

It is useful at this point to distinguish between a plan and a procedure. A procedure may be defined as a prescribed method for handling routine transactions. The problem with respect to a procedure is generally limited to one of relative efficiency, so that the establishment of procedures does not normally raise the policy issues which are involved in broader types of planning.

A market plan has already been defined as a program of action which specifies marketing goals and describes the means of attaining them in terms of time, money, and effort. From the viewpoint of the planner, policy may be regarded as setting up the framework within which planning takes place. More precisely, policy may be defined as a statement of the limits within which plans and procedures must operate or of the general direction which they should follow toward the attainment of marketing goals.

The first three stages in planning should determine the general type of plan, the scale of the effort, and the design of the plan as visualized in full operation. Consideration must then be given to procedures to be followed in launching the plan and the critical review of the plan in relation to conditions which may affect its success. All five of these stages will be described in the following sections.

The occasion for planning is usually presented by a specific marketing problem. A problem arises from uncertainty concerning the outcome of plans and procedures now in effect. Modern marketing management is inclined to meet its major problems and make its plans on the basis of analysis rather than being guided by experience and insight alone.

One way to conceive of this analysis is as a re-examination of the operating assumptions by which the executive has been guided. In day-to-day decisions, he necessarily makes some assumptions about the character of his market and the effectiveness of various types of effort applied to the market.

Before undertaking to improve on existing plans and procedures, it is essential that the factual basis of these operating assumptions be reviewed. The marketing executive may be visualized as operating on the basis of a sort of map. There are boundaries or limits marking off the class of products he is willing to sell or markets he wishes to serve. There are routes over which he can move in attaining his objectives which experience or investigation has indicated are better than other routes. This map has to be brought up to date by a validation or revision of operating assumptions before a new plan of action can be devised.

General Type of Plan.   In the initial stage of planning, the general type of plan should be determined. Often a list of three or four major alternatives can be set up for consideration. The selection among these alternatives can be tested against the marketing facts and the statement of marketing policies. At this stage the planner should be able to set down a brief description of the type of program that is visualized which will serve as the nucleus for the more detailed plan to be developed later.

Fundamental decisions as to type of marketing plan may include the issue of starting on a regional basis or beginning national distribution immediately, selling directly to retailers or distributing through wholesalers, or bringing the product out at a high price with a possibility of reducing it later as compared with pricing the product for the mass market immediately. A recent market-planning assignment involved a choice among several approaches to product promotion. The three alternatives considered were those of dramatizing the product, dramatizing the company, and dramatizing the user of the product. In this instance the marketing facts and the sales policies of the company pointed unmistakably to the third alternative.

Scale of Plan.   In determining the scale of a marketing operation, the aim of management is the adjustment of effort to opportunity. This process of adjustment is complicated by the fact that effort is expended through a plan or program in which the various parts must in turn be proportioned to each other. Usually, it is not practical to deal with the problem in terms of a simple continuous curve relating effort to opportunity.

It is possible, however, to set up limits as to scale and then attempt to determine the optimum scale of operation within these limits. The top limit might be called "the maximum effort plan." The starting point is an assumption as to the maximum amount of resources which might be available for putting the plan into effect. A rough proportioning of these total resources can then be undertaken, allocating time and money to each of the elements of the marketing operation.

The lower limit may be established by what might be called "the minimum result plan." The starting point in this case would be a statement of a minimum goal to be achieved during the first year or some other operating period. With this target in mind, an attempt should then be made to list the minimum essentials and to estimate the cost of such a minimum program. Conceivably, it will turn out that the maximum effort available is not sufficient to achieve the minimum result that is considered worth-while.

It may then be necessary to abandon the project or to reconsider the marketing goals in order to make it practical to proceed. For example, a decision might be reached to go ahead in a single region or sales territory rather than undertaking national distribution from the start. Generally speaking, there will be some range for planning decisions between the point of maximum effort and the point of minimum result. With these limits as guides, it should be easier to identify an optimum scale of operations which in the judgment of the planner represents the most effective application of effort to opportunity.

Decision as to the scale of operations is a major determinant in the design of detailed operating procedures. A procedure that is efficient at one level of operation may be quite inappropriate at a larger or smaller scale. Thus, determination of the optimum scale may lead directly to decisions as to whether brokers should be employed, whether salesmen should be specialized by products or solely by territories, and what should be the initial scope and character of the advertising program. Consideration of procedures may in turn lead to a revised judgment concerning the scale of operations. It may be obviously uneconomic to set up facilities for a restricted scale of operations if prospective growth will shortly render these facilities obsolete.

The Plan in Operation. Having decided on the general type and scale of operations, the next step is to design its structure in greater detail. A first problem is to determine the proper sequence of steps by which a product will move from its producer or sponsor to the ultimate consumer. The planner may start off by listing all the steps in what appears to him to be the natural order. This listing should then be reviewed to determine whether any of the steps are unnecessary or whether the sequence might be changed.

An important aid in determining the sequence of steps is what may be called "the principle of postponement." According to this principle, any change in the form of the product should be delayed to the last possible point in the distribution process; and any change in its location should be delayed until the last possible point in time. The principle of postponement is nothing more than a convenient device for testing each step for its position in the sequence in order to arrive at the most favorable arrangement of steps. In seeking to push a step as far ahead as possible, it sometimes becomes apparent that it can be eliminated altogether. There are other steps which exhibit strong resistance to postponement and thus establish their right to a position at or near the beginning of the sequence. Further applications of the principle of postponement will be considered in the next section.

Having established the sequence of steps, the next concern is with structural balance among them. That is to say that each step should be in scale with those which precede or follow it. No step should be allowed to become a bottleneck on the one hand or on the other a bulge in which resources are wasted needlessly.

Contingencies with respect to breakdowns in a process, as well as provision for normal operation, necessarily enter into this phase of planning. The next phase is the co-ordination of steps or processes which must proceed simultaneously or along parallel lines. Weaknesses in market planning are constantly showing up because of the failure to co-ordinate schedules. Goods are advertised to the consumer before they have been stocked in retail stores, point-of-display materials arrive too late for planned sales events, and inventories pile up during the course of changeovers in models or merchandising methods.

Launching the Plan. Too many times the planner visualizes a marketing plan in full operation but fails to work out the steps by which that point is to be reached. No planning job is complete unless it gives consideration to how the plan is to be launched or how the new operation or procedure is to be installed.

First of all is the question of timing. Whether it is opportune to launch a new plan may depend on the season, the business cycle, or a variety of factors in the current competitive situation. On purely strategic grounds, too much delay may put competitors on notice and dissipate much of the impact of a plan. Launching the plan too soon may mean slighting some of the conditions that are necessary to success. The most important single condition is that of making sure of adequate co-operation from all factors that will be involved in the plan. A marketing plan cannot be carried out by the sales executive himself; it will require co-operation from a number of branch offices or other units in his own organization and from various types of distributors and dealers.

Adequate incentives for co-operation should form a part of the marketing plan itself, but the sequence of steps by which co-operation will be obtained is a fundamental consideration in launching the plan.

Many marketing operations are wrecked at this point by unwise concessions or commitments which are made in an attempt to gain cooperation from key factors. These concessions limit the freedom of executive action, so that development thereafter is inevitably cramped and restricted. This hazard can be minimized by regarding the launching of the plan as a separate problem and determining in advance just how far to go in soliciting co-operation.

Critical Review of the Plan. The planning steps which have been described so far proceed on the basis of principles of design and internal consistency relating the plan to the goals to be achieved. The final step should be that of criticizing and reviewing the plan in terms of other conditions which may affect its success.

First of all, there are the secondary consequences of marketing operations. A plan may have a number of effects in addition to those that are intended. The proposed operation may be a very effective means of approaching a given market but may alienate other customers. It may stimulate counteraction on the part of competitors to an extent that largely nullifies its benefits. A partial plan intended to change one aspect of a marketing operation may set off a chain reaction which requires a whole series of changes.

A related and yet separate set of considerations pertains to the evaluation of market risks. A plan calling for expenditures over a period of years in the marketing of a product is subject to the hazard that the product may become obsolete during that time. A better product may be under development in the company's own laboratories or in those of competitors. It is highly desirable at the time a new product is introduced to make some judgment concerning the pressure for lower prices which will accumulate as competition enters the field. Not only the price at which the company can produce the product today, but the price at which it might be willing to sell it five years ahead may be essential to a marketing judgment.

Finally, there is the consideration of whether a plan is appropriate to the capacities of the marketing organization for which it is prepared. It might be a good plan in the abstract but require adjustments to a new type of market or to changed marketing methods which are beyond the capacity of the organization as presently constituted. As a final word of caution, it should be pointed out that the stages of planning cannot be separated as sharply in practice as they have been in exposition. Thus, suitability of the plan to the capacities of the organization is a criterion which the planner should have in mind from the first and not merely in the final critical review. The virtue of explicit planning procedures is to make sure that all these considerations are taken into account at some stage in the process. Some formalization of the planning process is required if market planning is to be widely accepted as a staff function.

MARKETING EFFICIENCY AND THE PRINCIPLE OF POSTPONEMENT

Marketing efficiency within a complete system of distribution can be promoted through application of the principle of postponement. Distribution cost analysis has been successfully applied in the past to problems of efficiency for individual marketing units. Less progress has been made in evaluating the efficiency of a complete system or marketing flow such as the movement of a major agricultural crop from grower to consumer.

Postponement in Product Differentiation. Changes in form may occur along the way, varying from elaborate fabrication and combination of raw materials to mere cleaning or packaging of a product which is to reach the consumer in essentially the same form as that in which it was produced. Changes in location of inventory occur as the product moves from farm to elevator, to factory, to warehouse, to retail store. Efficiency in the basic marketing processes depends on a proper ordering of these related steps involving changes in form, identity, or place.

The marketing process, like any other process, is extended in time. It can be viewed as a series of steps which need to be arranged in the most effective sequence. The process is marked by a definite direction which can be defined in terms of what is happening to the product along the way. The product starts out as materials which are relatively raw and unspecialized. It ends up as a relatively refined and specialized article, shaped to a type of need and fitted to the specific requirements of the individual consumer who buys it. To serve the individual consumer, the product must assume a special character as to its use qualities; these qualities must be adequately identified in relation to the proposed use; and it must be available at a convenient place when the consumer wants it.

All of these changes in form, identity, and location of the product are bracketed by the economist under the term "product differentiation." The closer the product is to the point of consumer purchase, the more differentiated it becomes. For many kinds of products the demand of the individual consumer is unique, or nearly so, when all of his special requirements are taken into account—including basic use, special features, color, size, and place of purchase. Mass production is made possible by the vast and intricate system of sorting which lies between the standardized output of farm or factory and the unique requirements of individual consumers.

Sorting as carried on by marketing agencies lays the foundation for mass production but raises its own problems of efficiency. How can the cost of sorting be controlled, so that it will not absorb all the savings in production costs made possible by sorting? One general method which can be applied in promoting the efficiency of a marketing system is the postponement of differentiation. As already stated, the principle of postponement requires that changes in form and identity occur at the latest possible point in the marketing flow; and changes in inventory location occur at the latest possible point in time.

The first aim of postponement is to permit sorting to occur to the greatest possible extent while the product is in a relatively undifferentiated state. Sorting by large lots is less costly per unit of product than sorting in small lots. Grading and refining of a product sets up separate identities which must be recognized in subsequent sorting. Dispersion of supply to a number of places reduces the scale on which sorting can proceed thereafter.

In addition to reducing the cost of sorting, postponement serves to reduce marketing risk. Every differentiation which makes a product more suitable for a specified segment of the market makes it less suitable for other segments. If a pair of shoes is to be purchased by the author of this book, it must be shaped to the size of 8½ double E. That differentiation makes the product unsuitable for purchase by the great majority of consumers. It must also be stocked by a store in Philadelphia, which eliminates it from practical consideration by men in San Francisco or New Orleans. To make up shoes to a certain size or last is to assume a marketing risk related to the reliability of the estimate of demand for that size. To take the additional step of shipping the shoes to Philadelphia involves a further risk as to the share of the market represented by this city. Each step in differentiation is taken on the basis of some prediction concerning demand for that differentiation at some future time. Postponement cuts down that risk by moving the differentiation nearer to the time of purchase.

The principle of postponement might be reduced to absurdity by concluding that it pointed to the complete postponement of every step in the process. Thus, materials would be turned over to the consumer in the raw state; and he would be asked to make the best of them. This absurdity is avoided because the product must at least be moved from its original source to the place of purchase, and that movement must be completed in time for the product to be available when the consumer expects to buy it. Similarly, there are other limits as to the postponability of each step in the process. Fabrication cannot be postponed beyond the point in the marketing process at which the necessary plant equipment and labor skills are available. Preservative processes for perishable goods must be applied soon enough in the marketing flow to be effective. Processes of refinement which greatly reduce the weight of raw material must be applied soon enough to avoid wasteful expenditure for transportation. Postponement as a technical concept is an aid in allocating the scarce resource of time and has no resemblance to wasting it through procrastination.

Orderly application of the principle of postponement means the separate consideration of limits for each step in the process. Each step in turn is regarded as a candidate for postponement. The limits of postponability with respect to each step are taken into account. The final outcome of this analysis is the arrangement of the steps in the most effective sequence. Each step has been postponed to the latest feasible point in the sequence.

Postponement of Changes in Inventory Location. With respect to the postponement of changes in inventory location, the analyst works back from the anticipated time of consumer purchase. Retail stocks should be replenished often enough to maintain adequate displays and to provide some margin of safety for unexpected variations in demand. Wholesale stocks should provide against similar contingencies, and wholesale purchases should allow for time in transit. A marketing agency that engaged in any form of processing would also have to allow for its normal production time. During any remaining time that the designated goods are in existence, the efficiency of the system would be enhanced by holding them as far back in the marketing flow as possible.

When the analyst is examining a going system of marketing for any product, he will usually find a partial but imperfect adherence to the principle of postponement. Some steps in the process are handled in a particular manner and at a particular place because the business grew up that way. Such a pattern often persists even though important changes have occurred in sources of raw materials, the character of demand, and technological possibilities as to processing and transportation. The principle of postponement provides a starting point for a critical examination of the present pattern and recommendations of changes which will promote efficiency.

Analysis and planning can speed up adjustments in a marketing system; but the principle of postponement tends to work itself out by less formal means, given enough time. Many of the changes in marketing in recent years can readily be interpreted as applications of this principle. The tremendous emphasis on rapid turnover of inventory in wholesale and retail establishments is one obvious application. This movement has been carried to extremes at times by merchants who made the highest possible turnover an end in itself. The correct rate of turnover could be determined in each case by a more conscious and precise application of the principle of postponement. Starting from the goal of postponing the replenishment of stocks, and giving due consideration to the factors limiting postponability, the question of turnover rate would answer itself.

Postponement of differentiation has brought about large savings in the marketing and handling of basic raw materials. The development of petroleum pipe lines capitalizes upon the fluid character of the original raw material and postpones as long as possible the breaking-down of supply into separate lots which must be loaded and unloaded into tank cars and trucks. Manufacturers of many products made of steel, from refrigerator cabinets to carpet tacks, purchase steel in relatively undifferentiated form from the rolling mills, with fairly uniform requirements as to physical handling in transportation and storage.

Elimination through Postponement. Another advantage in examining the postponability of a step is that it may turn out that it can be eliminated entirely. If a step is not performed prematurely, it may never have to be performed at all. Many years ago the author "bucked wheat" in the Palouse country of eastern Washington. That meant following a combine which was leaving sacks of wheat behind it and throwing the sacks onto a truck. Today the grain is not bagged at all. A truck with an open box body travels with the combine, and the loose grain pours directly into the box. When one truck is full and leaves for the elevator, another truck pulls into line. The same kind of change is now occurring in the case of dry edible beans and peas. At one time the whole crop was bagged in the field and then had to be dumped out at the elevator for cleaning. Today, about half the crop moves from farm to elevator in bulk.

The development of self-service food markets proves that differentiation can sometimes be avoided by passing certain steps on to the consumer. At first it seemed unlikely that the majority of consumers would want to give up the service of having groceries delivered to their homes or undertake the extra work of assembling their own orders in the store. It must always be kept in mind that the consumer is engaged in sorting also and may prefer an opportunity for effective selection to further differentiations undertaken by the seller. In the supermarket the urban housewife is able to make a rapid and efficient selection of the items she wants for one or more meals for her family. At one time, she may have made a similar selection from a well-stocked home larder. Like the retailer, she has reduced the size of her working stocks by postponing purchase now that the self-service store offers such a convenient assortment from which she can make her selection.

The principle of postponement is not presented as an answer to all planning problems in marketing. It is only one major analytical tool that can be derived from the view that sorting is the essential marketing function. This view, in turn, has its limitations, pertaining as it does to the external relations of exchange among marketing units. There are other problems which can best be approached from the standpoint of the internal unity of systems and the survival values inherent in organized systems. For this type of problem, it is appropriate to employ a different set of tools, derived from such concepts as market position and market organization, market opportunity and marketing effort.

PROCEDURE AND ORGANIZATION

At various places in this book the discussion has been concerned with the relation between function and structure. At this point, planning may well be defined in terms of this relationship. Planning facilitates marketing functions by providing a structure for effective action. A program or campaign is a blueprint for structured action, in which each step is designed to fit in with other steps. These steps are like the component parts of a machine; and the plan will not work unless it has sound components, properly integrated with each other. Planning creates other structures in marketing besides programs and campaigns. Among these are procedures for handling repetitive operations and modifications in the organization itself.

Design of Procedures. The analysis of systems and procedures is a well-established branch of management research, with its own special techniques and symbols for charting the flow of an operation. Yet the design of an internal procedure follows some of the principles of design which are utilized in the creation of marketing programs. Both plans and procedures may be produced by the same staff unit in all but the largest organizations. There are also some essential differences in these two aspects of scientific management. A marketing program meets the unique requirements of guiding a course of action during a specified period. A procedure is established as a means of handling an operating situation which is repetitive and subject to uniform treatment. A marketing program is not complete unless all the procedures it is to utilize have been specified. Within the framework of a marketing plan, procedures might be revised without altering the basic structure.

The magnitude of risk is obviously of a different order in adopting a marketing program as compared with a procedure. A fatal flaw in a program may result in complete failure in a major operation such as the introduction of a new product. Faulty procedures reduce efficiency, but the risk in perpetuating such procedures is usually limited to waste rather than failure. The revision of procedures usually comes about because of a gradual divergence between the character of the business and the type of transaction or process which prevailed when the procedure was originally devised. A method of billing customer orders may have applied at one time to 99 per cent of all transactions, with special handling required on only one per cent. As the nature of the business changes, it may reach a point where special handling applies to 35 to 40 per cent of all transactions. That would mean that the need to revise procedures has become urgent.

The design of procedures has developed as a technical art, but it will necessarily acquire a broader perspective as an adjunct of market planning. Improvement in procedures ordinarily has not involved any reconsideration of company goals or changes in basic policy. Management has felt more comfortable about delegating this function because of the limited area in which the procedural expert was expected to exercise judgment. The distinction between procedural analysis and programming can only be maintained, however, so long as procedural analysis deals with one restricted area of operations at a time. The problem of procedural analysis can also be posed as that of developing an integrated system of operations, with a whole set of procedures linked together to form a balanced and comprehensive process. Order handling, billing, inventory control, and procurement are no longer resolved by separate and individual consideration. All become phases of a master design for handling the flow of information and relating it to the flow of goods. This trend in procedural analysis was facilitated by applications of punch-card tabulating equipment. It is currently being greatly accelerated by the use of more advanced electronic computers and control devices. Any staff or consulting group engaged in the design of procedures will be obliged more and more to be adept in the application of such equipment as well as thinking in terms of the total operation.

One sequence of procedures concerned with the handling of goods from procurement to order filling has been mentioned for illustration. There are other procedural sequences in marketing, such as those pertaining to the selection, training, supervision, and compensation of salesmen. The procedural sequence in administering an advertising appropriation was discussed in Chapter XII. Better solutions in each of these areas are made possible by the new facilities for handling masses of information. The ideal goal of procedural analysis is to perfect all of these procedural sequences and to combine them in a total operating pattern which can cope with most situations without the intervention of executive command. An organization in which this happy result had been accomplished would be equipped for the execution of the marketing plans developed for successive operating periods.

One reason for periodic review of procedures in a marketing organization is to weed out unnecessary detail. Without such control, procedures will persist or even proliferate long after they have ceased to serve a useful function. One large retailer was using twenty-two separate printed forms for handling sales and purchase transactions. An analysis of his procedures resulted in a reduction to only three forms and an improvement in the operation. Records which are valuable on one type of product or class of customers can all too readily be extended to other products and customers for which simpler procedures would be sufficient. Procedures which involve customers can have a serious impact on sales if they are either inadequate or cumbersome. Reference was made in an earlier chapter to the problem of behavioral drift in organized behavior systems. All too frequently, the head of a marketing organization assumes erroneously that prescribed procedures are actually being followed in the treatment of customers.

MARKET ANALYSIS AND ORGANIZATION PLANNING

The structure of action provided by marketing plans and procedures leads back to the question of structure in the marketing organization. The appropriate form of organization is that which can carry out effective plans and procedures. The market, in turn, determines the plans and procedures which are likely to prove effective. A study of the market, for example, may indicate the need for selling through a market channel never used before. If the sales organization is handicapped by inexperience or the bias of its executives in making this shift, then perhaps the rational decision by top management is to change the organization. This might be called the marketing approach to organization planning, as opposed to taking the present organization structure as fixed and selecting marketing plans subject to the limitations of existing capacity and attitudes.

The marketing approach implies nothing less than functional or end-product thinking with respect to the firm as a whole. It assumes that the firm exists to serve a market and that the first step in making a critical study of an organization is to define the way it is presumed to function in the market. In other words, the organization analyst might well proceed as if he were writing a job specification for the firm as a whole before he attempted to specify the manner of functioning by smaller organization units or individuals. Conceptually, this means working down from the top in designing a structure; but procedurally, it would mean working in from the market and marketing channels, in order to gain a perspective for analyzing the central organization itself. The nucleus of the structure has the function of co-ordinating a system of action; and the system in its broadest term includes all who have dealings with the firm, as well as individuals on its payroll.

The approach recommended means literally that the place to start in an organization analysis is with the company's customers and the users of its products. The purchasing agent is in a preferred position to evaluate the selling job a company is doing as compared to its competitors. His impression of a company's policies, inferred from contact with its representatives, is often in startling contrast to what top management has announced or believes its policies to be. The present position of the company in the market rests on the attitudes of those who distribute or ultimately consume its products. Presumably, a cardinal objective of an organization review is to consolidate market position, to expand it, or to strike out in entirely new directions if the present outlook is for stagnation or decline. A judgment as to the character of the organization needed must spring from considerations as to what it is feasible and desirable to accomplish.

Organization planning can be understood as the creation or the modification of a system of action. In a marketing system the organization analyst may consider various possibilities as to where he will set the boundaries of the system of action. Certainly he cannot afford to make them identical with the limits of the organization proper. At the very least, he must include the firm's immediate customers in the system. The efficiency of the central organization is measured by its impact on its customers. The interaction between the firm and its regular customers is almost as stable and continuous as that taking place wholly inside the organization. Supplier and customers co-operate on common objectives and adjust to each other in various ways.

Suppose the firm under consideration is a manufacturer selling through wholesalers. The question then arises as to whether the retailers served by the wholesalers are also part of the relevant system of action. This extension of the planning perspective is inevitable as soon as any alternative methods of reaching the retailer are considered. One alternative would be direct sales by the manufacturer. Another would be the use of some other type of intermediary or wholesaler. Still others would consist in maintaining the present channels but supplementing the wholesalers' efforts with those of specialty salesmen. Various types of contracts or marketing plans for motivating the wholesaler might come up for consideration and comparison. Since all of these alternatives must be evaluated in terms of their impact on retailers, there is no escape from regarding the retailer as part of the pertinent system of action.

If the manufacturer is producing a consumer good, he may need more than one type of retailer for effective market coverage. He becomes concerned with the reactions among types of retailers, as well as their relative efficiency in serving the consumer. He may appeal to consumers directly through advertising, both for the purpose of influencing the consumer and as a means of establishing more satisfactory arrangements with retailers. The manufacturer may wish to reach a highly selected group of consumers, or he may strive for as broad a market as possible. Such considerations will have a vital effect on his policies as to product line, pricing, and promotion. The system of action must be conceived as embracing consumers if these issues are to be evaluated. The organization planner is actually using consumers, retailers, and wholesalers as building blocks for his system of action in deciding that effort should be concentrated on selected groups at each level. Finally, the organization proper is considered as the nuclear element in the system as a whole.

Not even this broad perspective can set the ultimate boundaries of the action system. As markets change, the relevant system of action is automatically modified. An organization which is only capable of meeting today's requirements is already obsolete in the face of the prospect for growth. An acceptable organization plan says what the system of action will look like three to five years ahead. An organization with a proper care for its survival and continued vigor is hiring men today and starting them on a course of training and experience which will qualify them for executive responsibility several years hence.

A complete plan is likely to picture an ideal organization for the future and to specify one or more transition stages. Structural changes designed to meet an immediate problem may be unwarranted unless they move in the direction of the pattern projected for the future. Under dynamic conditions the organization planner takes account not only of the market and marketing channels but of the kind and size of market the firm must serve the day after tomorrow.

COMMUNICATION ANALYSIS AND ORGANIZATION PLANNING

The nature and flow of communications which arise in the course of a business operation are matters of serious concern. Systems and procedures for both receiving and sending information are basic necessities for the general welfare of the firm. The subject of communications embraces a variety of highly developed techniques such as advertising, personal selling, marketing research, and employee relations. However, this section is concerned primarily with the transmission of information within the organizational structure rather than between the organizational structure and its market.

The Need for Analysis.   The findings of a communication study may lead to major changes in organization, in procedures, and even in the basic formulation of goals and objectives. Organizational faults disclosed by the study may consist either of deviations from the established structure or of defects in the structure itself. A few key individuals may tend to form bottlenecks in the flow of communications; too many individuals rely upon these key individuals for either information or decisions because of their greater ability, background, or willingness to assume responsibility. Too many fish may be swimming too far upstream in the form of detailed reports or questions which should be resolved at lower organizational levels. Too much independent investigation of the same issue and too little co-ordination may detract from efficient use of communication. There may be a great many memoranda concerning trivial matters, while major issues may be resolved purely by verbal communication and understanding.

While communication is not in itself either an end or a goal, it is management's most basic and universal tool for producing action. Broadly speaking, if no communications were passed through the organizational structure, all operational activity and policy direction would cease. On the other hand, by the establishment of an efficient and effective two-way communication system, a firm can create and maintain a dynamic program of policy formulation, along with appropriate actions and necessary controls.

In practice the effectiveness of a communication system lies between these two extremes. The nature of communication is so all-embracing that it cannot be separated or distinguished from the organizational structure which it serves. The status of executives or departments can largely be defined in relation to their position within the communication network. This becomes quite evident when each executive or department head is evaluated in accordance with the number and level of people who report to him, the number and level of people to whom he reports, the limits of his authority, and the extent of his ability to act upon the information he receives. A basically unsound organizational structure may contain a poor communication system simply because channels of authority and responsibility are confused. In such instances, messages are delayed or may never reach the proper individual, so that the right information is not at hand when issues must be resolved.

A fast and accurate flow of information is a basic prerequisite for a sound organizational structure. The best system of communication may not be the one that transmits the greatest quantity of information. Each matter must be reviewed in relation to its relevance and priority, which will largely be determined by operating considerations. These questions are of particular importance to an organization's marketing operations. Even if the original structure were conceived upon sound principles and staffed by competent individuals, inadequate exchange of information could eventually destroy the structure.

The continued effectiveness of an organizational structure is promoted by a periodic investigation and evaluation of communications. An investigation of the communication system affords an opportunity to study the organization while it is in action. More specifically, such a study provides insight into organizational difficulties and policy problem areas. The results of communication analysis can be evaluated in terms of the firm's goals, objectives, and policies. A firm's goals and objectives reflect management's long-range outlook concerning profits, sales, market position, plans for expansion, etc., while policies may be defined as rules which are formulated at a higher level of organization to guide decisions at lower levels. A good rule is one that minimizes the number of exceptions which require special treatment. An evaluation of the communication structure will indicate the extent to which a policy fulfills its original intent.

A study of communications and information flow is a complex undertaking because it involves the activities of all major departments and personnel. However, like most problems, the task can be simplified by limiting the study only to the matters of greatest importance. In addition, a variety of statistical sampling procedures can be utilized to simplify the analysis. Generally speaking, most current files and record-keeping systems are amenable to standard sampling procedures. The results may subsequently be classified and tabulated to facilitate analysis.

Solutions to problems are a matter of reducing uncertainty to a point at which a course of action can be adopted with confidence. However, reduction of uncertainty can only result from a systematic collection, classification, and analysis of facts. It is the purpose of this section to point out a variety of basic information categories which lend direction to a communications analysis. In a broad sense, there are three elements in the basic analytical framework: the content of the communication itself, the flow of information throughout the organizational structure, and the subsequent actions based on this information.

The Content of Communications. The content of written communications or records of verbal communications can be classified by such groupings as policy, operational, and facilitative matters. Those concerning policy deal with ideas and principles; those concerning operations, with people and current actions. Facilitative communications are of a more routine nature, acting as a lubricant in the conduct of both operational and policy matters. Several important findings result from this type of analysis. For example, it is possible to determine the number of people and the number of organizational levels or units which are involved in both the formulation of policy and the conduct of normal operations. Identification of positions allows an examination of delegations of authority and line-staff relationships.

Information content analysis can also be directed toward more specific subject matter groupings. Illustrations of such topics are customer relations, product usage, technical information, administrative procedure and control, market information, and competitive conditions. Analysis will show which matters receive the greatest amount of attention and interest. Similarly, it will also indicate those areas which receive only scant and perhaps insufficient attention. Another useful type of classification is that which distinguishes between communications issued to initiate action and those which control actions. The purpose is to determine which operational units and programs require the greatest degree of control, so that each can be reviewed and evaluated with a view toward organizational and policy adjustments.

The Flow of Information. A second broad area of communication analysis is concerned with the flow of information throughout the organizational structure. This analysis deals with the origin and destination of communications rather than their subject matter. For instance, it is possible to determine the number of communications that originate both inside and outside the central organization. There is a variety of additional analytical classifications which can also be used for determining the strong and weak segments of an organization. One rather simple measure is the number of people, departments, and organizational levels involved in a particular problem. Still another useful classification is the number of communications and the time span required to resolve policy or operating problems. A study of such interaction among individuals and departments can serve to determine the organizational level at which various types of problems should be resolved.

Special difficulties in communication arise in very large firms with far-flung operations. Certainly, as the chain of command is lengthened through the addition of organizational levels, sending and receiving information becomes disproportionately complex and retarded. Consequently, when time becomes a serious factor, levels are skipped, which eventually breeds inconsistency of action. On the other hand, if additional organizational levels are not added, far too many problems of a minor variety are forced upon executive personnel at the top levels. A periodic evaluation of communications seems necessary in order to preserve and maximize the benefits which accrue from large size and specialization of functions in an organizational structure.

Subsequent Actions.   Certainly, any evaluation of an organizational structure is incomplete until attention is also directed to actions which were specified or requested in communication. Generally speaking, a study of all communications relating to a particular problem or situation provides a higher degree of insight into the appropriateness of action than does a sample selected from the entire universe of communications. Communication case studies on selected situations offer an opportunity to evaluate the history and development of over-all strategy concerning operational problems. Of particular interest are the number, type, and nature of directives which are accepted without further negotiation between the sender and receiver and pressed into action successfully. The extent of negotiations and revision of planning which is necessary for successful action and results point to areas of organizational strength and weakness. Such an analysis is even more valuable when the nature and extent of control over a particular action or request for action is also considered, because it offers a concrete method of gaining insight into the problem of allocation of authority and responsibility.

Summary.   In summary, communication analysis is of considerable value as a method of studying an organization because it provides both an effective and an economical method for studying the organization in action. Like all research procedures, its scope and direction must be established in view of the problems on hand. However, three areas generally provide the framework for a well-rounded study of communications in an organizational structure. These three areas are an analysis of content, the flow of communications through the organizational structure, and the success of actions which result from communications and directives. Such a study can be accomplished by sampling, classifying, tabulating, and analyzing file material, followed by interviews in terms of well-defined issues conducted among the various individuals involved.

A communication study shows the relative rate of recurrence of various topics and questions. Routine handling procedures can be devised or improved for highly repetitive matters, and standard answers or programs can be prepared for questions and problems that frequently arise. Information requirements can be anticipated with respect to important issues which are expected to arise at less frequent intervals. A sharper distinction can be drawn between the responsibilities of staff people, who are primarily concerned with information, and line executives, who must have information at the right time and in the proper form if it is to influence decision. A better understanding of informational requirements should result as both line and staff personnel react to the findings of a communication study.

A study may show that while the organization is reasonably effective in reaching some of its objectives, it may be falling down with respect to others. For example, a company may be doing well in its existing business with large users, but failing to capitalize fully upon its growth potential. The operations of any company should substantially reflect the expectations of its customers. This may require considerable modification of what the company regards as its basic goals and objectives. The study of the communications of an organization in action may serve to clarify its goals, as well as to contribute to the means of achieving them.

TESTING MARKETING PLANS

The discussion of planning so far deals with principles of design parallel to those that might be applied by an engineer. While designing a marketing system is very different from designing a machine, some of the fundamentals of symmetry, balance, simplicity, and closure are as pertinent in one area as in the other. There still remains the problem common to both fields—that the beauty of a design is no guarantee that the system will work. Some essential conditions may have been overlooked by the builder, or failure may occur later on because of some unforeseen circumstances. In chemical and mechanical engineering a new operation goes through three stages before it is fully in effect. The first stage is the laboratory, in which a new chemical reaction is discovered and verified or a new engineering design is first subjected to critical analysis. The next stage is the pilot plant stage. Here the process is not purely experimental but represents a small-scale model of an operating plant. In the pilot plant stage the whole operation, with a normal flow of inputs or outputs, can be observed; and many defects can be corrected. This is a much more economical way of arriving at the final design for an operating plant than to have moved directly from laboratory to full-scale plant, with the hazard that the plant might have to be rebuilt before it would operate effectively.

Difficulties of Testing. Market planning as yet has no such definitely marked stages as laboratory, pilot plant, and full-scale operation. In many cases, both the laboratory and the pilot plant stages are missing. The marketing organization moves directly from a paper design to full-scale operation or, in the most flagrant cases, initiates full-scale operation immediately without being aware of the problem of design. This chapter has dealt primarily with what would correspond to preliminary design or blueprints in the case of engineering. The purpose of this section is to consider the possibilities for providing something which would parallel the laboratory and pilot plant stages of production. When this can be done, it should be the crowning step to establish professional planning in marketing. So long as there are no standard techniques for testing plans, the executive must rely on his own critical judgment in assessing their validity.

While techniques for testing marketing plans would be especially valuable, there are obvious difficulties obstructing such a development. Some of these difficulties are similar to those which the military forces are confronted with in their war games. The Army puts tremendous effort into test maneuvers to give its officers experience with the co-ordination of military units and to facilitate judgments concerning the relative strength of offensive and defensive tactics. It is impossible, of course, to reproduce the psychological conditions of genuine warfare and to learn how men and officers will stand the strain of unexpected crises and mortal danger. Similarly, it is difficult to test a marketing organization or program by anything short of actual marketing experience. Furthermore, the Army is able to carry out its tests with relative security from observation by prospective enemies. A real live test of a marketing plan, involving the co-operation of retailers and wholesalers and actual sales to consumers in a typical market, is fully open to observation by competitors. Hence, there is the danger that any test will deprive a plan of the advantage of surprise when the full-scale operation begins. A number of companies today use regular test cities, or select cities for a special test of a new marketing plan. There have even been instances in which a competitor who was fully aware of where a test was taking place has engaged in what might be called "jamming" by conducting operations of his own to upset conditions in the test city. An alternative procedure is to let the test go ahead without interference but to observe it so closely as to gain useful knowledge about how it operates at the expense of its originator.

The Pilot Plant. Despite these disadvantages, the use of live tests for marketing plans is a growing practice. A useful distinction can be drawn between a test market program and an introductory program. If the operation is strictly a test, the assumption is that it will determine the feasibility of the program and may end in the program being abandoned. An introductory program, by contrast, is one in which marketing begins in one city or region, with the full intention of moving across the country step by step until full national coverage is achieved. Some of the larger manufacturers of packaged products count on eighteen months to two years as the normal period for establishing national distribution of a new product. This procedure involves the assumption that no marketing program can be fully planned in advance and that it is better for the inevitable mistakes to occur on a small scale rather than allowing them to affect a nation-wide marketing program. An introductory program of this type gives the marketing organization something that is roughly comparable to the pilot plant operation in production. In fact, it might even be regarded as an improvement, since the scale of marketing can gradually be stepped up as the operation moves into one area after another. While an introductory marketing program is under way, a firm may still be making progressive improvements on the production side, so that both production and marketing are ready to move into high gear at the end of the introductory period.

The "Laboratory." The greatest need in market planning is to fill the gap now existing at the stage which would really correspond to the laboratory stage in production. Preferably, this phase of testing should take place behind the scenes, with complete security from observation by competitors. This would mean the use of testing techniques which did not involve the display of merchandise in actual retail stores or the disclosures which are inevitable as soon as the firm solicits trade cooperation. There are some aspects of marketing which offer opportunities for application of physical models. For example, some of the store planning undertaken by large manufacturers on behalf of their dealers involves the erection of either miniature or full-scale models in a store-planning laboratory. Physical models have contributed substantially to the development of self-service methods in retailing and to the streamlined operation of merchandise warehouses. In both these cases, it is possible to start from certain general principles and to experiment with various arrangements to determine which one is the best exemplification of the principles.

Possible principles as to the layout of a supermarket would include that of causing each foot of shelf space to produce the same volume of sales. An application of this principle would help to determine how much space to give to each product and what location to assign it in the store. A miniature model or a full-scale model could be useful in working out these applications, so long as the model offered complete flexibility for the arrangements of fixtures and merchandise. A possible principle to be exemplified in laying out a merchandise warehouse would be that of minimizing what might be called "foot-pounds." In other words, taking account of the weight of merchandise and the distance that merchandise has to be moved before it is finally shipped out to the customer, the warehouse may be laid out so as to minimize the product of the number of pounds and the average number of feet moved. Specialists in this field have made effective use of physical models in arriving at efficient designs.

For some aspects of marketing, an abstract model of some kind is indicated, rather than a physical model. An abstract model might be a formalization of the flow of goods and information through marketing channels. These abstract models need not take the form of mathematical equations and at this stage of market planning are likely to be somewhat less formal in character. The development of an abstract model and the testing of the model can be illustrated by some of the work being done in inventory control. The planner first tries to establish certain governing facts about demand for the firm's products, including seasonality and the lead time of orders over anticipated delivery dates. He ascertains similar key facts about production, such as the length of the production cycle and the minimum lot size for economic production. With these facts in hand and with a knowledge of the current inventory situation, the planner may design a scheme which is intended to minimize inventory without interfering with appropriate standards concerning service to customers. Once this inventory control plan has been designed, it can be tested on paper by using sales and production figures from the company's records for the preceding year. Past orders can be run through the system in a continuous process in a matter of days, rather than waiting for a year to elapse to get a test of the plan in actual operation. Similar tests can also be worked out pertaining to the information circuits which are such a basic element in the structure of marketing systems. To take a simple example, it is not necessary to introduce a product under a new brand name in order to evaluate the name as a vehicle for transmitting information or attitudes concerning the product. It is possible to find out through the use of laboratory subjects which of several names can be most easily remembered and which has favorable or unfavorable connotations in connection with the product. Psychological tests have also been devised for measuring the degree of confusion between a proposed name and trade-marks that have already been established.

Psychological Games.   Another possibility which is showing great promise is the use of psychological experiments and games for testing mental reactions both at the consumer level and within a marketing organization. The game is constructed in such a way as to parallel the decision structure that is believed to exist in the real-life situation. It has been used to test the reaction of consumers to various aspects of merchandising, such as breadth of assortment, depth of assortment, and price lines. It can be used to test reactions to advertising appeals or to the sales approach in a retail transaction.

The game approach is being utilized for testing elements of organization structure by institutions engaged in management research. Notable work in the application of psychological games has been carried on at the Massachusetts Institute of Technology, the Case Institute of Technology in Cleveland, and the University of Pennsylvania. What has been described so far is a series of methods for testing various aspects of a plan, such as the movement of goods and information, by measuring psychological reactions either by the consumer or within the marketing organization itself. A testing program for a marketing plan might proceed simultaneously with tests of each of these various segments. The final test would put all of these elements together in terms of an abstract model for the whole marketing program. Means may be found shortly for testing such a model on an analog computer. Similar tests are already being made by public utilities in planning their investment schedules. The network analog computer has been used in this way by setting up a structure on the computer which is analogous to the structure of the utility system and then studying the effect of making various alternative changes in the capacity of the system or the demands upon it.

Presentation of Sales Plans.   The final step in market planning is to prepare for the presentation of sales plans and programs to the sales force or to the brokers, retailers, or wholesalers on whom the producer depends for distribution of his product. The executives making such a presentation are not merely putting on a show but are contributing to the education of their audience. Techniques of showmanship and of education are involved; but such an occasion involves implicit negotiation, since both sides assume that action will result from the meeting. These occasions for the presentation of sales programs are of increasing significance in marketing. Sometimes every promotional activity and every page of advertising which is planned for six months or a year ahead is unveiled to the distributive organization. All of the arts of the platform speaker and of visual demonstration are mobilized to make such a presentation a success. At least an entire day is typically devoted to hearing from the managers of sales, advertising, sales promotion, and others who will play a vital part in the program. When such a meeting is well planned, it conveys a mass of information; but it also strikes a spark of enthusiasm which becomes more contagious because all of the people most directly concerned are gathered in one room.

The plan as presented has probably been the result of many kinds of effort and discussion, including talks between members of the sales organization and their various distributors. The plans have been shaped up gradually, taking into account what experienced distributors regard as most likely to prove effective or their reactions to past promotional plans sponsored by the company. Laying out an annual or semiannual program for a national sales organization is a truly prodigious task. In its final form, it has to be the product of a well-integrated team with an opportunity to work closely together. In producing this integrated program, the planning team represents all of those who have contributed suggestions or criticisms. The integrated program has been put together against a background of informal negotiation, but it achieves consistency and balance which could not have been attained by all interested parties working as a committee of the whole. Sometimes, more formal arrangements are made for representing the distributors involved. The executives of the sales organization rely on a council of brokers or wholesalers whom they may call into consultation in the early stages of formulating their plans.

It would be unrealistic to regard the presentation of these plans as having the force of a command within a single behavior system. The brokers or wholesalers present may listen with politeness or even enthusiasm, but that does not guarantee that all of them will conform or that the program will be carried out with uniform effectiveness. The presentation of a program is a bid for the support of distributive organizations. The degree of acceptance and the excellence of performance may reflect considerable variation. The presentation thus has the force of a mass negotiation in which an effective agreement is reached in some cases but not in others. Despite the lack of legal control in such a mass approach to marketing channels, the response is often as great or greater than that which is typically attained within a single firm.

The presentation of a sales program is a bid for something extra in the way of attention and effort for the sponsor's products. He is competing for these extras against other manufacturers using the same channels. He competes for full co-operation by trying to make his plans so good that his distributors will be convinced that the richest rewards for extra effort lie in co-operating with him. An effective plan is persuasive as well as sound. Planning can use the dramatic flair of the artist as well as tested principles of scientific technique.

Relation of Planning to Problem Solving. A final word of summary and emphasis seems essential since various facets of planning have been covered in this chapter. The full acceptance of the planning function by business and the more complete realization of professional planning techniques can be predicted with confidence. Staff planners more and more will be held responsible for the development of advance programs concerning both general structure and details of procedure. The essence of the executive function is decision, a responsibility which cannot be delegated. The delegation of planning can take place wherever management has sufficient assurance of the technical competence of the planners.

The staff groups serving marketing management, whether on a full-time or consulting basis, appear to have been climbing a sort of pyramid over the past 40 years. The broad foundation of the pyramid is technique —the knowledge and skill required for market investigation and market analysis. Techniques are only the foundation which give the staff analyst a place to stand. They are the tools of his trade and must be embodied in some type of output to be useful to management.

The next higher level in the pyramid is information, which represents the analyst's most elementary output. Management turns to him for more detailed or more reliable marketing information than that generated as a by-product of daily operation. Just above the information level is the problem-solving level. The assignment at this level transcends but does not exclude the collection and analysis of data. The essence of the assignment is to provide a solution to an operating problem or to suggest an answer to an issue of policy.

The fourth and highest level in the pyramid of staff services is planning or programming. Problem solving tends to be an intermittent activity, dependent on the executive's sense of urgency with respect to one crisis or another. Planning is a continuous function implying full collaboration between the staff group and the decision-making executive. It can bring technical competence to bear at the most vital point in management—namely, the continually evolving program which provides the framework for all operations.

The program mediates between the goals of the firm and the capacity of the organization. It is the means of reaching the goals and of making the most effective use of capacity. Management is constantly weighing these three elements in determining its policy, generally with a central concern for the program. This book generally emphasizes the problem-solving approach and the fact that both buyer and seller enter the market to solve problems. From the standpoint of executive action, programming carries executive foresight one stage further and avoids many acute problems by laying out an effective course of action in advance.

SELECTED REFERENCES

LORWIN, LOUIS L. *Time For Planning.* New York: Harper & Bros., 1945.

HART, ALBERT G. *Anticipation, Uncertainty, and Dynamic Planning.* Chicago: University of Chicago Press, 1950.

DAHL, ROBERT A., and LINDBLOM, C. E. *Politics, Economics and Welfare.* New York: Harper & Bros., 1953.

KOOPMANS, TJALLING C. (ed.). COWLES COMMISSION FOR RESEARCH IN ECONOMICS. *Activity Analysis of Production and Allocation.* New York: John Wiley & Sons, Inc., 1951.

DORFMAN, ROBERT. *Application of Linear Programming to the Theory of the Firm.* Berkeley: University of California Press, 1951.

No list of references on planning would be complete without the name of Louis Lorwin. The book cited discusses economic planning in a number of countries, but his influence was expressed through many channels. One was a famous seminar for government officials which he carried on for a number of years and which led directly to the establishment of the National Planning Association.

Hart recognized business planning as a vital part of the executive's role in meeting the uncertainties of the market. Dahl and Lindblom discuss planning within a perspective which transcends the boundaries of economics.

The volume of technical papers edited by Koopmans contains some discussions of military planning which are suggestive for the market planner.

Linear programming will doubtless make an increasing contribution to business planning. Dorfman relates this new technique to the decision-making process in the firm.

Chapter XV

A MARKETING VIEW OF BUSINESS POLICY

This book began with the objective of providing a useful perspective for marketing practice. In this final chapter the marketing viewpoint will be considered as an approach to business policy in general. The range of its application will be illustrated by a number of cases in which the problems of the policy maker lie wholly or partially outside the field of marketing operations.

The task of policy is to deal with issues affecting business operations. Some of the most important decisions confronting the chief executive are marketing issues. Others concern the reconciliation or co-ordination of marketing with production, finance, and engineering. Still others pertain to the place of the firm in the broader community, the outlook for the firm and the people who comprise it, and the impact of business policy on the evolving society of which business is a part.

The marketing viewpoint rests on the functional analysis of group behavior, which is here extended to the highest level of business responsibility—that is, the weighing of policy issues by the top executive. Marketing theory provides a perspective for determining when and how these key issues are to be resolved.

SOME APPLICATIONS OF THE MARKETING VIEWPOINT

Business policy may be defined as a set of working rules governing the use of the resources of the firm in gaining the firm's objectives. Policy rests on key decisions concerning the general course to be followed and guides executives in the day-to-day decisions involved in carrying out a detailed program. A business firm or any other operating organization can be analyzed in terms of inputs and outputs. The primary output of the typical business firm is a flow of salable products. It is this output which justifies the existence of the enterprise and from which are derived such secondary but highly essential outputs as profits, wages, and payments to suppliers. The inputs to be acquired and utilized in the business include labor, raw materials, plant equipment, working capital, and

444

executive talent. Issues arise in business as to the character of outputs and the direction in which inputs are to be expended, not merely their allocation within a fixed frame of reference. The function of policy is to deal with these issues.

Marketing considerations are the necessary foundation of policy in dealing with a complex pattern of relationships between inputs and outputs. This statement would be self-evident to any group of business executives were it not for the fact that so many have grown up in aspects of management which on the surface appear more stable and precise than marketing. Often, an executive who has spent all his working years in production, engineering, or finance takes over as the head of a company. It can well be a chilling thought that his most important decisions thereafter will be concerned with the uncertainties of the market place. There is no intention to deny that many successful executives have risen by these diverse routes. But they succeeded precisely because of their creative capacity to cope with uncertainty. Whether they recognize it or not, they are marketing men first of all from the time they accept top responsibility for the determination of company policy.

The pertinence of marketing considerations to every aspect of management will first be illustrated by a series of cases from the records of a consulting firm. These cases show how every major decision turns out to be a marketing decision or to be heavily involved with marketing decisions. Later sections will consider the formulation of policy within the marketing department, the relation of marketing department to to other departments, and the approach to company goals and their attainment in marketing terms. There will inevitably be some repetition of matters covered in earlier chapters in the effort to crystallize and summarize all that has gone before from the viewpoint of the chief executive. The intention is to picture the way in which such an executive would operate if he adopted the perspective provided by marketing theory.

Marketing Decisions and Production Methods. While marketing is the essential background for business policy, not all of the decisions governed by policy are marketing decisions. In fact, policy would not be very effective if it did not enable department heads and their subordinates to make decisions within a much narrower frame of reference than that required of the chief executive. Many decisions about the management of company resources can be defined as problems of plant layout, materials handling, inventory control, quality control, labor relations, or administrative organization. Some examples from the notebook of a management consultant will serve to illustrate the range of problems and policy issues arising in business firms, large and small. Ten examples will be presented, in five related pairs. Marketing considerations relevant to each case will be mentioned briefly. The succeeding sections will present in more general terms a conception of the place of marketing in policy formulation.

A moderate-sized plastics fabricator entered the postwar period with a reputation for quality work but with a prospective loss in volume through completion of government contracts. The principals were men of some ingenuity in product engineering and design, but they lacked management experience. The inefficiency of production methods was obvious on the most casual inspection. Bench workers processing plastic components had to stoop down to get each blank from a box placed on the floor and stoop over again to place the finished piece in another box. Little thought appeared to have been given to the placement of machines in relation to the normal sequence of steps in the process.

A much larger plant was turning out vinyl film and plastic-coated textiles for upholstery and other purposes. While the machinery was largely automatic, the plant employed a surprising amount of unskilled labor. Materials used by each machine were brought in as needed on hand trucks or by small tractors from a warehouse a block away. Similarly, the finished product from each machine had to be carted some distance for storage. The business was growing, and the available floor space was crowded with equipment. It would have taken a major reorganization to bring stocks of raw materials up to the production line at one end and provide for more efficient movement of the product into storage at the other.

These cases would appear to call for the services of experts in plant layout and materials handling. Such specialists would necessarily have been involved in any program to make either plant fully efficient. Yet, marketing decisions had to be made before the production engineers could go to work. The plastic-fabricating plant had survived despite its inefficiency because of the high operating margin it enjoyed. The crucial issue was whether it could maintain an adequate volume in that class of work or whether it would have to be converted to the mass production of more competitive products. The process of tuning up the plant for efficient production would be quite different according to the outcome of that marketing decision. In the larger plant, nothing less than a major investment and construction program would have sufficed. Rapid shifts were going on in the demand for the various types of products the company manufactured. Plant reorganization could not be undertaken without key decisions concerning an investment program. The first requirement was for long-range forecasts based on thoroughgoing market studies.

Marketing Approach to Quality Control.   The next pair of cases is concerned with quality control. One company was a leader in its field, with procedures for quality control surpassing those of any of its competitors. One of its products had originated as a high-quality specialty and was manufactured to strict standards, including sanitary requirements. Later a volume market developed for a very similar product in a much less exacting field of use. Yet the control laboratory continued to employ the same strict standards, regardless of end use. With a quality level that was excessive in relation to actual use requirements, the volume product found it increasingly difficult to meet price competition.

The other case represented an extreme in the opposite direction. Because of numerous customer complaints, this firm introduced quality control, but with little conception of its significance. The method employed was 100 per cent inspection, but with no objective standards. In fact, the supervisor of the inspection crew was instructed to reject 3 per cent of the units produced each week, neither more nor less. This method was costly and ineffective and could scarcely be expected to lead to either a genuine improvement in the product or greater efficiency in production.

Both cases illustrate the need to begin with the market in designing appropriate quality control procedures. A study of each product in use would have disclosed the realistic requirements. An orderly method of recording, analyzing, and servicing complaints would provide a place to start. Rather than standardizing the percentage of rejects, it would be more to the point to standardize the number of complaints relative to volume of sales by adjusting the quality level upward or downward. The second company needed to apply objective procedures which would reduce the number of complaints to tolerable limits. The first company should actually have been concerned about the lack of complaints, which meant that it was producing a product which was both too perfect and too expensive for the particular need.

Marketing and Control Procedures.   The third pair of cases is concerned with internal records and controls. A large retail jeweler was burdened with paperwork which had little real bearing on operating problems. Procedures have a way of accumulating in old and well-established companies, and persisting after the operating heads have forgotten that they exist. In the jewelry trade a most laborious type of inventory records developed, based on the identification and registry of individual pieces. This method, appropriate to gems of great value, was gradually extended to each new line that was added, including some costume jewelry, plated silver, and handbags. Despite this elaborate set of records, there was little current information for the guidance of buyers in the store under study. New business forms had been adopted to cover each aspect of purchase and sales transactions until more than twenty were in use.

The other extreme in record keeping was represented by a manufacturer of specialty leathers. There was nothing resembling a perpetual inventory control, and the occasional physical inventories were scarcely more than a collection of estimates. Inventory continued to accumulate on some items which were being manufactured to stock, even though demand had been declining for several years. There were great variations in seasonal demand, item by item; and it seemed necessary to build up stocks months in advance of each peak. Capital was tied up in finished goods inventory, some of it of doubtful salability. Funds were lacking for effective purchasing of hides to take advantage of changes in the market. Management had attempted to improve its situation by instituting controls designed to reduce labor costs.

Solutions of both problems were attained without the use of extensive market surveys, although both were approached from a marketing viewpoint. The valuation of outputs, essential to the proper control of inputs, can sometimes be achieved by relatively simple means. One of the principal tools employed in these instances was sales analysis. The jewelry retailer agreed that there was little point in maintaining registry of pieces retailing for less than $30. Much to his surprise, an analysis of sales by size showed that 95 per cent of customer sales slips were for less than that amount, so that the items still requiring registry accounted for only 5 per cent of the sales transactions. Similarly, an analysis of the basic elements of both purchase and sales transactions showed that it was easily possible to standardize business forms, using only two as compared to more than ten times that number.

A somewhat more elaborate analytical procedure was followed in coping with the inventory problem of the leather manufacturer. An inventory control system was developed which would operate on the basis of advance orders, established seasonal patterns for each class of product, and daily records of production and shipment. The entire business of the previous year was then put through this system as a dry run. The result of this test was to confirm the judgment that the inventory actually required to run the business and give satisfactory service to customers was only one third as great as the existing inventory. This finding not only made possible a great improvement in the financial position of the firm but also laid the basis for new policies in purchasing, sales, and production.

Marketing Analysis and Organization Problems. The fourth pair of cases has to do with organization difficulties and the delegation of executive responsibility. One very large company sold its entire line of products through territorial salesmen, with a single important exception. Included in its line was a class of products formerly manufactured by an independent company which had been acquired twenty years before. Actually, this firm had never been fully absorbed but continued to operate like a company within a company. Its products were originally consumed by a single industry, and it was argued that only men specializing in this industry could supply it successfully. Territorial salesmen were not allowed to call on plants of this type, and the particular product division continued to maintain its own national sales force.

The second case, out of many involving organization difficulties, is selected because of an interesting parallel to the first case. It was another instance of an enclave or a semiautonomous unit persisting within a larger organization. A manufacturer had disposed of his entire output for many years through a single manufacturer's agent. Upon the death of the founder of the sales company, it was acquired by the manufacturer. The intention was to have it become the sales department of the producing company. Assimilation was not easy because some of the sales executives continued to maintain the viewpoint appropriate to a separate company. They saw their primary function as that of keeping their traditional customers happy while drawing on a single source of supply for this purpose. It was especially difficult for sales and production to see eye to eye on new product possibilities, particularly when their proper development might involve new channels of trade.

Both of these organization problems were resolved by extensive market surveys. In the first case, involving industrial selling entirely, interviews were made with buyers representing all classes of customer firms. The purpose was to find out what kind of service these buyers expected from suppliers and to decide on the type of sales organization best equipped to give it to them. The conclusion was in favor of an intensification of territorial selling, with product specialists on call when the salesmen needed help. As to the semiautonomous product division, the survey disclosed three trends which enabled management to see it in a new perspective. All of the companies in the industry served by the division were prospects for other products made by the company. Some of the leaders of this industry had expanded into new fields, so that it was no longer correct to regard them as belonging to a single industrial classification. Finally, some of the products originally sold to this group of firms only were now in demand in other industries.

In the case of the company absorbing the independent sales agency, it was found that the established methods and channels were still serving some segments of the market quite well, but missing the mark in others. While the company continued to enjoy a moderate growth in total sales, it was being outdistanced by competitors in some major new fields of use. The traditional distributors which the sales company had relied upon were not equipped to develop or serve these new markets. Appropriate changes were recommended in the sales program and sales organization. The real point of this story is that making policy from a marketing viewpoint does not necessarily mean relying on the judgment of the sales department. In the instance cited, the pressure for exploring broader marketing possibilities came from company executives whose background was in engineering and finance.

Marketing and Investment Planning. The final pair of cases deals with investment problems. They were chosen because of the contrasting attitudes of company executives. In one case it was recognized that investment decisions must rest eventually on marketing considerations, while in the other case it was not. The first company was one of the largest in the United States, long accustomed to gearing its tremendous operations to the market. It had developed a specialty product during the war which met certain needs of the military services. The demand was so great that a plant normally making other products was devoted exclusively to its production. After the war, this plant went back to its normal operations; and the question arose as to whether to invest millions of dollars in a plant to manufacture the new product. The problem was promptly defined as one of estimating the civilian demand for the product over the period required for the plant to pay for itself. An extensive market survey was undertaken, covering all the major fields of possible use. The survey results included a maximum and minimum estimate of the volume attainable within three years. These forecasts were considered under various assumptions as to the price of the product and the intensity of promotion. The minimum was only .40 per cent of the maximum. Even the minimum estimate, based on the most conservative assumptions, was so large that the proposed plant investment was amply justified.

The other case was that of a branch department store operating in a thriving suburban shopping center, but with indifferent success. A market survey, conducted at the instance of the landlord, indicated that the store was not living up to the potentialities of its location. Residents of the community appreciated the convenience of a neighborhood store but demanded goods of higher quality than this store provided. The survey results were shown to the department store manager. The landlord agreed to enlarge the store, maintaining the same percentage lease basis, if the manager would undertake the relatively minor investment of improving and expanding the assortment of goods the store offered. The manager was skeptical about the survey findings concerning the market area and said that they did not check with his knowledge of his own customers. When pressed, he fell back on the argument that his downtown buyers were not experienced in higher-priced merchandise lines and he could not afford to have two sets of buyers. The landlord and the manager could not get together, and the lease was canceled shortly thereafter when it came up for renewal. Another organization occupied the store and accepted the survey findings as the basis of their merchandising program. During their first year, they did four times as much business as the previous tenant had done the year before. Floor space has been increased three times to accommodate the steadily expanding business.

After this discussion of concrete instances, it remains to offer some general comments on the relation between marketing and management policy. Marketing is concerned with the primary output of a firm, which determines the outlook for its survival and growth. Marketing perspective is essential to the formulation of policy concerning production, finance, and engineering. Finally, the marketing viewpoint should enter into policy making with respect to some problems precipitated by indefinite growth and expansion. These are problems for the whole community as well as for business, involving nothing less than the destiny of our free market economy and our society.

MARKETING AND PRODUCTION

The mass-production industries of today have arisen out of economies of scale. It is possible to perform many operations at a much lower cost per unit if the operation is to be performed a thousand or a million times rather than ten or twenty. Economies of scale have been in the forefront of both economic theory and business thinking in recent decades. This principle is a convenient place to begin in considering the relations between marketing policy and production policy.

Scale of Production. There has been a tendency to regard economies of scale as a benefit accruing automatically as the size of business operations increases. Actually, the existence of a large volume of business under a single control does not in itself result in economies; it merely provides the opportunity to achieve them. Judgments as to the impact of economies of scale upon the individual firm or upon society as a whole have been both too optimistic and too pessimistic. Businessmen have too often assumed that if they could break into a specified volume range, costs would decline and profits increase. They often remark that there is nothing wrong with their company which cannot be fixed by an increase in volume. This cheerful outlook overlooks the fact that the achievement of economies of scale in certain phases of an operation may be accompanied by increases of cost in other phases. The most important example for our present purpose is the fact that the attainment of the volume which will result in the economies of large-scale production is often accompanied by large marketing expenditures to attain the necessary volume. It is true that the increase in marketing costs may often be less than the reduction in total cost. Nevertheless, there is little ground for the pessimistic view of economies of scale which has been expressed by some economic theorists. This is to the effect that the large firm, by achieving a much lower cost per unit, would soon be able to put all its small competitors out of business. The simple historic fact is that this gloomy prophecy has not been fulfilled, even though it has been made repeatedly for more than one hundred years.

There is an obvious and significant distinction between having plant capacity for a large volume of business and actually attaining that volume in any given year. Management must provide large capacity on the chance of achieving economies of scale; but capacity in itself merely represents large overhead costs, with constant uncertainty as to whether the volume will accrue to absorb these costs. The plant must operate close to capacity if the firm is to achieve the low production costs which it counted on in building the plant. Far from being able to rest securely in a monopolistic position, the management of such a firm is faced with a constant drive for volume to absorb its overhead.

This drive for volume tends to hold prices down to a competitive level established by other large firms with a similar need for volume. At the same time, it may push marketing costs up until the firm is obtaining only moderate profits and, frequently, a lower rate of profits than it earned when its volume of business was smaller. Marketing decisions must be made concerning the extent to which the economies achieved through mass production can be utilized in reducing prices and to what extent these funds must be used in advertising and selling as alternative methods of increasing volume. The decision will turn on the extent of substitutability of the products of the firm for the products of competitors. If there were perfect substitutability among all products used for the same general purpose, then the large firm would doubtless utilize the low cost of the product for drastic price decreases, which might then put all small competitors out of business.

For most of the products of mass production, substitutability is very imperfect indeed. To enlarge its market share, a firm must persuade more and more consumers who lie on the fringe of its market position to buy. They must be convinced that they obtain a better value in buying the standardized product, even though it does not fit their needs or preferences quite so well as some competitive products. It takes large sums of money to carry out such a program of mass persuasion. The more that has to be spent for the purpose, the less remains of the margin of price advantage, which may be one of the claims made for the product. Marketing judgments must balance these two considerations and try to find the most favorable combination of an actually greater value and mass persuasion to convince consumers that a greater value is being offered.

Market Segmentation. Another basic issue in the relations between marketing and production has to do with market segmentation and the degree to which the product will be differentiated to match differences in need and preferences from one segment to another. Assuming that there is a continuous range of variation as to the needs of consumers, the market for a given type of product might be divided into two, five, ten, or even more numerous segments. If only two product variations are offered, then it is obvious that differences in demand cannot be matched as precisely as if ten product variations were offered. Frequently, however, there is an inherent conflict in the requirements of marketing and production. The greater the range of product differentiation to meet consumer requirements, the less the opportunity to achieve economies of scale in production. Even assuming that all ten products can be made on the same machinery, there is a loss in efficiency in reducing the lot size and being obliged to make frequent changeovers in the plant from one product to another.

Sometimes, industries which grew up on the foundation of mass-production economies are obliged to dissipate these economies almost completely to meet variations in demand. Running a small lot through a plant built for continuous mass production is not the most efficient way of using plant equipment. It is the lesser of two evils, however, since the plant might be standing idle a large part of the time if it refused to make the various products demanded. The textile mills making upholstery fabrics provide an outstanding example of the dissipation of mass-production economies. At one time, looms could be set up to run for months at a time, with no variation in the pattern or color of the product. Today a plant that once made half a dozen patterns is making hundreds of variations in color and fabric. Each changeover from one lot to another is very expensive. Even though the loom is a prime example of mass-production equipment once it is set to run, a skilled worker has to tie some three thousand knots by hand in setting up the loom to run each new lot.

There are other mass-production industries which are somewhat more fortunate in their ability to adapt themselves to product variations. The first big automobile plants were operated on the assumption that any variations in the product would destroy the advantages of mass production. Today, improvement in production scheduling and in the control of both component parts and assembly make it possible for cars with many variations to roll in a steady stream from the same production line. The Ford Motor Company was known in the beginning for its rigid standardization on a single model. Today, it is said that Ford could produce a million and a half automobiles, no two of them exactly alike, without ever slowing up the production line. Somewhat similar achievements in production engineering have occurred in the great steel rolling mills. Several hundred variations in product can come off the rollers in the same day, without any interruption in the process. This result is achieved by a system of co-ordinated adjustments at various stages along the line as the new order reaches that stage in the process.

These partial reconciliations of marketing and production requirements are of great economic value and can doubtless be extended to many product fields. There are obvious limitations, depending on the character of product variations. Thus, while Ford might handle a million and a half variations in automobiles on the same assembly line, it obviously could not switch to refrigerators and then to watches and then back to cars again. The difficulty with the production of upholstery fabrics is that the switch from one lot to another in the character of the fabric is more like the change from automobiles to refrigerators than it is like a shift from blue to gray in the color of the automobile. For all mass-production industries, a cardinal issue of policy will continue to be that of market segmentation on the one hand versus economies of scale on the other.

The segmentation of a market can be made by geographic areas rather than by models of the product. The problem of whether to manufacture in a single large plant or in a number of smaller and scattered plants is largely a question of balancing transportation costs against the economies of mass production. Some economists have assumed that if production is to occur in decentralized plants, there is no economic justification for them to be under the control of a single firm. The weakness of this view is that it overlooks economies in marketing that can be achieved in a nation-wide operation. A unified sales organization supported by advertising through national media can sell a standardized product turned out by these localized plants more effectively than could be done by separate sales organizations and purely local advertising. Sometimes, however, decentralization of production is designed to meet marketing requirements as well as production requirements. The local plant may be able to give prompter and more individualized service to its major customers. In some cases, both production and marketing are rather fully decentralized, so that the economic advantage of the large concern lies in financial considerations and centralized staff services for research and planning.

Importance of Production. A basic aim of management in most firms is the stabilization of production. Marketing programs are generally designed with this objective in mind. Production usually involves a larger number of workers as well as a much greater amount of fixed investment. It is better for the fluctuations and uncertainties of the market place to register their impact on marketing costs rather than on production costs. Stability of production in the short range requires production scheduling. Stability in the long range requires investment planning. The attempt to achieve these requisites of stable production may result in large expenditures on the marketing side, either on a regular or on an emergency basis.

Another reason for giving priority to the operating problems of production is the conservation of materials. Marketing contributes to this end by foreseeing demand and cutting down on the production of unwanted items. It also helps to keep finished goods inventory at reasonable levels, thus reducing inventory losses and the cost of carrying inventory. Keeping inventory within the limitations required by service to customers helps to remove a speculative element from business inherent in the possibility of major changes in demand or supply.

Importance of Marketing. While there are all these reasons for giving priority to stability in production, management should not lose sight of the fact that the values achieved in production rest to a large extent on marketing decisions and marketing effort. Neither should the opportunity to reduce marketing costs be overlooked. The definition of the marketing task must take account of the fixed requirements of production. Once the marketing task is specified, functional analysis can be utilized, in order that the task may be performed as economically as possible.

There are some areas in which marketing economies should be given prior consideration. This would apply to products for which production costs are relatively small, such as packaged products in the drug and cosmetic fields. The largest possible savings in production might not be a critical factor in deciding the price at which such a product should be sold or the way it should be presented to consumers. Firms in this field must have a sound marketing program, first of all, in order to survive. Actually, many well-known companies in the drug and cosmetic industry are strictly marketing organizations, which have their products manufactured for them by someone else. It is true that they forego a manufacturing profit under this arrangement, but that is a minor loss compared to freeing themselves from manufacturing problems and financial hazards in order to concentrate on marketing. There are a number of other fields in which a company which plans to erect its own production facilities eventually may depend on outside production at the time a new product is launched. This policy is indicated when the market hazards are so great that a major plant investment might not pay off.

In summary, it might be said that marketing necessarily takes the lead in solving the issues that arise between marketing and production. In some cases the first concern of policy is stability and economy in production through appropriate marketing decisions. In other industries, where the cost structure is very different, it is appropriate for marketing to solve its own problems first because of the much greater magnitude of marketing costs and risks.

MARKETING AND FINANCE

The subject of finance is concerned with the value of assets as compared to the preoccupation of marketing with the value of products. The first principle to be recognized in relating marketing and finance is that these two sets of values are not independent. The value of assets rests on the actual or potential output of products which can be achieved through their use. The term "product" is used here to embrace all of the aspects of utility which an article has when it reaches the hands of the ultimate consumer. The assets involved in producing this utility consist of the capacity to market goods as well as the capacity to produce them. Assets employed in manufacturing are easier to evaluate, since they consist in large part of physical plant and equipment. The asset value of a well-integrated sales organization, with good morale based on an experience of success, has no value as collateral in floating a loan and, until quite recently, has had little recognition in financial analysis. The new emphasis on evaluating the market position of a firm and its ability to generate future sales may be regarded as a postwar phenomenon. This type of analysis is now frequently undertaken in considering mergers or acquisitions. The fact that statistical studies show that a high percentage of mergers have failed to live up to advance expectations is doubtless due in part to the very casual attention to marketing which was once prevalent in financial evaluation.

Both finance and marketing are concerned with the growth aspects of firms, the one from the standpoint of an expanding market position and the other from that of the accumulation of assets needed in transacting a larger volume of business. In financial terms, a firm can grow in two principal ways. One is to finance its growth by retaining some of the earnings generated by the company's operations. The other is to acquire either new capital or new assets from the outside. This growth from external sources may be effected by issues of stocks and bonds, followed by the purchase of the necessary equipment; or it can be effected by merger and the exchange of stock between two companies.

Growth through Retained Earnings.   Growth through retained earnings has been criticized by economists as tending to remove from the market place some of the crucial decisions about the allocation of resources. Theoretically, if a company had to finance all expansion through the capital market, a sounder allocation would be made to precisely those users who were able to outbid all others in their demand for capital. First of all, it is obvious that small enterprise could seldom obtain its initial capital in this way. The owner or manager, by putting up his own funds, has a commitment to make the business succeed which is essential to its survival during the period of establishment. Even though a business may be well along its way toward gaining a solid foothold, it does not always have access to the public market for capital. The uncertainties may be too great and the integrity and drive of the management too dominant a consideration for capital to be obtained from outside sources. The chief way in which any small business can grow at all, therefore, is by financing growth through retained earnings. There are something like eleven hundred stocks listed on the New York Stock Exchange, or only a tiny fraction of all the companies which are interested in continued growth. Even among these listed stocks, most of the activity pertains to those of a few giant corporations.

These very large companies also depend to a considerable extent on retained earnings in financing expansion, but for a somewhat different set of reasons. Of paramount importance are the tax laws in inducing corporate management to retain earnings rather than paying out the entire net earnings in dividends and then seeking capital funds for expansion. Retained surplus, within the legal limits, is subject to corporate taxes only, whereas dividends paid out and then reinvested are subject to both corporate taxes and personal taxes. The large company does not necessarily reinvest retained surplus in its own operations. Many companies have large portfolios of other stocks. Thus the criterion of a free market choice is at least partially observed, since a company treasurer and its board of directors will tend to invest surplus funds as profitably as possible, whether the assets they represent are used in the same company or in other companies. A large corporation is to some degree eliminating the middleman in its financial operations. That is to say that it generates large amounts of capital which it allocates to the most profitable uses available, without pouring it into the capital market and then calling it back to meet future uses.

This tendency in corporate policy is supported and reinforced by the prevailing attitudes of individual investors. Perhaps the majority are less interested in dividends than in increased values which can provide capital gains. The tax laws are again responsible for the predominant interest in capital gains. Since the owners of stocks want to see a company increase the value of its assets through growth, there is a constant pressure on management to move into new markets and to pioneer technical developments. The result is a highly competitive economy with moderate dividend rates, a constant drive for expansion, and a large part of total income being reinvested to support expansion. The specialist in finance who long ignored the marketing side of business now indirectly helps to generate the pressure which makes marketing the crucial aspect of business today. The tax and fiscal policies of the government also support this trend, although they were not designed for this purpose.

Growth through New Capital.   The same forces are at work in a somewhat different way when a company requires outside capital for expansion. Many companies have growth goals which cannot be financed entirely from the inside because they call for a rate of growth which could not be sustained with retained earnings alone. For these companies, marketing considerations can play an important part in the effort to obtain new capital. To get money from outside investors, a firm must be well known to the public. Some companies have been engineering research. The marketing staff provides the chan. which the engineer can make contact with the needs and pret consumers. Just as the manufacturer needs retail stores as ou his product, so the engineering staff must rely on the marketin, as an outlet for the technical possibilities at its command. As a t. engineering and marketing are concerned with expanding technolo and changing markets and the best possible adjustment of one to th other.

Some leading companies have become increasingly concerned about the co-ordination of technical and marketing research. It is no longer regarded as efficient to complete a program of technical research resulting in a new product design and then to start a program of market research to find out how and where to sell the new product. The two types of research must work together from the inception of the product idea until its successful introduction on the market. A series of five steps has been suggested by B. F. Bowman as a convenient way of laying out such a co-ordinated program. These stages move from preliminary explorations through test marketing to the final launching of a full-scale marketing and production program. At each stage, there are essential activities on both the technical and the marketing side.

Aspects of Co-ordination. While seeking co-ordination of marketing and technical research, there must be room for each to develop according to its own best possibilities. Neither one should be put in a strait jacket by being made too closely dependent on the other. At least three approaches can be observed in the engineering research of large companies, each having its most appropriate field of use. At the extremes are the basic research approach and the customer service approach. Some companies have emphasized basic research, assuming that the best results would be obtained by recruiting the finest talent available and giving it broad freedom for investigation in a general area. The expectation here is that discoveries and designs of novelty and value will emerge from time to time and that only the ideas of obvious merit will be considered for market introduction.

The customer service approach starts with the problems or complaints of individual customers and tries to develop new products or product improvements to meet customers' requirements. While this approach would appear on the surface to be one of matching technical skill directly against customer needs, it has serious disadvantages in many situations. The design which satisfies an individual customer may be so specialized that it cannot be sold to many other customers. The cost of developing the design may be so great that neither the

able to establish a public prestige which is out of proportion either to their size or to a cold-blooded evaluation of their relative prospects. Among the instruments which have been used in achieving standing with the public are public relations, institutional advertising, and product promotion. A management with a good public relations sense uses every favorable development to build up a public image of itself which leads to confidence. Some companies succeed in getting capital funds relatively cheaply year after year. That is to say that they attract the money they need without paying out large dividends, although dividend payments are a factor of some importance in creating public interest in a company. Some of these companies early saw the value of institutional advertising and have spent large appropriations which were ostensibly aimed at customers for products but ultimately were directed at the purchasers of stock.

A refinement of this procedure is to advertise products but to make each product advertisement serve an institutional purpose. The product is presented as an example of the scientific ingenuity and management skill which the company exhibits in its operations generally. It may be described as one of a family of products, each offering exceptional values to the industrial or household consumer. This use of product promotion as an aspect of a financial program, in turn, determines in some degree the company's marketing and product development program. Consumer products are more potent than industrial products in making a company known to the public. A company which derives its income largely from industrial markets may produce or sell one or more consumer products as a means of attaining public recognition. There is also a tendency for its financial policies to push a company in the direction of novel and newsworthy products. A new product may do more to gain prestige and, eventually, financial support than a much larger volume of sales in ordinary products.

Growth through Acquisition of Assets. Another way in which a large company continues to expand is by acquiring the assets of small companies. If the small company fits neatly into the established growth program of a larger company, its acquisition may represent a great saving in time as compared with the same expansion achieved from the inside. Acquisitions are frequently advantageous to both sides from a financial viewpoint. The larger firm, in effect, pays for the acquisition out of income generated by the new assets. The owners of the small firm may obtain a substantial amount of money which is subject to the capital gains tax only and which it would take many years to accumulate out of current income.

The tendency of firms of moderate size to sell out to larger companies is having an important effect on the size distribution of firms in the United States. Much of the uneasiness about the concentration of economic power and apparent trend toward monopoly is the result of this phenomenon. In many cases the initiative is on the side of the large firm looking to acquisitions in the effort to meet the pressure for steadily expanding sales. In other cases the initiative is exercised by the management of a smaller firm which has built up substantial productive assets but may no longer be interested in the day-to-day operation of the firm. This state of mind may result from the fact that the head of the firm is nearing retirement age. In other cases the deliberate aim is to build up an operation which some larger firm would be willing to buy. In getting ready to offer a company for sale, managements have been known to make drastic changes in policy, such as reducing prices and taking on new marketing channels in order to build up volume as quickly as possible while looking for a buyer.

Reference was made in an earlier chapter to the presumption of immortality implicit in the corporate form of organization. It may be that the true immortals consist of the limited number of large firms which are nationally known and whose shares are regularly traded on the stock exchange. Smaller companies, even though they adopt the corporate form of organization, may turn out to be mortal after all. In our present fiscal climate, there are thousands of small and moderate-sized firms in existence at any one time, because new ones are constantly being created. Only a very few of these will ever grow large enough to join the select circle of the great corporations. Of those which show enough vitality to survive the difficult periods of establishment and expansion, the great majority may disappear as independent entities by the route of acquisition. If this be true, it need not mean that the economy as a whole is any less effective or competitive. Earlier versions of the theory of the firm made the company the reflection of a single individual known as the "entrepreneur." A firm which survives only during the active career of an individual or a small group of principals is quite consistent with this earlier conception of business enterprise. Thus the dynamics of economic development involves continued interaction between the financial status of individuals and the marketing operations of firms. The resulting economic system is a mixed system in the sense that it consists of a limited number of large organizations, which may be expected to survive for the indefinite future, and many thousands of smaller organizations, which serve important marketing

nd financial objectives both while they are operating and as they c o operate.

MARKETING AND ENGINEERING

Of the many staff activities which are a part of modern busi engineering is the oldest and possibly the most universal today. Ma ing covers both staff and line activities, on the staff side being cerned with market research and market planning. These relati new staff activities have had to make a place for themselves in a bus environment in which the engineering staff was already well establis As in nearly all other phases of organization activities, the engine staff and the marketing staff are partly competitive and partly con mentary. The engineers in a company, aside from their functior plant maintenance or product design, have usually been recogr as the group specifically trained for systematic planning. As the ma ing staff has progressed from fact finding to planning and prol solving, it has brought a new point of view and a competitive clain the confidence of management. The potential conflict between staff groups which are not competing for line authority should n difficult to resolve. Each is bringing its own technical perspecti problems of planning and policy making. Their joint aim is to illum these problems, which they should be able to do without was duplication of effort and with a useful difference in emphasis.

The Need for Co-ordination. If the marketing staff and th gineering staff can work as a unified team, they can be the spear for company growth and expansion. As a member of this team, appropriate for the marketing man to assume that his fundamenta is to find adequate outlets for the engineering and production ski his company. These skills are usually embodied in products as a n of harnessing them to demand, but the product is the vehicl technology. Its command of technical know-how is what the com really has to sell.

A corresponding attitude on the part of the research engineer v be that of being engaged in helping consumers and industrial solve their problems. While there is a place for some research basic or general character in a large company, engineering resear concerned with application. Usually, there are many more probler a technical nature than could be scheduled for effective work b engineering staff. The assignment of priorities to problems reg; as of a higher degree of urgency is paramount in the manageme

supplier nor the customer is willing to absorb it. The customer is not always competent to define his own needs, and a better solution might be discovered by approaching the problem in a more general way.

The intermediate approach is probably the one which is more suitable in the majority of situations. It might be designated as the "selected problem approach." That is to say that out of a screening of ideas from customers and the technical staff, but with over-all guidance from marketing research, certain problems are given priority as the ones which will meet the needs of the greatest number of customers or which offer the greatest potential volume for business. Engineering research is assigned these selected problems, which are broader than problems of particular customers but more specific than those which might be identified from the viewpoint of basic research. A continuous process of screening to identify these selected problems may often result in the definition of whole families of related problems. Where this is true, research of a more basic nature may be undertaken in the underlying field to facilitate the solution of individual problems.

BUSINESS GROWTH AND PUBLIC POLICY

The marketing view of business activity presented in this book is closely linked with a philosophy of economic expansion and innovation. Attempts of businessmen to solve their problems in the market tend inevitably to increase the scale or modify the character of their operations. Growth and change solve some problems for the firm but tend to precipitate other problems. The growth of business in the aggregate creates problems for the whole economy which are the proper concern of public policy and hence of public-spirited business executives. Growth seems often to go through alternating phases, which might be called "hypertrophy" and "compensation." Instead of growing steadily and equally in all directions at once, a system may exhibit a burst of growth in a single direction which may persist for a considerable period of time. Sometimes, this drive seems to get out of control, carrying the organism or the behavior system further and further away from a condition of adjustment to the environment. The "normal" tendency, in the sense that it contributes to the survival and adjustment of the system, is for compensating forces to intervene to offset a lopsided development. A business firm may undergo a rapid development in the field of engineering research because of the competence and drive of the members of the engineering department. They may develop new ideas much faster than the firm is able to put them to use in salable products. Usually, there comes a time in such a development when the marketing activities of the firm will have to be strengthened, so that there will be a better balance between engineering and production. Unless this is done, the steady drive in engineering research will eventually grind to a stop because the business is not generating enough income to support it.

Growth by compensating phases is typical of fast-growing marketing organizations. This may be due partly to the inescapable limits of time and executive talent, since making genuine progress in even a single aspect of a great enterprise can well occupy all the attention of the top executive group for a considerable period. The compensating phase of growth is directed toward filling in or rounding out the activities of the organization. In a sense, it is the sustained drive, which first carries the system out of balance, that creates the need for the other organization elements or activities. In many cases, there is a constant struggle for a balanced structure which is never quite achieved as long as the system continues to grow. This fact may be illustrated by the example of a small city which makes a determined effort to attract new industry in order to achieve a higher level of employment. If this effort succeeds, the new plants may require more workers than the community can provide. Once the plants are built, attention must be shifted to new problems, such as the building of homes and schools and the requirements for civic planning and administration which have been created by industrial development.

One of the forces which brings about invention and innovation of all kinds is the stresses set up in a system because of unbalanced development. An incomplete and unbalanced system of action is prepared to accept and utilize the elements which will complete the system. The new element has to appear on the scene in some manner in order to be selected for survival as part of the balanced system. The elements available for selection are drawn from various sources. They may be borrowed or imitated from the neighboring tribe, the principal competitor, or the family next door. On the other hand, the new development may appear as an original act of invention on the part of someone inside the system who senses the need and works out the means for gratifying it.

Habitability of the Environment. The activities of any economic system react upon its surroundings and may affect the habitability of the environment. Habitability is the capacity of the environment to sustain life or promote survival for this or any similar behavior system. The reaction to the system may be reflected in a steady tendency toward decreasing habitability. In some fortunate cases the trend is in the other direction. Boulding regards the tendency to foul the environment and eventually render it unfit for habitation as almost universal. Primitive agriculture in many places meant slashing and burning an area in the forest and then moving on after a few years of cultivation had exhausted the soil. This type of patch agriculture for the growing of corn is still practiced in Central America. It may have been the basic cause of the migratory character of the Maya civilization, which built one large city after another, only to abandon each in turn after a few generations.

In modern times the westward migration of cotton agriculture before the Civil War illustrates declining habitability because of the adverse reaction of behavior groups on the capacity of their environment to promote survival. Industries foul streams by the discharge of waste or otherwise make an area less healthy or attractive to the people that industry needs. Los Angeles provides a spectacular example of a city which attracted masses of people because of its climate but lost some of its climatic advantage bacause of the smog resulting from the activities growing out of having so many people in the area.

Habitability declines most disastrously because of the exhaustion of resources upon which activity was based. The ghost towns in mining regions and the barren wastes of cut-over timber lands are the aftermath of great activity at some earlier time. The greatest crime of colonialism in many parts of the world is that it brought native populations into concentrated settlements to exploit some natural resource and then left these populations stranded when the resource was exhausted. Such exploitation of resources is destructive because the promoters had no intention of making a permanent residence in the area and the natives gave up their previous method of making a living without realizing that the new way of life could be only temporary. Similar problems can be found much nearer home. The government of the state of Pennsylvania is concerned just now about stranded populations in the coal regions who no longer obtain adequate employment in the mines and are difficult to resettle either by migration or by the development of new industries in their home territory.

While the reaction of behavior groups on an environment is too often of an adverse character, it can also result in increasing habitability. The introduction of irrigation, the terracing of hillsides to conserve the soil, and the more advanced methods of modern agriculture illustrate this tendency. Conservation methods of many kinds are directed toward less wasteful use of resources that cannot be replaced and some form of cultivation or management of resources which can replace themselves under favorable conditions. The forest industries of the Pacific Northwest are struggling to reach a point of balance at which the new growth will about offset the annual cut. Oyster beds are maintained on a permanent basis in Chesapeake Bay, and streams are constantly being restocked with fish throughout the country.

These considerations are important to marketing in two respects. On the one hand, the location of people and industrial activities determines the task that is to be performed by marketing channels. Investment in marketing facilities should take account of future decline or expansion, area by area. There is also a more direct parallel in that marketing activities can react on the population which constitutes the market in such a way as to foreclose opportunities on the one hand or conversely to open them up more rapidly. Laws against false advertising, as well as many other aspects of trade regulation and the activities of such groups as the Better Business Bureau, are all directed toward restraining marketing organizations from fouling the environment for themselves and others. A substantial part of the promotional and service activities of large marketing organizations is directed toward keeping the customer sold after the sale has been made. Dissatisfied customers may be regarded as a form of infection in the market environment which is likely to ruin prospects for further sales.

From another viewpoint, it may be said that the environment should never be regarded as a static concept, but is constantly being redefined in terms of new technology available within the behavior system. Ores which were thrown away at an earlier stage become valuable under new methods of refining. Other mineral resources are disregarded altogether, until new discoveries make them useful in alloys. Aspects of the environment which have no meaning for one form of culture become vital distinctions in the geography of a region under another. A classic illustration is provided by Preston James in discussing the geography of Argentina. So long as the great central plain was largely devoted to wheat growing, it seemed to be all of about the same character. When cattle raising became an important industry, there turned out to be a dividing line of critical importance running north and south through the middle of this region. Cattle-tick infestation was common on one side of the line but not on the other, because of moderate differences in climate which had not materially affected the yield of wheat. Thus, it can be said that the same geographical region was two quite different environments from the standpoint of the wheat grower and the cattle grower.

In general, new technologies increase the resources available for human activity, although they may also cause precipitate changes in the location of industry. The ability to use what was once an inferior resource, which enjoys the advantage of being close to market, may react against an area with good resources with a long haul to market. New technologies can also lead to a decline in habitability because they mean a more rapid extraction and hence exhaustion of resources. Technological advantage may be regarded as a hopeful trend, but it points toward a tempered optimism. The current faith in the wonders of science is too ready to assume that miracles of invention and discovery will always be able to get mankind out of the tight spots it gets into through careless and wasteful exploitation of resources. Just now, it is easy to assume that atomic energy will replace oil, coal, and water power in time, so that there is no cause to be concerned about conservation of these resources.

One flaw in this reasoning is that human activities may come to be limited by some of the simple and basic requirements for life which we tend to take for granted as free goods. A prime example is water for consumer and industrial use. There are some leading American cities for which further growth seems problematic because there are no means of meeting the added demand for water. The industrial development possibilities of many regions are limited to activities which are not major consumers of water. The gradual dropping of the water table in most sections of the United States may spell trouble in the long run for agriculture as well as for urban development. The consequences for marketing lie in the dislocation of marketing channels and the decline of sales in the areas most affected. Marketing may also play a part in the efforts to make good the deficit. Numerous inventions will be made for the purpose of utilizing limited water supplies more effectively or for tapping such resources as sea water. These devices will be adopted and become effective over a considerable period, with continuous interaction between market exploration and product development.

Part of our public philosophy in the United States is that capitalism or the free market economy confers greater benefits on its participants than any possible alternative. The preservation of the values that are presumably inherent in the free market is a goal which is accepted by most citizens. The goal of maintaining free competition appears more complicated when it is recognized that one of the essential freedoms is freedom to compete in organizing a market. The question arises as to whether competitive efforts at market organization can lead to a change in structure such that free competition will largely disappear.

The Fate of Our Economy According to Marx. The idea that capitalism is doomed and must eventually follow early forms of organization such as feudalism into oblivion has been maintained by both the enemies and the friends of capitalism. Specific examples of particular interest are Karl Marx on one side and Joseph Schumpeter on the other. Marx, a deadly foe of capitalism, believed that it would destroy itself by carrying certain inherent tendencies to their inevitable conclusion. Schumpeter was one of the most conservative of economists in his general social viewpoint and in his advocacy of the essential values of capitalism. Many of the practices which other economists condemned as monopolistic appeared to Schumpeter as only part of the essential and beneficent processes of economic development. He too maintained in one of his latest and best-known works that capitalism would pass, but this he regarded as a calamity rather than a crowning achievement of irresistible historical forces.

Marx formed his critical ideas concerning capitalism in the mid-nineteenth century, based on observation of what turned out to be the relatively modest beginnings of free enterprise as compared to the gigantic corporations which are so important in the economic structure today. Reasoning from a conception of the inevitable logic of history, Marx foretold the rise of an industrial proletariat to supreme power. This was to be the final stage in the long story of the class struggle by which the rising middle classes had overthrown feudalism and the workers were destined to destroy capitalism. An essential part of this train of argument is what Marx called "the principle of capitalist accumulation." That was the idea that big firms would always destroy or displace small firms, until the concentration of integrated power became monopolistic, industry by industry. Once each industry, or possibly the whole economy, was under the control of one huge monopoly, the remaining one issue would be that of control and the consequences of control with respect to sharing the output of industry. As the monopolies became more firmly entrenched, they would necessarily become more oppressive, building up a pressure of resistance which could find no outlet except in revolutionary overthrow. Once the proletariat took over, the political machinery of the state would wither away because there would no longer be any essential difference between government and industry, or any need for external control of industrial operations, since management would be in the hands of the workers.

Nothing which has happened in the world since that time does Marx much credit as a prophet. As industry has become stronger, the worker has experienced better conditions rather than degenerating into abject poverty and near-slavery, as Marx predicted. It is true that the larger enterprises now operate on a scale which would have staggered the imagination of Marx or his contemporaries. It is also true that in an economy such as that of the United States the total number of independent firms has not declined but continues to increase year after year at about the same rate as the increase in population. Instead of regarding themselves as a downtrodden class preparing for the ultimate violent struggle, the majority of workers are conservative in their political and economic views and recognize their great stake in the continued advance of industry.

Turning to Russia, it is almost equally difficult to find any indication that the ultimate solution forecast by Marx is getting any closer. A new governing class has risen to power under the ideological umbrella of the "dictatorship of the proletariat." There is no evidence whatever that this dictatorship will pass or that this new elite will suddenly agree at some indefinite date in the future to surrender its privileges. In fact, there is considerable continuity between the old ruling class and the present one because of the dominant position the army occupies in Russia today. Many army officers and their families represent a continuation of the old aristocratic tradition carried forward from the officers' corps of the Czar's army. Instead of the leveling influence which had been predicted, differences in income and status in Russia today are steadily widening, so that currently the income distribution of the people is not very different from that in the United States. In many fields, such as taxation and labor relations, Russia may be regarded as being far to the right, rather than to the left, of policies prevailing in the United States.

The Fate of Our Economy According to Schumpeter. The criticism of Schumpeter is harder to meet, coming as it does from one with a deep understanding and sympathy for modern capitalism. He did not expect to see capitalism fall apart but predicted instead that it would be carried forward into a new and different type of structure because of its own tolerance and, indeed, encouragement of innovation. In a free society in which there is unrestrained freedom to innovate, he foresaw that the changes devised or advocated at various levels might carry capitalistic society far away from its natural foundations. There is always the possibility that freedom will be exercised to give up freedom, or that political innovation can take the form of prohibiting or restricting many types of economic innovation.

At the level of the national economy, it is impossible to draw a sharp line of distinction between political and economic power. Individuals or interest groups struggle for status or differential advantage within the system as a whole. As long as a secure position or a margin of an advantage can be obtained, few are really concerned as to whether the advantage is economic or political in its ultimate nature. Economic organizations use political means wherever available to gain their ends. Not only the large corporations seek favors from government, but representatives from small business as well are continuously advocating legislation to obtain advantages for their clients. Politicians use various means to maintain themselves in power, including that of currying favor with economic organizations which can provide the sinews of war for their political campaigns. Nearly all agree that free and untrammeled economic competition is a good thing in general. Few believe that there is any need for intensification of the competition faced by themselves.

Year after year, there is a constant flow of legislation changing the framework within which business must operate. While the character of this legislation may differ in detail under a conservative or a liberal administration, the volume of it continues unabated. The flood of legislation designed to regulate economic activity poses a dilemma whereby the dire prophecies of Schumpeter could be fulfilled in one direction or the other. Assume, on the one hand, that legislation of this type is badly needed, because it is necessary to curb the power of the larger economic organizations which might organize the market to suit their special interests. In that case the attempt to preserve the free market by legislation may be too little and too late. The consequences of economic action may already have been carried so far that no law can prevent or remedy the damage. For example, it might be easier to preserve small business while it was still vigorous than it would be to resuscitate small enterprise after great segments of it had been wiped out or absorbed by its large competitors.

Assume, on the other hand, that much of this political action is mistaken. Suppose that it rests on an inadequate conception of how the economy really works. Historians feel that political and economic systems have fallen in the past because they were never really understood by their principal beneficiaries. Thus, many of those today who have been loudest in proclaiming their devotion to a system of capitalism or free enterprise may have little understanding of how competition operates in producing its beneficent economic results. Certainly, the view of these processes which is here designated as "functionalism," and which stresses the central role of differential advantage, is distinctly different from the view of competition underlying many of the present or proposed laws for regulating economic activity. The essential mechanism of economic progress, as first made plain by Schumpeter, consists of the constant drive toward a unique and secure market position, which has generally been categorized and condemned as a tendency toward monopoly. What seems like an essential attempt to restore balance under one view appears under another to strike at the very heart of the system governed by individual incentives.

The Fate of Our Economy According to Roos.   Much political and regulative action has been directed toward economic stability, particularly as a result of the deep economic depression suffered in the United States and in most countries around the world in the early thirties. Stabilization as a goal is not entirely consistent with the goal of vigorous and continuous growth. As a matter of fact, much of the economic discussion at that time accepted the relative stagnation of the mature economy as a basic premise. So much has happened in the past twenty years to expand the scale of economic activity and to proliferate both business opportunities and the consumer's way of life as to make the economic structure of the thirties seem very immature by comparison. The question remains as to whether policies left over from those days are placing a harmful curb on the continuous growth in productivity. Charles Roos, a well-known economist, contends that this is what has happened. He says that some of our regulative agencies, such as the Federal Reserve Board, are making economic policy on the assumption that it is adequate to maintain a 2 per cent annual growth rate in per capita production. He contrasts this situation with that of Russia, where informed opinion holds that annual productivity is increasing at a rate of at least 7 per cent. He raises the question of whether political action directed toward the maintenance of economic stability might turn the United States into a second-rate power by persisting in policies which would slow down growth in productive capacity. In a free economy the productive power of the nation as a whole is the sum total of the capacity of the individual productive units which constitute the economy. The Communist critic of capitalism believes that it is always vulnerable in terms of the threat of depression and chronic unemployment. It might turn out that we had made an unhappy choice indeed if, in the effort to avoid fluctuations, we halted the rise in economic productivity, out of which all improvement in our way of life must come. It would be much harder to catch up once we had legislated or regulated ourselves into stagnation than it might be to stay abreast in the beginning. These questions are tied up with the military security of the United States, since the nation which we regard as most likely to be the enemy in case of war is also the one which threatens to catch up with us or to take the lead in the expansion of productive capacity.

The Viewpoint of Functionalism.   Functionalism provides a middle way concerning our political and economic future. It does not accept the extremes of *laissez faire* on the one hand or of the inevitable development of a socialistic state on the other. It visualizes instead a continuous process of reorganization, in line with continuous expansion and functional differentiation. Just as geographical assignment of functions may undergo steady change in an expanding trading area, so the assignment of functions between private enterprise and government must change steadily if balance is to be maintained. Meanwhile, government policies should be less concerned about curbing monopoly than with the avoidance of government action which contributes to the creation of monopoly. Genuine monopoly power in an advanced economy can hardly exist except on the basis of special rights conferred on business firms or other organizations by the government.

A national policy geared to the basic goal of expanding productive capacity would be an interesting alternative to one which placed exclusive emphasis on economic stability. If the resources of government could be added to those of private enterprise in removing the obstacles to further economic growth, it is conceivable that our annual increases in productivity might be two or three times what they are today. Given such a continuous thrust toward the expansion of productive capacity, a substantial contribution to stability might be achieved as a by-product. The momentum of the upward movement might be sufficient to avoid downturns if government and business were collaborating fully in a program of expansion. The role of government under such a policy would be to undertake projects which were beyond the scope of individual enterprise or to act as a facilitating agency in overcoming obstacles which proved too formidable to be overcome by individual and unorganized attack. This type of policy might mean less antitrust regulation but more developments like the Tennessee Valley Authority. It might mean less concern about the curse of bigness, but a greatly expanded system of staff services for small enterprise, something like the system of experiment stations and county agents by which government has given encouragement and support to agriculture. It might mean a declining use of tariffs and restrictions to protect American business against foreign competition, and more active government leadership in assisting business to develop export markets.

Certainly, it should mean a more explicit recognition that the skills and knowledge of our people constitute our most fundamental resource.

This should lead to a far more liberal attitude toward the support of education, with government participation and leadership in creating educational facilities and promoting the kind of training which an expanding economy requires in increasing measure. It is estimated by students of the Russian economy that Russia is spending at least four times as large a percentage of its national income on education as is the United States. Because of our greater wealth, we still have a larger proportion of our young people receiving education at the college level. The Russians, however, are currently turning out half again as many scientists and twice as many engineers annually as we are. We will need to double our facilities for college education in the next twenty years if we are to keep pace with the thrust of dynamic technology.

What are the essential values of a free enterprise system which we should be vigilant to maintain despite the changes which will involve increasing collaboration of government and business at certain crucial points? We want freedom of choice for the consumer and freedom of enterprise for the business organization. Freedom of choice for the consumer begins with freedom to select the merchandise that he considers most suitable for his needs from adequate and conveniently located retail assortments. This freedom to choose stands as a symbol for an even more fundamental principle—that is, the right of every individual to have a part in defining the basic values of life so far as he is concerned. No matter how lavish the way of life which a successful dictatorship might eventually provide, it would be built on a fallacy if the individual had no part in determining this pattern. There is little likelihood, actually, that a dictatorship can ever provide a superior way of life for the individual, since this freedom of self-determination is so basic for the acceptance of innovation and the gradual expansion of the physical basis of life. Every individual, similarly, needs the opportunity to perform in a framework which gives him a chance to develop and make effective use of whatever creative talent he may possess. So long as the system provides adequate freedom for the individual, both in living and in earning a living, it makes relatively little difference by what label the system is called.

SELECTED REFERENCES

CLARK, JOHN MAURICE. *Alternative to Serfdom.* New York: Alfred A. Knopf, 1948.

BAUMOL, WILLIAM J. *Welfare Economics and the Theory of the State.* Cambridge, Mass.: Harvard University Press, 1952.

KAPLAN, ABRAHAM D. H. *Big Enterprise.* Washington, D.C.: Brookings Institution, 1954.

OGLE, M. B.; SCHNEIDER, and WILEY. *Power, Order and the Economy.* New York: Harper & Bros., 1954.

VOGT, WILLIAM. *Road to Survival.* New York: William Sloane Associates, Inc., 1948.

WALES, HUGH G. (ed.). *Changing Perspectives in Marketing.* Urbana: University of Illinois Press, 1954.

GRETHER, E. T.; VAILE, R. S.; and COX, R. *Marketing in the American Economy.* New York: Ronald Press, 1952.

In the book cited, Clark makes a plea for greater responsibility on the part of businessmen in a society which gives them considerable action. As a student of welfare economics, Baumol illuminates the problem of building a bridge between business policy and government policy.

Kaplan expresses a generally optimistic view of the place of big business in an expanding economy. Ogle, Schneider, and Wiley survey some critical contemporary problems of policy, both national and international.

Vogt is a conservationist with a pessimistic view as to what is happening to world resources. He is cited in connection with the discussion of habitability in this chapter.

The last two references illustrate the development of a broad perspective on public policy in the marketing field. The volume edited by Wales grew out of the first Paul D. Converse Award symposium. Grether, Vaile, and Cox are marketing teachers whose textbook reflects both broad theoretical grasp and participation in numerous research projects.

INDEX

INDEX

Rothschild, Kurt, 103
Routinization
  credit phase, 299
  durable goods, 301
  lease, 302
  prepacking, 303
  problems, 301
  reaction against, 311–15
  types, 297

S

Sales organization
  asset value, 457
  construction, 373
  sales assignments basis, 375
  sales coverage plans, 373
  sales plan presentation, 440
Samuelson, Paul A., 80, 258
Schiff, Michael, 320
Schneider, Louis, 474
Schrecker, Paul, 351
Schumpeter, Joseph A., 267, 291, 468, 469
Search theory, 410
Second survival theorem, 56
Sellers, market organization power, 333
Seriality, 75
Set theory, 225
Shannon, Claude E., 47, 48, 64, 176
Shelford, V. E., 63
Shils, E. A., 33
Shopping
  brand loyalty, 182, 278
  communication with retailer, 153–56
  husband's role, 180
  implicit negotiation, 146
  store preference, 183
  wife's role, 180
Shove, G. F., 200, 206, 227
Shultz, Henry, 240
Singer, Edgar, 385
Smith, Adam, 19, 103, 345
Snygg, Donald, 189, 191, 291
Sociology, 8, 12, 13, 14
Sorting
  intermediate
    contact cost, 217
    economics, 217–23
    goods handling, 221
    information handling, 222
    item flow, 218
    location pattern, 220
    railroad freight, 216
    risk, 223–25
    storage capacity, 221
  postponement principle, 424
  types, 201
    accumulation, 204
    allocation, 207

Sorting—*Cont.*
  types—*Cont.*
    assorting, 209
    sorting out, 202
    utility of assortment achieved, 198
Sorting out, 202
Spencer, Herbert, 18
Staff activities
  centralization, 378
  co-ordination with line, 376
  placement, 380
  planning, 442
Stagner, Ross, 172
Status
  analogy with product, 196
  as form of competition, 325
  importance to system, 30
  principle of behavior system, 322
  survival of behavior system, 55
Stigler, George Joseph, 20, 80
Structural postulate of marketing, 81
Suboptimization, 222
Supply and demand, 109, 155, 200, 233, 285, 355
Surface, S. M., 320
Survival conditions, 113
Survival theorems, 55, 56, 57
Symbiosis, 53
Symbolic logic, 225
Symbolization, 192
Systasy, 287
  defined, 326
  location of trading center, 337
  trade policy, 344
System
  atomistic, 27
  closed, 117
  ecological, 29
  goals, 52–60
  mechanical, 28
  open, 115
  status in, 30
System, communication, 36
System, input-output
  division of labor, 71–75
  in marketing, 68–71
  in a modern economy, 67
  operation, 65–97
  in primitive economy, 66
System, operating
  allocation of resources, 89–90
  concurrence
    centrality, 78
    parallelism, 76
  control-communication relationship, 90
  decision centers, 87
  and efficiency, 79–87
  negotiation, 133
  related to power structure, 85

*This book has been set on the Linotype in 12
and 10 point Garamond No. 3, leaded 1 point.
Chapter numbers are in 24 point Bank Script
and 18 point Lydian Bold and chapter titles are
in 18 point Lydian Bold. The size of the type
page is 27 by 46½ picas.*

A CENTURY OF MARKETING

An Arno Press Collection

Alderson, Wroe. **Marketing Behavior and Executive Action.** 1957

Assael, Henry, editor. **The Collected Works of C. C. Parlin.** 1978

Assael, Henry, editor. **Early Development and Conceptualization of the Field of Marketing.** 1978

Assael, Henry, editor. **A Pioneer in Marketing, L. D. H. Weld.** 1978

Bartels, Robert D. W. **Marketing Literature: Development and Appraisal.** 1978

Blankenship, Albert B. **Consumer and Opinion Research.** 1943

Borden, Neil H. **Advertising in Our Economy.** 1945

Breyer, Ralph F. **The Marketing Institution.** 1934

Breyer, Ralph F. **Quantitative Systemic Analysis and Control.** 1949

Clark, Fred E. **Principles of Marketing.** 1922

Clark, Lincoln H., editor. **Consumer Behavior.** 1958

Coles, Jessie V. **The Consumer-Buyer and the Market.** 1938

Collins, V[irgil] D[ewey]. **World Marketing.** 1935

Converse, Paul D. **The Beginning of Marketing Thought in the U.S.** *and* **Fifty Years of Marketing in Retrospect.** 1959

Copeland, Melvin Thomas. **Principles of Merchandising.** 1924

The Ethical Problems of Modern Advertising. 1931

Frederick, John H. **Industrial Marketing.** 1934

Frederick, J. George. **Modern Salesmanagement.** 1921

Hower, Ralph M. **The History of an Advertising Agency.** 1939

Longman, Donald R. **Distribution Cost Analysis.** 1941

Lyon, Leverett S. **Salesmen in Marketing Strategy.** 1926

The Men Who Advertise. 1870

Nystrom, Paul H. **Economics of Retailing.** 1930

Reilly, William J. **Marketing Investigations.** 1929

Revzan, David A. **Wholesaling in Marketing Organization.** 1961

Rosenberg, Larry J., editor. **The Roots of Marketing Strategy.** 1978

Scott, Walter Dill. **The Psychology of Advertising.** 1913

Sorenson, Helen. **The Consumer Movement.** 1941

Starch, Daniel. **Advertising Principles.** 1927

Terry, Samuel Hough. **The Retailer's Manual.** 1869

Tosdal, Harry R. **Principles of Personal Selling.** 1925

White, Percival. **Advertising Research.** 1927

White, Percival. **Scientific Marketing Management.** 1927